Teaching

as a Sacramental Act

Teaching

as a Sacramental Act

MARY ELIZABETH MULLINO MOORE

THE
PILGRIM
PRESS
Cleveland

*To Mama, Mother, MaMere — Elizabeth Heaton Mullino —
the matriarch who tended us, prayed for us daily, and lived her life fully.
She was strong, vulnerable, and loving beyond measure.*

*This book is also dedicated to the churches that have loved, nurtured, and sobered me
into seeing myself and others as precious children of God —
entrusted with care for God's vineyard,
stirred by glimpses of God's New Creation,
and blessed by grace without end.*

The Pilgrim Press, 700 Prospect Avenue
Cleveland, Ohio 44115-1100, U.S.A.
thepilgrimpress.com

© 2004 by Mary Elizabeth Mullino Moore

All rights reserved. Published 2004

Printed in the United States of America on acid-free paper

09 08 07 06 05 04   5 4 3 2 1

Library of Congress Cataloging-in-Publication Data

Moore, Mary Elizabeth, 1945-
    Teaching as a sacramental act / Mary Elizabeth Mullino Moore.
      p. cm.
    Includes bibliographical references (p.).
    ISBN 0-8298-1647-X (alk. paper)
    1. Christian education – Philosophy.   I. Title.
    BV1464.M67 2004
    268'.01 – dc22

                                    2004058749

Contents

Preface

I have written this book during one of the most difficult and powerful decades of my life. During the past six years, I have moved across the country, leaving a treasured institution where I studied and taught for twenty-five years, and entering another valued institution where I was a stranger, but came to make my home. In the past four years, my home country has been attacked by terrorist actions (the Oklahoma City bombing, 9/11 attacks, and street violence across the nation); it has also perpetrated terror on others and is now torn in a debate among diverse values and worldviews. During the past two years, our son-in-law was killed in a tragic accident, which brought out the best in our family and, eventually, frayed our edges. During the past three months, I nursed my mother and sat with her while she died, intensifying my love of life and helping to restitch the edges of our family and the center of my soul. I share these experiences to confess the contextual particularity of my life as author of this book and, more importantly, to identify the book as a work arising from the raw tragedy, hard work, and joyful beauty of life.

One particular experience of the past illumines the center of the work. A few years ago, I was invited to respond to an interreligious panel — Jewish, Christian, and Muslim. Earlier in that day, a colleague and I drove a round trip of five hours to visit a mutual friend who was near death. We had both visited her before, but this visit was to be different. In a journey of many years, this woman and her husband had lived courageously with her lung disease, and finally with a lung transplant. Her body had initially accepted the new lung but had now clearly rejected it; she and we realized that her life was near an end. Walking into her room that day, all of us laughed and cried and prayed. We held her hand, and then left with words of love and a "thumbs up" sign.

As my colleague and I rushed back to the interfaith panel, I knew that responding would be difficult in my emotionally exhausted state. Complicating matters, I had no advance manuscripts, but was to listen intently and respond on my feet. The panelists had prepared well, but I kept asking myself what such a discourse had to do with my friend's dying moments. I began my response with that question and the story of my dying friend. I concluded that what finally binds people across religious communities is not common beliefs, or even respect for diverse

beliefs, but a shared reverence for life. Such reverence is experienced in holy moments, like the journey with my dying friend, and it is expressed in commitments
to treasure and sustain life in all its forms. This moment of awareness was to open
a new dimension of sacramentality for me — one that I interpret through Christian faith, one that I share with people of other traditions. As if to underscore
this insight, a friend came to me after the panel discussion that day. She cried as
she described how my words had helped her see something holy in her husband's
death that she had missed before. This friend is Muslim, but she and I shared,
in that moment, a sense of awe that transcended our diverse and equally deep
religious commitments. We knew the presence of sacrality, and that was enough!

Sacrality is the center of this book. I approach it as a Christian theologian and
educator, recognizing that the sacred transcends human words and actions, even
transcending well-developed religious traditions. At the same time, those very
words and actions are sometimes all we have to name and reflect upon what is
awe-full. Thus, I enter this project with humility and daring, hoping to touch and
vivify the sacred, while offering guidance for spiritual life and sacred teaching.

History of the Project

I cannot say when this project began, probably when my mother and father cared
for me as an infant. Since then, many church and friendship communities have
nourished the project, as have academic colleagues. The project has been further
nourished by ethogenic studies, which have uncovered the power of congregations
to reveal sacred realities, as well as their yearnings to seek God and God's ways
for their common life.[1]

---

1. Mary Elizabeth Mullino Moore, "Dynamics of Religious Culture: Theological Wisdom and Ethical Guidance from Diverse Urban Communities," *International Journal of Practical Theology* 2 (1998):
240–62. Other publications have come from this work, but this particular essay includes some introduction to the method as well as a report on two of the studies. The ethogenic method is akin to
ethnography, with an accent on collecting and negotiating accounts from different sources in order to
ascertain insight into the origins and meanings of the structures of community life and patterns of behavior. See also Mary Elizabeth Moore, "Education in Congregational Context," in *Rethinking Christian
Education: Explorations in Theory and Practice*, ed. David S. Schuller (St. Louis: Chalice, 1993), 31–46;
Mary Elizabeth and Allen J. Moore, "Denominational Identity and the Church School — Teasing Out
a Relationship," in *Beyond Establishment: Protestant Identity in a Post-Protestant Age*, ed. Jackson W. Car-
roll and Wade Clark Roof (Louisville: Westminster John Knox, 1993), 54–73; Mary Elizabeth Moore,
"Walking with Youth: Youth Ministry in Many Cultures," in *At-Risk Youth, At-Risk Church: What Jesus
Christ and American Teenagers Are Saying to the Mainline Church* (Princeton, N.J.: Institute for Youth
Ministry, Princeton Theological Seminary, 1998), 47–61; "Volcanic Eruptions: Eruptive Youth Ministry," in *At-Risk Youth, At-Risk Church*, 63–72; "Promises and Practices for Tomorrow: Transforming
Youth Leaders and Transforming Culture," in *At-Risk Youth, At-Risk Church*, 73–84; "Communautés
urbaines et traditions culturelles: La dynamique de la culture religieuse," in *Dieu en ville: Evangile et
eglises dans l'espace urbain*, ed. Jean-Guy Nadeau and Marc Pelchat (Outremont, Quebec: Novalis,
1998); and Mary Elizabeth Moore, Gabriele Mayer, and Steve Marlatt, "Following a Tradition: Seeking a Vision," in *People of a Compassionate God*, ed. Janet F. Fishburn (Nashville: Abingdon, 2003),
39–61.

The project is also rooted in my study of Christian spirituality, particularly in the study of women mystics such as Julian of Norwich, whose lives were grounded in a sense of spiritual aliveness in each moment and each being. In the tradition of these mystics, my project is further shaped by countless experiences of wonder — wonder at daffodils springing from the ground at the close of winter; wonder at pin oak trees growing on sheer ledges of granite in the Sierra Nevada mountains; wonder at the salmon's return to spawning grounds against powerful river currents; wonder at my children's first steps; wonder at precious, hard-earned relationships with my stepchildren; wonder at the tender, strong love between my husband and me; wonder at the tender, strong love between gay and lesbian couples whose families have rejected them; wonder at the determined love of people who lead justice movements; and wonder at the fragile fear and deep determination of peoples who rebuild their worlds after suffering untold oppression — rebuilding a family after violence or rebuilding a nation after apartheid.

In a similar way, this book is rooted in years of work for environmental justice and stewardship, brought to expression in *Ministering with the Earth* and other publications, as well as in communal work with students, faculty, and staff at two institutions of higher education — Claremont School of Theology in California and Emory University in Georgia.[2] *Teaching as a Sacramental Act* builds on the reverence for creation expressed in these works; here, however, the sacred is named as sacramental, uncovering dimensions of spirituality and teaching that have been hitherto neglected or minimized.

Women's theologies have also shaped this project, including feminist, womanist, *mujerista*, Asian women's, and ordinary women's theologies. These theologies have helped me wrestle with hard questions, reminding me that I stand in a long line of soft-hearted, tough-minded women and men who do theology differently from dominant traditions. In particular, these theologians call attention to mediations of God that are not part of the mainstream, and they cast fresh light on mediations that *are* part of the mainstream, such as Augustine's *Confessions*.[3]

Thanksgiving

My thanks go to people who have lived and reflected with me on ideas in this book. I drafted the first version of *Teaching as a Sacramental Act* for the Association

---

2. Mary Elizabeth Moore, *Ministering with the Earth* (St. Louis: Chalice, 1998); "Richness in Religious Education: Ethnic, Religious and Biodiversity," *The Fourth R for the Third Millennium: Education in Religion and Values for the Global Future*, ed. Leslie J. Francis, Jeff Astley, and Mandy Robbins (Dublin: Lindisfarne Books, 2001), 115–35; "Stewards of the Good News of Creation I and II," in *Steward: Living as Disciples in Everyday Life*, ed. Bruce C. Birch and Charles R. Foster (Nashville: Abingdon, 2000), 17–38.

3. One example is Margaret R. Miles, *Desire and Delight: A New Reading of Augustine's Confessions* (New York: Crossroad, 1992); Augustine, *Confessions*, trans. R. S. Pine-Coffin (Harmondsworth, U.K.: Penguin Books, 1961).

of Presbyterian Christian Educators.[4] I continue to be grateful to that community and many other church groups (local and judicatory) of diverse traditions for their sparkling insights and nagging questions. Likewise, I appreciate faculty colleagues at Claremont and Candler Schools of Theology who read and responded to early drafts of two chapters.

Many students have also walked with me in the making of this book. I taught the course "Sacred Teaching" three times at Claremont, and the class and I produced a volume called *Sacred Teaching Book of Resources* each time. At Candler, several individual students have assisted with research, especially Carmen Homola-Brock, Susan Witty, Rebecca Andrews, Kristina Ringland, Joshua Noblitt, Jennifer Ayres, and Erin Maddox. Ayanna Abi-Kyles and Jennie Knight have kept the Women in Theology and Ministry Program flourishing during my sabbatical absence, and numerous students and colleagues have inspired me in conversations about their work or mine.

Along with theological colleagues and students, I was blessed by a copious, wise, and gracious editor, Ulrike Guthrie. Uli persisted in support and wise counsel, especially through this past year of major revisions. Thanks also go to John Eagleson for his meticulous copy-editing and primary work on the book's bibliography.

The largest thanksgiving goes to my family. Allen has been my sacred partner and intellectual companion for twenty-eight years of marriage. Our children — Rebecca, Cliff and Sheryl, Nan and Mike, Joyce, and Glenda — have always been priests and prophets to us, even as we have loved and cared for them. The final thanks goes to my mother, Elizabeth Heaton Mullino, who died in the final days of editing and to whom I dedicate this book. Through all of life's ups and downs, I always knew that my mother prayed for me *every* morning and periodically through the day. Often, her trust in God sustained me, and I already miss her prayers; yet, her sacramental presence endures!

---

4. "Teaching as Sacrament," lecture presented to Association of Presbyterian Christian Educators, Dallas, Texas, January 1994.

Chapter One

Searching for the Sacred

✡

A group of youth stands on a street corner jeering at an old man as he crosses the street; they feel agile and youthful by comparison. The man does not notice because he is watching a ragged woman walking beside him. The woman with unkempt hair and dirty clothes looks pathetic, he thinks, not successful like him. Meanwhile, the woman, who is white, looks grumpily back at the man, who is black. She resents the way he holds his head high; she deems his race inferior to hers and does not like his "uppity ways."

Across town, a young woman sits at home, whining about her unhappy life to a neighbor, "The only times I am happy are when I am eating or shopping."

Down the street, a young boy is drinking with his friends. He turned to alcohol at the age of twelve, discovering that his friends were impressed. These friends were his only hope for acceptance. His family had rejected him when he was a small boy, and his efforts to get their attention by acting out in school had only assured that his teachers also rejected him. A girl from this boy's class sees him on the street today. When she realizes he is drunk, she is frightened; then she realizes it is just like him to do something stupid like that. By comparison, she feels stable, and wise, knowing that she would never get drunk.

These snapshots reveal the lives of real people, and the challenges that churches face in teaching ministry. Each story is more complex than what is presented; however, taken together, they reveal people who are searching — searching to feel youthful, wealthy, successful, superior, happy, accepted, stable and wise. In fact, these people are searching for more than appears on the surface. Youth, wealth, and all of the other goods named here are simply poor substitutes for the larger Good that people seek. One way to describe this larger Good is in terms of relationships — uplifting relationships with the Holy (the deeper reality that transcends our lives), genuine relationships with other people, and meaningful relationships with creation. Yet how can teaching encourage people to seek these larger goods? That is the challenge of this book.

1

In the vignettes introducing this chapter, all of the characters are settling for some form of pretense and escape. The street corner youth who are jeering at the old man are youthful and agile, but they seek joy in comparing themselves favorably with the man. The man, likewise, depends on comparing himself with a raggedy woman. The woman depends on comparing herself with him. The young woman escapes in a different way, not through comparisons, but through acquisition; more specifically, she delights in acquiring food (eating) and material goods (shopping). The twelve-year-old boy likewise seeks acceptance by acquisition, in his case, filling up on alcohol. Finally, the boy's schoolmate, the young girl, depends on comparing herself with the drunken boy. If we are honest, most of us will see ourselves in these characters, *seeking to give meaning to our lives by comparing and acquiring, rather than communing and sharing.* These are fundamental problems in human life, pointing to the human dilemma that underlies this book. This dilemma marks individuals, and it also marks human communities — neighborhoods, ethnic communities, religious communities, villages, cities, and nations.

Given the human willingness to settle for lesser goods, *Teaching as a Sacramental Act* focuses on two primary questions. What is the nature of Christian vocation? What kind of teaching is needed to inspire and equip people toward that vocation? To travel with these questions, we begin by exploring the landscape — exploring contours of human searching, the project itself, and sacramental theology and teaching.

Human Searching and Spiritual Living

Living texts, in the form of case studies, frame the questions of this book. Readers will recognize similar experiences in their own lives and in the communities they know best. *People everywhere are searching for meaning, for answers to difficult questions, and for ways to live fully in a world of beauty and harshness.* Consider the child who sat with me after his grandmother's funeral, asking what happens to people after they die and proceeding to tell me what he thought about the question. Consider Jake, a homeless man who approached Jim (fictitious names) and asked how God might help him get through his job interview tomorrow. Consider the church youth group that decided they could make a difference in the poor governance of their school, beginning with a sit-in in the school library. Consider the father who sat on the snowy top of a mountain for three hours, watching his son sled gleefully down the slope and trudge back up to do it again. Consider the group of mothers who meet weekly to work on violence prevention in their children's school and to address human needs in their community that contribute to violence. Consider the local church's justice group that went to City Council and objected to racial injustices in their local community, or the caring teams of local congregations around the world that visit people who are lonely and infirm.

These are all snapshots of sacramental teaching, offering authentic responses to the searching concerns and distorted attitudes with which this chapter began. Sacred teaching mediates God's grace to people who search for God's Goodness in a world oriented toward lesser goods and despair. Two educational cases will reveal more of the textures of human searching and the hunger for spiritual living to which sacred teaching responds.

A few years ago, a friend told me about her husband's Bible study group. She said it had formed a couple of years earlier because the men simply wanted to know the Bible better. They continued to meet once a week, and while they were together, they talked about their lives and prayed, in addition to studying the Bible. What they discovered in the second year is that they had come to know each other well and, also, to feel comfortable in talking and praying together. This trust — toward one another and toward God — was a Godsend, for almost every man in the group went through a major life change during that second year — death of a loved one, loss of a job, financial reversal, or a difficult ethical decision to make. My friend described what happened: "They realized that the group was doing much more than studying the Bible; they were supporting one another and helping one another to deepen in faith."

Much is revealed in this simple story about human searching and spiritual living. First, the focus of the group was a common yearning — the yearning to deepen their faith. Second, they focused on their common Christian tradition; in this case, they focused on the Bible. Third, the men committed themselves to meeting regularly; they met once a week and agreed not to miss unless they had strong reasons to do so. Fourth, the men engaged in sharing what was important in their lives. Sharing in small, safe ways built relationships in which they could later share shattering vulnerability, overwhelming joy, and deep distress. Fifth, the group was bound together by prayer. They prayed each week when they met. In the end, this group came to know themselves as a sacramental community — a community in which they mediated God's grace with one another.

Ministries that are most significant are those in which people come to know themselves as sacramental people in sacramental communities with sacramental vocations. Often these ministries emerge unexpectedly, as this men's group did. Similar surprises have happened before, as in the class meetings of eighteenth-century England.

John Wesley and other leaders of the Methodist movement wanted to build a chapel in Bristol. To raise money, they asked that everyone give one penny a week. In order to collect the money more effectively and give people a spiritual opportunity at the same time, they organized class bands (as classes were originally called). The people came together to give their pennies, study the Bible, reflect on their lives, pray, sing, and make decisions for their actions in the coming week. They discovered, however, that the value of classes far surpassed anyone's expectations, and the classes continued for many decades after the Bristol chapel had been fully funded and built.

As in my friend's Bible study class, these people originally came together around a common need or yearning; in this case, it was to raise money for a chapel. Similarly, they focused on a significant part of their common Christian tradition — the Bible and hymnody. As in the other story, the people committed themselves to meeting regularly (once a week), and they shared their lives; however, the classes' sharing was more formal and regularized. Each week, class members shared the state of their souls, laid themselves open for scrutinizing questions and suggestions, and reflected on what God was calling them to do. The classes were challenging, but members were bound together with prayer, praying together each week and encouraging one another in daily prayer.

These two stories suggest much about human searching and spiritual living; yet, spirituality has become a fluff word in much of contemporary conversation, referring particularly to that which is personal, ephemeral, and often conventional. I propose that the stories suggest more than this. They suggest forms of spirituality that involve searching, facing vulnerability, opening to God, and facing radical transformation. They suggest forms of religious education that go beyond transmitting knowledge, addressing biblical literacy, responding to personal needs, providing happy fellowship, or offering comfort. These stories call us to *understand spirituality and Christian religious education as engagement with God and God's creation.* Engagement with God includes biblical engagement, yes, but it also includes engagement with God in prayer, in the deeps of God's forests, and in the whirlwind of God's hurting world.

We can begin to do these things only when teachers open themselves to wonder and are blessed by the mysteries of God. We can begin only when searching questions and practical needs are honored. We can begin only when ordinary gatherings of people are understood as holy, filled with unimagined possibilities. We can begin only when we honor and wait for the movements of God in the midst of human gathering.

Grounding a Project

The intention of this book is to face these realities and hopes. To do so requires planting seeds for educational reform, which are fed by the past, but open to a radically new future. Seeds can grow, however, only if the ground is nourishing; thus, we turn to the grounds of this project, especially the assumptions, assertions, and approach.

Assumptions

The book is grounded, first, in two assumptions: *that God is the primary Teacher and that God's sacred creation is a source for learning.* The relationship between God and the world is primal. Ordinary reality mediates God's grace, and ordinary people, situations, and objects are vessels of the Holy. Thus, all aspects of life — even the margins of society — are imbued with God's presence. To acknowledge this is to call forth reverence.[1] Yet with a few exceptions (often in women's liturgical and educational writing), theologies of ministry often deemphasize or omit a sense of awe.[2]

Assertions

The central assertion of this book is that *religious teaching needs to be re-envisioned as sacred teaching — mediating the Holy.* The more specific assertion is that *Christian teaching needs to be envisioned as sacramental, with the purpose of mediating God, and with approaches that mediate God's grace and God's call to the human community for the sake of human sanctification and creation's well-being.*   ●

The first statement is general, addressed to diverse religious traditions and to education that takes place in schools, colleges and universities where students, faculty, and subject matters also represent diverse traditions. The longer statement focuses on the Christian tradition, which is my tradition and context, as well as the tradition and context of most of my sources. My hope is to speak broadly but not imperialistically. I will draw connections with other traditions, but avoid unwarranted assumptions about the sameness or transferability of ideas from one religious context to another. For this reason, I will make some references to *religious* education, pointing to that which is broadly shared. I will make other references to *Christian* education or educational ministry, recognizing that much of the book derives from uniquely Christian contexts and purposes.

Reflecting on the stories with which this chapter began, one can see that sacred teaching does not have to be explicitly religious, much less does it have to do with the sacraments of the church. Many stories in this book will have religious themes because the focus is primarily on education in religion or education in communities of faith; on the other hand, sacramental teaching can be understood as mediating the Holy without explicit reference to that which is mediated. This focus distinguishes the book from other works on teaching and the sacraments. It is different from works that focus on teaching *about* the sacraments, teaching *for* sacramental participation, or teaching *by way of* the sacraments (sacraments as educative events).[3] It does however build on this work, which

---

1. Mary Elizabeth Mullino Moore, *Teaching from the Heart: Theology and Educational Method* (Valley Forge, Pa.: Trinity Press International, 1998), 220–24. In this book, I discuss the educational importance of revering. An aspect of reverence is revering the ordinary, which, when valued, becomes "extraordinarily ordinary" (224).

2. One discussion of the liturgical emphases is found in Marjorie Procter-Smith, *In Her Own Rite: Constructing Feminist Liturgical Tradition* (Akron, Ohio: OSL Publications, 2000; Nashville: Abingdon Press, 1990), v–ix, 130, 135. A discussion of the educational emphasis is found in Maria Harris, *Women and Teaching: Themes for a Spirituality of Pedagogy* (New York: Paulist Press, 1988).

3. Robert L. Browning and Roy A. Reed, *The Sacraments in Religious Education and Liturgy: An Ecumenical Model* (Birmingham: Religious Education Press, 1985); Elizabeth Francis Caldwell, *Come unto Me: Rethinking the Sacraments for Children* (Cleveland: United Church Press, 1996); James Michael

has opened paths for the more fundamental reorientation offered in the present volume.

Extending the comparisons, I can highlight the distinctive intentions of *Teaching as a Sacramental Act* by comparing it with related work.

- Recent work on *sacramental living* draws evocative pictures of God's movements and human vocation, focusing attention on the sacramentality of daily life.[4] *Teaching as a Sacramental Act,* in probing depths of sacramentality and teaching, can enrich sacramental theology and stir visions of education to enhance sacramental living.

- Another body of recent literature attends to *Christian practices.*[5] *Teaching as a Sacramental Act* expands on such work by attending to sacramental practice in particular. The focus on sacramentality pushes the boundaries of earlier work toward a more grounded and integrated pattern of practice.

- Also important are works on *sacramental theology and ecclesiology.* For many theologians, a deep understanding of the sacraments stands at the heart of Christian faith and ecclesiology.[6] A few of these focus on connections between sacramental theology and the church's life, especially worship but with some attention to teaching and preaching.[7] The present work extends these emphases to focus more fully on teaching and prophetic action, integrating insights that are usually placed in separate boxes of thought.

Lee, *The Sacrament of Teaching: A Social Science Approach* (Birmingham: Religious Education Press, 2000).

4. Dwight W. and Linda J. Vogel, *Sacramental Living: Falling Stars and Coloring Outside the Lines* (Nashville: Upper Room Books, 1999); Sue Bender, *Everyday Sacred: A Woman's Journey Home* (San Francisco: HarperSanFrancisco, 1995); and Anne Simpkinson, Charles Simpkinson, and Rose Solari, eds., *Nourishing the Soul: Discovering the Sacred in Everyday Life* (San Francisco: HarperCollins, 1995).

5. Thomas H. Groome, *Sharing Faith: A Comprehensive Approach to Religious Education* (San Francisco: HarperSanFrancisco, 1991); Maria Harris, *Teaching and Religious Imagination: An Essay in the Theology of Teaching* (San Francisco: Harper & Row, 1987); Dorothy C. Bass, ed., *Practicing Our Faith: A Way of Life for a Searching People* (San Francisco: Jossey-Bass, 1997); and Craig Dykstra, *Growing in the Life of Faith: Education and Christian Practices* (Louisville: Geneva Press, 1999).

6. Leonardo Boff, *Sacraments of Life: Life of the Sacraments* (Washington, D.C.: Pastoral Press, 1987); Bernard J. Cooke, *Sacraments and Sacramentality* (Mystic, Conn.: Twenty-Third Publications, 1983); Jürgen Moltmann, *The Church in the Power of the Spirit: A Contribution to Messianic Ecclesiology* (New York: Harper & Row, 1977); Alexander Schmemann, *For the Life of the World: Sacraments and Orthodoxy* (Crestwood, N.Y.: St. Vladimir's Seminary Press, 1973); Edward Schillebeeckx, *Christ the Sacrament of the Encounter with God* (New York: Sheed and Ward, 1965).

7. Don E. Saliers, *Worship Come to Its Senses* (Nashville: Abingdon, 1996); Saliers, *Worship as Theology: Foretaste of Glory Divine* (Nashville: Abingdon, 1994); Henri J. M. Nouwen, *Can You Drink the Cup?* (Notre Dame, Ind.: Ave Maria, 1996); Alexander Schmemann, "Theology and Eucharist," in *Liturgy and Tradition,* ed. Thomas Fisch (Crestwood, N.Y.: St. Vladimir's Seminary, 1990, 1961), 69–88, esp. 72.; Joanmarie Smith, *Teaching as Eucharist* (Williston Park, N.Y.: Resurrection Press, 1999); Mary Catherine Hilkert, *Naming Grace: Preaching and the Sacramental Imagination* (New York: Continuum, 1997).

- One last genre of literature focuses on *the relationship between spirituality and prophetic action*.[8] This literature paves the way for *Teaching as a Sacramental Act*'s more specific focus on sacramentality and social witness.

Building on these trends, *Teaching as a Sacramental Act* further disrupts dichotomies of worship and education, sacredness and secularity, belief and action, spirituality and social witness. It is grounded in God's sacramental relationship with creation and the human vocation to receive and mediate God's presence in an aching world.

The grounding of this book is broad; the hope is grand. To align teaching with the sacramental nature of God's creation is to admit the power and responsibility of teaching. It is to focus teaching on the Good rather than settling for lesser goods. Lesser goods *may* be pathways to the Good, but they may also be cul-de-sacs from which people cannot escape. Those who teach or administer educational programs have the awe-full, awesome task to discern and act sacramentally.

Approach

The very approach of this book involves a series of practices, which I will describe to satisfy curious readers and to provide educational clues for sacred teaching. The practices were somewhat sequential in my work, but with considerable movement back and forth.

1. *Awakening to the sacramentality of life.* Awakening involves attending to the details of life. In the making of this book, awakening was not intentional at first. It was a gift from communities that loved me, which I later nurtured. Much sacred teaching begins this way — as a gift that people receive and later nurture by attending to life.

2. *Study of teaching, sacramentality, and ecclesiology.* The second practice was research. Taking seriously the many forms of revelation, I turned to diverse sources: books and essays; ethnographic observations in churches; observations of teaching in church and school settings; and interviews with religious teachers, seekers, and learners.

3. *Analyzing the theory and practices of teaching alongside the theory and practices of sacraments.* The back and forth movement between these two analyses eventually shaped a framework for understanding sacramental teaching. Continuing the analysis led to my reshaping the framework at least three times. The chapters on remembering the dismembered and thanksgiving were not part of the original framework. The study of teaching cases led me to include the former; the study

---

8. Representatives of this genre are Alton B. Pollard, *Mysticism and Social Change: The Social Witness of Howard Thurman* (New York: P. Lang, 1992); Luther Smith, *Howard Thurman: The Mystic as Prophet* (Washington, D.C.: University Press of America, 1981).

of liturgical theology led me to include the latter. Thus, educational experiences, experiences of the larger world, and sacramental theology corrected and enlarged one another.

4. *Interpreting the research data as a multidimensional whole.* Interpretation was a process of standing back and looking at the whole, exploring and imagining patterns and possibilities in light of the preceding study and analyses.

5. *Making proposals for future action.* This movement was an extension of interpretation. To say that teaching is sacred suggests that certain attitudes (such as expectation and reverence) are critical for teachers and learners. Though these attitudes are central, a book in practical theology needs to go farther, making explicit proposals for future action, and sometimes pointing to practices that are overlooked in other works. Thanksgiving, for example, is not commonly included in theories of teaching and learning (although commonly practiced in strong learning communities). A focus on sacramental teaching yields proposals for the educational practice of thanksgiving.

In the actual crafting of this book, the five practices named here are not completely separate; they are woven in and out of one another. At the same time, each chapter does begin with case studies, followed by analysis, interpretation, and proposals for practice. In this way, readers can trace the ideas from living texts and written texts to interpretive visions and concrete practices. The structure offers a rhythmic pattern, roughly reflecting the method of crafting the book. The method resembles that of an artist. Proposals for action emerge after a vision is stirred in the artist (awakening); after training with other artists, experimenting with different media and subjects, and detailed study of the subject of this new painting (research); after reflecting on the vision from many angles, perhaps even painting small versions or small parts of the whole (analyzing); and after the artist finally begins to paint the vision onto a large canvas (interpretation). The vision stirred for me was sacramental teaching, but research and analysis were necessary before I put paint on canvas. Interpretation finally demanded response in the form of proposals for action.

This work is not complete, of course, until others engage with it. As a former student, Amy Gafford, says of her paintings, "My work is not complete until others interact with it; a painting hidden in a closet is never really finished."[9] Amy's insight suggests that this book is also not complete until others engage it. My hope is that readers will be sparked to fresh insights that go far beyond the book: raising profound questions; stirring holy visions; engaging in educational experiments, renovations, and innovations; and leading to further interpretation and proposals for practice.

---

9. Amy Gafford, Reading Course in Process Theology, Candler School of Theology, May 2001.

Understanding Sacraments and Sacramentality

With this sense of awe, we turn now to sacraments, worship, and teaching. Each has a particular and a broad meaning. Sacrament signifies Jesus Christ, the incarnation of God. Yet God's incarnational presence is active in all times and places; thus, all creation is sacramental. Similarly, worship is understood as giving service and praise to God in the gathered assembly, but it also includes serving and praising God in the streets. And teaching is sharing faith in a gathered learning community, but it also includes sharing faith in other times and places and in a multitude of forms. Sacraments, worship, and teaching are alike in resisting narrow categorization. Further, they are closely related with one another. With this in mind we turn to more precise definitions.

Sacrament

The definitions of sacrament are many, but the most common and enduring is *an outward and visible sign of an inward and spiritual grace.*[10] Some of the more recent work on the sacraments affirms that all of creation is sacred, and that the formal sacraments of the church awaken people to the sacredness of God's whole creation, mediating God's grace and enabling the community to participate more fully in the grace of God that is everywhere revealed.[11] Most Protestant churches acknowledge two sacraments — Baptism and Eucharist — as the two instituted by Christ. The Roman Catholic Church acknowledges seven sacraments, but the Roman Church also gives special priority to Baptism and Eucharist. The ecumenical discussions and publications on the sacraments have been profuse in the past twenty years, and the churches seem to be moving closer together on many of the issues that have previously divided.

To say that teaching is sacramental is not to add to the number of formal sacraments but to emphasize the role of education in mediating God. In fact,

---

10. James F. White traces the origins of the key terms to Augustine, who introduced the phrases "visible form" and "invisible grace"; the later development of the definition is the work of Gratian and Lombard. See James F. White, *Introduction to Christian Worship*, rev. ed. (Nashville: Abingdon, 1990, 1980), 173–76. Augustine used this language in various ways, including his description of animal sacrifices of old and the self-giving sacrifice of ourselves to God. These are to be understood as "a visible sacrament of an invisible sacrifice." See Augustine, *City of God against the Pagans*, Book X.5, ed. and trans. R. W. Dyson (Cambridge: Cambridge University, 1998), 397; cf: Peter Lombard, "Peter Lombard: The Four Books of Sentences, IV," trans. Owen R. Orr, in *A Scholastic Miscellany: Anselm to Ockham*, Library of Christian Classics 10, ed. Eugene R. Fairweather (Philadelphia: Westminster Press, 1956), 338–40; Lombard, *Peter Lombard and the Sacramental System*, trans. Elizabeth Frances Rogers (Merrick, N.Y.: Richwood Publishing Co., 1976), 122. Many centuries later (1559), John Calvin elaborated definitions of sacraments, drawing upon Augustine in discussing "a visible sign" or "visible word" and "an invisible grace." See John Calvin, *Calvin: Institutes of the Christian Religion*, IV, 14, 1–26 (1559), trans. Ford Lewis Battles, Library of Christian Classics 21 (Philadelphia: Westminster Press, 1960), 1276–1303, esp. 1280–81, 1290.

11. Karl Rahner, *Theological Investigations*, 14 (London: Darton, Longman & Todd, 1976), esp. 166; Browning and Reed, *The Sacraments in Religious Education and Liturgy*, 3–25, esp. 11–15.

the number of sacraments has varied widely through Christian history, with as many as thirty at one time. What has been consistent, however, has been the role of the sacraments in conveying God's grace through signs in creation (water in baptism, and bread and wine/grape juice in Eucharist) for the sanctification of human beings.[12]

In view of God's work in and through all creation, the definition expands: *Sacraments are the conveyance of God's grace through signs in creation for the sanctification of human beings and the well-being of all God's creation.* Adding the last phrase harmonizes with recent writing on sacraments and with a growing consciousness of God's work in the whole creation.

All of this suggests, in plain language, that *the heart of sacramental teaching is mediating the grace of God through the concrete stuff of creation for the sanctification of human communities and the well-being of all God's creation.* My purpose in this book is to cast a bright light on the sacramental nature of religious education in mediating the Holy for human sanctification and creation's good. How is that, then, different from worship?

Worship

Religious educators have long debated the distinctions, or lack of distinction, between worship and education.[13] I uphold both. Worship and education are different and cannot be collapsed into one. Yet the distinctions are not fully distinct. Good liturgy is educationally powerful, as good education is liturgically rich. So what is worship?

Worship is the responsive service and praise of God in the gathered and scattered community. It is, first, responsive to God's action — an idea running deep in Christian tradition. Evelyn Underhill, for example, describes worship as "the response of the creature to the Eternal."[14] Further, worship includes and relates the gathered and scattered community — another traditional Christian emphasis that is being recovered. Don Saliers describes worship as *"performed liturgy,* the actual 'lived' liturgy that throws together our lives and what we do in the assembly."[15]

---

12. Thomas Aquinas, "Fourth Article: Whether a Sacrament Is Always Something Sensible?" *Summa Theologica,* Part III, 60, trans. Fathers of the English Dominican Province (New York: Benziger Bros., 1947). According to Thomas Aquinas, a sacrament is "the sign of a sacred thing inasmuch as thereby man [people] is [are] sanctified" (2347). For Augustine, the practice of sacrifice, including the animal sacrifices of earlier times, is to draw nearer to God and to help our neighbors draw near as well (Augustine, *City of God,* 397). See also Lombard, "Four Sentences," 340–41.

13. Some years ago, Howard Grimes argued that worship and Christian education are distinct and should not be confused; however, he continued to insist that they are complementary. See Howard Grimes, *The Church Redemptive* (New York: Abingdon Press, 1958). John Westerhoff sought to blur the distinctions by emphasizing that liturgical formation is part of education, or what he preferred to call enculturation. See John Westerhoff and Gwen Kennedy Neville, *Learning through Liturgy* (New York: Seabury, 1978). Westerhoff discussed this in later books, but this particular presentation was foundational for what was to come.

14. Evelyn Underhill, *Worship* (New York: Crossroad, 1982, 1936), 3.

15. Saliers, *Worship as Theology,* 16; emphasis in the original.

Such an intimate connection binds life into a whole and shapes theology: "It is the worship of God in cultic enactment *and* service of God in life that constitutes the 'primary theology.' "[16]

Central to this discussion is the centrality of praise to worship. This accent goes back to the disciples and forward to the hunger for praise music today. Don Saliers describes worship as blessing and praise: "Communal worship is first and last blessing God, praising and giving thanks."[17] Praise, in his view, centers on God's self-giving in Christ: "Christian liturgy is the ongoing prayer, act, and word flowing from the cross and empty tomb."[18] Such self-giving stirs gratitude, and also participation: participation in the rites; participation as a church (the Body of Christ); and participation in God's life (communing with God and living with hope in God).[19] Worship, then, has particular and broad definitions, but it finally transcends that which is observable and describable.

Worship is difficult to define, but it contains recurring elements: response, service, praise, gathered community, and community in the world.[20] According to James White, the German word *Gottesdienst* is richer, requiring seven English words to translate its full meaning: " 'God's service and our service to God.' "[21] The presence of God's action and human response, gathering in and scattering, service and praise, service in assembly and on the streets expresses the wholeness of worship, preventing any one definition or practice from becoming the boundary-setter. This also means that the boundaries between worship and education are opened wide for mutual indwelling.

The relation between worship and education has long been important. In 1903, Pope Pius XII described the purpose of worship as "the glory of God and the sanctification and edification of the faithful."[22] Worship is thus educational. In 1937, Evelyn Underhill urged teachers to have a "spirit of worship" in their teaching, which is the only way "to educate in the true sense of the word."[23] She described the spirit of worship as "the habit of looking up and out beyond the frontiers of the useful and the obvious, and finding beyond those frontiers a beloved Reality which gives significance to the useful and the obvious."[24] Such a spirit is possible in *all* education and not just religious education. It has to

---

16. Ibid.
17. Ibid., 25.
18. Ibid., 45.
19. Ibid., 47–48.
20. White, *Introduction to Christian Worship*, 21; cf. 21–37.
21. Ibid., 31.
22. *Tra le sollecitudini*, in *The New Liturgy*, ed. Kevin Seasoltz, O.S.B. (New York: Herder & Herder, 1966), 4; quoted in White, *Introduction*, 29.
23. Evelyn Underhill, "Education and the Spirit of Worship," in *Collected Papers of Evelyn Underhill*, ed. Lucy Menzies (London: Longmans, Green and Co., 1946), 189–90. This was originally presented as the Winifred Mercier Memorial Lecture, Whitelands College, Putney, November 1937.
24. Ibid., 190.

do with "that deep reverence for life which alone enables us to interpret life."[25] These reminders from Pope Pius XII and Evelyn Underhill vivify the link between worship and education, leading naturally into questions of teaching.

Teaching

Just as worship has multiple definitions, so does teaching. Consider the word "pedagogy," used interchangeably in this book with teaching. Despite historic associations of pedagogy with children, it has a broad meaning in popular education parlance.[26] More troublesome are some of the related words: "pedantic," "pedant," "pedantry." For a teacher to be called pedantic is not a compliment. A pedant is "a person who puts unnecessary stress on minor or trivial points of learning," or "a narrow-minded teacher who insists on exact adherence to a set of arbitrary rules."[27] Similarly, pedantry is defined as "ostentatious display of knowledge" or "an arbitrary adherence to rules and forms."[28]

On the other hand, the word "pedagogy" comes from two Greek roots: *pais* (child) and *pedon* (ground). The latter is related to *pes* (foot). These roots suggest two perspectives. As a combination of *pais* and *agein* (to lead), the word "pedagogy" is understood as *the act of leading a child.* Knowledgeable people teach the young in the knowledge they need. As a combination of *pedon* and *agein*, "pedagogy" is understood as *the act of leading people on a journey,* or leading across the earth. This involves walking with people, offering guidance when needed, and providing opportunities for people to discover new knowledge as they need it on their journey. Movement is primary here, as it is in related words: "expedition" (a journey), "expedite" (the act of speeding a movement or action), or "impede" (the act of hindering movement or progress).

In modern usage, pedagogy has, until the last twenty years, been associated largely with the first genre of definition.[29] It has re-entered the vocabulary of modern education with expanded meanings, however. Paulo Freire and others have raised issues regarding the basic nature of pedagogy, echoing the morphology and

---

25. Ibid. See also Moore, *Teaching from the Heart,* 220–24.

26. Malcolm S. Knowles, *The Modern Practice of Adult Education: Andragogy versus Pedagogy* (New York: Association Press, 1970), 37–55. Knowles proposes andragogy ("the art and science of helping adults learn") to complement pedagogy (38). Although his argument is compelling, the use of two separate words creates rather sharp distinctions regarding how adults and children learn, which I would like to avoid. Further, the use of the word "pedagogy" in recent literature has been sufficiently broad that Knowles's greatest fears do not seem to be insurmountable. At the same time, Knowles's concern, as well as that of others, have led me to emphasize definitions of pedagogy that are not exclusively focused on children.

27. Victoria Neufeldt, ed., *Webster's New World Dictionary,* Third College Edition (New York: Simon & Schuster, 1988), 995.

28. Ibid.

29. Ibid. In English, the two most common dictionary definitions have been: (1) teaching, or the actual profession or function of a teacher, and (2) "the art or science of teaching," with special attention to teaching methods.

multiple origins of the word itself. Freire, for example, poses educational questions regarding transmission vs. reconstruction in the starkest possible manner, reminding educators that education is never neutral; education always endorses the status quo or contributes to the revolution of the world. Because of this awareness, Freire argues for a pedagogy of the oppressed, which will contribute to the work of the oppressed to liberate themselves as well as their oppressors. Because of this awareness, Freire also argues for a pedagogy in process — a work of the people as they seek to practice freedom.[30]

Given these diverse associations, one can describe pedagogy, or teaching, as *an act of walking with, sharing with, acting with, remembering with, and constructing meaning with people in a learning community.* Teaching is what Thomas Groome describes as "sharing faith"; teachers are wise companions on the journey.[31] Christian education thus includes the full life of the church — sharing and reflecting in classrooms, praying and planning with others, recreation, worship, and service in the community.

Concluding Reflections

With these multiple associations in mind, we conclude by returning to the beginning. Reflecting on the snapshots with which this chapter began, I see reason for despair and reason for hope. Despair comes from people's willingness to settle for lesser goods, especially the goods sought by comparing and acquiring rather than communing and sharing. Yet people continue to ask soul-searching questions; they continue to seek the Good. The teaching challenge is to enable people to discern the God who responds to these questions. The challenge is to kindle hope and to nurture life-sustaining relationships with God, other people, and God's creation. The challenge is to equip people to respond to God with their lives.

The test of this book is how adequately it can respond to human hungers and God's tugs and promises. Stories of this chapter point in hopeful directions, but sacred teaching is still an eschatological vision — present but not yet. Chapter 2 introduces six dimensions of sacramental teaching; chapters 3 to 8 explores each in turn. Chapter 9 is a culmination, posing ways to design, resource, and embody teaching in living communities, thus to inspire and equip people in sacramental living. May this book and all practices of sacred teaching, wherever they are found, bear much fruit!

---

30. Paulo Freire, *Pedagogy of the Oppressed,* trans. Myra B. Ramos (New York: Herder & Herder, 1970); Paulo Freire, *Pedagogy in Process* (New York: Seabury, 1978).

31. Thomas H. Groome, *Sharing Faith;* Mary Elizabeth Moore, *Education for Continuity and Change* (Nashville: Abingdon, 1983), 175, 179; cf. Thomas Groome, *Christian Religious Education* (San Francisco: Jossey-Bass, 1999, 1980); Moore, *Teaching from the Heart.*

Reflecting Further

Below are possibilities for further reflection on the issues of this chapter.

1. Gather with others in your church, school, family, or other community to ponder the life of your community and the individuals within it. What kind of searching are people doing? What questions are they asking? What concerns them most, both on the surface and below?

2. In light of your community's searching, what hopes do you have from God? From the church? From the teaching ministry of the church?

Chapter Two

Sacred Teaching:
Education as Sacrament

In what kind of world do we live? What are the promises of sacred teaching for such a world? These are central questions for chapter 2.[1] I will include images and stories (as in chapter 1) throughout the book, thus grounding the work in realities that people can recognize and feel in their bones. The stories below begin with "imagine," but the stories are real. One is from history, one from an ethogenic study of a living community, and one from the Bible. As case studies, the stories reveal something of the world in which others have lived, and where we live today.

Imagine yourself worshiping in St. Giles Cathedral atop Castle Hill in Edinburgh, Scotland. *The year is 1637, and King Charles I has insisted that the church in Scotland join with churches in England to read Archbishop Laud's Liturgy. King Charles is tightening his grip because the Parliamentarian forces of Oliver Cromwell, with their Puritan values, are threatening his control of government and religion. On this Sunday, Jenny Geddes stands and glares at James Hannay, the dean of St. Giles, as he reads that liturgy for the first time. She hurls her anger at him, then hurls her stool; it misses the mark but hits one of the stone columns of the sanctuary, making a mark that remains to this day. The column now bears a plaque commemorating the act of Jenny Geddes, and in 1992 the artist Merilyn Smith crafted a cutty stool for St. Giles, which the Scotswomen dedicated to Jenny Geddes. Imagine and remember Jenny Geddes.*

Return now to the image of St. Giles on that fateful day of 1637. *Dean Hannay, knowing the frustrations of his people and pressures of Archbishop Laud, stands to read the liturgy, but Jenny Geddes unleashes her fury. Over time, people have also remembered Dean Hannay. Another column in the cathedral bears a plaque inscribed:*

---

1. A version of this chapter was published as Mary Elizabeth Moore, "Sacramental Teaching: Mediating the Holy," in *Forging a Better Religious Education for the Third Millennium*, ed. James Michael Lee (Birmingham: Religious Education Press, 2000), 41–68. The earlier chapter was a prolegomena for this book. It included the same opening cases, plus four of the six educational practices presented here. The section on "Sacramental Theology" is entirely new, as are parts of the presentation throughout.

TO JAMES HANNAY DD
1634–1639
HE WAS THE FIRST AND THE LAST WHO READ
THE SERVICE BOOK IN THIS CHURCH.
THIS MEMORIAL IS ERECTED IN HAPPIER TIMES
BY HIS DESCENDENTS.[2]

Imagine and remember James Hannay.

Now, imagine yourself worshiping in Lavington United Church, Nairobi, Kenya. *The year is 1986, and the day is Confirmation Sunday. A group of young people sit in the front with their families and godparents. In this united church — Presbyterian, Methodist, and Anglican — the young people will be confirmed into all three denominations; thus, the presiding ministers on this day include the Methodist minister of the church, the moderator of the Presbyterian Church and the bishop of the Anglican Church. Early leaders of this congregation, and of the three denominations, were missionaries, but no more; for more than twenty years, the members and leaders have been native Kenyans.*

The service begins after the overflowing crowd squeezes into the pews, with people saying to one another, "There's always room for one more."[3] The Methodist minister introduces the service, the Anglican bishop leads the liturgy, and the Presbyterian moderator preaches. The liturgy crescendos in the reading of scripture, preaching of the Word, and service of confirmation, in which all three ministers participate. When the time comes for the sermon, the pastor invites the entire congregation to welcome the preacher for the morning with singing, "Lord, speak to me, that I may speak." And the preacher does speak — with passion and fire.

The Presbyterian moderator begins with these words, "The churches are populated with people who haven't come to full knowledge of Jesus Christ." He elaborates by describing how churches say the Lord's Prayer and Apostles' Creed, but do not always know Jesus Christ. The preacher then turns to the text of the day, beginning with 2 Corinthians 5:17 — "So if any one is in Christ, there is a new creation: everything old has passed away; see, everything has become new!" (NRSV). Here in this united church in Nairobi, people are being warned of the social and personal evil in their land, and they are being invited to new life in Christ. Confirmation follows. Imagine the people who gave themselves for new life in Christ on this August day in 1986; imagine the people of years past who united this church, and remember.

I invite you now to imagine yourself as a member of the first-century church of Rome. *Someone else established your church, but Paul, the famous missionary, is coming to visit. For some reason, Paul seems eager to communicate with your church,*

---

2. Inscription on column of St. Giles Cathedral, Edinburgh, Scotland.
3. The description presented here is taken from Mary Elizabeth Moore, Kenyan field notes, August 10, 1986. These were part of an extended ethnographic study of the Nairobi congregation.

so he writes a long letter and sends it ahead. In the letter, he reminds Roman Christians: "Do not be conformed to this world, but be transformed by the renewing of your minds, so that you may discern what is the will of God — what is good and acceptable and perfect" (12:2, NRSV). Paul expresses concerns in this long, careful letter. But why?

Imagine yourself in this divided Roman Christian community. Some people are Jewish Christians who were exiled by the emperor Claudius and are now returning; some are Gentile Christians. These diverse Christians, as those in Jerusalem, have many questions about the relationship of Christianity to Judaism, and Gentile Christians to Jewish Christians.[4] Their issues seem important to Paul as he writes to them before departing to Jerusalem, and later proceeding to Rome. Some disagreements in Rome are intense: whether the Ten Commandments are binding on Christians and what foods are lawful to eat. The community is alive with different views, and Paul urges constraint among Jewish and Gentile Christians alike. Paul seems particularly concerned about those Jewish Christians who insist that Christians obey all of Jewish law.[5] Paul, a Jewish Christian himself, insists in chapter 3 that Jews and Greeks alike are "under the power of sin" (Rom. 3:9), and they are also alike as recipients of God's care.

---

4. Leander E. Keck, "The Letter of Paul to the Romans: Introduction," in *The HarperCollins Study Bible*, ed. Wayne A. Meeks (New York: HarperCollins, 1993), 2114–16. The issues in Jerusalem and Rome were different; the Jerusalem church was largely Gentile, and the Roman church was mixed. Both communities struggled, however, to interpret the relationship between Judaism and Christianity. Paul's purposes in writing Romans are difficult to discern. One interpretation is that Paul wrote to introduce himself for the sake of his future mission and to defend himself against criticisms regarding his views on Jewish and Gentile Christian practice (a controversial issue in many locales). Another is that Paul had heard about serious divisions and disputes in the Roman Christian community. Another is that Paul anticipated and feared conflicts in Rome that he had seen elsewhere. Whichever interpretation one makes, Paul's letter clearly addresses issues of communal conflict. He apparently believed that these issues were important for him to address and for Roman Christians to hear. For further discussion of Paul's purposes and the Roman context, see A. Katherine Grieb, *The Story of Romans: A Narrative Defense of God's Righteousness* (Louisville: Westminster John Knox, 2002), 14–16; James C. Miller, *The Obedience of Faith, the Eschatological People of God, and the Purpose of Romans* (Atlanta: Society of Biblical Literature, 2000), 2–19; Anthony J. Guerra, *Romans and the Apologetic Tradition: The Purpose, Genre and Audience of Paul's Letter* (Cambridge: Cambridge University Press, 1995), 22–42; James Christopher Walters, *Ethnic Issues in Paul's Letter to the Romans: An Analysis in Light of the Changing Self-Definition of Early Christianity in Rome*, dissertation, Boston University (Ann Arbor: University Microfilms International, 1991); Neil Elliott, *The Rhetoric of Romans: Argumentative Constraint and Strategy and Paul's Dialogue with Judaism*, Supplement Series 45 (Sheffield: JSOT, 1990), 43–59.

5. Douglas Campbell, "Righteousness in Romans Revisited," lecture, Centre for Advanced Biblical Studies, King's College, London, January 28, 1994. Campbell argues that Paul's rhetorical interjections reveal the contentious context to which he was writing, and the particular contentiousness of militant Jewish Christians. He argues that the tendency to ignore this context in the Reformation, Methodism, and neo-Orthodoxy has been a methodological shortfall and has led to misunderstandings of Romans, which, like Paul's other letters, was addressed to particular concerns of particular people. Several texts in Romans 3 and 16 illustrate this point. See also Douglas Atchison Campbell, *The Rhetoric of Righteousness in Romans 3:21–26* (Sheffield: JSOT, 1992). For a different view, see Mark D. Nanos, *The Mystery of Romans: The Jewish Context of Paul's Letter* (Minneapolis: Fortress, 1996), 9–40. Nanos argues that Paul was centrally concerned with Israel's restoration — to the Jew first, and also to the Greek — and was more concerned with gentile Christian exclusivism than many interpreters believe. For both Campbell and Nanos, Paul is strongly concerned about contentions and exclusivist practices in the Roman church.

Or is God the God of the Jews only? Is he not the God of Gentiles also? Yes, of
Gentiles also, since God is one; and he will justify the circumcised on the ground
of faith and the uncircumcised through that same faith (Rom. 3:29–30, NRSV).

In the same chapter, Paul intensifies his point, repeating his testimony four times that
salvation is for the whole community through Jesus Christ (21–26). Imagine this
diverse and divided Roman community, and Paul's message for them: remember!

Texts Explored

Thus far, I have invited readers to imagine and remember. What does that have
to do with teaching as sacramental? What does it have to do with mediating
God's grace? As with any texts, blessing comes with wrestling; thus, we dive into
these texts from different periods of Christian history and different parts of the
world. We cannot be exhaustive here, but I suggest three themes that emerge
from the texts.

Communities in Conflict and Pain

The first theme is common to all of the texts: the communities were living with
conflict and pain. At St. Giles, the conflict was most obvious because Jenny
Geddes, full of fury, threw a stool during worship. This woman represented a
large number of people in the congregation, who resented the actions of King
Charles I and Archbishop Laud to impose the Anglican *Book of Common Prayer*
upon the church in Scotland. The conflict at St. Giles is made obvious again when
we see the words of Dean Hannay's descendants; they recognized the finality of
Hannay's reading from the Service Book, and the pain of his role in a seventeenth-
century church fraught with power struggles and theological tension. The conflict
here was not mild, nor was it creatively resolved to everyone's satisfaction; the
conflict began more than a century earlier and was to last for several decades
to come. Further, it was filled with pain, some of which persists today (albeit
in milder forms) in relations between England and Scotland and between the
Church of England and the Church of Scotland. The conflict and pain signal a
broken community.

Conflict and pain is less evident in the text from Lavington Church in Nairobi.
We see here a miracle story of a united church, uniting the Presbyterian, Anglican,
and Methodist traditions that were torn asunder in sixteenth-, seventeenth-, and
eighteenth-century Britain. We see here a local church uniting denominations
whose leaders had divided the mission field of Kenya many years before, so that
churches would evangelize in different locales with different tribes. But conflict
and pain are present still — in the pains of giving birth to a postcolonial church
and in efforts to foster communication and support between the wealthier and
poorer congregations of the church, congregations who speak different primary

languages. Conflict and pain are also represented in lingering tensions among the three denominations, creeping into power struggles within the church and among the denominational leaders.

Conflict and pain were not on the surface in 1986, but they bubbled up from time to time, even in disjunctions of the confirmation service. When the Presbyterian preacher ended his sermon with a call to conversion, he invited people to come to the altar if they were "ready to turn their lives around." He also invited the young confirmands to come forward. The young people remained seated, apparently confused about an invitation to conversion in the middle of a service in which the entire liturgy was leading to the climax of their confirmation. Though the liturgy was a united one and developed collegially by denominations in East Africa, some differences were unresolved. In the congregation's story, conflicts were not explosive, but they were reminders of discord under the surface of many ecumenical efforts and local church ministries in which people of divergent beliefs and values are held together in a sometimes awkward, sometimes conflicted, community. And when conflicts turn to pain, we see signs of broken community.

We turn finally to the church community who received Paul's letter to the Romans — a community in which we can see conflict, but we can only guess how much of the conflict was above and below the surface. Paul seemed eager for the Romans to hear his message. He wrote with fiery passion at many points, as in the last chapter:

> I implore you, my friends, keep your eye on those who stir up quarrels and lead others astray, contrary to the teaching you received. Avoid them, for such people are servants not of Christ our Lord but of their own appetites, and they seduce the minds of innocent people with smooth and specious words. (Rom. 16:17–18)

These are strong words! According to Douglas Campbell of New Zealand, the Christian church has made a mistake in reading Romans without attention to the contentious context of Rome.[6] The tendency is to read the letter as a general theological statement and to miss Paul's intent to respond to concrete issues in the Roman community.

Many distortions and abuses have actually been created by the tendency to abstract Romans into theological dogma. One distortion is the tendency to read the letter as a message of individual salvation and miss Paul's concern for divisions in the community. Another distortion, which has become a serious abuse over the centuries, is the tendency to read Romans as a message to the Jews rather than a message to a particular community in which many Jews had been exiled in the past and some were militant in the present. Texts in Romans have been used for centuries to reinforce anti-Semitism and anti-Judaism, even to justify

---

6. Campbell, "Righteousness in Romans Revisited."

the extinction of six million Jews in the Holocaust. What if we reread Romans and discover in the particularity of the church at Rome the particularity of our own churches with their squabbles and conflicts? In those conflicts and pains of community life, we might see signals of broken community.

A World in Turmoil

In addition to communities in conflict and pain, the texts with which I began also signal a world in turmoil. The conflict and pain within these communities did not arise apart from turmoil in the world around them. The conflicts in St. Giles in 1637 were surrounded by longstanding political conflicts between the govern-ments of Scotland and England and between the churches in both countries. In 1560 (seventy-seven years earlier) the Scots Parliament had declared an end to the authority of the pope in Scotland, and in 1562 the General Assembly adopted John Knox's *Book of Common Order.* John Knox became the minister of St. Giles, and the new church was born. Disagreements about church government persisted, however, and emerged strongly in 1633 when King Charles I ruled that Scottish Presbyterianism should be replaced with the episcopacy. He made St. Giles a cathedral and required the use of the *Book of Common Prayer* across Britain, thus setting the stage for the action of Jenny Geddes in 1637. By the following year, the Scots had signed the National Covenant, pledging to Presbyterianism in Scot-land. This was not the end, however: civil war broke out in Britain, Charles I was beheaded, a Parliamentarian government governed for a time, and then King Charles II was crowned in 1660, launching further persecution of Presbyterians until the end of his reign in 1688. This brief history scans 128 years of turmoil, preceded and succeeded by still more struggle. The 1637 church of Jenny Geddes and James Hannay was engulfed in turmoil.

Likewise, the 1986 united church in Nairobi was surrounded by social turmoil that seeped into the life of the church. Among other things, the congregation lived in a world in which the three denominations of their union had disagree-ments among themselves. They also faced difficult decisions regarding how they should respond to the social upheaval in Kenyan society, such as the movement of people away from rural areas and traditional rural values, increasing problems of poverty, and immigration of people from other countries into Kenya for jobs and stability. Further, the church faced problems of how best to relate to the Kenyan government with its remarkable postcolonial accomplishments, its en-couragement and support of Christianity, its silencing of dissident voices, and its preferential representation and treatment of some tribes over others. These pres-sures intensified the commitment of the congregation to its unity and aliveness, but the pressures strained the community as it lived daily in a world of turmoil.

Finally, a look at the first-century church of Rome calls up the memory of many religious communities in the same region — Jewish, Christian, Hellenistic,

Roman, and other — that were divided among themselves and within themselves as they sought to live faithfully in a world of religious conflict and Roman imperialism. The diversity of peoples, economic and political inequities, and recurring conflicts over religious truth created a stressful world and intense questing for identity. This questing added fuel to debates within the Roman church over Christian belief and practice. The people lived in a world of turmoil, and their Christian faith did not exempt them from feeling it.

Communities Seeking New Life

To say that these texts reveal internal conflict and pain and an external world of turmoil is not all there is. The three communities were also seeking new life. The very effort of the people in Scotland to determine their own future and to struggle against domination represents their search for new life. The effort of the Nairobi congregation to live as a unified church represents its search for new life. The particulars of what these churches were trying to do were different, but both were seeking after God and witnessing to truth insofar as they could discern it — witnessing to a truth that they thought important to their community life and to the world in which they lived. The church in Scotland was struggling to be a participatory, liberating, and reformed church. The church in Nairobi was struggling to create a church community that would symbolize and contribute to *harambee* — the motto of Kenya, meaning "Let us pull together."

Turning finally to the church in Rome, we see a church (through Paul's lens) in which people were willing to put their commitments forward, to struggle with difficult questions, to seek understanding of the Gospel, and to follow Jesus Christ. On the other hand, we see a church touched by mean-spiritedness, and we see Paul urging the people to be transformed into a community befitting the Gospel that they proclaimed. This discussion leads to the familiar text in Romans: "Do not be conformed to this world, but be transformed by the renewing of your minds, so that you may discern what is the will of God — what is good and acceptable and perfect" (12:2, NRSV). Paul called this Roman community to be transformed — not conformed to the combative turmoil of the world, but transformed by the renewing of their minds. As the people were transformed into a new life in Christ, they would be equipped to witness to new life in the world.

Sacramental Theology — Roots of Hope

We cannot presume that all Christian communities are identical to those we have explored thus far. We *can* presume, however, that most communities face conflict and pain — sometimes visible, sometimes under the surface. We can also presume that most live in a world of turmoil, and most hunger and search for new life. In such a broken church and tumultuous world, where then is hope? What is God's call for Christians?

The invitation of this book is to understand *God's call to practice sacramental living* — *living that mediates divine grace in the church and world.* Because sacramental living is grounded in God, we turn to sacramental theology — the study of God and the signs of God's grace in the world — to discover hope. Sacramental theology is like a towering tree, impressively large and bountiful with fruit. What is less apparent is the deep roots that hold the tree in the ground, sending nourishment to its branches. Each root reaches far under the ground, intertwining with others, as roots are wont to do.

Encounter with God

The first root of hope in sacramental theology is the *understanding of sacrament as an encounter with God.* The sense of encounter has been associated with sacraments since New Testament times.[7] These powerful encounters mark people with grace, and also with vulnerability to what God will reveal and ask of them. According to dominant traditions, when people are baptized into the Body of Christ, they die to sin and arise to new life — a transformation described as both joyful and demanding.

To explore the joy of baptism, reflect on the African American community. Melva Costen describes joyful baptisms, even during early days of slavery in North America:

> Baptisms by immersion were particularly dramatic and celebrative. Both slave and free, representing many denominations, were known to have walked as far as ten miles to share in the excitement of these important and memorable occasions.[8]

This baptismal joy was powerfully joined with a sense of responsibility; many people sought earnestly to forgive and be forgiven before they went forth for baptism. The ex-slave Isaiah Jeffries vivifies the practice when he describes what his mother did:

> She went around to all de people dat she had done wrong and begged dere forgiveness. She sent fer dem dat had wronged her, and told dem dat she was born again and a new woman, and dat she would forgive dem. She wanted everybody dat was not saved to go up wid her.[9]

Such an accent on joy and responsibility continues in African American communities today.

---

7. James F. White, *Introduction to Christian Worship,* rev. ed. (Nashville: Abingdon, 1990), 166. White describes this encounter as God's love made visible (165–91). See also White, *Sacraments as God's Self-Giving* (Nashville: Abingdon, 1983).

8. Melva Wilson Costen, *African American Christian Worship* (Nashville: Abingdon, 1993), 62.

9. Ibid., 63; cf. George P. Rawick, ed., *The American Slave: A Composite Autobiography,* vol. 3 (Westport, Conn.: Greenwood, 1972, 1941), "South Carolina Narratives," part 3, 19.

In addition to joy and responsibility, however, baptism can also be joined with anger, as when slave owners *denied* baptism to slaves. The owners did not want slaves to demand rights and privileges as a result of their inclusion in the Christian community. Indeed, anger raged when African American slaves who *were* baptized were denied freedom, even the right to earn their freedom, from slavery.[10] Looking at the African American community, we can see what is true for many communities — tensions between baptismal claims and human distortions. Marjorie Procter-Smith points out how ambiguous the revelation of God can be when symbols of baptism and eucharist simultaneously communicate power, strength, and alienation to women. Yet baptism has the power to transform human distortions when the church reclaims "the early church's understanding of baptism as a multivalent symbol, representing rebirth, death and resurrection, messianic anointing, incorporation into a priestly people, to name but a few."[11] Facing the ambiguity, multiplicity, and power of baptism simply underlines its power to reveal God. Baptism is an encounter with God that marks people with joy, responsibility, belonging, and expectation, and with anger or disappointment when expectations are not fulfilled and belonging is not actualized.

Remembrance

The second root of hope in sacramental theology is the *understanding of sacrament as remembrance.* In some traditions, the Lord's Supper is understood as a memorial, remembering particularly the sacrifice of Jesus for humanity. For all Christian traditions, the Lord's Supper is accompanied with remembrance of Jesus' life, death, and resurrection. Remembering is also part of baptism, especially remembering God's Spirit moving across the face of the waters, God's delivery of Israel across the Red Sea, and the baptism of Jesus. Similarly, remembering is central to the sacramental acts of Jews — Passover, remembering the delivery of their ancestors from slavery in Egypt, and circumcision, remembering God's covenant with Abraham and his male descendants. In both traditions, the act of recalling the past evokes God's promises for the future.

In Christian eucharist, the words of institution are actually words of remembrance, reported in Mark's Gospel in this way: "While they were eating, he took a loaf of bread, and after blessing it he broke it, gave it to them, and said, 'Take; this is my body'" (14:22, NRSV; cf. 22–25). Similar words of institution are found in Matthew 26:26–29, Luke 22:17–20, and 1 Corinthians 11:23–26. In Luke and 1 Corinthians, the word *anamnesis* appears, translated inexactly into English as remembrance, recalling, representation, and experiencing anew. Remembrance is thus central in the biblical narratives and in the celebration of eucharist, in which remembering is embodied both in words and actions. According to James White,

---

10. Costen, *African American Christian Worship,* 33–34.

11. Marjorie Procter-Smith, *In Her Own Rite: Constructing Feminist Liturgical Tradition* (Akron, Ohio: OSL Publications, 2000; Nashville: Abingdon Press, 1990), 128; cf. 123–24, 132.

"*Anamnesis* expresses the sense that in repeating these actions one experiences once again the reality of Jesus himself present."[12] The remembering also expands to the broad sweep of God's works, and *anamnesis* is identified with the memory of all God's acts, including but not limited to Jesus' last meal with the disciples.[13] Many of these acts are named in the eucharistic thanksgiving.

   Sacramental remembering is not limited to remembering God, however. As Don Saliers notes, Christian liturgy is where human pathos and divine ethos meet. He says, "The very act of remembering who God is and what God has done confers dignity and honor and deepens the pathos of those who gather."[14] In particular, the sacraments are sacred times of remembering God's work throughout history; Jesus' life, death, and resurrection; *and* realities of human history, including tragic human history. The danger, of course, is that people will distance tragedy and ig-nore the more recent and still present tragic memories — tragedies in their own lives and tragedies of oppressed peoples and oppressed parts of creation. This dan-ger is sometimes addressed in the liturgies of marginalized people, such as women, which is why their liturgies are so important to the larger tradition. According to Marjorie Procter-Smith, "Honest expressions of grief, anger, and lament, rarely affirmed in traditional liturgies, are a common and respected element of many feminist liturgies."[15] Such liturgies are vital for awaking the larger church. The sacraments, especially eucharist, give courage to face destructive and horrifying realities, as well as hopeful and life-giving ones.

Encounter with New Creation

The third root of hope in sacramental theology is the *understanding of sacrament as an encounter with New Creation.* This understanding is often overlooked in practice, but the sacraments are profoundly eschatological in character, looking back in remembrance and looking forward in hope for God's New Creation.[16]

---

   12. White, *Introduction to Christian Worship*, 223, cf. 222–24; White, *Sacraments as God's Self-Giving*, 24–27. R. J. Halliburton recognizes the particular power of thanksgiving (*eucharistia*) and commem-oration (*anamnesis*) during the patristic period, for salvation was understood to come through God's redeeming action in Christ — the central focus of thanksgiving and memorial in the eucharist. Both thanksgiving and commemoration evoke gratefulness to God and prayers for continued blessing; the patterns parallel thanksgivings and memorials in Judaism. See Halliburton, "The Patristic Theology of the Eucharist," in *The Study of Liturgy*, ed. Cheslyn Jones, Geoffrey Wainwright, and Edward Yarnold, S.J. (New York: Oxford University Press, 1978), 203–5. The power of the liturgical actions is partic-ularly evident in the Byzantine liturgy. See Hugh Wybrew, "Thy Byzantine Liturgy from the *Apostolic Constitutions* to the Present Day," in *The Study of Liturgy*, ed. Jones, Wainwright, and Yarnold, 208–19.
   13. Procter-Smith, *In Her Own Rite*, 30–32; Halliburton, "The Patristic Theology of the Eucharist," 205; Geoffrey Wainwright, "Recent Eucharistic Revision," in *The Study of Liturgy*, 287; John Chrysos-tom, *The Homilies of St. John Chrysostom on the Gospel of St. Matthew* (Oxford: John Henry Parker, 1852), Homily 25.4, 380 82.
   14. Don Saliers, *Worship as Theology: Foretaste of Glory Divine* (Nashville: Abingdon, 1994), 26; cf. 21–38, esp. 25–28.
   15. Procter-Smith, *In Her Own Rite*, v; cf. vii.
   16. This view is prominent in the literature of sacramental theology. See, for example, Saliers, *Worship as Theology*, 14 and entire book; Don E. Saliers, *Worship and Spirituality*, 2nd ed. (Akron,

Petros Vassiliadis, writing from an Orthodox perspective, calls this a "costly eucharistic vision," for it points to the fundamental unity between the church's sacramental acts and its sociocosmic responsibilities.[17] The eschatological nature of the eucharist points to the eschatological and diaconal nature of the church; it calls forth an active response from the church that celebrates the holy meal. This radical claim may be why many churches deemphasize the encounter with New Creation; it *is* threatening.

The connection between memory and vision is more radical than it frequently seems in the literature. A dramatic contrast often exists between memory and hope — the memory of Jesus' self-giving and human hopes for comfort, the memory of human distortions and hopes for a new humanity, the memory of human alienation from God's creation and hopes for New Creation. Some authors identify these contrasts, especially in relation to women and the poor and hungry;[18] however, common sacramental practice does not always accent the encounter with New Creation. Nor does common practice stir hope that the world's pain will be touched by sacramental practice.

Even more threatening are contrasts between God realities communicated through the sacraments and hurtful human realities in the church that celebrates. Procter-Smith, for example, describes how the sacraments can be alienating for women, who are struck by the contrast between promises celebrated and the patriarchal church in which the sacraments are enacted.[19] These issues call for at least four responses: (1) remembering eschatological dimension of the sacraments, pointing toward a world of justice and peace; (2) drawing upon sacramental promises to measure destructive realities of the present; (3) attending to the contexts in which sacraments are celebrated so that people might seek transformation within those contexts; and (4) exercising sacramental imagination, imagining the world toward which sacraments point and the sacramental potential to subvert destructive worlds of the present and past.[20] The last point regarding imagination is often neglected in sacramental theology; yet it permeates the sacraments:

Ohio: OSL Publications, 1996, 1984), esp. 79–90, 43, 67–68; Procter-Smith, *In Her Own Rite*, 30; Leonardo Boff, *Sacraments of Life: Life of the Sacraments* (Washington, D.C.: Pastoral Press, 1987); Bernard J. Cooke, *Sacraments and Sacramentality* (Mystic, Conn.: Twenty-Third Publications, 1983); Alexander Schmemann, *The Eucharist: Sacrament of the Kingdom,* trans. Paul Kachur (Crestwood, N.Y.: St. Vladimir's Seminary Press, 1988, 1987).

17. Petros Vassiliadis, *Eucharist and Witness: Orthodox Perspectives on the Unity and Mission of the Church* (Geneva: WCC Publications, 1998), 1–2; cf. 1–6, 49–51.

18. See, for example: Procter-Smith, *In Her Own Rite*, 37–38; Tissa Balasuriya, *The Eucharist and Human Liberation* (Maryknoll, N.Y.: Orbis, 1979, 1977), 1–27, 128–45.

19. Procter-Smith, *In Her Own Rite*, 123–27, 130–31.

20. On the first point, two prominent spokespersons are White, *Sacraments*, 94; Saliers, *Worship as Theology*, 185–90. On the second point, see Procter-Smith, *In Her Own Rite*, 131–38. On the third, see Rafael Avila, *Worship and Politics* (Maryknoll, N.Y.: Orbis, 1981, 1977), 100. On the fourth, see Procter-Smith, 37–38, 43–44.

Only by understanding liturgy as a deeply imaginative act can we account for liturgy's claim that a bowl of water is the Red Sea, the cosmic waters of chaos, the River Jordan, the uterine waters of new birth, or that a loaf of bread and a cup of wine are the body and blood of the Risen Christ, the foretaste of the messianic banquet, the food of angels.[21]

The sacraments can inspire and terrify people with new vision. And their visions may require action, as in the radical practice of forgiveness among many slaves at the time of baptism. Vision may also require letting go of old habits and familiar practices, destructive church structures, oppressive cultural forms, and distorted worldviews.

Symbol of God's Work in Creation

The fourth root of hope in sacramental theology is the *understanding of sacrament as a symbol of God's work in creation, the source of praise and thanksgiving.* The sacraments are, at their heart, acts of thanksgiving, stirred by the gracious acts of God. Thanksgiving has been particularly expounded in relation to the eucharist, for the very name of the sacrament derives from the Greek word *eucharistia*, giving thanks to God. Not only is thanksgiving at the heart of eucharistic liturgies; it appears in most New Testament eucharistic texts as well. James White points out that the emphasis is not primarily on human gratitude; the primary focus is on "thankful commemoration of God's works and prayer for their continuance."[22] Thanksgiving for God's actions is surely a powerful source of hope in sacramental theology.

While the sacraments draw upon symbols (water, bread and wine), the ritual action is itself a symbol of God's gifts to creation.[23] The sacraments thus point to, participate in, and enact the work of God. Most obviously, the Christian sacraments point to God's work in Christ — the ministry of Jesus Christ and his life, death, and resurrection. They also point to the eschatological vision at the center of Jesus' ministry and to God's acts throughout history. In baptism, the

---

21. Procter-Smith, *In Her Own Rite,* 43. Note that Procter-Smith's references to imagination are grounded in historic imagery, reflecting the close relation between God's movements in history and God's invitation to future.

22. White, *Sacraments as God's Self-Giving,* 54.

23. This view is somewhat different from that of Evelyn Underhill, who distinguishes between sacrament and symbols. She acknowledges that symbols are important to sacraments, but that sacraments are "far more than a symbol; since here the supernatural is not merely suggested but actually conveyed." Underhill, *Man and the Supernatural* (London: Methuen, 1927), 176; cf. 175–78. For her, symbols "suggest and represent; but sacraments work" (ibid.; cf. Underhill, *Worship* [London: Nisbet, 1936], 42–43, cf. 42 47). In her earliest book, Underhill's distinction between symbol and sacrament was suggested, but less sharply. See Underhill, *Mysticism: A Study in the Nature and Development of Man's Spiritual Consciousness,* 12th ed., rev. (London: Methuen, 1930, 1911), 163–64. Though Underhill increased her emphasis on the transcendent action of God and the stark contrast between Creator and creature (ibid., vii–viii), she did not revise *Mysticism* as regards the mediating power of symbols, sacraments, and mysteries, which is more akin to my presentation.

assembly remembers God's acts of creating, delivering, and baptizing. Similarly in the eucharist, the prayer of thanksgiving includes remembering God's works from the beginning of creation.

To say that the sacraments symbolize God's gracious action is to encounter God's self-giving through them.[24] Sacramental acts re-present the giving nature of God, clearing a sacred space for the community to *receive from* God and *participate in* the being of God. Sacramental acts are thus transformative, opening the way for God to continue acting in human lives and creation. God's self-giving in Christ is more than a blessed memory; it evokes a congregation's own self-giving.[25] First, however, it evokes gratitude to God, as noted in the church's earliest collection of formal teaching:

> In the first century or early second century, the *Didache* instructs: "Now, about the Eucharist: This is how to give thanks and begins, 'We thank you, our Father, for....' In good Jewish fashion, Christians then remembered God's saving acts past and petitioned for those yet to come."[26]

We see here the central eucharistic act of thanksgiving, a response to God's actions in the past and into the future. Hope is grounded again and again in God.

Communion

The fifth root of hope is the *understanding of sacrament as communion*. In the sacraments, God enters genuine communion with the people. Unfortunately, this idea is easily converted into an abstraction, or interpreted as coming only through the priesthood. According to Alexander Schmemann, however, priestly participation in the sacraments is not valid without the congregation.[27] According to Petros Vassiliadis, communion is "the culminating and most important act of the eucharistic rite."[28] The sacraments thus herald the unity of the church and ministry. God communes with the whole Body, and *every* part is important to the whole. Such a theology puts communities to shame when they destroy one another. When they come together at the Table, they are called to be in community

---

24. White, *Sacraments as God's Self-Giving*, esp. 13–33; cf. White, *Introduction to Christian Worship*, 165–91; Underhill, *Man and the Supernatural*, 175–89.

25. Augustine, *City of God against the Pagans*, Book X.5–6, ed. and trans. R. W. Dyson (Cambridge: Cambridge University Press, 1998), 396–400. According to Augustine, the sacrifice God wants is "a contrite heart," marked by love of God and neighbor. More pointedly, "mercy is the true sacrifice" (397–98).

26. White, *Sacraments as God's Self-Giving*, 55. See the full *Didache* text in Cyril Richardson, ed., *Early Christian Fathers* (Philadelphia: Westminster Press, 1953), 175.

27. Alexander Schmemann, *The Eucharist: Sacrament of the Kingdom*, trans. Paul Kachur (Crestwood, N.Y.: St. Vladimir's Seminary Press, 1988), 14–26; Schmemann, *For the Life of the World: Sacraments and Orthodoxy* (Crestwood, N.Y.: St. Vladimir's Seminary Press, 1973, 1963), 25–28.

28. Vassiliadis, *Eucharist and Witness*, 57. Vassiliadis makes this point (originally to Orthodox theological schools) as part of his critique of the church's decreasing involvement of the entire people in celebrating the Eucharist (49–66).

with one another, not in competition or mutual hatred. This theology also shames the early missionaries in South America and Africa who baptized people en masse, a tool of manipulating a social body rather than a sacrament of grace. One of the most sobering practices comes from slave history when masses of Africans were baptized as they were taken into slavery, without any prior teaching or choice in the matter.[29]

The communal nature of sacrament is grounded in the power of the community, not in people's feeling good about one another. In fact, the feelings and moral state of the celebrant and congregants are not critical to the power of the sacraments. Augustine (400 c.e.) was clear that the holiness of baptism did not rely on the holiness of the minister and recipient; Thomas Aquinas (1271) carried the same emphasis regarding all sacraments, as did the Council of Trent (1547); Evelyn Underhill, many centuries later (1909), reiterated the theme with particular attention to the eucharist.[30] Of course, churches have, from time to time through history, placed restrictions on celebrants and congregants, but the weight of Christian tradition is to see the communal nature of the sacraments as present regardless of the state of mind and soul of those who gather at the water or the table. Communion is a gift of God.

The communal nature of sacrament also requires response from the community, a theme discussed in feminist liturgical literature. Feminist liturgy generally emphasizes shared leadership and responsibility and values diversity and relationships.[31] Such relationships are based, not on agreement and agreeability, but on honesty, a sense of interconnection, and resistance to oppression. Feminist liturgies point to ways in which the sacraments themselves might more fully embody the communion they proclaim.

Efficacy

One final root of hope will be named here, but others could also be named. This is the *understanding of sacrament as efficacious.* Sacraments are efficacious in invoking

---

29. Costen, *African American Christian Worship*, 27; cf. Eugene D. Genovese, *Roll, Jordan, Roll: The World the Slaves Made* (New York: Pantheon Books, 1974), 176. Such communal baptisms have a complex history from the fourth century. Many missionaries sincerely trusted the power of baptism to begin people on a journey of faith; however, even with good intentions, such baptisms were sometimes conjoined with manipulation and enslavement.

30. Augustine, *On Baptism against the Donatists*, Book IV, Ch. 11.18 (c. 400), trans. J. R. King, rev. Chester D. Hartranft, in *Nicene and Post-Nicene Fathers of the Christian Church*, vol. 4, ed. Philip Schaff (Grand Rapids, Mich.: Wm. B. Eerdmans, 1956), 454; Thomas Aquinas, "Fifth Article: Whether the Sacraments Can Be Conferred by Evil Ministers?" *Summa Theologica*, Part III, 64, trans. Fathers of the English Dominican Province (New York: Benziger Brothers, 1947), II, 2369–74; Aquinas, "Ninth Article: Whether Faith Is Required of Necessity in the Minister of a Sacrament?" ibid.; Council of Trent, "Canon XII," *The Canons and Decrees of the Council of Trent* (1547), trans. Philip Schaff, *The Creeds of Christendom* (Grand Rapids, Mich.: Baker Book House, n.d.), 2:119–22; Evelyn Underhill, "To M.R. (St. Patrick's Day, 1909)," in *The Letters of Evelyn Underhill*, ed. Charles Williams (London: Longmans, Green, 1943), 96. See also White, *Sacraments as God's Self-Giving*, 33.

31. Procter-Smith, *In Her Own Rite*, iii–v.

the power of God's Spirit and God's work through history, embracing the pain of
the past, creating new life within individuals and communities, and transforming
the old into new. They make a difference in people's lives and in the life of God's
creation. The sacraments are efficacious, first, in the sense that God truly gives
God's Self.[32] Sacraments manifest God's love, which is critical so that people can
know and be supported and guided by God. The former archbishop of Canterbury
Arthur Michael Ramsey described this efficacy in vivid language: "The sacrifice of
Christ on Calvary is present in the here and now in its timeless potency, and the
homely bread and wine of a contemporary meal are made the effectual signs of
Christ's self-giving."[33] This leads to a second dimension of efficacy, namely, that
the sacraments actually change the present situation. According to Ramsey, the
eucharist equips people to face the world: "to tackle the tasks of the present with
realism and to face the future with hope."[34] According to Evelyn Underhill, "A
valid sacrament . . . always leaves the situation different from what it was before."[35]
In short, sacraments do change the world.

The sacraments are made efficacious, not by the perfectly performed liturgy,
but by the Holy Spirit. Central to the sacraments of baptism and eucharist is
the *epiclesis*, the prayer by which God is asked to send the Holy Spirit upon
the sacramental water, bread, or wine so that the Holy Spirit may act through
it.[36] Because of the Spirit's movement in the sacraments, people treasure their
liturgies; for the same reason, they sometimes feel compelled to critique, renew,
and reform them.[37] For example, people have questioned the tendency in some
traditions to deemphasize the sacramental participation of the whole people, or

---

32. Underhill, *Man and the Supernatural*, 175–80; cf. 175–89. See also White, *Sacraments as God's
Self-Giving*, 23. White points to John Calvin's emphasis on the weak human faith that requires visible
signs of God's love. For Calvin, a sacrament is "an outward sign by which the Lord seals on our
consciences the promises of his good will toward us in order to sustain the weakness of our faith."
See *Calvin: Institutes of the Christian Religion*, IV, 14, 1–26 (1559), trans. Ford Lewis Battles, Library
of Christian Classics 21 (Philadelphia: Westminster Press, 1960), 1277.

33. Arthur Michael Ramsey, *God, Christ and the World: A Study of Contemporary Theology* (London:
SCM, 1969), 116.

34. Ibid.

35. Underhill, *Worship*, 43. She elaborates that the sacrament "effects a communication of the
Wholly Other"; thus, it is "an acknowledgement of the presence and priority of the divine, and is
directed towards the sanctification of life" (ibid.). James White notes that sacramental efficacy has
been debated due to the subjectivity involved in judging the results; nevertheless, "Roman Catholics
and many Protestants consider sacraments to be divinely given means of grace wherein God's self-
giving occurs here and now. In this sense, they affirm that God does act anew in the sacraments"
(*Sacraments as God's Self-Giving*, 32–33).

36. E. J. Yarnold, S.J., "The Fourth and Fifth Centuries," in *The Study of Liturgy*, ed. Jones,
Wainwright, and Yarnold, 102; Yarnold, "The Liturgy of the Faithful in the Fourth and Early Fifth
Centuries," ibid., 192, 196.

37. Vassiliadis, *Eucharist and Witness*, 61; cf. 57–62. He says: "The moral and social responsibility
of the church . . . is the logical consequence of its ecclesial consciousness. It is therefore only by a
massive reaffirmation of the eucharistic identity of the church through a radical *liturgical renewal* that
our Orthodox church can bear witness to its fundamental characteristics of unity and catholicity"
(emphasis his).

the tendency to engage with Christ in ways that disrespect Christians of different Christian communions and proselytize people of other religious traditions.
People also question the failure of Christians to remember and enact the connection between the sacraments and the well-being of the larger world, such as the
connection between eucharistic food and food for hungry people.

The efficacious nature of sacraments sometimes evokes an experimental quality, as is common in feminist liturgies. By experimenting, people seek to enhance
the sacramental possibilities in their present situation. When this is done by
marginalized women and oppressed people, the sacrament stirs self-criticism and
moral vision oriented to empowering and liberating them.[38] Whether the sacraments are celebrated in a historic liturgy, unchanged through centuries of church
history, or celebrated with some degree of experimentation, they are efficacious.
They make a *difference* in the world.

Sacramental Teaching

With hope bubbling up from liturgical theology, we turn now to sacramental
living and the particular focus of this book, sacramental teaching. Sacramental
living is a way of life fueled by God's hope, incarnate in Jesus Christ. This is not
naïve hope, nor gentle hope without pain. It is a powerful, God-centered hope
that evokes self-giving and full living. This hope cost Jesus his life; it also opened
the way for new life to emerge. This is the same hope that ordinary people and
flawed human communities are promised. The promise itself calls forth the need
for sacramental teaching so that God's hope might be proclaimed and actualized
in people's lives.

As I said in chapter 1, my purpose is not to multiply the number of formal
sacraments in the church by adding a sacrament of teaching alongside others;
my purpose is to cast a bright light on the sacramental nature of teaching. The
close relationship between sacraments and education is natural. Baptism is a rite
of initiation, and eucharist, a rite of ongoing nurture. These are functions of
education, as of liturgy.

In both initiation and nurture, the results may be damaging, as well as positive.
Consider the dangers of initiating and nurturing people into patriarchal communities: "The rites themselves, because they are rites of initiation and sustenance,
serve to initiate both women and men into a patriarchal ecclesial structure and
to maintain their identity with that structure even when it is oppressive."[39] The
alternative is to be alert to danger and alert to the empowering, converting, liberating work of sacraments. We need, thus, to engage in lifelong learning, to revere
sacramental power, to critique distortions in the church, and to open ourselves

---

38. Procter-Smith, *In Her Own Rite,* v–vi.
39. Ibid., 125; cf. 123, 140–51.

for ongoing transformation. In short, we need sacramental teaching that, like the sacraments, mediates God in the church and world.

Expect the Unexpected

The first act of sacramental teaching is to *expect the unexpected* — to expect that God *is* present and *will* act. One mark of the sacraments is that they convey mystery and point to mystery even beyond what they can convey. Expecting the unexpected has to do with traveling with others on the long journey of faith, expecting surprises along the way. The surprise may be the end of apartheid in South Africa, or the amazing strides in that same country to re-create its many selves into the "New South Africa." It may be the recovery journey of an alcoholic from binding addiction, or a family's recovery from a longstanding feud. Expecting the unexpected, in its many guises, evokes the first theological theme discussed earlier — *encounter with God.*

Congregational studies uncover such unexpected encounters with God as these:

- In an intergenerational weekend retreat, a young girl withdrew to the side-lines. She ignored other children and walked away when adults reached out to her. An older woman decided to spend time with this child, inviting her to make hand puppets and, later, to join a session of storytelling. The girl followed along, but showed no interest, never cracked a smile. The older woman, exasperated, decided to stop reaching out to this child, who was not responding. The next morning, all of the retreatants — young and old — were asked to paint a rock to give someone as a sign of their love. The room buzzed with activity as people painted rocks and set them aside to dry. At the end of the morning, people were invited to give their rocks to someone in the room or to pack them away to share back home. The little girl who had been withdrawn throughout the weekend ran across the room to give her rock to the older woman who, by that time, had given up on her. The rock was painted bright green with black letters that read "You Are My Sunshine." The unexpected had happened!

- A small group in a local church was appalled at the ecological destruction in their community. The community had no recycling programs, no one talked about the toxic waste dump down the road, and green space was being paved over every day. The small group decided to address the problems, beginning with a small recycling program within their church, then with a plea to the City Council to begin a city-wide program. They studied toxic waste in their region, as well as the loss of green space. When they delivered their findings to the City Council, two of their members were appointed to a city commission to work on solutions. Later the congregation began a vegetable garden on the church grounds and the youth planted and watered several fruit trees, reclaiming an area that had been used as a dump for unwanted construction materials. On Earth Day, just two years after they had begun, the small group (now tripled in size) rehearsed their journey and expressed surprise at the wonders that had come from their dreams. One man said he was glad they had "reached for the impossible."

These stories reveal the power of expecting the unexpected, which sometimes comes after we have abandoned hope and sometimes when we are walking boldly with naïve optimism. In chapter 1, I described teaching as walking with, sharing with, acting with, remembering with, and constructing meaning with people in a learning community. If this journey is permeated with God's presence, it will be filled with surprises, as in the two cases. Teaching for such a journey is planned with prayer, enacted with prayer, and opened to unexpected movements of God's Spirit.

Remember the Dismembered

A second act of sacramental teaching is to *remember the dismembered*. Initially, this act was not included in plans for this book, but two classroom encounters (told in chapter 3) raised my consciousness that such remembering is urgent for teaching. Consider a congregation that has experienced the death of its pastor while preaching in the pulpit, or a congregation that has lived through the death of several youth within a span of six months, or a congregation that has struggled with the hasty departure of their choir director and a choir member, who had an affair and left their respective spouses to live with one another. These are difficult times for congregations as they mourn their losses and struggle with ethical issues. The same *remembrance* discussed in relation to sacramental theology is needed for such communities to be freed from the debilitating effects of hidden memory and to witness God's Spirit amid tragedy and loss.

One surprising insight arising from congregational studies is the degree of dysfunction that creeps into a congregation when it experiences tragedy or loss and does not take time to grieve, reflect, and rebuild. Some congregations become known for their squabbling, unjust expectations of pastoral leaders, or instability. Consider some cases:

- One thriving congregation experienced the suicide of its beloved pastor forty years ago, and the sudden death of another a few years later. This congregation developed a relational pattern that isolated its pastoral leaders thereafter, while expecting them to do miracles in resolving their internal conflicts.

- Another congregation survived the departure of its priest with a parishioner, but became increasingly hostile toward its new priest and increasingly combative with one another.

- A congregation committed to being multicultural within the tense racial environment of its city gave twenty years to developing a unique ministry. The ministry blossomed and became a beacon to other congregations. In time, however, the congregation was torn by competition among factions within the congregation, particularly by one faction that had a different vision from others. When competition became intense, the congregation sought denominational support, but the denomination had no images of a congregation without an ethnic or language majority. Receiving no support, groups within this congregation began to isolate themselves, refusing to deal openly with their concerns or collaborate in ministries. This marked the end of the multicultural efforts; the congregation soon returned to being a single ethnic and language group.

- Another congregation had quietly arranged to move its pastor to another church after alleged affairs with several young people in the congregation. Twenty years later, they discovered that they had never dealt with their anger and grief. They had driven the young people out of the church, blaming them for the troubles. They had removed the offending pastor from collective memory and repressed their feelings about the situation, only to put heavy pressure on their pastoral and lay leaders from that time forward. The result was that yet another pastor (twelve years later) had an affair with a congregant, and the church's lay leaders continued to bicker among themselves. In the meantime, the young people who had left the congregation during the first uproar never returned to that church or any other.

These stories could be multiplied, but the heart of each is the dismemberment of people within a congregation, effecting dismemberment of the congregation. Submerged memory contributed to further dismemberment and to diminished relationships with God, one another, and the church's mission. While these cases do not suggest easy answers, and no one "solution" is called for, the need for remembering the dismembered is clear.

Seek Reversals

A third act of sacramental teaching is to *seek reversals*. In the Kenyan confirmation story, the Presbyterian moderator preached from 2 Corinthians 5:17: "Therefore, if anyone is in Christ, [that person] is a new creation;...behold, the new has come." The sermon invited an encounter with New Creation, the third theological theme discussed above, which is usually a bold reversal in the status quo. Jewish and Christian traditions abound with such reversals, which are nowhere more evident than in the Bible.

Note the reversals in Exodus 3:1–6. Moses, an immigrant child and a shepherd in Midian, sees a burning bush while tending sheep. First, the bush was not consumed. Second, God was speaking out of the burning bush — the God of

Moses' ancestors — but God was not appearing in conventional ways. Further, God was mourning the pain of the people and sending Moses to Pharaoh to deliver the people (the same Moses who had fled the former Pharaoh after he murdered an Egyptian).

Consider the New Testament tradition, which reveals Jesus — the teller of parables — as the one who proclaims reversals at every turning, whose very life is a reversal. As Luke tells the story, Jesus' birth is announced to Mary by an angel — a reversal — and Mary responds by sharing the news with her cousin Elizabeth in the Magnificat — a song of reversals:

> My soul magnifies the Lord, ... for [God] has looked with favor on the lowliness of [God's] servant. ... [God] has brought down the powerful from their thrones, and lifted up the lowly; [God] has filled the hungry with good things and sent the rich away empty. (Luke 1:47–48, 52–53, NRSV)

The opening chapter of Luke prepares people to seek reversals in the life of Jesus. And Luke, as a teacher seeking reversals, leads readers through the birth of Jesus in a stable, the revelation of this mystery to common shepherds and to Simeon and Anna, the curiosity and wisdom of twelve-year-old Jesus, the subversive teachings of the man who ate with sinners and told the parable of the prodigal son, the death and resurrection, and the suspenseful ending when Jesus ascended into the heavens while his confused disciples looked on. Readers remain in suspense until Luke's next installment in the book of Acts, which opens with the same ascension theme.

In Luke, as in the other Gospels, we see Jesus' life and teachings as a parable,[40] a life that "brought down the powerful from their thrones and lifted up the lowly," a life that stirred reversals. To follow this man Jesus and to live in the biblical tradition that we inherit is to seek reversals and to participate in reversal living: "Do not be conformed to this world, but be transformed by the renewing of your minds" (Rom. 12:2a).

So how do we engage in sacramental living in such a tradition? I will draw a few clues from this hasty journey through our reversal tradition: (1) Christians can *expect* the tradition to offer as many questions as answers and to upset comfortable beliefs, values, and social structures; (2) teaching can be an opportunity to follow Jesus in telling parables and follow Luke in telling the parable of Jesus; (3) teaching can open questions without answers, as Jesus did with his parables and Luke did with his Jesus stories; (4) teaching can engage people with tradition when they are confused, and can support people when they find no comfort in their tradition — when it introduces new questions, upsets the status quo, or gives rise to something new (new insight, new action, new life).

---

40. John Dominic Crossan, *In Parables: The Challenge of the Historical Jesus* (New York: Harper & Row, 1973), esp. 53–78; Sallie McFague, *Speaking in Parables: A Study in Metaphor and Theology* (Philadelphia: Fortress, 1975), 3.

Give Thanks

A fourth act of sacramental teaching is to *give thanks*. This act came to my consciousness through the study of sacramental theology, which is permeated with *symbols of God's work in creation* (fourth theological theme above). Giving thanks is an act of wonder before God. Consider the texts with which this chapter began.

- In the stories of Jenny Geddes and James Hannay, little joy seemed evident on the fateful day of 1637, but later generations have continued to remember and appreciate them. Rather than casting from memory the brazen woman who threw the stool, or the dean of the cathedral who read from the unpopular service book, the people of St. Giles have chosen to remember them both. They remember them with sympathetic appreciation and, in the case of Jenny Geddes, with gratitude for her daring. St. Giles is filled with other symbols of gratitude as well, including plaques of commemoration, markers honoring people who have died for their country, and a central table for communion, symbolizing God's gift of the Table, as well as the Church of Scotland's departure from Anglican practices and movement toward a liturgy that centers on eucharist.

- In the Kenyan congregation, the spirit of thanksgiving is even more evident, expressed in many ways. The children are celebrated on their birthdays in a large Sunday school assembly, where some two hundred children sing to them and teachers give thanks for their lives. In the same congregation, people express gratitude for the freedom of their country and the possibility of Kenya's giving leadership in Africa and the world — in social, political, and ecological relations. They openly identify problems that face their country, but quickly reiterate their thankfulness for the opportunity to build a strong nation in the spirit of *harambee*.

- Paul opens his letter to the Romans with a greeting, followed with a prayer of thanksgiving: "First, I thank my God through Jesus Christ for all of you, because your faith is proclaimed throughout the world" (1:8, NRSV). As in the Kenyan congregation, thanksgiving is the foundation upon which the Roman community can continue to build, even as Paul lays out his concerns and challenges.

In these three cases, we see teaching as giving thanks. In different ways, the people of St. Giles and the people of the Kenyan congregation have made intentional decisions to be thankful. They pass on their thankfulness by acts of commemoration, celebration, and conversation. In Paul's letter to the Romans, he gives thanksgiving through prayer — a practice that also marks the Kenyan church, whenever people gather.

Nourish New Life

This leads to the fifth act of teaching as sacrament — to *nourish new life.* In the earlier analysis, we discovered that the opening stories reveal communities embroiled in conflict and pain and living in a world of turmoil; we also recognized their avid search for life. Sacramental teaching is teaching that encourages people to look for the promise of new life in every text they study, and to look for the promise of new life in their own lives. In so doing, sacramental teaching embodies the theological theme of *communion,* for God's work is discovered in relating fully and deeply with diverse peoples and communities, diverse texts and situations.

The sacramental role of teachers is to nourish seeds of new life wherever they are found. In the first text of Jenny Geddes, the seeds may have been in Jenny's anger, and in James Hannay's bearing his leadership role through angry times. In the church in Kenya, seeds of life may have been efforts of this local congregation to be unified and to witness to their unity in a confirmation service with young people who would soon be leaders of their country. In the church of Rome, the seeds may have been in the community's questions and conflicts, and also in Paul's urging of the community to be transformed by the renewing of their minds. Though more could be said, the challenge for sacramental teaching is to seek and nourish seeds of new life, even unpleasant ones, in ordinary communities.

How can teaching respond to such communities and texts? To answer that question, we turn to a story. I knew a woman in a small town in Louisiana who gave leadership to a five-member Presbyterian church. Together the five congregants cleaned and polished their sacred space, maintained the grounds, and kept the sanctuary alive with growing plants. The congregation rented their manse for income and brought ministers from all over Louisiana to preach and administer the sacraments. They always paid the ministers and gave them a nice meal after the service; the ministers often returned the money, however, because they enjoyed being with the community.

The life of this congregation, when viewed from the outside, was minimal; however, viewed from the inside, they were a community that nourished life in one another and in their town. They visited the ill, welcomed visitors, and often joined with other churches for ecumenical events. When the leader of the congregation spoke, she never mentioned the woes of her church, although she laughed when the congregation dwindled to two on a Sunday morning and the music was off-key. What she did discuss was her excitement about what happened last Sunday, or what their little church would be doing with the Methodists next month.

Reflecting on this story as a metaphor for sacramental teaching, one sees that: (1) small communities can be powerful teachers in their way of *being* community;

(2) sacramental teaching involves caring for the space and daily routine of church life — tending the church as sacred space and tending Sundays as Sabbath time; (3) sacramental teaching can be done by one energetic, loving leader, who includes others and inspires them to join her; and (4) sacramental teaching is an act of joy that mediates the joy of God's Spirit to others. To say that teaching is sacramental is to say that it nourishes life, even when life is a small seed or remnant. If life is God's creation, then nourishing life is participating with God in the creation and care of the world.

Reconstruct Community and Repair the World

This leads to one final act of sacramental teaching — to *reconstruct community and repair the world.* Some readers may be nervous in reading the last story because denominational leaders often worry about churches that hold on when they dwindle to five people. The purpose here is not to evaluate any particular congregation in this regard, but rather to suggest how communities can *be transformed* and can *be agents of transformation.* After all, the last theological theme named in this chapter was *efficacy;* the sacraments make a difference in the world.

Sometimes the promise of transformation calls a congregation to fan sparks of life from their dying embers; sometimes a congregation is called to die and be reconstituted; and sometimes congregations are led into ministries quite different from those they have practiced in the past. The question I raise now is not directed toward one kind of community, but to all communities that are dwindling in their ministry, aliveness, or sense of direction. What does sacramental teaching have to do with them?

Sacramental teaching has to do with more than expecting, remembering, seeking, thanking, and nourishing; it has also to do with mediating God's prophetic call in the church and world. The accent in Christian tradition has often been on prophecy as the ministry of a few daring and charismatic leaders — Jeremiah, Amos, Martin Luther King Jr. But prophecy is an action of God to be received and enacted by *all* God's people; the roles of Jeremiahs, Amoses, and Kings is to mediate the call of God to the whole people — to call the people into prophetic action.

James Lawson argues that Martin Luther King Jr. would have accomplished nothing had it not been for "the trampling of feet."[41] The decision to involve people in marching and campaigning for voting rights was critical to the civil rights movement. The result was to mobilize and empower an already impassioned people. King went through another struggle regarding children who wanted to participate. He first discouraged them, later deciding that children should be allowed to march for their rights and for the freedom of their people. In these

---

41. James Lawson, "Remembering King," lecture presented at the School of Theology at Claremont in honor of Martin Luther King Jr., February 9, 1993.

decisions, King could be called a sacramental teacher, for he was mediating the prophetic call he heard from God. In these actions, King was concerned with reconstructing Christian community, for he valued the quality of Christian action. He was also concerned with repairing the world, for he valued the quality of justice in the world. For him, the quality of Christian community and the quality of global justice were intertwined.

What is needed today is a new way of thinking about leadership, particularly about prophetic leadership. Rather than bemoaning the lack of leaders, people might look toward prophetic *communities* — sacramental communities that seek to discern God's call and to respond by reconstructing their community life and repairing the world. Sacramental teaching would thus have to do with building the community, praying and listening together for God's call, and acting together to protest the destruction of life and to reconstruct communities and social structures that can protect and nourish life.

Sacramental teaching takes place when we recognize and respond to the drama in our particular place and time in history, just as the Scots and Kenyans and Romans were called to respond. Sacramental teaching has to do with facing into conflict and pain — seeking ways to express and negotiate conflict and to mourn and heal pain. This is not just good psychology; it is sacramental, for God is the Holy One who knows the suffering of creation. God came to Moses in the burning bush, saying, "I have observed the misery of my people who are in Egypt; I have heard their cry.... Indeed, I know their sufferings" (Exod. 3:7). To mediate God's love is to mediate God's empathy toward creation. Sacramental teaching thus requires naming and analyzing the conflicts and turmoil of the world and then responding as prophetic people. Sacramental teaching requires courage to face the world as it is and to seek new life, even amid brokenness and suffering.

Concluding Reflections

I have named six acts of sacramental teaching: expect the unexpected, remember the dismembered, seek reversals, give thanks, nourish new life, and reconstruct community and repair the world. These acts will be the subjects of chapters 3 through 8. What is most central, however, is to recognize that all of these acts mediate God's grace. The unexpected is God in our midst; the dismembered are those for whom God cries; reversals are God's parables; thanksgiving is God's spirit of delight; new life is God's New Creation; and acts of reconstruction and repair are God's redemptive works, empowering people to be transformed and to participate in the transformation of a broken world. When our communities see teaching as sacramental, they will see God's presence in every teaching act and God's transformative power in every educative event. Teaching can indeed mediate God's grace and bless the earth!

Reflecting Further

Below are suggestions for engaging with the ideas of this chapter.

1. The following meditation can be done alone or in a group: In silence, meditate on that which stirs or storms *around* you.... Turn your meditation to that which stirs or storms *within* you.... Breathe deeply and know the presence of God in you, with you, under you, and throughout the earth.... Continue meditating with Psalm 29 in the style of *Lectio Divina,* reading very slowly while you breathe in Spirit and breathe out Spirit. Allow God to speak to you through these words. Amen.

2. Remember the most vivid experiences you have had with baptism or eucharist. Meditate on those moments. Reflect on what your experience of baptism and eucharist adds to or questions in the presentation of this chapter. In light of your experience, what would you expect from sacramental teaching? How does that relate to the educational practices sketched in the chapter?

3. Consider your congregation or ethnic community. What do their experiences of baptism and eucharist suggest about the sacraments and sacramental teaching?

Chapter Three

Expecting the Unexpected

If a teacher or teaching community is committed to sacred teaching, where do they begin? While teaching begins in many places at once, the first teaching act developed in this book is expecting the unexpected. This is an attitude and action, important to sacramental teaching because it represents the expectation that God works wonders in the world. The stories that introduce this chapter raise the possibility of expecting wonder. They also call attention to many dimensions of expectation. The stories themselves are autobiographical tales told by three remarkable people.

Madeleine L'Engle tells her story of writing A Wrinkle in Time.[1] *When she finished writing, she sent her manuscript to a publisher. She mailed it with a prayer, and with hope for prompt publication. She received a negative reply, and several others after that. She was not pleased with herself or with God. Ten years later, when her book was finally published, she thanked God in a surge of gratitude. In that moment, she realized that the publication was much better timed than when she first submitted it. Readers were now eager for such a book as this. She was astonished!*

Howard Thurman tells stories of his grandmother, an ex-slave, who welcomed him when he came home from school as a child. His father had died, and his mother did domestic work to support the family; his grandmother was a prominent presence in his life. When Howard was twelve, he went to his Baptist church to be interviewed in preparation for baptism and joining the church. The deacons asked him many questions, which he answered with care. The final question was, "Howard, why do you come before us?" to which Howard replied, "I want to be a Christian." The deacons were not pleased with the answer; they told Howard that he needed to take more time. When he was ready to tell them of his conversion, then they wanted him to return. Howard went home, dejected. When he told his grandmother about the delay, she took his hand, and they marched back to the church. They arrived before the deacons had dispersed, and

---

1. Madeleine L'Engle, interview conducted in *Sharing Our Faith* series (Nashville: United Methodist Communications, n.d.); cf. L'Engle, *Madeleine L'Engle Herself: Reflections on a Writing Life*, comp. Carole F. Chase (Colorado Springs, Colo.: WaterBrook, 2001), 78–79.

Howard's grandmother addressed the chairman, "How dare you turn this boy down? He is a Christian and was one long before he came to you today. Maybe you did not understand his words, but shame on you if you do not know his heart. Now you take this boy into the church right now — before you close this meeting!"[2] The deacons were astonished! And Howard Thurman was baptized the next Sunday.

John Hull, a British scholar in religious education, describes his adult journey into blindness. He struggled with depression for three years, having been an active and productive person whose professional life centered around reading books and writing them, and whose family life revolved around caring for his small children, teaching them how to read and traveling with them to interesting places. Suddenly his world was changing. He could not read books, play in familiar ways with his children, or write the essays for which he was appreciated.

In time, Hull discovered reading machines and books on tape. He was again able to prepare his classes, and he read the Bible every day, making new discoveries about God. One day, many months after he lost his sight, he was standing at a busy street corner waiting for the bleeps that would tell him he could safely cross to his home. He suddenly realized that people driving by probably noticed this blind man and wondered how he was going to cross, especially without a dog. Then John thought about how he would step off the curb, cross the street, and make his way home. He later wrote, "Looking back now, I think that this was the first time I had a feeling of calmness and confidence as a blind person in a blind person's world."[3] John was astonished by his own confidence! Several months later, John's son Thomas asked him, "Why doesn't God help you?" John replied, "God does help me, in lots of ways." The baffled Thomas asked, "How?" John replied, "Well, [God] makes me strong. [God] gives me courage."[4] Thomas needed to ponder that mystery some more.

These three stories reveal people with sincere faith, but people for whom transitional moments were fueled by the unexpected. In recent years, the church talks a great deal about biblical literacy and teaching people how "to live good lives." These themes are especially dominant when congregations, judicatories, and denominations discuss formation and educational ministries. In this chapter, we will seek an alternate vision to biblical literacy and moral rules. The opening stories offer clues.

As described in chapter 1, the spirituality beneath this book is marked by searching, facing vulnerability, opening to God, and facing radical transformation. The opening stories point to the heart of spirituality and education — engaging

---

2. Howard Thurman, *With Head and Heart: The Autobiography of Howard Thurman* (New York: Harcourt Brace Jovanovich, 1979), 18.

3. John M. Hull, *On Sight and Insight: A Journey into the World of Blindness* (Oxford: Oneworld Publications, 1997, 1990), 132–33.

4. Ibid., 172–73.

with God and God's creation. To engage with God is to seek God's movements in every ordinary and extraordinary moment of every day. The dream underlying this particular chapter is *that the Christian community might catch a vision of expecting the unexpected — expecting the wonder of God's work in the midst of everydayness, including moments of joy, routine, and tragedy!* This happens when teachers and learning communities open themselves to God's wonders and unleash their imaginations to be blessed by mystery.

Contemporary churches are hungry for wonder. They often move to praise worship to satisfy this hunger; however, contemporary approaches to praise often follow rigid formulas, not unlike those of so-called traditional worship. Churches often do not know how to enhance expectation, confusing particular liturgies or new innovations (screens, new music, etc.) with wonder.[5] This chapter is an attempt to dive below the surface of these discussions and discover the heart of wonder, exploring how sacramental teaching can enhance human openness to the Creator's unfathomable gifts. We begin by exploring the power of expecting the unexpected and then turn to roots of expectation in church practice and to a theology and hermeneutic of wonder. These sources can shape educational practice to evoke expectation in a world filled with Holy Presence.

Power in Expecting the Unexpected

The opening stories are clearly not focused on mastery, whether of biblical knowledge, doctrines, or moral principles; neither do they witness to particular innovations in worship. They focus instead on *engagement with God,* the *source* of power. When you engage something, you enter into a lively interchange that transforms you from within and without. Biblical literacy is cognitive in connotation, but biblical engagement is cognitive, affective, volitional, and physical — total. The same is true of doctrinal literacy in contrast with doctrinal engagement, or moral literacy in contrast with moral engagement, or worship innovation in contrast with deepening worship. What is needed for expecting the unexpected is not literacy, but engagement with God and God's creation. Insofar as encounters with the Bible, doctrine, moral teachings, and diverse styles of worship enhance such engagement, they are rich indeed; insofar as they become ends in themselves, they deter people from experiencing holy wonder. In this chapter, I encourage deep engagement, looking to the opening stories, in dialogue with biblical stories, for insight.

Consider first what the opening stories have in common. I suggest that they are all sacramental moments — ordinary moments when God is revealed in unexpected ways. All have an element of surprise, but not the kind of surprise that

---

5. The analysis and reconstruction in this chapter resonate with Thomas G. Long, *Beyond the Worship Wars: Building Vital and Faithful Worship* (Bethesda, Md.: Alban Institute, 2001).

people control, as in planning a surprise party. All reveal an unexpected turn of events, or a reversal in how people think. In each story, the characters are astonished. Further, the stories reveal people living with conflict or discouragement, whether in L'Engle's book rejections, Thurman's initial postponement for baptism, or Hull's living with blindness. The people of these stories are not fully pleased with God, and they ask difficult questions about what God is doing. They may even wish they could control God's actions — get the results or the healing they want. In each story, however, God's response does come. The answers are not the expected or hoped for answers, but they *are* a response from God all the same.

Power of Surprise

The stories reveal the *power of surprise*. One is tempted to identify surprise with positive thinking — seeking a constant flow of inspiration and cultivating optimism. The analysis here is not so naïve. Consider John Hull. After he became blind, even simple tasks took extra time and effort. Daily steps into the unknown, like walking home from the university, demanded unreasonable courage. During the months of adjustment, John questioned himself and many of his old images of God. Further, people often talked about John as if he could not hear. In church, a verger asked his wife if John wanted to go forward for communion, using what John called the "does he take sugar?" approach to disabled people.[6] While John knew that he *could* hear, he also knew that he could not do many other things. Further, the encouragement of religious folks to participate in healing services diminished his hope further. What we see in John Hull is not the instant healing that these well-intended people urged upon him, but a slow, painstaking journey that required faith in the God who travels *with* people. Hull's story points to a disabled God — a God who rarely waves problems away in a flash, but plods and aches and works with creation in the daily struggles of life.[7]

Engaging with biblical texts sheds further light on the unexpected ways of God in relation to human life. Consider Matthew 22:15–22, a story of the Pharisees trying to trap Jesus with a question — forcing him into rejecting taxes (thus angering the Romans) or supporting taxes (angering people weighed down by taxes). Knowing that the Pharisees produced coins in the Temple precincts, Jesus requested a coin and responded, "Give therefore to the emperor the things that are the emperor's, and to God the things that are God's" (21, NRSV). According to Matthew's story, the Pharisees "were amazed" (22). Their trap had not worked. Unable to stir a conflict or to control Jesus, they went away.

---

6. Ibid., 101.

7. Nancy Eiesland, *The Disabled God* (Nashville: Abingdon, 1994); John Hull, "Blindness and the Face of God: Toward a Theology of Disability," in *The Human Image of God*, ed. Hans-Georg Ziebertz et al. (Leiden: Brill, 2001), 215–29.

The unexpected for the Pharisees was to discover not only that Jesus was clever, but also that people had more than two options for taxes. People already knew they could judge taxes good or bad. In a world that wanted neat categories of good and bad, right and wrong, Jesus was saying: You can find another way — a way in which taxes do have a place, but their place is limited. His proposal was simple but unexpected, that people give to the emperor what is the emperor's and to God what is God's. The unexpected came from Jesus' teaching that the predictable world of two choices — either/or — was not so predictable after all. Such is the nature of surprise, and such is its power: to stop people from their superficial assumptions (e.g., about blindness), their common understandings (e.g., of healing), their efforts to damage others (e.g., the Pharisees' effort to trap Jesus), and their limited patterns of thought (e.g., either-or thinking).

Power of Engaging with God in Good Times and Bad

The stories of this chapter also suggest the *power of engaging with God in good times and bad*. The people faced real struggles, a theme common to the biblical witness as well. Consider the story recounted in Exodus 33:12–23, a struggle in the wilderness. It follows shortly after Moses became angry with his wandering people and threw down the stone tablets he had received from God (32:15–20). The commandments were shattered, as were the people, condemned for worshiping a golden calf. After much discussion, a plague, and God's instructions to continue the journey, Moses entered the tent of meeting to implore with God: "Now if I have found favor in your sight, show me your ways, so that I may know you and find favor in your sight. Consider too that this nation is your people" (33:13). Moses was asking God to take care of everything, and show him God's glory.[8] God responded dramatically: "I will make all my goodness pass before you, and will proclaim before you the name, 'The Lord'; and I will be gracious to whom I will be gracious, and will show mercy on whom I will show mercy." Then came a qualification, "But . . . you cannot see my face; for no one shall see me and live" (19–20). God would put Moses in a cleft of the rock and cover him while the divine glory passed. Later, God would remove the hand, and Moses would be able to see God's back.

Is that enough? Could Moses or anyone else be satisfied living behind God's back? This is not simply an issue from the ancient past. In 1992, after the civil uprising in Los Angeles, the *New Yorker* published an article by Stuart Hall, a black British social critic. The article had been written after the Tottenham riots in London:

---

8. God had earlier refused to go among the people as they traveled, explaining to Moses, "I will not go up among you, or I would consume you on the way, for you are a stiff-necked people" (Exod. 33:3, NRSV).

> Britain has a long and distinguished history of urban and rural riot.... It results from a long and grueling period of deepening poverty and neglect, so that people begin to feel as if they are permanently out of sight of the society at large: living behind God's back.[9]

Living behind God's back is like being severed from directly witnessing God; and in Tottenham, being severed from society's concern as well. Surely Moses felt some distancing, as did the people who passed down Moses' story through countless generations. Whether or not Moses was satisfied with seeing God's glory from behind, the divine drama continued. In the next scene, we see God giving Moses instructions to cut two more tablets of stone and climb Mount Sinai — no glory here, just more work (34:1–8). Moses did it. Then God actually came and stood with Moses, proclaimed the name "The Lord," and made a covenant with Moses and the people. We are told, "Moses quickly bowed his head toward the earth, and worshiped" (8, NRSV). Having traveled with God through good times and bad, Moses experienced wonder yet again.

Power of God's Response to the World

A third power of expecting the unexpected is *God's response to the world.* In light of Moses' story, one might say that living behind God's back has its rewards. Behind God's back, one can see God's handiwork; one can touch it and taste it. But people can also feel neglected, even destroyed by the ravages of a harsh world. Sometimes people are angry with God for sending them on impossible missions against their better judgment, not even guaranteeing the results. According to Exodus, Moses was distraught when the people turned away from God to worship a golden calf. He was angry with the people *and* with God. The promise in the Moses story is not glib. It is simply this — that God *does* come and God *does* act and God *does* make covenant, but we can neither know nor control what God does and how.

Does this analysis suggest that people are helpless — that God controls every event? God's control is certainly not featured in the Moses story. In Exodus, we read that the people *chose* to make a golden calf. Similarly, human decisions about social structures and economic practices contributed to poverty and hopelessness for youth in Tottenham before the riots there. In the Exodus account, Moses is at least convinced that he can plead with God for himself and his people. God listens and responds with direct action and covenant-making. In a world that wants to see God face to face, that wants predictable promises, people are given a similar option — to plead with God and trust that God will listen, even if we are only to see God's back. In these encounters, we see a God of surprises who

---

9. Stuart Hall, quoted in the *New Yorker,* June 8, 1992, 28. Michael Warren first shared this quote with me.

comes in sacramental moments every day, but not always as people imagine. In God's surprises, we awaken to the power of expecting the unexpected.

Roots of Expecting the Unexpected in Church Practice

We turn now to roots of expecting the unexpected in church practice, some obvious and some more difficult to discern. If God is the primal source of wonder, then expectation can take root wherever and whenever God is revealed. Even church life can be a mirror of God — not equal or adequate to God, but a mirror all the same. Indeed, expectation dwells in much of ecclesial life, but nowhere more visibly than Advent, the season of expectation, and the sacraments, bearers of holy mystery. Church practice, of course, can also hide the wonder of God; it can be a vacuous routine, a series of power plays, an empty show, and so forth. Even with its human limitations, however, church practice has potential to communicate the wonder and mystery of God.

Advent

Advent is a time of waiting for the coming Messiah. Every year, Christians await Jesus' birth. Traditionally, this is also a time for awaiting God's New Creation, called by many names — Jesus' Second Coming, Kingdom of God, Kin-dom of God, Kingdom of Heaven, and others. Historically, Advent has been a time of repenting, asking and giving forgiveness, fasting, and preparing for baptism or spiritual renewal (for those already baptized). Whenever Christians reduce Advent to Christmas preparations and celebrations, they sacrifice the opportunity to engage in expectation — to analyze and mourn the troubles of this world and to expect God's redemptive and creative action.

Expecting the unexpected is not easy; this may be one reason that Advent is undercelebrated in the Christian church. Perhaps people jump quickly to Christmas celebrations because Advent is demanding. It involves analyzing the horrors and divisions of our world and daring to hope that God will heal and remake that world. When we practice Advent, we expect that peace *can* come to the Middle East, Sudan, and Bosnia; that reunification *can* come to Korea; that wounded victims of child abuse *can* be healed; that wounded teachers *can* be healers; that God suffers with creation and God will keep Her promise to repair the world (*tikkun olam*).

Such expectation is not positive thinking theology. Sermons on positive thinking encourage people to be confident that their hopes can come true. The accent is placed on human action and individual well-being. In one such sermon, the preacher gave three pronouncements: "If you expect to fulfill your personal goals in the coming year, you *will*. If you expect to have another crummy year, you *will.* If you expect to die, you probably *will.*"[10] In truth, human expectations can have a self-fulfilling character. On the other hand, this approach emphasizes individual willpower, belittling other social factors and the role of God. Further, the approach focuses on individual wants and needs, giving little attention to the larger society.

This critique does not mean that human expectations have nothing to do with human choices; yet they are more complex and more God-filled than positive thinkers generally claim. In a recent interview, Maya Angelou described how she quit her thirty-year smoking habit. Her story reveals the possibility of genuine transformation, but avoids simplistic do-it-yourself assumptions. One day on a train ride, Angelou saw full-page anti-smoking ads in the *New York Times* and *USA Today:* "Don't smoke tomorrow. Join America's Great Smoke Out." Angelou saw the ads as a sign that someone cared for her life more than she did. She decided to reduce her smoking the next day, waiting until 4:00 to smoke the first cigarette. She did this, and discovered that the 4:00 cigarette did not even taste good. She continued the goal-setting routine for the rest of that day and the next. At 7:00 on the second day, lighting up a cigarette and disliking its taste yet again, she realized that she had stopped smoking. Angelou concludes:

> Because I could do it, I did do it. Because we can live without hate, we might do it. Some might do it. I suppose if a hundred people saw that ad, maybe 10 stopped smoking forever. Well, there we are, you see. We are new. We're the last group made. We have all sorts of chances to do wonderful things.[11]

Angelou's interview was accessible to a broad readership, as positive thinking books are. Yet her story embodies more complexity than most positive thinking messages. It is an Advent story, expressing hope for genuine change without assuming that all people will change at once. It also attributes transformation to a Maker ("We're the last group made"), a theme that is more explicit in her writing. At the same time, Angelou acknowledges that human decision and action contribute to transformation. Finally, she links personal goals, as breaking a harmful habit, with larger social goals of ending hate. These are some of the textures of Advent expectation.

Sacraments

Continuing this reflection, we turn to the sacraments. Wonder is central to the eucharist, expressed in praise (considered further in chapter 6). Wonder is also active in baptism, evident in the early church's sense of occasion, in 250 years of African American tradition, and in many parts of the world today. In this section

---

10. This quote is drawn from field notes in an ethnographic study of television evangelism, 2002.
11. Teree Caruthers, "Southerners," *Southern Living* (March 2001): 67.

we explore textures of sacramental practice through another case study. Though no case can fully embody sacramental practice, each can point to holy realities. This particular case is a baptism in which I was involved.

A few years ago, I was privileged to be in England for the baptism of a friend's child, Alexander. The presiding pastor was an old friend of the infant's family and ours. After the service, I thanked the pastor for the sacrament and his preaching. He laughed, saying how touched he was when the family invited him, but how nervous he had become in succeeding weeks; he wanted everything to be just right for the family on this important occasion. Turning to the sermon, I shared how I admire his ability to communicate profound truth with simplicity and aliveness. I suggested that he publish a book of sermons. Laughing uproariously, he said, "I sometimes get caught up in the Spirit, and the preaching really takes off. When I look at my notes later, I realize that I left out this bit and that bit, and added other bits, to my prepared notes."

This pastor was engaged in sacramental expectation. He administered the sacrament of baptism, but he did more: he recognized in advance the significance of the event with excitement and nervousness. When the day arrived, he welcomed the congregation to the holy event; he thanked God for the sacred gift of Alexander and his family; he read the traditional liturgy, baptized with the traditional water, and gave Alexander the traditional holy kiss. Then he smiled the untraditional smile, lifted Alexander into the air, and processed up and down the center aisle while the congregation sang and grinned. With these initial observations, we return to the case.

The sacrament was a celebration with many elements. The small children sang a welcome to Alexander; later they turned to the congregation and spoke a blessing to the community before departing for their classes. In the sermon, the pastor referred back to the baptism as he interpreted scripture and told stories of Jesus telling stories. We had been prepared by the opening words of the pastor and lay leader to expect something wonderful, and that is what happened throughout worship. Further, close friends of the family gathered later in the church hall to enjoy a feast prepared by Alexander's mother. The friends helped lay out the feast as they chattered with one another.

A vivid part of the baptismal service was the "passing of Alexander." Initially, Alexander was near the front, held by family friends. The parents and sister were nowhere in sight. They were delivering food for the meal and speaking with the minister; they came in later and retrieved their son, but only momentarily. Alexander's six-year-old sister and his mother held him for a while, but they passed him again to a godparent, who took him forward and held him for the first part of the liturgy. After the anointing with water, the pastor gave Alexander to his father, but only temporarily. The pastor took Alexander again during the hymn and processed through the congregation.

This baptism uncovers many qualities of expecting the unexpected. As soon as the parents began to plan, the unexpected began to happen. The pastor's excitement betrayed his expectations of the unexpected; the family's hours of preparation for the sacrament and meal betrayed their excitement. The god-parents did not know what to expect, but were apparently prepared for anything. Friends were even less clear, but the family had stirred their expectations by tele-phone: "You are special to us, this is a special time for us, could you come?" The entire congregation was invited into expectancy when they arrived. The service was, from beginning to end, a celebration of baptism, full of unexpected moments of music and laughter amid expected moments of blessing.

Alexander's baptism was a sacrament of the church, rich with clues for sacra-mental teaching: (1) the event pointed to God's wonder in Alexander's life and in the community; (2) the family invited the pastor and many congregants to be part of the sacramental event; (3) the formal teacher — the pastor in this case — was in awe of the joy and responsibility in his role; (4) everyone in the community had a role and many people had special roles, such as holding Alexan-der, bringing food, serving food, and so forth; (5) the children also had a role; and (6) the shared meal was *part of* the sacramental act. Consider the children. Alexander was the center of our attention and prayers, but other children played roles in the unfolding drama. Alexander's sister held him; children of the church sang welcome to him and blessed the congregation. Consider also the meal — a gift from Alexander's family, prepared with delight and care; it was a covenant meal in which we all shared. The textures of this case point to a theology of wonder.

Theology of Wonder

Beneath the sacramental practice of expecting the unexpected is a theology of wonder, rooted in the wonder of God and God's creation. Such theology pushes the edges of common theological thinking, especially in regard to wonder, immanence and transcendence, incarnation, and sacramental presence.

1. God and God's Creation Are Full of Wonder

In Alexander's baptism, the *real power was God's work* — work that was at once transcendent, immanent, and incarnate. Consider the pastor's sense that he was caught up in the Spirit. He knew that God transformed his prepara-tions into something beyond his doing. The power was greater than him and beyond his reach, yet mysteriously working through him. At the same time, the pastor and congregation sensed God's immediate presence in Alexander, in chil-dren's singing, in family joy. The membrane separating Creator and creatures seemed thin and God's immanence was consciously felt. The larger-than-life and closer-than-skin God was incarnate in the moment.

The sense of holy wonder expands when Alexander's baptism is connected with Gospel accounts of Jesus' baptism. Matthew tells the story with particular fullness (3:13–17), but all the Gospels include accounts (Mark 1:9–11; Luke 3:21–22;

John 1:31–34). Matthew's story is preceded by John the Baptist's announcement: "I baptize you with water for repentance, but one who is more powerful than I is coming after me; I am not worthy to carry his sandals. He will baptize you with the Holy Spirit and fire" (3:11). John's words prepare readers to see the gap between himself and Jesus, emphasizing that Jesus transcended him in might and ministry. John hesitated to baptize Jesus: "I need to be baptized by you, and do you come to me?" (14). He finally agreed to honor Jesus' request, perhaps responding to Jesus' persuasive power and the divine significance of baptism. The story concludes as Jesus rises from the water, the Spirit descends, and God speaks, "This is my Son, the Beloved, with whom I am well pleased" (17).

The other Gospels also include a contrast between John's announcement of the one who would come after him and the later descent of the Spirit, although these focus more on the Spirit. Matthew stresses the human-divine distance as background to the dramatic ingression of God's Spirit. Jesus and the Spirit are awesome *and* immediate. Further, God pronounces the incarnation, "This is my beloved Son." Immanence and transcendence co-mingle, and people glimpse the incarnation.

Reflecting on Matthew's account in relation to Alexander's baptism, we see humility and awe in both presiders. John the Baptist, in the ancient story, and the pastor, in the recent one, both sensed a distance between themselves and God; yet the chasm was bridged by the touch of God in an unexpected moment. In Matthew, transformation was linked with Jesus' unexpected request and the descent of God's Spirit, both initiated by the Divine. In the modern story, transformation began with the family's request for Alexander's baptism, and it continued through preparation days, the baptismal liturgy, and the family feast. In both events, a spirit of wonder was stirring from beginning to end, declared in the greatness and nearness of God, and in incarnation. This interpretation evokes wonder, but it disrupts dominant traditions. First, it suggests no easy dichotomy between transcendence and immanence. Second, it broadens the common understanding of incarnation. Third, it broadens the understanding of sacraments.

2. God Is Transcendentally Immanent and Immanently Transcendent

Moving into the first theological disruption, the challenge is to wonder at God's greatness and "beyondness," and also wonder at the presence of Spirit in every event of creation. Such wonder pushes beyond dichotomies — recognizing that *God is transcendentally immanent and immanently transcendent.* The distinction between God's transcendence and immanence has long been an issue in theology. One of the most widely read liturgical theologians of the last century was conflicted in these discussions and underwent a theological shift over her life.[12] In

---

12. Underhill actively discussed these issues with her mentor Baron Friedrich von Hügel. One description is found in Michael Ramsey, "The Mysticism of Evelyn Underhill," in *Evelyn Underhill:*

her first book, Evelyn Underhill accented human religious experience, social and psychological influences, and God's immanence. In later works, Underhill emphasized the distance between God and humanity, explaining that a human being needs assurance of "the utter and childlike dependence of his [sic] tiny spirit on God's Being."[13] For Underhill, this is grace, and sacraments provide "an access of Supernature" through the natural paths of the senses.[14]

Underhill described her theological shift to transcendence in the 1930 edition of *Mysticism*, originally published in 1911. She said that she would state her arguments differently if beginning the book anew. She would give greater emphasis:

(a) to the concrete, richly living yet unchanging character of the Reality over against the mystic . . . ; (b) to that paradox of utter contrast yet profound relation between the Creator and the creature . . . ; (c) to the predominant part played . . . by the free and prevenient action of the Supernatural . . . as against all merely evolutionary or emergent theories of spiritual transcendence.[15]

Underhill chose not to do a major revision of the book; she simply named shifts in her thinking and did modest revisions. Her revisions regarding contemplation show how subtle the different accents can be (additions noted by italics, deletions by strike-through).

(A) Whatever terms he may employ to describe it, . . . the mystic's experience in Contemplation is the experience of the All, *and this experience seems to him to be given rather than attained*. It is *indeed* the Absolute which ~~he has attained~~ *is revealed to him* . . . (B) This ~~attainment is brought about this knowledge gained~~ *revealed Reality is apprehended* by way of participation, not by way of observation.[16]

Anglican Mystic, ed. A. M. Ramsey and A. M. Allchin (Oxford: Sisters of the Love of God Press, 1996), 5–14, esp. 5, 9, 12; cf. Dana Greene, *Evelyn Underhill: Artist of the Infinite Life* (New York: Crossroad, 1990), 77–97.

13. Evelyn Underhill, *Man and the Supernatural* (London: Methuen, 1927), 179. In this later emphasis, Underhill is closer to von Hügel. See, for example: von Hügel, "The Facts and Truths Concerning God and the Soul Which Are of Most Importance in the Life of Prayer," *Essays and Addresses on the Philosophy of Religion, First Series* (London: J. M. Dent & Sons, 1928, 1921), 217–26.

14. Underhill, *Man and the Supernatural*, 179–80. In her view, the thirst for the Infinite cannot be satisfied by human effort. "That Infinite must come to us before we can go to it . . . the whole of man's [sic] spiritual history, both corporate and solitary, involves and entirely rests in the free self-giving of God" (180).

15. Evelyn Underhill, *Mysticism: A Study in the Nature and Development of Man's Spiritual Consciousness*, rev. 12th ed. (London: Methuen, 1930, 1911), viii. In this same 1930 introduction, she attributes von Hügel with "recovery of the concept of the Supernatural — a word which no respectable theologian of the last generation cared to use" (ix).

16. Ibid., 333; cf. Underhill, *Mysticism: A Study in the Nature and Development of Man's Spiritual Consciousness* (London: Methuen, 1911), 397. I have superimposed the two editions.

Underhill's new emphases were God-focused: The mystical experience is given by God rather than attained; it is revealed by the Absolute and apprehended by the mystic. The initiative is God's, freely acting and disclosing to the human soul, which simply responds.

Unlike Underhill and her mentor Baron von Hügel, I argue that a dichotomy between immanence and transcendence distracts from God's wonder. The traditional debate locks people into either/or debates about where God is. The deeper truth is that God *is* and God *dwells* everywhere — above and below, within and without, near and far. A pan*en*theistic view of God affirms the transcendence and presence of God with equal fervor. God and creation are not the same, but God indwells the created world and the world lives in God.

3. God Is Incarnate in Jesus and in All Creation

This leads to the second theological shift uncovered in my analysis — an enlarged view of incarnation, namely, that *God is incarnate in Jesus and in all creation.* Jesus' life is traditionally understood as the incarnation of God, yet God's wonders are incarnate in many moments of life, as in Madeleine L'Engle, Howard Thurman and his grandmother, John Hull and his son, and Alexander. *Incarnation is the embodiment of God in creation, in every event in which God's purposes are even partially enfleshed.* This view recognizes the totality of Jesus' incarnation, yet acknowledges other embodiments of the Holy, however minimal and flawed they are beside God's full indwelling in Jesus.

This view offers a fitting interpretation to the story of Jesus' baptism. John's sense of vocation in proclaiming the One to come and his willingness to baptize Jesus reveal a sense of God's presence in, around, and through him. At the same time, his hesitation to baptize Jesus and his witness of the descending Spirit reveal a sense of humility before God. These are more than competing claims about God's whereabouts; they reveal the *work* of God. God's work is beyond John — in the future One whom John proclaims and in the descending Spirit; God's work is also through John — in John's baptizing and his proclaiming expectation and awe. Incarnation is, thus, part of the entire act of baptism, most fully in Jesus but also in John's actions and in the waters of baptism.

4. God Dwells in the Sacraments and in the Sacramental

This analysis leads to a broad view of the sacraments, affirming that *God dwells in the sacraments and, also, in the sacramental.* The sacraments convey mystery and point to mystery even beyond what they convey. This mystery is not a puzzle to be solved; it is a precious gift and transformative act. Traditionally, baptism and eucharist are associated with the Paschal mystery — the death and resurrection of Jesus Christ; however, the mystery of Christ includes *all* aspects of Jesus' remarkable life — his birth, baptism, teaching, healing, transfiguration, as well as his death and resurrection.[17] As God's primary sacrament, Jesus reveals and mediates God's grace to the world. At the same time, the mysterious workings of God are everywhere. Spirit was present from the earliest creating days, and Spirit still moves in creation — hearing, seeing, and responding to the world's moans and laughter. The sacraments thus represent Jesus' death and resurrection, as well as the work of God in all of Jesus' life and in the life of the world.

In baptism and eucharist, God dwells in the elements and in the people and their actions. The eucharistic traditions of transubstantiation and consubstantiation are thus affirmed and conjoined. The bread and wine are filled with Christ; thus, one can say they *become* the body and blood of Christ (transubstantiation); they are also *accompanied by* the living presence of Christ (consubstantiation). God thus dwells in and with the bread and wine; they are holy food. God also dwells in those who receive the food, however incompletely. God works in, around, and through the bread and wine, and God works in, around, and through the gathered community. Such a view honors the Real Presence of Christ in the eucharist, as it honors traditions of transubstantiation and consubstantiation, but without being absorbed in debates between them.

Hermeneutic of Wonder

The analysis thus far invites people to practice a hermeneutic of wonder — *to seek mystery and open to deeper relations with God and creation.* This hermeneutic is at work in the Psalms, as in Jewish and Christian contemplatives for whom the Psalms are a source of nourishment. Walter Brueggemann describes the Psalms as a source of "abiding astonishment."[18] Thomas Merton saw them as a way of opening to God.[19] A hermeneutic of wonder works through creation and other human art forms as well. Not surprising, many contemplatives in history have been nature lovers, musicians, poets, and artists, drawing upon wonders of creation to touch God.

---

17. "Sacrament/Sacramental," in *Dictionary of Theology*, ed. Louis Bouyer, trans. Rev. Charles Underhill Quinn (New York: Desclée, 1965), 363–66. See also Odo Casel, *The Mystery of Christian Worship and Other Writings*, ed. Burkhard Neunheuser, O.S.B. (Westminster, Md.: Newman, 1962). As a Benedictine writing in the 1920s and 1930s, Casel redirected sacramental theology by placing emphasis on the quality of mystery. He also drew connections between Christian sacraments and Hellenistic mystery rites (50–62). Consistent with perspectives of my book is also Casel's understanding of the Christian year as mystery, which embodies the union of the Christ of history and Christ of faith (63–70).

18. Walter Brueggemann, *Abiding Astonishment: Psalms, Modernity, and the Making of History* (Louisville: Westminster John Knox, 1991), 29–35, 54–61.

19. Thomas Merton, *Bread in the Wilderness* (Collegeville, Minn.: Liturgical Press, 1986, 1953), 71–81.

If God's world and human art convey dramatic power, interpreters need a hermeneutic to discern the heights and depths to which they point.[20] A hermeneutic of wonder can uncover revelation, though creation is inevitably limited in expressing mysteries of the universe. A person can never fully know a tree or its Creator; nor can poetry or paintings fully reveal mystery. According to Heschel, "A sensitive person knows that the intrinsic, the most essential, is never expressed."[21] Since people never fully know mystery, a hermeneutic of wonder can help them walk to the edge of knowing; it stands beside them as they gaze into canyons of mystery. Beyond that is simply awe.

A hermeneutic of wonder responds to a basic human yearning. In this era, the yearning for wonder seems to be rising, evident in survey studies of spirituality in the United States. In the past thirteen years, the percentage of people who reported to Gallup pollsters that searching for the meaning of life is important to them has risen. Nine of ten people report that they pray; most of these say prayer is heard and effects change.[22] How these surveys relate to behavior is unclear; they do reveal an expressed spiritual yearning.

A hermeneutic of wonder responds to this human searching, yet it emerges from more than human longing; it rises from a belief that wonder actually exists. Heschel calls this "radical amazement," arguing that philosophy originates from seeking what is beyond knowledge.[23] I suggest that theology also arises from mysteries that are not fully knowable and expressible. For Heschel, and for me, wonder is a spiritual necessity: "Spiritually we cannot live by merely reiterating borrowed or inherited knowledge."[24] Howard Thurman expresses a similar emphasis. Writing for the *Bulletin* during his years as dean of the Boston University Chapel, he urges people to experience life deeply, not simply to dwell on what

---

20. Similar ideas are developed in Mary Elizabeth Mullino Moore, "Poetry, Prophecy, and Power," *Religious Education* 93, no. 3 (Summer 1998): 268–87; Abraham Joshua Heschel, *Man Is Not Alone: A Philosophy of Religion* (New York: Farrar, Straus and Giroux, 1951), 40–41.

21. Heschel, *Man Is not Alone*, 4. He says, "The attempt to convey what we see and cannot say is the everlasting theme of mankind's unfinished symphony, a venture in which adequacy is never achieved" (4, cf. 13–16). For Heschel, the ineffable includes the dramatic and ordinary: "The ineffable inhabits the magnificent and the common.... Some people sense this quality at distant intervals in extraordinary events; others sense it in the ordinary events, in every fold, in every nook; day after day, hour after hour" (5). See also Karl Rahner, *Theological Investigations* 4 (Baltimore: Helicon, 1966).

22. George H. Gallup Jr., "Measuring America's Spiritual Hunger," *The Christian Science Monitor,* December 16, 1998, 9; The Gallup Poll, "Gallup Poll Topics A–Z: Religion" (www.gallup.com/poll/releases/pr991224.asp). In 2003, 61 percent people in the U.S. reported that religion is important in their lives, up from 58 percent in 1992 (www.gallup.com, Religion).

23. Abraham Joshua Heschel, *Man Is Not Alone*, 11–13. Radical amazement is broader in scope than other human action, as it reaches to all reality — "not only to what we see, but also to the very act of seeing as well as to our own selves, to the selves that see and are amazed at their ability to see" (13). See also Heschel, *God in Search of Man: A Philosophy of Judaism* (New York: Farrar, Straus & Cudahy, 1955), 43–53.

24. Heschel, *Man Is Not Alone*, 12. He also compares wonder and doubt: "Doubt may come to an end, wonder lasts forever" (ibid). Doubt and logic are secondary in value to wonder or radical amazement.

they know through their senses. For Thurman, "We are most alive when we are brought face to face with the response of the deepest thing in us to the deepest thing in life."[25] Prayer at its best opens people to these deepest things.

A hermeneutic of wonder is *the art of dwelling on another (a text, person, sunset, or tree) with full attention to its wholeness, its complexity and simplicity, its intricate patterns of relationship.* Whether we focus on Brueggemann's abiding astonishment, Heschel's radical amazement, or Thurman's deepest things, we see the power of this hermeneutic. Practiced in dramatic and simple moments, it uncovers "blessings so intimate, so closely binding, that they do not seem to be blessings at all."[26] Such blessings are important in themselves, but they also build a life of wonder, awaking people to moments that delight, annoy, and teach them about God and God's world.

Whether approaching a biblical text or walking in the woods, one may actively seek wonder (through biblical criticism), practice disciplines of stillness (*lectio divina*), or contemplate in silence. The result may be a sense of communion with the forest or the text, which transcends the obvious and reveals God in the commonplace. "One becomes an indistinguishable part of a single rhythm, a single pulse."[27] These experiences are treasures, and while they do not happen in every moment, they can potentially color the rest of our lives with rainbows of bright assurance.

Educational Practices:
Teaching through Expectation

How does this relate to teaching? How does it shape classes, prayer groups, work teams, and fellowship gatherings? The cases studies of this chapter are suggestive. In Madeleine L'Engle, we glimpse the value of trusting and persevering. L'Engle trusted in God when she first mailed her manuscript, and she persevered in sending it, even after rejections. To teach with this spirit is to *trust and persevere, even in moments when discouragement looms large.* In Howard Thurman's grandmother, we glimpse the importance of taking bold action. She responded quickly when the church's deacons rejected Howard for baptism. She boldly advocated for her grandson, knowing him better than the deacons ever would. Her courage inspires teachers to *take bold action without knowing what the results will be or what others will think.* In John Hull, we glimpse the importance of struggling and seeking. Hull was willing to struggle for a new life after he became blind, even when the struggle required endless effort and led into depression. He sought new ways to

---

25. Howard Thurman, *The Inward Journey* (Richmond, Ind.: Friends United Press, 1961), 19. He adds: "The sunset opens a door in us and to us, to another dimension, timeless in quality, that can be described only as ineffable, awe-inspiring" (19–20).

26. Ibid., 45; cf. 74.

27. Ibid., 51.

relate with his children, new images and experiences of God, new ways to conduct the ordinary business of daily life, thus inspiring teachers to *respect and support people as they struggle and seek.*

These insights are practical in themselves, but I will expand them in relation to the earlier theological analysis, seeking educational practices that empower people to expect the unexpected. Sacramental teaching is giving reverence to the Holy and mysterious God whose work transcends our imagination, yet whose presence in ordinary moments of life can be taken for granted. Such reverence is embodied in the waiting and hoping of Advent and the wonder of the sacraments. It is also embodied in teaching that encourages the active practices of engagement, wonder, expectancy, and hope.

1. Engage with God and Creation

As we reflect back on the wonder of God and God's creation, the first practice that emerges is engagement. *To engage with God is to seek God's movements in every ordinary and extraordinary moment of every day. To engage with creation is to be awake to its pains and joys.* This sounds like fun, but it requires the kind of trust and perseverance we saw in Madeleine L'Engle. It requires high energy effort to let go.

One Saturday I had a very bad day, which had escalated into a sleepless night. With *no* excitement on Sunday morning, I dragged myself to worship. I was glad we would not celebrate communion that morning, aware that the eucharist would require more of me than I wanted to give. Upon entering the sanctuary, I felt dread; people looked too joyful on that sunshiny morning. I sat through the service, hoping nothing significant would happen. The sermon focused on hope, and I stayed as removed from it as possible. Occasionally, a word from the sermon, a giggle from a child, or the power of the instrumental music would touch me, but I kept the worship experience at a distance. I had built a fence around myself after some searing disappointments during the preceding week, perhaps protecting myself from expectation or another disappointment.

This personal experience points to how easy it is to block engagement, but how important engagement is. Sometimes engagement is *physical,* dragging oneself to church. Runners know that the act of running can energize them for new ventures, and scientists know that vigorous exercise releases energy into the body through a complex hormonal and cardiovascular interplay. Sometimes engagement is *psychological,* such as my growing awareness on that Sabbath day of how sad and disappointed I was. Though painful, the awareness was at least honest; it eventually enabled me to let go of my "pity party." Engagement may also be *spiritual* — engaging with God, with community, with creation. These are all part of spirituality. In all of its forms, engagement connects people with the Holy and stirs wonder in their souls.

Teachers and spiritual guides can clear paths for wonder with intentional planning, as Anabel Proffitt urges in her work.[28] They can also engage people with God and creation through disciplines of stillness. Further, engagement may arise unexpectedly as one is "grasped" by awe. In all forms of wonder, whether actively sought, evoked in stillness, or arising unexpectedly, human engagement is important. Engagement is not control; it is letting go, self-emptying, anticipating, and experiencing a moment in time.

Practice Attentiveness to God

A first form of engagement is *to practice attentiveness to God — letting go of work, sorrows, accomplishments, preoccupations, and clearing space to breathe Spirit.* Attuning with God's wonder is enhanced by empty spaces. When Madeleine L'Engle dropped her manuscript in the mailbox, she whispered a prayer; she was letting go of the manuscript and waiting for God. The wonder that came was not what she expected. Publication did finally come; however, her dialogue with God embraced wonder of a different kind — a quiet, waiting kind.

Teachers can teach attentiveness to God in a myriad of ways. They can invite people to *attend to God in physical ways* — participating in active liturgies, engaging in the manual labor of one's job, working in a garden, walking in the woods, swimming in the sea, playing with children, wind-surfing, or marching in a protest march. These physical actions are intentionally wide-ranging, for the wonder of God is waiting to be discovered in the active involvements of people's lives, whatever their life circumstances and wherever they take momentary pauses (however brief) to attend to God.

Teachers can also encourage people to *attend to God in powerful human experiences.* The most awesome moments in my life were the births of my two birth children. I knew, without being told, that my children were miracles of God. I knew that God was moving in the conception, carrying, birthing, and growing of these children. Other awesome moments are social events, as when the first U.S. civil rights legislation was signed into being, and when the Berlin Wall tumbled down, with people delighting in the streets where war and bondage had once prevailed. Teaching cannot fully prepare people for these moments; they are often unexpected, even when people have worked long and hard for them. What we *can* do is to imagine them, work and pray for them, and celebrate them when they happen. We can cultivate what Don Saliers calls a "habit of beholding."[29]

Finally, teachers can invite people to *attend to God in traditional spiritual practices.* Especially important are prayer, contemplation, and meditation. Consider the power of regular prayer times, centering prayer, minute-prayers, or

---

28. Anabel Colman Proffitt, "The Importance of Wonder in Religious Education," *Religious Education* 93, no. 1 (1998): 102–13.

29. Don E. Saliers, *Worship Come to Its Senses* (Nashville: Abingdon, 1996), 32.

breath-prayers during the course of a day, and simple moments of stillness for contemplating God and the things of God. When people pray, their lives are transformed. One of my daily disciplines is to pray the Lord's Prayer upon awaking, then again as I drive to school, and usually again later in the day. Something happens to me when I pray: "Hallowed be Thy name; Thy Kingdom come, Thy will be done, on earth as it is in heaven." The nagging questions and fears of my day fall into perspective, and I realize that I am living this day with and for God. Something wonderful also happens when I begin prayer with a time of centering, breathing deeply and becoming aware of my center in God. Again, I experience a reorientation of self, and prayers flow that I did not plan or expect — prayers for hurting children and for people suffering from war and drought.

These practices of prayer, contemplation, and meditation are not limited to individuals. Some of the most overwhelming moments in the decision-making of large church bodies have come in the context of prayer-filled gathering. The civil rights movement was powered by prayer in communities of faith, as have been many church decisions that have shifted an entire congregation or denomination toward a more compassionate and just decision. Of course, church decisions, as individual ones, are not always compassionate and just, and prayer does not guarantee a particular outcome. People do not even perceive the same responses in prayer. On the other hand, a river of prayers offered day in and day out can carry us into the flow of God's will and work. Further, this attentiveness to God will help us be more attentive to those around us.

Practice Attentiveness to Creation

This leads naturally to *practices of attentiveness to creation.* Consider first the practice of *being still before God's world* — a practice sung by psalmists and later generations who gather for worship or walk on starry nights: "When I look at your heavens, the work of your fingers, the moon and the stars that you have established; what are human beings that you are mindful of them, mortals that you care for them?" (Psalm 8:3–4). Strangely, these moments of feeling small in relation to the universe are also moments of hope. I remember drawing hope from storms during a difficult time in my life. I would sit by my window and watch lightning rage across the desert. The wonder of lightning was comforting, pointing me to the Holy, raining on creation.

Teaching can also enhance attentiveness by *lifting other people into consciousness.* Howard Thurman, in his university setting, encouraged people to be aware of children:

> Let us bring before our spirits the children of the world! The children born in refugee camps where all is tentative and shadowy, except the hardness of the constant anguish and anxiety that have settled deep within the eyes of

those who answer when the call is "Mommy" or "Daddy"... the numberless host of orphans corralled like sheep in places of refuge.[30]

Such teaching — in prayer, worship, and classrooms — invites people to attend to others.

Sacramental teaching also enhances attentiveness through *presenting facts and theories.* Don Saliers describes a childhood memory of learning that the earth is on the edge of the galaxy. With this new knowledge, he was astonished one winter night to see the "stunning brilliance of the Milky Way." In that moment, his new knowledge intensified his wonder, drawing together "the sight of the starry heavens with the knowledge of galaxies."[31] If information and theories of the universe enhance wonder, we need teaching that connects people in multiple ways with the stars, rivers, mountains, and seas — both the wonder and travail in creation's life.

Elsewhere I have discussed the value of richness to education, especially the richness that comes from *engaging people with diversity* — diverse people, environments, ideas, and ways of knowing.[32] In studies of animals, researchers have discovered that environmental changes enhance alertness and health; thus, in many animal preserves, people create rich environments for animals by changing their habitats from time to time. Since the early work of Jean Piaget, children's intellectual development has also been associated with rich, interactive learning environments. Novelty stirs new questions and rethinking of earlier ideas; thus, what is typical of the unexpected movements of God is also vital for the full living of people and other creatures.

2. Search for Wonder

Building on the earlier hermeneutical discussion, we turn now to the educational practice of wonder —*searching actively for wonder and reflecting upon wonders that come unexpectedly.* The hermeneutic of wonder is a discipline of spiritual searching, to be practiced, whether or not we are inspired. I suspect that my half-hearted participation in worship in the earlier story was at least a minimal practice of the hermeneutic, a semi-active search for wonder. Alas, it may have contributed to my letting go of grumpiness (finally!), though a hermeneutic of wonder has no guaranteed results; seeking is significant in itself.

When people practice attentiveness to God, they encounter the strange and familiar — unknown and known. Thurman describes this experience as hearing "a strange Voice — but not quite a stranger."[33] The strange and familiar God

---

30. Thurman, *The Inward Journey*, 109.
31. Saliers, *Worship Come to Its Senses*, 21.
32. Mary Elizabeth Mullino Moore, "Richness in Religious Education: Ethnic, Religious and Bio-diversity," in *The Fourth R for the Third Millennium: Education in Religion and Values for the Global Future*, ed. Leslie J. Francis, Jeff Astley, and Mandy Robbins (Dublin: Lindisfarne Books, 2001), 115–35.
33. Thurman, *The Inward Journey*, 135–36.

awakens people to the Holy, subverting the typical theological dualisms between immanence and transcendence discussed earlier. It awakens people to transcendent experiences of divine immanence — knowing God's immediate presence so strongly that it evokes a sense of transcendence. It also awakens people to immanent experiences of God's transcendence — glimpsing God's surpassing qualities so strongly that it stirs a sense of immediacy and presence.

Engage People in Searching Their Religious Traditions

Wonder can arise in the birth of a baby, a dramatic political change, or an experience in nature; it can also occur through religious traditions, most of which arose as vessels of wonder. A hermeneutic of wonder can *engage people with their religious traditions — searching, questioning, yearning, opening self, and committing.* For Heschel, wonder is a *legacy* of tradition, and only through wonder can we understand and worship God. Further, wonder can shape daily living: "Indifference to the sublime wonder of living is the root of sin."[34] In this light, wonder is a necessity for good living, concerned with the ultimate questions to which religion responds. Heschel calls this "depth-theology," which focuses people on the act of believing more than on content.[35]

Educationally, the practice of engaging with tradition is similar; it emphasizes active searching. Jewish education is a model, with its traditions of inspiring awe (as in the Psalms), searching texts, questioning traditions, and interpreting tradition for the sake of understanding and action. Hanan Alexander argues that the "tradition of query and response is rooted in the biblical text itself."[36] It is at the heart of rabbinic teaching and instructions to parents and communities on teaching children. Consider the familiar pattern: "And when your children ask you . . . you shall say" (Exod. 12:24–27; cf. 13:8; Deut. 6:20) This is a kind of teaching that is immersed in, and reflective upon, the tradition. It emerges from a searching engagement with religious traditions.

Invite People to Seek Wonder in Daily Living

The search for wonder also inspires people *to seek wonder in their religious experience and daily action.* This seeking may be inspired by religious traditions, yet many experiences and actions take place outside of self-conscious religious life. When people have religious experiences, whether adults or children, they often welcome opportunities to express and explore them.[37] People are less apt to search their

---

34. Heschel, *God in Search of Man,* 43.

35. Ibid., 3–4, 7–8.

36. Hanan A. Alexander, "A Jewish View of Human Learning," *International Journal of Children's Spirituality* 4, no. 2 (1999): 157; cf. 155–59.

37. One recent study regarding divine dreams in children documents this experience. See Kate Adams, "God Talks to Me in My Dreams: The Occurrence and Significance of Children's Dreams about God," *International Journal of Children's Spirituality* 6, no. 1 (2001): 99–111.

daily routine for signs of wonder; yet action-reflection can uncover wonder in ordinary life, as well as missed opportunities and future opportunities.

Such education is common in Jewish educational traditions, as in Christian traditions and recent philosophies of education. Jewish education does not focus on gathering information, but on "understanding for the sake of doing," on life for God.[38] In many Christian practices (Latin American base communities and early Wesleyan class meetings), people reflect on personal and social action as a spiritual discipline. In educational philosophy, John Dewey emphasizes learning in the encounter with life problems that beg to be solved — reflective action that contributes to learners' growth and larger social purposes.[39] These approaches all tap the human propensity to search; they maximize the wonder of learning and maximize its value for society. Such reflective participation can reshape action (a theme of chapter 8) as it uncovers daily wonders.

3. Practice Expectancy

A hermeneutic of wonder stirs expectation, and sacred teaching encourages the *practice of expectancy*. As Advent is a season of waiting, so every educational event and every day can be a time of awakening and awaiting God's incarnation in the world.

Celebrate the Waiting of Advent

A central practice, then, is to *celebrate the waiting of Advent,* which is often eclipsed by Christmas in North America. For many people, Christmas day marks the end of Christmas, rather than the beginning of Christmastide with its twelve days concluding in Epiphany. Such hurried practices obscure the blessings of the season, most especially of Advent. For people accustomed to putting Christmas trees up before Advent begins, and taking them down immediately after Christmas day, changing habits can be difficult. For teachers the challenge is to awaken people to the expectancy of Advent without trampling valued family traditions. One approach is to focus on additions rather than deletions. Teachers can introduce practices of Advent candles and home services of candle-lighting, daily meditations, Advent banners (based on lectionary texts for the four Advent Sundays), wearing purple, and celebrating the December saints' days (St. Nicholas on December 6 and St. Lucia on December 13) as Advent practices. People can

---

38. Alexander, "A Jewish View of Human Learning," 160. Alexander builds on ideas of Martin Buber and Franz Rosenzweig. He says, "What distinguishes mere *learning* from *teaching,* or dry *law* from *enlivening commandment,* is what Buber called 'inner power,' the willingness to accept that which is learned not merely as objective knowledge, but as a knowledge that has sufficient subjective meaning to drive one's life path" (160, emphases his). See also Hanan A. Alexander, *Reclaiming Goodness: Education and the Spiritual Quest* (Notre Dame, Ind.: University of Notre Dame, 2001).

39. John Dewey, *Experience and Education* (New York: Collier Books, 1977, 1938), 58–60, 67–72; John Dewey and Evelyn Dewey, *Schools of Tomorrow* (New York, E. P. Dutton, 1962, 1915), 121–31; John Dewey, *The Child and the Curriculum* (Chicago: University of Chicago Press, 1971), 3–29.

also study traditions from the past and different parts of the world, reflecting on diverse ways of celebrating Advent, Christmas, and Epiphany.

More important, people can study the significance of awaiting the Christ child while also awaiting God's New Creation, or the Second Coming of Christ. This is a time to name devastations in the present world and to pray fervently for the world's repair. This is a time to study historical traditions of Advent: fasting and baptism preparation; traditions of Eastern Christianity (in which Advent is a longer season); and traditions of solemnity, still reflected in the Roman Catholic practice of omitting "Gloria in Excelsis" in Sunday Mass during Advent. This is a season to rehearse the story and sing "O Come, O Come, Emmanuel."[40] When a community celebrates Advent with expectancy, they open themselves to appreciate the significance of Christmas for the present world.

Practice Sabbath

Another approach to expectancy is to *practice Sabbath — Sabbath rest and expectation for God's New Creation.* Practices include honoring the Sabbath day, honoring Sabbath times in every day, and taking Sabbath moments throughout each day. They include Sabbath seasons when people let go of their normal work and possessions and work toward justice for God's creation. The practice of Sabbath described in Exodus 23:10–13 is more than "self-care." Anticipating God's Reign is central to Sabbath, as to Advent. It is a time of rest and expectancy for the whole community, indeed the whole creation and a time of caring for God's gifts (Lev. 19:3; 25; Deut. 15:1–18; Gen. 2:1–3; Exod. 20:11; 21:1–6).[41] Sacred teaching invites people to reflect upon these Sabbath traditions and to practice Sabbath in ways that enhance life for others.

Sabbath replaces busy-ness, distractions, and efforts to control with expectancy. Maria Harris describes practices as: attunement to holiness in time (listening to what we are called to do in time), cessation (letting land lie fallow and practicing "not-doing"), and recreation in community.[42] Howard Thurman emphasizes letting go, urging people to let go the "idol of togetherness" and the effort to control others. He urges people to treasure private times, so that shared life can be enhanced by solitary experience, and to release themselves from controlling others.[43] Sacred teaching invites people to consider such practical ways of clearing Sabbath space to expect God's New Creation.

---

40. This hymn, based on the O-Antiphons, is traditionally sung during Advent or during the seven days before Christmas Eve. The "O" meditations begin with "O Wisdom" and end with "O Emmanuel."

41. Find more on keeping Sabbath in Mary Elizabeth Moore, *Ministering with the Earth* (St. Louis: Chalice, 1998), 146–51; Maria Harris, *Proclaim Jubilee! A Spirituality for the Twenty-first Century* (Louisville: Westminster John Knox, 1996); Tilden Edwards, *Sabbath Time* (Nashville: Upper Room, 1992); Abraham Joshua Heschel, *The Earth Is the Lord's and the Sabbath* (New York: Harper & Row, 1962).

42. Harris, *Proclaim Jubilee!*, 26–35.

43. Thurman, *The Inward Journey*, 110–11, 127, 137; 118–19.

4. Practice Hope

The discussion of expectancy points to the *practice of hope*. This practice responds to God's sacramental presence in the sacraments and in creation. Don Saliers identifies hope as an essential quality of true and relevant Christian worship, along with awe, delight, and truthfulness. He asks, "Why do we settle for so little when God offers so much in Word, sacrament, and song?"[44] True worship awakens people to wonder and stirs hope, as does sacred teaching. Two specific practices are particularly important.

Engage People with the God of Hope

If the source of hope is God, we can cultivate hope by inviting people to *engage with the God of promises*. As discussed earlier, hope is distinct from optimism. Optimism is a psychological state; hope is a theological decision to trust God's untiring devotion to creation. Optimism can encourage people to hope, but it can also obscure hope. It can lead people to think of God as a magician who will make things like *they* want them, or to think of human beings as capable of doing anything they dream by the sheer power of their will.

To engage with God's hope is to study the promise-making and promise-keeping God of the Bible, studying God's movements over time and praying for God's hope-filled response to the present world. In light of God's presence in the sacraments, we can also expect God to renew promises through sacramental action. The earlier case of the baptism service was filled with invitations to practice hope. The case gives clues for engaging people with the God of hope: (1) pointing people to God's gift of hope to the world, including hope embodied in the sacraments; (2) recognizing possibilities for the entire community to teach God's hope, including the children; and (3) celebrating covenant with God in worship, sacraments, formal preaching and teaching, and common meals.

Engage People with a Community of Hope

This points to a second practice — to *engage people with a community of hope*. Often when people meet life struggles, such as death, divorce, or political disruption, they realize their need for community. People sometimes seek a religious community (or wish for one) during these times. Sacramental teaching has to do with creating such communities and inviting people to be involved in them.

Earlier I described a Sabbath worship where I worked hard to remain disengaged and to avoid expectation. A friend recently described a similar experience; in her case, an unexpected event took place after she dragged herself to worship. During the celebration of eucharist, she approached the altar to receive the bread and grape juice; as it happened, she walked behind a gay couple whom

---

44. Saliers, *Worship Come to Its Senses*, 15; cf. 14–17.

she knew and admired. One of the men had recently had surgery, and his partner of thirty years was helping him down the aisle. Walking behind this devoted
couple, my friend's spirits lifted. She was touched by human compassion; she was
touched by the Holy.

Engaging with a community of hope guides restless souls to hope, sometimes
for the first time and sometimes in repeated returns. In a learning community,
people need to engage in life together — in praying, studying, playing, breaking
bread, and working — so that hope can be nourished. People need opportunities
to take on roles of sharing and leading, as well as listening to, collaborating
with, and following others. When people are thus engaged, hope is embodied and
intensified in the community.

Concluding Reflections

We live with a God of surprises, who always comes, but not always as we imagine.
One central sacramental practice of education is to expect the unexpected. This
requires a spirit of expectation among teachers and learning communities. The
challenge is to cultivate a capacity for astonishment and be prepared for what
follows. The next chapters reveal some of that ongoing journey, which emerges
from the gift of wonder.

Reflecting Further

To reflect further on expecting the unexpected, people might do the following:

1. Study patterns of expectation in your congregation. Reflect on what stand-
    ing traditions and recent experiences have contributed to a sense of wonder.
    What has blocked it? How might your congregation or group encourage
    expectancy, both within the community and in the larger world? Which
    practices of this chapter would contribute most to sacred teaching in your
    context?

2. Consider making an Advent banner, adding a symbol each week. You can do
    this intergenerationally or with children, sharing it each Sunday in worship,
    classes, or homes. Symbols can be based on lectionary lessons: a potter's
    hand with a pot (Isa. 64:1–9); a path in the wilderness (Isa. 40:1–11); a
    descending dove and broken chain (Isa. 61:1–4, 8–11); building materials
    for the house of the Lord (2 Sam. 7:1–16); and, for Christmas, an angel in
    a burst of light (Luke 2:1–20).[45]

---

45. These lections are for Year B of the Revised Common Lectionary (1992). One source is *The
United Methodist Book of Worship* (Nashville: United Methodist Publishing House, 1992), 227–28.

Chapter Four

Remembering the Dismembered

✡

A short time ago, a wrenching event happened in one of my classes. From this event come questions for sacred teaching: Why and how might faith communities be engaged in the work of remembering the dismembered and identifying with the suffering of God? How does God's suffering contribute to hope? This is the story:

We were near the end of term when a student cried in anger about the assigned reading. She said the author was blaming victims for their suffering. Through tears, she told about a woman who was beaten, stabbed in the head, and left on the floor to die. The woman was her mother. Never could she believe that her mother deserved to die in this horrible way. Various students in the class tried to explain their interpretations of the author to the distressed woman. They argued that the author was not blaming victims, citing pages and paragraphs to support their arguments. One student offered the woman an alternate explanation of suffering that was meaningful to her. The woman was not consoled; she repeated her cries. For her, dwelling with pain was more important in this moment than understanding another person's book or another person's answers.

Why did this event happen spontaneously in a theological classroom? Why did people seek answers for the distressed woman, and why did she want to dwell on painful memory? What did the various members of this community yearn to know? Such questions emerge when people engage honestly with life. Alongside this story are others from adult study groups, spiritual retreats, youth groups, and children's classes. Together, they alert religious communities to the significance of remembering the dismembered — a critical element in sacred teaching. I borrow the term from Jong Chun Park, who sees "remembering the dismembered" as critical to theological reflection and construction.[1] I believe it is also critical to educational theory and practice.

In this chapter, we focus on the role of tragic memory in sacred teaching, helping people respond to the world, both its sacrality and its woundedness. This aspect of sacramental teaching mediates the memory of God's suffering

---

1. Jong Chun Park, presentation to faculty of Candler School of Theology, Emory University, October 18, 1999. See also Jong Chun Park, *Crawl with God, Dance in the Spirit! A Creative Formation of Korean Theology of the Spirit* (Nashville: Abingdon, 1998).

with hurts of creation and links Jesus' death upon a cross with the continuing presence of suffering in the world. Remembering the dismembered connects people with tragedies in vast historical events and painful memories in their families, churches, and communities. It connects people with violent legacies of their people, whether slavery, war, land removal, class oppression, racial oppression, or genocide. Though pain is ever-present, people hesitate to rehearse it, fearing that it will disrupt rather than heal; yet, South Africa's Truth and Reconciliation Commission reveals the power of remembering (truth-telling in a carefully designed process) to heal a nation.[2] How might education be an agent of such healing?

While the focus of this book is Christian, people can also approach tragic memory with an interreligious view — important in a world where much suffering is caused or escalated by religious conflict. Sacred teaching is mediating holiness and goodness in response to a broken world for the sake of healing. Most religions include stories, rituals, and worldviews that account for brokenness and promise repair in some form.[3] Whether we focus on Christianity or diverse religious traditions, *the heart of teaching in the presence of pain is to help people grieve destruction, discern Holy touch, and find hope and direction without denying or belittling tragedy.* The primary purpose of this chapter is to consider the educational potential of remembering the dismembered, turning first to the power of tragic memory and concluding with approaches to religious education that enhance people's ability to remember the dismembered and respond to an aching world.

Power in Remembering the Dismembered

In the opening case, the passion for remembering arose from a student rather than the teacher, yet it was powerful for the whole class. In spite of the educational potential, teachers usually discourage such painful remembering; the challenges are too great. Teachers are often tempted to focus education on general themes or less evocative details. This temptation is ironic in Christian education: the faith was born from the particularity of Jesus' life; it is devoted to the God who cares for birds of the air and lilies of the field (Matt. 6:25–34; Luke 12:22–31).[4] On the other hand, teachers hesitate to stir the difficult human dynamics of painful memory, a palpable challenge in the case. This temptation is also ironic in light of Jesus' courage in facing conflict and death.

---

2. Desmond Mpilo Tutu, *No Future without Forgiveness* (New York: Doubleday, 1999).

3. William James, *The Varieties of Religious Experience: A Study in Human Nature* (New York: University Books, 1963, 1902), 508; cf. 507–15. James described the commonality among religions as knowing that something is wrong with the world and that people can be saved by connecting with a higher power.

4. Paul Santmire, *Nature Reborn* (Minneapolis: Fortress, 2000), 29–31. Santmire urges Christians to focus on particularities and to include all creation.

A teacher can avoid such situations by discouraging personal sharing in the classroom, inviting a troubled student to meet for further conversation later, or giving protective reassurance. One can also create an educational climate that discourages people from sharing intense personal concerns. All of these responses are appropriate in certain circumstances, and all have limitations. Personal sharing can distract from educational purposes, as well as enlarge them. In some cases, personal sharing is a sign of psychological trauma and is best served with a protective response. Further, structured educational settings are important for some educational communities and purposes. Even in the case situation, diverse responses were plausible, depending on circumstances, educational purposes, and the ability and experience of teachers and learners. In fact, remembering the dismembered does not require personal sharing; it can take place in many ways. What is important is not to advocate one particular response but to advocate teaching that helps people meet truth and healing in the face of wounding memories. This is what I learned from the student who cried out. With her cries ringing, together with painful cries from history, we analyze the power of remembering the dismembered.

Power of Releasing Terrifying Memories

In the opening case study, the *power of release* is evident — *the cathartic sharing of painful memory*. The student found release (by her later account) in returning to the terror. Her intuitive wisdom diverged from the common human tendency to be silent about past horrors. Silence is more evident in other instances — the lengthy time before Holocaust victims began to tell their stories, or the long repressed tragedies that underlie slavery, economic oppression, and other forms of human and ecological destruction.

Korean theologians have been particularly courageous in regard to actively remembering historical terror. Park's emphasis on "remembering the dismembered" encourages people to *mourn the silencing* of Korean people through history: the silencing of Korean traditional religions by Christian missionaries; silencing of Korean language and culture during the last thirty-six year Japanese occupation; silencing of "comfort women" used as sex slaves by Japanese soldiers in World War II; and silencing of civilian murders during the Korean War. In light of this dreadful history, Park argues that the strongest need is not reconciliation, but inscribing tragedies of the past in our memories. I conclude from this that the power of remembering transcends its contributions to activist agendas; it is powerful because it breaks forced silence, releasing people to integrate horrific parts of life into the whole.

Power of Uncovering Hidden Hurts

Closely related is the *power of uncovering hidden hurts* — *revealing painful memories beneath the surface that shape the social fabric*. The opening case took place in a southern university. The U.S. South is not more or less racist than most other places, but racist attitudes are often visible here, running deep and evoking awareness and shame. In this context, people often feel compelled to tell raw stories of racism. Even here, however, the urge to remember the dismembered is too painful to be a permanent place of dwelling. People often leap to provide answers, as students did when they insisted that our text's author was not blaming victims or justifying violence. One person tried to hasten a resolution further, encouraging the distressed student to adopt a belief and attitude that worked for her. Neither response was adequate. The woman needed to uncover deep hurts of the past. She seemed to know that redemption and reconciliation required her dwelling, at least for now, in a horrible, dismembering tragedy.

The student in this story was African American, as was the author we read that day, as was the student who offered advice. All three sought to respond, albeit in diverse ways, to issues in dominant white societies with racial overtones — uncovering and responding to hidden hurts. Similarly, indigenous peoples (Native Americans, Canadians, Hawaiians, and others) often set aside sacred places to remember past tragedies, thus honoring ancestors and their pain. In light of the case study and indigenous practices, I conclude that people *need* to know hidden hurts, thus need education that remembers.

Power of Taking Time

The difficulty of releasing terrifying memory and uncovering hidden hurt points to another *power — taking time.* Remembering tragedy cannot be hurried. If Jesus could not, in his lifetime, bring the reign of peace and justice into the world, why do we expect that of ourselves? Jesus *did* bring the reign of God, but it was both present and future. In Luke's Gospel, he likened the Kingdom of God to a mustard seed that grew into a great tree where birds could nest, and he likened it to yeast that could leaven three measures of flour (13:18–20). These images reflect the significance of small beginnings and waiting over time. They do not promise God's instant "fixing" of a broken world; they plant hope that small actions, even ours, might contribute to a good present and better future. Taylor and June McConnell and Lynn Bridgers accent the importance of time for building multicultural relationships.[5] Building on their ideas, I suggest that time is needed to explore the depths of tragic memory and to build life-giving relationships.

Consider the post–Civil War South, where racism and memories of slavery are receiving new attention. A child of the South, I am now teaching in the South

---

5. Taylor McConnell, "Family Ministry through Cross-Cultural Education," *Religious Education* 76, no. 3 (May–June 1981): 271–79; Mary Elizabeth Moore, Boyung Lee, Katherine Turpin, Ralph Casas, Lynn Bridgers, and Veronice Miles, "Realities, Visions and Promises of a Multicultural Future," *Religious Education* 99, no. 3 (Summer 2004): 287–315, esp. 304–7.

after more than thirty years of living in the West. I knew, when I decided to move, that I would have a fresh encounter with difficult memories of my own family; some owned slaves and some drove Native people off their lands so they could increase their prosperity. People who live honestly with such a heritage inevitably discover that racism is deeply embedded in their cultures and family relations. As a white Southern woman writing her classic *Killers of the Dream* in the 1940s, Lillian Smith recognized that lingering racist patterns haunt even those white folk who are most determined to free themselves of hateful judgments.[6] More recently, Thandeka has analyzed these patterns. She has brought her African American astuteness to reflect on how white racism is learned, arguing that white families teach racism in subtle but sure ways; it is very difficult to resist.[7] I have come to realize that I can never walk through my white racism if I do not face the dismembered tragedies that my ancestors perpetrated, however long that process may take. Even more challenging is to live with the dismembered tragedies that I myself have perpetrated.

Power of Memory for Repentance and Reconstruction

Eventually, many people yearn to turn around (repent) and reshape the world, thus unleashing the *power of memory for repentance and reconstruction*. Consider efforts to build post-Holocaust (*Shoah*) reconciliation around the world. The Museum of Tolerance (Los Angeles) is one example, specializing in research, educational displays, and events. Another is the educational work of Björn Krondorfer and Gabriele Meyer. Krondorfer engages German and Jewish students in travel seminars, visiting historic sites, meeting with people involved in contemporary efforts to reeducate and rebuild, and relating intensely with one another. Meyer focuses on post-Shoah education with German Christian women.[8] Analyzing post-Holocaust silence, she argues that German Christian women, victims themselves of patriarchal domination, have perpetuated silence and denied their complicity in the Holocaust. She argues that remembering is an important first step toward repenting and reconstructing identity and action. These studies reveal the need for remembering that embraces more than personal memory; it must also embrace the communal memory of violence perpetrated by ordinary people, thus evoking hope for repentance and reconciliation.

---

6. Lillian Eugenia Smith, *Killers of the Dream* (New York: Norton, 1994, 1949).

7. Thandeka, *Learning to Be White: Money, Race, and God in America* (New York: Continuum, 1999).

8. Björn Krondorfer, *Remembrance and Reconciliation: Encounters between Young Jews and Germans* (New Haven: Yale University Press, 1995); Gabriele Mayer, *Post-Holocaust Religious Education for German Women* (Münster: LIT Verlag, 2003).

Roots of Tragic Memory in Church Practice

Every corner of the world has its legacy of tragedy, and people yearn to face their tragedies, whether in mourning, protesting, healing, or some other response. At its best, the church invokes such memories from time to time; at its best, it allows safe space for pain to be felt and wrestling to be done. If we are awake to these moments, we will discover God in the middle of the pain and wrestling. In this section, we explore roots of tragic memory in church practice, especially that which attunes people to the world's pain and to God's co-suffering and hope-stirring presence in the midst of creation.

Lent and Holy Week

Just as Advent is the season that marks expecting the unexpected, so Lent and Holy Week mark remembering the dismembered. These are times for entering into Jesus' passion. A youth once expressed concern to me that blood and pain are central to Christianity. As a result, he chose not to participate in celebrating eucharist, nor in Good Friday services; he was disturbed by the suffering and death symbolism. I understand his concern, yet the Gospels, particularly Mark, are captivated by the passion. Why?

In truth, people who have suffered much often find their greatest hope in Jesus' suffering. Is this because it *justifies* their suffering? I doubt it. Yet the suffering of Jesus does *honor* and *identify* with their suffering. It is not strange, therefore, that, in parts of the world where poverty and oppression are intense, so is devotion to the crucified Christ. It is not strange that people in the early Christian church crawled on their knees up the steps in Rome that were traditionally thought to be the steps Jesus walked to meet Pilate. It is not strange that the Holy Sepulchre in Jerusalem, where Jesus is thought to have been crucified and buried, is shared by six churches — Latin Catholic, Greek Orthodox, Armenian, Syrian, Coptic, and Ethiopian. It is not strange that the same church is a pilgrimage site for thousands of people each year. People yearn for God when they suffer. They yearn to know that God is *with* them and *suffers with* them. The young man's concern about glorified suffering is real; so is the power of knowing that God suffers with creation, and that God offers consolation and meaning amid tragedy.

One way to respond to suffering without glorifying it is to be mindful of suffering in our present world. *Lent is a time for such remembering.* It is a time for remembering the painful competition among Christian groups who all claim to revere Jesus Christ and grieve his sacrifice. Consider the Holy Sepulchre mentioned above. The six Christian communities who share this holy space sometimes exercise "jealous possessiveness" and "watch one another suspiciously for any infringement of rights."[9] Jerome Murphy-O'Connor, O.P., elaborates: "The frailty

---

9. Jerome Murphy-O'Connor, O.P., *The Holy Land: An Oxford Archaeological Guide from Earliest Times to 1700* (Oxford: Oxford University Press, 1998), 45.

of humanity is nowhere more apparent than here; it epitomizes the human con-dition."[10] Lent is a time to remember moments of destructive competition among diverse religious communities. It is a time to remember people who struggle in poverty and people who live in war-torn countries, shedding their blood in human conflict. It is a time to remember the woman Mary who shed her blood in birthing Jesus, the women who suffered at the foot of the cross, and the countless women today who are denied safety and opportunity in a world where gender oppression is still rampant. These are hurting ones with whom God suffers, people whose pain calls us to remember and respond.

Lent is also a time of preparation, marked by fasting and penance. It is a time to rehearse the story — to walk with Jesus on the dusty roads to Jerusalem; it is a time to search our souls. During Lent and Holy Week, people recall Jesus' suffering and death and make explicit connections between those memories and the present suffering of creation. This is not primarily a time for thinking of suffering as a thing that Jesus did for abstract humanity or that God did *to* Jesus to retrieve sinful humanity from the devil, although these views have meaning for some Christians. This is a time for people to *grieve* Jesus' suffering and *confess* our lack of response to the world's suffering. Confession and repentance come to the fore, expressed in penitential practices of letting go and taking on — letting go of certain festivities and pleasures, and taking on more active religious observance and more generous giving to others.

The remembering and soul-searching of Lent may be less explicitly religious. In a recent interview, the owner of a small global company searched his soul with me. He can no longer bear to buy the cheapest products in Southeast Asia, knowing they may be produced by child labor or by workers in unbearable conditions with non-living wages. At the same time, he knows that his company, which buys products and sells them to larger retail companies, has limited options if it is to remain viable. His company can enter long-term partnerships with Asian companies that have more just personnel practices, seeking to benefit both the producers and their countries. Unfortunately, his company depends on retailers who will readily purchase from other suppliers if they discover similar goods for a penny cheaper. The retailers will insist that his company abandon their carefully selected producers and move elsewhere for lower prices. This man is caught in conflicting tugs — his ethical standards, the needs of his suppliers and retailers, the hometown that relies on his company's viability, buyers who want quality goods at low prices, and his sense that many people would happily pay a penny more if they had the opportunity and knew the consequences. This is a complex ethical dilemma.

---

10. Ibid. Murphy-O'Connor makes a case for pilgrims to allow this holy site to address them, saying: "Those who permit the church to question them may begin to understand why hundreds of thousands thought it worthwhile to risk death or slavery in order to pray here" (ibid.).

The man in this interview is not involved in a religious community; yet he daily searches his soul, which may eventually lead to major changes in his company. This is the work of Lent. If he makes the difficult choice to change his approach to work, he may face rebuke, coercion by others, or economic downturn. In such a case, he suffers the consequences of his ethical choices, economically, socially, and personally. This is the work of Holy Week. Lent and Holy Week are times of remembering and responding to the dismembered, both past and present. It is a time of remembering and responding to God's own suffering and God's movement in the midst of sorrow and tragedy.

Sacraments

We have already acknowledged that the eucharist has, at its heart, the remembrance of Jesus' death. Also part of the service of eucharist in many traditions is the prayer of humble access: "We do not presume to come to this thy table, O merciful Lord, trusting in our own righteousness, but in thy manifold and great mercies. We are not worthy so much as to gather up the crumbs under thy table."[11] In these words, as in the words that recall Christ's suffering and death, the eucharist is grounded in tragedies — those that befell Jesus and those that dwell in broken human life. Tragedy is further recognized in the offertory of a traditional eucharistic liturgy. The offertory begins with collecting alms — remembering those who are poor and responding to realities of poverty.

The service of baptism is also rooted in tragedy, both in Jesus' death and in human sin. As people are lowered into the baptismal water or anointed with water on their heads, they symbolically enter into Jesus' death and rise to a new life. The radical experience of dying and rising is symbolized in practices of the African American slave community described in chapter 2, especially in the practice of asking others for forgiveness. These slaves recognized that in baptism they would leave one life and enter another.[12] Their symbolic death and new birth would transform their daily relations.

Some tragedies are less frequently remembered in traditional services of eucharist and baptism, as the tragedy of women's missing presence in the sacraments themselves. In traditions where women are not ordained, women often know the pain of being eliminated by their gender from presiding in the sacraments, as well as the narrowness of defining sacraments in relation to clerical orders.[13] Another problem is the emphasis on Jesus' blood and the priests' mediation of the power of that blood, without any connection to the blood of women's monthly cycles or

11. This particular form is found in The United Methodist Book of Worship (Nashville: United Methodist Publishing House, 1992), 49.

12. Melva Wilson Costen, African American Christian Worship (Nashville: Abingdon, 1993), 62–63.

13. Susan A. Ross, "God's Embodiment and Women: Sacraments," in Freeing Theology: The Essentials of Theology in Feminist Perspective, ed. Catherine Mowry LaCugna (San Francisco: Harper, 1993), 185–209; Rosemary Radford Ruether, Women-Church: Theology and Practice of Feminist Liturgical Communities (New York: Crossroad, 1985), 4.

childbirth.[14] Remembering women's bodies and women's collective past, including their dismembered past, is critical to a full celebration of the sacraments.

This discussion reveals that the power of the sacraments is affected by the quality of remembering. According to Marjorie Procter-Smith, the *anamnesis* in the eucharistic prayer (the words that connect the past event in Jesus' life with the present act of offering bread and wine) reminds the people and God of that past and generates an encounter with God in the present.[15] The recovery of women's memory in the *anamnesis* is critical for the sacraments.[16] It is critical for the full inclusion of women in the church and for reminding people of women's presence and pain, even their sense of abandonment by the church and God. It is also critical for reclaiming and reconstructing sacramental traditions, making connections with women's stories, such as the Gospel story of the woman anointing Jesus.[17] Similar reclaiming is needed in regard to the poor, children, and other systemically neglected communities.

We see in this brief exploration of sacramental practice that remembering the dismembered is part of traditional church practice, and it is critical to the God-human relationship. We also see that what is liturgically ignored is easily minimized and negated, as in the case of women. Add to this the nearly complete silence regarding the nonhuman creation. Remembering the dismembered, if it is to be honest and whole, will be an act of remembering the suffering and death of Jesus, the suffering of humanity, the pain of the cosmos, and God's empathic suffering with a hurting creation.

Theology of Suffering

Tragedy stands in the foreground of sacramental theology, along with wonder. Christians gather at the table of eucharist to remember the dismembered Jesus: "On the night on which he was betrayed.... This is my body, broken for you. ...This is my blood...." Similarly in teaching, remembering the dismembered honors the tragic in Jesus' life. It also honors tragedy in the Christian community past and present, in the larger human community, and in the cosmos. In teaching children, such remembering honors children's nightmares and the harsh realities that stir them. In teaching diverse religious traditions in schools, remembering

---

14. Christine Gudorf, "The Power to Create: Sacraments and Men's Need to Birth," *Horizons* 14 (1987): 296–309.

15. Marjorie Procter-Smith, *In Her Own Rite: Constructing Feminist Liturgical Tradition* (Akron, Ohio: Order of St. Luke, 2000, 1990), 32–33. Procter-Smith makes a case for this view in relation to oppression: "For oppressed people ... and any who have felt abandoned by God, the 'reminding God' aspect is critically important" (33). She explains that this reminding of God "recognizes a fundamental truth: to be forgotten by God is to die; to be remembered by God is to live" (ibid).

16. Ibid., 34–43. This is a work of reclamation and reconstruction (42).

17. Ibid., 43–47; Elisabeth Schüssler Fiorenza, *In Memory of Her: A Feminist Theological Reconstruction of Christian Origins* (New York: Crossroad, 1983), xiii–xiv.

is a way to acknowledge diverse concerns for tragedy in diverse traditions, and the often-tragic relations among religious communities. For people of all ages, remembering brings to light the tragic dimensions of life. Tragedy and suffering thus demand theological reflection and stir strong affirmations about the sacred.

1. God Suffers with and Responds to Creation

The first affirmation is that *God suffers with and responds to creation*. Of particular note are traditions recalling God's engagement (re-membering) with creation: the creation stories of Genesis (1:1–2:4; 2:5–25) and Proverbs (8:22–31); God's hearing the cries of the people in bondage (Exod. 3:7–12); God's response to Job's cry (38:1–42:9); Jesus' weeping over Jerusalem because the people had not recognized "the things that make for peace!" (Luke 19:41–44); and Jesus' driving money changers from the temple (Luke 19:45–46). These texts reveal God as creating, discerning pain, speaking to people in distress, weeping at human failure, and expressing anger. We could add other texts, but these are sufficient to reveal the biblical God as One who *feels* with creation and *responds* to creation's joys and groans.

The Christian journey through Lent and Holy Week is a pilgrimage with that tragedy. People are faced with the suffering and crucifixion of God, *not* a cruel act of sacrifice by a distant God. People are faced with the helplessness of the cross and God's plaintive cry for human efforts, however feeble, in redeeming the world. People are faced with the suffering of Jesus' community and of all communities that endure abuse and oppression.

God's suffering has captured theological interest in recent decades, perhaps a natural outgrowth of the world's intense suffering. Jürgen Moltmann struck a chord when he wrote *The Crucified God* in 1972.[18] Arguing that *God* died on the cross, he uncovered the identity of God with pain. Feminist work has continued and reshaped the emphasis, critiquing the idea of necessary suffering, which is easily used to glorify and justify suffering. For Rita Nakashima Brock and Rebecca Parker, Jesus' suffering is tied to the suffering of Jesus' community and must also be interpreted through the suffering of contemporary communities.[19] For Marjorie Suchocki, God is relationally bound with the world; thus, the world's

---

18. Jürgen Moltmann, *The Crucified God: The Cross of Christ as the Foundation and Criticism of Christian Theology*, trans. R. A. Wilson and John Bowden (San Francisco: HarperSanFrancisco, 1991, 1974, 1972).

19. Rita Nakashima Brock, *Journeys by Heart: A Christology of Erotic Power* (New York: Crossroad, 1988); Rita Nakashima Brock and Rebecca Ann Parker, *Proverbs of Ashes: Violence, Redemptive Suffering, and the Search for What Saves Us* (Boston: Beacon, 2001). See also Christine E. Gudorf, *Victimization: Examining Christian Complicity* (Philadelphia: Trinity Press International, 1992); Nancy M. Victorin-Vangerud, *The Raging Hearth: Spirit in the Household of God* (St. Louis: Chalice, 2000), 150–53, 167–86.

suffering inevitably enters into God's life and becomes God's suffering.[20] In these views, as in mine, the Holy One is revealed as a suffering presence, not removing creation's suffering with acts of magic, but feeling and responding to it.

2. God Receives and Transforms Creation's Hurt and Anger

The first affirmation seems to some as a weak view of God, but how can compassion (suffering with) be seen as weak? It is also not the last word, however. *God actually takes creation's woes into God's Self, thus opening the possibility of transforming those woes into a new reality.* Job railed against God, and his spirits turned when God responded (Job 42:1–6); hope came from anguish. Similarly in recent times, theologians who reflect on tragedy often dwell on hope as well. Jürgen Moltmann embeds his theology of hope within the tragedies of Jesus and the oppressed.[21] His view neither glances over tragedy, nor glorifies it; he simply claims the hope of future, pulling creation beyond present terrors. While memories of dismemberment may be depressing as nighttime reading, they do not run counter to hope. In fact, encountering tragedy can strengthen people to search for and claim hope, even to argue with God as Job did; ironically, it can also disarm people from depending on wishful thinking or their own powers. The irony is critical. People are strengthened by remembering the dismembered to relate authentically with God, the Giver of all good things, and to relate honestly with tragedy, an undeniable reality of life in this world.

To say that God receives the sadness, hurt, and anger of creation is not just to acknowledge God's listening ear; it is to know that God carries these aches in God's own being and transforms that which can be transformed. For Suchocki, this transformation carries into everlasting; for Alfred North Whitehead, it promises the apotheosis of the world.[22] God not only receives the aches of creation, but saves the world as it enters into the divine life. God's judgment has "a tenderness which loses nothing that can be saved" and "a wisdom which uses what in the temporal world is mere wreckage."[23]

3. Creation's Grief and Effort Enhance God's Work

This leads to another affirmation, that *God needs creation's grief and participation to transform suffering into hope.* This radical affirmation is an assertion that creation's

---

20. See Marjorie Hewitt Suchocki, *The Fall to Violence: Original Sin in Relational Theology* (New York: Continuum, 1994), 63–64. Similarly sin against creation (violation of creation) also violates God.

21. Jürgen Moltmann, *Theology of Hope: On the Ground and the Implications of a Christian Eschatology,* trans. James W. Leitch and preface trans. Margaret Kohl (San Francisco: HarperSanFrancisco, 1991, 1975).

22. Marjorie Hewitt Suchocki, *The End of Evil: Process Eschatology in Historical Context* (Albany: State University of New York Press, 1988), 97–114; Whitehead, *Process and Reality: An Essay in Cosmology,* ed. David Ray Griffin and Donald W. Sherburne (New York: Free Press, Macmillan, 1978), 348, 346–49.

23. Whitehead, *Process and Reality,* 346.

grieving — often seen as an act of neediness before God — is important to God. Mourning opens possibilities for deeper relations *with* God and more effective response *by* God. Further, Jesus' weeping over Jerusalem and prayer in the Garden of Gethsemane reveal his divinity as well as his humanity; they reveal God's suffering and also human suffering in solidarity with God, both important to God's work.

The grief process involves what Sue Nelson describes as "returning to the original rupturing experience(s)," analyzing what happened, grieving hurt, and "allowing it to be a part of our *past* history."[24] The return to pain does not obliterate the past, but analyzes and feels it until people are ready to let it reshape the future. This suggests an active human process of co-creating with God, described in diverse ways. Carter Heyward framed the issues in terms of God's limited power, accenting the total self-giving of Jesus that led to devastating consequences and God's need for human effort in the ongoing redemption of the world.[25] Others have added relational images of the suffering Christa community and the wounded heart of God.[26] Each portrait portrays God's yearning, indeed God's need, for people to participate in the transformation of suffering into hope.

4. God Reconciles and Calls Creation to Reconciliation

This discussion begs the question of what kind of transformation is promised. The fourth affirmation is that *God transforms tragedy, violation, and sin into whatever is possible within the present world, seeking to reconcile God's Self with creation and to reconcile every part of creation with the whole.* To understand this, we need to recognize the pain of being violated and alienated by a hostile world; we cannot simply talk about human sin as errors of omission and commission. We need to look at what some have named "the other side of sin," to recognize evil and the devastation experienced by the sinned-against.[27] With a genuine sense of evil in a relational world, people are asked to build relations of trust and love. To be human is to build bridges and "to know the reality of broken bridges"; it is also "to know the possibility of reconciliation."[28] Reconciliation is a human yearning,

---

24. Susan L. Nelson, "For Shame, for Shame, the Shame of It All: Postures of Refusal and the Broken Heart," in *The Other Side of Sin: Woundedness from the Perspective of the Sinned-Against*, ed. Andrew Sung Park and Susan L. Nelson (Albany: State University of New York Press, 2001), 82.

25. Carter Heyward, *The Redemption of God: A Theology of Mutual Relation* (Washington, D.C.: University Press of America, 1982); cf. Carter Heyward, *God in the Balance: Christian Spirituality in Times of Terror* (Cleveland: Pilgrim, 2002).

26. Brock, *Journeys by Heart*; Park, *The Wounded Heart of God: The Asian Concept of Han and the Christian Doctrine of Sin* (Nashville: Abingdon, 1993).

27. Andrew Sung Park and Susan L. Nelson, eds., *The Other Side of Sin*, 2–3; cf. 1–23. Park and Nelson build on their earlier works, as on Mary Potter Engel's idea of "the other side." See Engel, "Evil, Sin, and Violation of the Vulnerable," in *Lift Every Voice: Constructing Christian Theologies from the Underside*, ed. Susan Brooks Thistlethwaite and Mary Potter Engel (San Francisco: HarperCollins, 1990), 152–64.

28. Nelson, "For Shame, for Shame, the Shame of It All," 78–79.

as well as a promise and command of God; however, it does not emerge without God's transformative grace and the human work of building bridges.

Hermeneutic of Tragic Memory

This discussion leads to a hermeneutic of tragic memory — *engaging people in remembering and interpreting the painful past, and in confronting the dynamics of tragedy, including their own complicity in perpetuating pain.* Through a hermeneutic of tragic memory, people ponder memories in biblical texts and living situations, as well as memories that lie behind these texts and situations. In biblical studies, the historical-critical approach contributes to a hermeneutic of memory, as do rhetorical analysis and other analytic forms. In studying historical and living texts, the analysis of historical-social context is equally critical. Consider another case study.

The Candler women's colloquy group met every Friday. The group had been together for almost three years of seminary, and we had become close. This was the last semester before graduation for most of the students, and on this Friday, we had read Katie's Canon in preparation. In the book, Katie Cannon describes her ethical passions for African Americans who have endured capture in their African homeland, slavery in the United States, and the enduring racism that lingers in attitudes and laws, even 140 years since Emancipation put an end to slavery.[29] In the class, we sought to follow Cannon's pattern by identifying our own ethical passions before proceeding to analysis.

One African American in the group named her passion to overcome racism. She told about her family's first visit with her in seminary. She had booked a room in advance, but, when her family arrived, the hotel operator saw the color of their skin and turned them away, saying that he did not have a room after all. If this had been an isolated incident, the woman would have assumed another explanation — a mistake in the booking, an unexpected overload in the hotel, or an isolated act of racism; however, this woman and her family have had this experience many times. They have learned that racism is alive in the United States.

This story would have been enough to raise the class's consciousness to the tragedy of dismembering. The student continued, however, telling a story of her own experience several years ago with a lesbian colleague. She described how her attitude toward that woman changed when she learned that the woman was lesbian; she described how she judged the woman and began to keep her child at a distance. As she told the story, her tears flowed. The class fell into deep silence. She ended by saying that her ethical concern is for people who are rejected because of racism, but she is overwhelmed when she realizes that she has done the same thing, rejecting someone because of sexual orientation. . . . After some moments, others added their stories.

---

29. Katie G. Cannon, *Katie's Canon: Womanism and the Soul of the Black Community* (New York: Continuum, 1995).

What is striking about this student's story is that she was aware of her ethical concerns in an embodied way. They were tied to her life experience and that of her family and closest friends. They were tied to her sense of hurt and anger, and also to her self-reflection as one who sometimes rejects others. The student could not tell her story without tears. Her ethical passions were so deep that nothing but tears could speak them. This is the wrenching hurt of remembering the dismembered.

This case reinforces an educational insight for me as a teacher. The insight is that *a community can best understand a text (or other work) by employing the same approach to interpretation that the author has used in writing or creating.* Approaching Katie Cannon's text with an analysis of the class's passions reflected her own approach to the writing, beginning as she did with *her* passions. This approach not only uncovered important insights in the class, but also led to a deeper understanding of the text itself. In addition, the case study reinforces some more commonly acknowledged educational insights. Certainly, *the quality of the learning community contributed to the level of sharing.* Compassion and empathy were strong among these students, who had become colleagues and close friends through the colloquy and other shared experiences. Further, *the class had cultivated a spirit of openness to hear one another as deeply as possible.* Finally, *the seminar was sufficiently structured to ask challenging questions and sufficiently flexible to support people in whatever answers they shared.* A hermeneutic of memory is well served by these qualities of learning together in community.

In addition to insights, however, the case also raises an unsettling educational question. What is the appropriate educational response to remembering the dismembered? As discussed earlier, I do not assume that educators have only one good option. In some contexts, a pause for caregiving is appropriate. In other contexts, moving quickly to the next set of questions is best. A quick movement allows the exposed person to rest and avoid pressure for further sharing. In this case situation, I chose to sit with silence, then thank the student for her sharing. Two white women also thanked her and confessed their shame for white racism. After a few moments, I asked if anyone wanted to show respect for the student's sharing by sharing another ethical passion. Someone said, "I would like to share my passion for allowing people to speak out of their pain." The earlier story had raised her awareness that painful sharing is vital and people (especially women) are often not allowed to speak from pain.

When the class closed that day, I knew that the student who initiated our discussion had given the class a treasure. She had been honest, self-aware, critical of the world, and open to dwelling in dismembering realities. I also realized that the group's natural response was to offer care. We did that briefly; however, I encouraged people to continue reflecting on their ethical concerns and then turn to the reading. I had discerned some compelling educational challenges in the situation: dwelling silently in pain, avoiding quick responses, and making connections with complex ethical issues. For that, we needed a hermeneutic of memory and the courage to face discomforts and ethical challenges that the hermeneutic uncovered. As teacher, I followed countercultural intuitions — countering cultural norms of caregiving or dismissing the personal sharing. I chose a third alternative — listening, interpreting, and developing larger communal understandings and responses. This interpretive alternative does not replace other responses, but it encourages people to dwell in painful remembrance and to interpret the truths it discloses. Such acts of remembrance call forth educational practices.

Educational Practices:
Teaching through Memory

Thus far, we have dwelt on remembering the dismembered — *rehearsing stories of people and parts of creation in which destructive forces have taken away some or all of their life.* People often know instinctively that they need to remember, as the two classroom stories indicate. The cases also reveal that conscious remembering can be stirred in contexts of disciplined study and intellectual wrestling. No neat division of intellectual and existential issues is suggested here. On the other hand, people often work hard to forget terror and pain, as revealed by speedy responses in the first case study and, also, by society's common denial of global racism and genocide. The natural temptation is to repress or deny tragedy; however, many leaders in global healing have developed countercultural alternatives, encouraging people to remember for the sake of repairing the world. In crafting educational practices, we will reflect on some of these saints, especially as they inform practices of love, truth-telling, mourning, and reconciliation.

1. Practice Love: Listening and Empathizing

The cultivation of love is a primary dimension of religious education, not in the sense of sentimental feeling, but as *compassion for others and concern for their well-being.* Compassion represents *"feeling with"* others, *including suffering with them.* This is a form of re-membering. Concern for others' well-being is *active hope and work for the flowering of their lives — flowering in justice, spiritual strength, physical health, loving relations and joy.* Love empowers others to be more fully themselves, to be who they are created to be in the image of God. Love also contributes to a more just and humane social order.

In the two cases of this chapter, students shared intimate details of their lives and, even, their own motivations and responses. In so doing, they mirrored God's suffering with creation. Such sharing was possible because members of the two classes had been practicing love throughout the term. Through gathering rituals, text analysis, personal sharing, and wrestling with theological ideas, students had explored depths of human struggle, empathized with others, and celebrated the sacred. One class had also gone on retreat, sharing laughter, food, stories, and truth-telling.

While these practices are generally valued in human community, they are often not associated with education. I join with bell hooks, however, in proposing that love is fundamental to learning, as it is, also, to social critique and transformation.[30] The lack of love is a source of fear and violence in the world; the practice of love is a fundamental movement toward touching human lives and transforming the world. This basic assumption is embedded in the work of Martin Luther King Jr., who sought to transform fear into hope through the practice of love, citing 1 John 4:18: "There is no fear in love; but perfect love casteth out fear" (KJV). He urged people to face fears honestly, take courage, practice love (even to those who hate you), and live with faith. These were not vague generalizations for King; they were practices that empower people to relate courageously to harsh realities, whether war, economic displacement, or racial injustice. His seemingly simple response was to love: "Hate is rooted in fear, and the only cure for fear-hate is love."[31] Love points people beyond themselves and beyond the fears that debilitate them; love asks people to participate in a more hopeful world.

These practices are the stuff of sermons and devotional writing, even of psalms, but what of religious education? Love often abounds in educational settings, but it can also be enhanced. Consider practices of listening and empathizing, through which people remember God in the sinews of daily living and face harsh and awesome realities of this world. Practicing love prepares the soil so that knowledge of God and the world can grow. Thus, *educators are urged to cultivate love and nonviolence so that people can know God more fully and prepare themselves to meet sorrow with compassion, and injustice with active work for justice.* In religious education, this involves such practices as the following:

- *Develop empathy with biblical texts* — analyzing texts to discern what is revealed about God and creation, and to imagine the community to whom this text was first addressed and the communities that have read it through time.

- *Develop empathy with the creators of historic and contemporary works,* whether creeds, hymns, diaries, novels, newspapers, paintings, musical compositions, movies, or other creations. Meditate on these creations to discern their multiple meanings. Analyze their structure and style, seeking to understand their creators — their relation with the Holy and their cultures, concerns, and passions.

---

30. bell hooks, *Communion: The Female Search for Love* (New York: William Morrow, 2002); bell hooks, *Salvation: Black People and Love* (New York: William Morrow, 2001).

31. Martin Luther King Jr., *Strength to Love* (Minneapolis: Fortress, 1981, 1963), 120, 117–26.

- *Listen intently to one another in the learning community,* creating ways to share (such as sharing circles or collaborative projects) by which each person can contribute and others can receive their contributions. People can share life stories, or share in the work of interpreting texts. Children can produce a video of their concerns, youth a collection of oral history interviews. Possibilities are endless.

- *Practice mirroring and other forms of empathic listening* — asking people to mirror or interpret what others have said (whether or not they agree), and to take the role of the creator of a particular work, explaining why they (in the role of creator) had to create this text or movie and how they interpret it. This can be done in meditative listening, discussion, role-play, and other ways.

Through such practices, learning communities develop the capacity to re-member and love others, and to contribute to the just world for which they long.

2. Practice Truth-Telling

The two cases of this chapter and the hermeneutic of tragic memory reveal the significance of *telling truth about tragedy and pain.* In the global picture, people devastated by genocide and violent oppression often feel compelled to remember the dismembered and to interpret those memories. The post-Holocaust cry, "Never forget," is painful in tone and urgent in demand. Martin Luther King Jr. heard in it a cry for prophetic vision and action, as in the tragic death of Jesus and the human folly leading to Socrates' death.[32] Prophetic leaders are persistent heralds for memory — memories from different ages and places, woven into a garment of tragedy that warns the world against destruction and points it toward hope.

Like King, Archbishop Desmond Tutu connects his work in South Africa with post-Holocaust truth-telling, citing the words of George Santayana posted over the death camp at Dachau, "Those who forget the past are doomed to repeat it." Tutu says that people who negotiated South Africa's future knew that failure to face the past would preserve it as a "baneful blight" on the future. National amnesia would impede efforts to reshape the future and victimize the victims of apartheid yet again. South Africans also studied history for positive guidance, seeking an approach to justice that went beyond the retributive justice of the Nuremberg trials. They looked to Namibia, where no reprisals were made against whites and where people sought the spirit of *ubuntu* (generosity, hospitality, care, and compassion).[33] Struggling for honest memory and compassionate

---

32. Ibid., 16, 43.
33. Tutu, *No Future without Forgiveness,* 29, 31–32.

justice, Tutu and others created the Truth and Reconciliation Commission (TRC), which granted amnesty to people who testified, but required reparations to society.[34] The hearings uncovered ghastly atrocities of the past; yet, the new South Africa emerged.

Reflecting on his country today, Tutu says, "God does have a sense of humor. Who in their right minds could ever have imagined South Africa to be an example of anything but the most ghastly awfulness, of how not to order a nation's race relations and its governance?" Instead, the new South Africa is a model for the world, and Tutu gives credit to God: "Our experiment is going to succeed because God wants us to succeed....God wants to show that there is life after conflict and repression — that because of forgiveness there is a future."[35] The South African journey reveals the power of collective memory in the human struggle to transcend horror.

Truth-telling is not easy to hear, and it demands a response, whether by individual action or social policy. Native Americans make this clear in the United States, asking the government to acknowledge atrocities against their people. Vine Deloria also addresses the Christian Church, which has forced "opinions, myths, and superstitions on us." He adds: "You have never chosen to know us. You have only come to us to confront and conquer us."[36] Deloria's cry echoes the cries of South Africa and elsewhere, where generations of people have been denied basic human rights. Like Tutu, he knows the significance of memory, including the memory of pain and horror.

Such memory cannot be ignored; neither is it the last word. *Religious educators need to engage people with life's messiness — struggles and pain, alongside survival and transformation.* Teachers will find natural opportunities and create others, encouraging people to name and analyze tragedy — past and present — and to see the destruction and transformation that has emerged from it. Consider some possibilities:

- *Practice truth-telling* in your congregation or local community, and develop ways to seek God and negotiate new patterns of relationship within those truths.

- *Study biblical and historical narratives of dismemberment*, seeking to understand the multiple dimensions of dismemberment and God's response. What do they reveal about God, the world, suffering, and hope?

---

34. Ibid., 49–50. The TRC was established by the Promotion of National Unity and Reconciliation Act. It required people who testified to focus on acts during the period 1960–94 that were politically motivated and to give full disclosure, in addition to further conditions that Tutu describes.

35. Ibid., 282.

36. Vine Deloria Jr., "Open Letter to the Heads of the Christian Churches in America," *For This Land: Writings on Religion in America* (New York: Routledge, 1999), 79.

Truth-telling about tragic realities creates transitional space through which people can move toward justice and freedom.[37] Dismemberment is not an end in itself, yet moving *beyond* hatred and fear requires courage to face dismemberment and learn from it.

3. Practice Mourning and Repenting — Making Space for Forgiving

This discussion leads into mourning and repentance — *the acts of grieving the destruction of life and turning away from perspectives and practices that contribute to that destruction.* Recall the second case study when a student told her story about being victimized as a black woman while, at the same time, victimizing another person who was lesbian; she engaged in mourning and repentance simultaneously. This woman awakened me as an educator to the power and interconnection of these acts. Doing both, the student subverted the class's either-or tendency to offer only sympathy or judgment (whether negative or reassuring judgment). The class initially wanted to move into caregiving; I sensed that was too easy. I asked the class to allow their colleague's mourning and repentance to teach us, then to continue reflecting on ethical passions. They did so, and the cycle of mourning and repentance continued. Later in the session, a lesbian woman shared her ethical passion. She then turned to the first woman, saying, "You are forgiven," and she meant it.

Without my knowing it in advance, this event created an opportunity to express grief and probe existential truth. It also cleared a space for forgiveness, though the gift of forgiveness can never be guaranteed or forced. The case poses urgent educational questions, which Maria Harris has addressed more profoundly than most. Harris emphasizes remembrance, mourning, and new birth, in combination with aesthetics. From these concerns, she proposes to reform religious education.[38] For her, mourning is part of the natural educational process, yet it *is* a process; thus, Harris encourages people to move *through* mourning, but to return as often as they need to return. She also encourages aesthetic expression of tragedy and hope, and aesthetic creation (shaping) of new possibilities. Indeed, Harris recommends other educational practices of this chapter — cultivating love, truth-telling, and reconciling with the past — which are more fully developed in her later work.[39] In all of her work, however, she encourages teachers to combine educational practices into a dance. Each movement is important, and one movement (mourning) leads into another (letting go and form-giving) and back

---

37. A good educational example of this is found in Marsha Foster Boyd and Carolyn Stahl Bohler, "Womanist-Feminist Alliances: Meeting on the Bridge," in *Feminist and Womanist Pastoral Theology,* ed. Bonnie J. Miller-McLemore and Brita L. Gill-Austern (Nashville: Abingdon, 1999), 189–209.

38. Maria Harris, *Women and Teaching: Themes for a Spirituality of Pedagogy* (New York: Paulist, 1988); Maria Harris, *Teaching and Religious Imagination: An Essay in the Theology of Teaching* (San Francisco: HarperSanFrancisco, 1991, 1987).

39. Maria Harris, *Proclaim Jubilee! A Spirituality for the Twenty-first Century* (Louisville: Westminster John Knox, 1996).

again. The teacher's role is to teach, guide, and be present as people engage in the dance.

While Harris's educational emphasis is on mourning and turning around (repenting), the emphasis on forgiving is stronger in African and African American communities. Building on Jesus' injunction to "love your enemies" (Matt. 5:43–45), Martin Luther King Jr. recognized this as a necessary command — one that cannot easily be fulfilled, but is necessary to counter hate in the world. Even in the face of debilitating histories, the practice of loving our enemies begins with developing and maintaining the capacity to forgive. King described forgiveness as lifting a burden or canceling a debt, but never as a glib act: "Forgiveness does not mean ignoring what has been done or putting a false label on an evil act. It means, rather, that the evil act no longer remains as a barrier to the relationship." In this spirit of building relationships, King made two other assertions: the evil deed of one's enemy "never quite expresses all that [the person] is" and the goal is not "to defeat or humiliate the enemy but to win his friendship and understanding."[40]

However idealistic these words may sound, King was not purely altruistic in developing the ideas. He recognized that hate destroys those who hate; thus, eliminating hate is important to the self: "Like an unchecked cancer, hate corrodes the personality and eats away its vital unity." Further, it causes a person "to describe the beautiful as ugly and the ugly as beautiful, and to confuse the true with the false and the false with the true."[41] In short, hate distorts people's perceptions and their lives, eating away their souls and destroying others' lives. These are reasons that I have combined educational practices of mourning, repentance, and forgiveness in this section. One without the others is too easily false. The challenge for educators is to develop practices that *empower people to participate in rituals, stories, music, and art to express their suffering and sin in relation to their longing for a better world.* Intentional practices might include the following:

- *Create spaces for people to express sorrow, ritualize mourning, and pray.* These spaces may be physical, like a "mourning chapel," or spaces of time, like a time of remembrance and prayer.

- *Deliberate hard questions regarding the relation of mourning, repentance, and forgiveness.*

- *Draw upon historic and global liturgies to create rituals for your community's mourning, repentance, and forgiveness.*

These practices lead naturally to efforts to reconcile with the past, stirring people to respond to despair with a search for hope.

---

40. King, *Strength to Love*, 50–51.
41. Ibid., 53.

4. Practice Reconciliation with the Past

This discussion leads to the human yearning to be reconciled with a hurtful past. Reconciliation with the past is *a movement toward honest acceptance of painful realities and their legacy, for good and for ill.* Acceptance is different from condoning the past; it is acknowledging realities, as well as choices that people now have for response. Acceptance creates space for people to be transformed by the past and to participate in the ongoing process of transforming the world. Reconciliation builds on practices of love, truth-telling, and mourning, bringing people into life-giving relationship with what is past, even horrid histories. Such reconciliation cannot be forced, for force yields premature or false harmony. True reconciliation with the past helps people to understand why and how, and to envision new possibilities for present action. It nurtures the work of reconciliation in the present world, to which we will return in chapter 7.

Reconciling with the past is undermined when people gloss over pain, blame themselves or others for tragedy, or seek glib words of comfort. These are common responses, however. Painful parts of the Bible are rarely the subject of sermons or Bible study in Christian churches. People often carry large burdens of unresolved guilt on their backs, which they hesitate to reveal in their churches, much less to expect absolution or renewal. Scapegoating is an international pastime, soaking into our various religious communities as ink soaks into a garment, staining our communities forever with practices of looking for other people to blame for ills in our world. Further, people often seek solace in painful times by scouring the Bible and devotional books for comforting words. Dietrich Bonhoeffer notwithstanding, "cheap grace" is attractive. To reconcile with the past, however, we need a deeper response. Three approaches are promising.

Preserve Memory

Reconciling with the past begins with *honoring the memory of forebears* — *those who lost their lives and dignity to dismemberment, and those who survived, even thrived, in spite of oppression.* No one is more adept at preserving memory than African American women, who look to women of the past for clues to living with the triple oppression of race, gender, and social class. Katie Cannon and Emilie Townes draw ethical hope from their suffering and wise forebears. Townes explains:

> Womanist wisdom springs out of the experience of African American women as they have been daughters, wives, partners, aunts, grandmothers, mothers, other mothers, comrades, worshipers, protesters, wisdom bearers, murderers, and saints in African American culture and society — and in the life of the church. This perspective — which flows from surviving, as women, in a society based on inequalities rather than justice — is one that yearns for glory.[42]

---

42. Emilie M. Townes, *In a Blaze of Glory: Womanist Spirituality as Social Witness* (Nashville: Abingdon, 1995), 10.

The hope of which Townes speaks looks toward glory — a new future in which justice and love are supreme. Such hope permeates the heritage of her people.

Within every human community, including every religious community, are wellsprings of hope. Our task is to find and honor them — to draw hope from the strong spirits and enduring goodness of our forebears. Our ancestors were flawed, as we are, but they left a legacy of survival, protest, courage, righteousness, love-making, and justice-building as well. In their unique and sometimes distorted ways, they were often faithful to the God who guided and inspired them; thus, we seek educational practices such as the following:

- *Reflect theologically on biographies, documentaries and historical novels and movies,* asking what they reveal about God, the world, suffering, and hope;

- *Study patterns of grief, protest, and response to dismemberment in diverse cultures,* seeking alternatives for the present.

Through such practices, we preserve memory for posterity, discover practices that we can determine not to repeat and find memories to guide our faithfulness and hope.

Preserve and Visit Sacred Memorials

Hope does come from remembering people, but also from *preserving and making pilgrimage to sacred places that memorialize tragedy,* like the Garden of Gethsemane or Golgotha. To reconcile with the past is to remember pain that the earth has seen, whether human oppression, ecological destruction, or life-destroying war. People seemingly *need* to memorialize the past in such sacred places. "Unfortunately," as Vine Deloria says, "many of these places are related to instances of human violence." Consider Gettysburg National Cemetery and Wounded Knee, South Dakota — one a site of military burial, one of massacre. These places evoke tragic memory, but also contribute to a community's ongoing life: "They help to instill a sense of social cohesion in the people and remind them of the passage of the generations. . . . A society that cannot remember its past and honor it is in peril of losing its soul.[43] Such remembering also has potential to deter future destruction, which is a conscious motivation of many recent memorials: the Oklahoma City memorial of the bombed federal building (1995), the Columbine memorial of fourteen murdered youth (1998), the New York memorial at the former World Trade Center (2001), and Argentina's Museum of Memory on the site of a former death camp.

In sacred memorials, people remember the dismembered and connect with their ancestors; they also attune with the human passion for life that transcends history. If this is true, people need to create memorials where strip-mining or toxic dumping has destroyed land and water as well; we need to remember the full range

---

43. Deloria, "Open Letter to the Heads of the Christian Churches in America," 207; cf. 250–60.

of destruction to creation. Why? The act of preserving and making pilgrimage to memorials can inspire prayer and renew people's resolve to work toward justice and well-being for the earth. Sacred places are alive with the Holy and with the spirits of wounded peoples and wounded earth. Educational practices can help people connect with these wounds:

- *Visit historic sites of tragedy* to meditate and reflect on suffering and hope.

- *Create a tour of tragedy in your home community*, visiting sites of human and environmental destruction and pausing to pray and reflect.

Preserving and visiting such places is a powerful educational act, moving people toward reconciliation with the past and clearing a path for reconciliation in the present.

Reshape Tradition and Religious Practice in Light of Tragedy

To reconcile with the past is to engage with hard realities, which finally requires *critiquing and reforming theological traditions and religious practices in light of those realities.* Historical critique is not an empty exercise; it points to real flaws in historical traditions. To say this is to align with Irvin Greenberg's post-Holocaust analysis — to recognize that no theology is adequate if it does not make sense in the presence of burning children.[44] If anti-Judaism and anti-Islam are part of Christian history and have led to dismemberment of others, we need to reflect critically on traditions that made that possible. If Christian theology has aligned with oppressors and ignored the oppressed, we need to revisit and reshape our traditions in light of Jesus' central teaching of love toward God and neighbor.

Some Christian theologians are bold in reflecting on hard memories in the work of transformation, revealing what all Christian people *can* do through education. We find exemplars in womanist ethics, as in many Korean theologies. In Jong Chun Park's theology of the Spirit, Park grieves Korea's history of oppression and division, and seeks paths for healing and transformation. He ponders the Jubilee tradition to illumine God's character: "God of Jubilee takes sides with those who crawl in history and judges those who step on the crawlers and fly over them." The "crawling God" humbled himself in the incarnation, and continues to inspire human response: "God who crawled in Jesus Christ provides the *minjung* with courage to resist the tendency of resignation and fatalism or the cynicism of power."[45] As in my theological analysis of suffering, Park seeks to guide Christian living in the present world. He proposes "a new spirituality that climbs down to the market place as well as climbing up the holy mountain," recognizing that

---

44. Irvin Greenberg, "Cloud of Smoke, Pillar of Fire: Judaism, Christianity and Modernity after the Holocaust," in *Auschwitz: Beginning of a New Era?*, ed. Eva Fleischner (New York: KTAV, 1977), 23.
45. Jong Chun Park, *Crawl with God*, 11–12.

God is present in the journey to the cross and the joy of Pentecost.[46] Park's own journey to these images is by way of the painful memories of Jesus and his people.

Similarly, Andrew Sung Park begins theological reflection by analyzing problems of the world. He recognizes that the church's concern with human sin "has largely overlooked an important factor in human evil: the pain of the *victims* of sin" (emphasis added). This concern leads Park to the Korean notion of *han* — the "critical wound of the heart" that is caused by oppression and repression.[47] The consideration of *han* shifts theology to include victims as well as sinners and oppressors. It expands Christian traditions to emphasize forgiveness along with repentance, justice with justification, and the resolution of *han* with salvation. Such proposals reshape tradition in ways we cannot fully imagine. People can sometimes join the reshaping efforts of others, but they will sometimes need to engage in the terrifying work of shaping forms that are not yet imagined.

The continuing work of education is to participate in reshaping traditional constructs and actions toward God and creation.

- *Identify theological questions that arise in your community from tragedies in the past;* wrestle with alternative responses.

- *Create prayers, drama, and other art forms that express a community's theology and active response to suffering.*

Such practices engage people in reconciling with the past — reshaping religious practices and traditions in response to histories of violation.

Concluding Reflections

The conclusion of this chapter is heavy. The educational practices are alien to some communities and cannot be practiced superficially. While remembering the dismembered is vital for sacramental living, it challenges teachers and learners:

- *Love* — Cultivate a spirit of love and nonviolence, preparing people to meet sorrow with compassion, and injustice with active work for justice. Such love is demanding, extending far beyond the bounds of one's own community. Yet just as King learned love from the African American church, and nonviolence from Mahatma Gandhi, so we need to learn these practices from others.

---

46. Ibid., 42; cf. 36–45. Park's theology is inspired by the *minjung*, people who struggle with poverty and social inequities. He also draws upon the Asian understanding of *ki*, or vital power, to describe spiritual reality as fully immanent and fully transcendent — a linkage that he also sees in Jesus, for whom "holy mountain climbing and the cosmic sanctification of the market were closely related" (45).

47. Sung Park, *The Wounded Heart of God*, 10, cf. 13.

- *Truth-telling* — Engage people with history, including the history of struggle and pain, and the history of survival, transformation, and repair. Some truth-telling will come easily; other truths are more difficult to discover and harder to face.

- *Mourning* — Engage people in rituals, stories, music, and art to grieve suffering, repent sin, and clear space for forgiveness. Pain may be so evident that we mourn instinctively; it may be so far beyond our experience that we have to exert ourselves to find and grieve it. Moving into repentance and forgiveness is even more demanding, as we open ourselves for genuine transformation.

- *Reconciling with the past* — Engage people in preserving memory and sacred places, and in reshaping traditions and practices in light of historical violations.

Such remembering is difficult; it is also life-giving. It deepens faith and awakens a sense of God's presence in adversity. It draws wisdom from struggle, and envisions genuine transformation. To remember the dismembered and the suffering God of history is to plant seeds of memory, from which a garden of future hope can grow.

Reflecting Further

The reflection opportunities in this chapter revolve around the suffering of God and creation, the season of Lent, and practices of remembering.

1. Reflect on the following biblical texts, asking what they reveal about how God responds to creation during hard times: Exodus 3:7–12; Job 38:1–42:9; and Luke 19:41–46. Approach them with a hermeneutic of tragic memory, asking what they reveal about God, the world, suffering, and hope.

2. Recall hard memories of your life or hard memories of your community. What do these reveal about God, the world, suffering, and hope?

3. During Lent, rehearse the radical journey of Jesus, and ponder the life journeys that you and your community are called to walk. Meditate on the journey of Lent:

> Lent is a journey into the unknown
>   a journey to the end of what we have known,
> A journey where Jesus' words echo:
> "The one who would follow me must take up her cross,
>   take up his cross, and follow;
> The last shall be first,
>   and the first shall be last."

And, then, Jesus speaks with more than words:
"Where I am going does not promise ease or praise;
It promises hard-walking, love-talking, justice-making;
If you are prepared, or even if you are not,
     come and follow me.
I will walk the walk with you,
     provide the love you need,
          and journey by your side as you labor, protest,
               and give your life for justice."

Lent is a journey into the unknown
     a journey to the end of what we have known,
          a journey where all are welcomed,
               and each is valued,
                    and all are needed in the repair of broken hearts,
                         broken lives, broken communities and institutions,
                         broken ecologies and nations,
          a journey where you are welcomed,
               you are valued,
                    you are needed in the holy priesthood of *all*
                         God's people —
     the people of God who journey *together* into the unknown
          with God before and behind and with us as we walk.
                    AMEN! AMEN![48]

4. Recall a moment in your life or your community's life in which people
   practiced one or more of the educational practices described in this chapter.
   What emerged from the practice? What further needs to happen to respond
   to the feelings, insights, and yearnings that were uncovered?

48. Mary Elizabeth Moore, "Lenten Journey," 1998.

Chapter Five

Seeking Reversals

We live in a world where people long for neatness and order; yet education, at its best, upsets the world as much as it orders it. We live in a world where people experience boredom and go to great lengths to avoid being bored — buying "toys" for entertainment and staying busy in work and play; yet education at its best challenges people to look beneath boredom to big questions. We live in a world of unexpected wonder and a long history of tragedy (chapters 3 and 4); yet education at its best challenges people to seek meaning and direction in *all* of life's circumstances, reaching beyond the obvious toward the not-yet known and not-yet future. This chapter is about searching — about education that upsets the world, probes beneath boredom to big questions, and searches beyond the obvious for meaning and direction. Such education carries on the reversal tradition of the Bible and bears the sacramental power of reversals. Its textures are varied; thus we begin with diverse narratives.

A young woman (Sarah) traveled home on a mud-soaked mountain road. Halfway down the mountain, she was forced to turn around; the road had washed out. Driving uphill again, she proceeded slowly; however, her car spun out of control, careened against the mountainside, and turned upside down. When the car stopped, Sarah was hanging upside down, uninjured in the protective grasp of her shoulder belt. A concerned motorist stopped, helping her exit the car through a broken window. A young family, returning home from a weekend in the mountains, waited with the frightened Sarah for an hour until paramedics arrived. Then they offered to drive her home, which, with the weather and washed-out roads, was to be a long drive. The family, who lived nowhere near Sarah, delayed their own arrival home by several hours.

The next day, Sarah's mother called the family to thank them again. The man responded, "Thank you for calling, but we simply did what we wanted and needed to do. People have stopped for us when we needed help, and we believe that helping other people is what we are expected to do as Christians."

I once worked with a church youth counselor who saw his vocation as "devil's advocate." He liked to prod the older youth with whom he met on Sunday nights. He explained his philosophy this way: "By the time these youth get to be fifteen, they have heard one another's views on most subjects. I want them to think, so I constantly ask questions like: 'Do you really believe that? What in the world leads you to that conclusion?' "

A young woman, Sonya Wu, tutored immigrant and refugee children during her seminary years.[1] After many weeks of tutoring Nermina, a twelve-year-old Bosnian girl, Nermina's mother asked Sonya to join her in a parent-teacher conference. Nermina's work and behavior were problems in school. The math teacher said that Nermina never finished her homework, and when the teacher gave in-class assignments, she copied other students' work. The teacher said with a disgusted look, "She turns her head around like a wild animal." Nermina's mother, understanding the teacher's expression, asked Sonya if the teachers knew that Nermina had had only one year of schooling five years earlier before coming to the United States. Sonya explained that to the teachers. Nermina's English teacher responded with a look of astonishment, "That changes everything."

These stories raise questions regarding reversal living, echoing the Christian tradition of reversals. In the first case, the helping family, with actions and words, reversed normal human responses to a demanding situation. In the second, a youth counselor developed strong relations with young people and was able to ask probing questions without intimidating the group. In the third, a young woman was able to interpret the unusual behavior of an immigrant child; she took time to reverse her own thinking and understand the child's world. All of these narratives reveal a spirituality of reversals, marked by suspicion and searching. In this chapter, I analyze the power, roots, and theology of this spirituality, and then focus on reversal teaching — equipping people to live with unresolved questions and face the daily challenges of parable and paradox.

Power in Seeking Reversals

To link spirituality, suspicion, and searching seems anachronistic, but they are powerful companions. Suspicion and searching invite people to live more faithfully — to transcend existing social structures and worldviews and to face radical questions regarding Christian tradition and holy living. A spirituality of reversals bears power.

Power of Reshaping Relations with the Past

Building on insights of chapter 4, we see that one power of reversals is to reshape people's relation with the past — the *power to draw strength, courage, and redirection from the past, as well as to find an anchor in storms.* Much religious education

---

1. This story is elaborated in Mary Elizabeth Moore, "Spiritual Leadership in a Beautiful, Broken World," *Christians in Education* 7, no. 2 (Spring 2001): 1–4. Nermina is a fictitious name; the story is true.

has focused on transmitting the past as an unchanging body of belief and instruction. Much has focused on creating something new and ignoring the past. Both approaches have the lure of simplicity; both are inadequate. The former distorts the past by extracting it from contexts of time and place; the latter negates the past and floats on erratic winds of fad. The Christian challenge is to journey deep into the past to be confronted by questions and wisdom that dwell therein, and to walk boldly into the deep of the future to be reshaped, renewed, and radically transformed.[2]

The chambered nautilus offers a valuable image. With its spiral shell, it looks like a large sea snail, making people think it crawls on the ocean floor. Actually, the nautilus swims three hundred feet below the surface, moving in every direction, and sometimes plunging as deep as fifteen hundred feet. Why would such a simple-looking animal have such versatility of movement? One answer lies in its deceptively complex structure. As the nautilus grows, it leaves its old chambers and dwells in newly constructed ones. Oliver Wendell Holmes was correct when he wrote that the chambered nautilus "left the past year's dwelling for the new," but his biology was not correct when he concluded that the nautilus "knew the old no more."[3] In fact, the chambered nautilus remains in contact with its older chambers through a thread of living tissue. Through that thread, the nautilus regulates gas and fluid in its chambers, thus allowing flexible movement and adjustment to conditions at varying depths of the ocean. The chambered nautilus, far from being a simplistic creature that discards the past in favor of the new, is a living creature. It survives by constructing and moving into new chambers while preserving relations with the old.

A spirituality of reversals has similar power to link people with the stability *and* flexibility of tradition. People look to the past for norms, yet the fluid relation between past and present allows people to construct new norms and live in changing seas. To maintain strong roots and a flexible relation with them, a community needs to seek reversals. As described in chapter 2, these lie deep in Christian tradition, and they promise to lead people into greater faithfulness as they engage them honestly.

---

2. A further development of these ideas is offered in Mary Elizabeth Moore, *Education for Continuity and Change* (Nashville: Abingdon, 1983). Catherine Keller stresses the limits of linear views of time, thus encouraging an encounter with mysteries that indwell complex movements of creation in any time and all time. See Catherine Keller, *Face of the Deep: A Theology of Becoming* (New York: Routledge, 2003), xv–xviii. I have also attended to limits of linearity, with a turn toward cyclical time in *Ministering with the Earth* (St. Louis: Chalice, 1998). These various views are important for deep encounter with realities in time.

3. Oliver Wendell Holmes, "The Chambered Nautilus," in *Yale Book of American Verse*, ed. Thomas R. Lounsbury (New Haven: Yale University Press, 1912), lines 18 and 21. I am indebted to Bishop Roy Sano for his analysis of the chambered nautilus in relation to Christian living: Sano, sermon, California-Pacific Annual Conference, United Methodist Church, June 1997.

Power of Transformed Lives

A second form of power is the *transformation of human lives through reversal living over time*. In the first story of this chapter, the family who helped the young woman made a decision for reversal living. They allowed all of their normal internal voices about tired bodies, tired children, and the need to get home at a sensible hour to be replaced with concern for the young woman who had had a frightening accident. In so doing, they offered genuine help, and they witnessed to the possibility of full self-giving.

Reversal living is not as easy as it sounds. Sometimes help is not helpful, and sometimes people have to make difficult decisions between equal goods or equal evils. Reversal living has to do with entering into that ambiguity and discerning as well as possible the response to which God is calling, knowing that God's pull might upset normal patterns and assumptions. Such decisions do not usually fall from the sky. As in the opening story, they are informed by Christian tradition ("We believe that helping other people is what we are expected to do as Christians") and past experience ("People have stopped for us when we needed help"). Reversal living is not one isolated action; it is a courageous pattern of life over time that creates new patterns and new possibilities.

Power of Transformed Thinking

A third kind of power is *transformed thinking — the result of probing beneath the surface and considering alternative perspectives*. The youth counselor in the second story knew that the young people yearned to probe deep questions; he challenged them to question even their most treasured beliefs and attitudes and to uncover new insights and new questions. In the last story, Sonya Wu had so internalized the practice of reversal thinking that she could imagine the experience of Nermina. Sonya actively *sought* reversals that would illumine Nermina's situation and communicate with her teachers.

> Nermina, who had survived a war as the oldest in her family, had seen to it that her six younger siblings had as well. She was now surviving in the most resourceful way she knew. She was being asked to do pre-algebra when she didn't know how to subtract. Of course, she knew that the way to get through difficult times was to work together and help each other, and that was exactly what she was doing.[4]

Sonya was able to see this reversal because she had come to know Nermina well. Weeks of compassionate listening had opened the door for reversals.

---

4. Sonya Wu, presentation, Religious Education Retreat, Candler School of Theology, Emory University, Atlanta, February 2001 (used with permission).

Sonya had also been prepared for reversal thinking by her background. She grew up in Singapore, where her bicultural parents were missionaries. Her father still teaches and her mother collaborates with people in various countries to develop curriculum resources that reflect their contexts, gifts, and issues. Sonya learned much about cultural sensitivity from her family, suggesting that reversal thinking can be taught through family and congregational culture from one generation to another.

Roots of Reversal in Church Practice

Reversals are deeply rooted in church practice, even witnessed among early Jesus-followers. John's Gospel tells of Jesus washing the disciples' feet and Peter's resisting the radicality: "You will never wash my feet" (John 13:8a; cf. 1–20). All four Gospels describe Jesus' offering the disciples a covenant meal, knowing that one of them would betray him and others would flee (Matt. 26:17–35; Mark 14:12–31; Luke 22:7–34; John 13:21–30, 36–38). The Gospels describe Jesus' first postresurrection appearances to women, though women would not have counted as legal witnesses in the courts (Matt. 28:1–10; Mark 16:1–9, or 1–8 in the earlier ending; Luke 24:1–12; John 20:1–18). In Acts, Luke describes Pentecost — the birth of the church from a ragged group of followers who, not knowing what to do, simply gathered together and were surprised by the Spirit (Acts 2:1–47). These dramatic accounts of Jesus and his friends reveal reversal upon reversal. The fact that the Gospel writers emphasized these stories by telling them and framing them within dramatic literary contexts suggests that the reversals had considerable power for the early church. They have power for modern followers of Jesus as well.

Christmas and Easter

Several seasons of the church year can be identified with reversals. Advent is marked by the angel's pronouncement of reversals to Mary and the church's prayers for God's New Creation — the New Heaven and New Earth. The reversal tradition is further embodied in Mary's song when she shares her experience of the angel's visitation with Elizabeth (Luke 1:46–55). One can also make a case for reversals in other seasons, for the Christian story is permeated with reversals from beginning to end. Even so, two seasons are particularly marked by reversal — Christmas and Easter. In the Christian stories of Christmas and Easter, God's dramatic actions reverse the ways of the world; they also reverse people's experience and understanding of God. Christmas celebrates God's birth in an infant boy, and Easter, God's gift of life beyond death. Whether one takes these events literally or symbolically, they represent radical reversal. God is incarnate in a tiny child, revealing God's identification with human life at its most vulnerable; then Jesus dies; then Jesus rises from the dead — every chapter marked by reversal.

Incarnation and resurrection pose challenging questions: how does God relate with the world, what is the nature and work of Jesus, how are we to relate with mystery. In Christmas and Easter, we see God active in the world, but not in expected, or even desirable, ways. The birth of God in an infant seems an in-effectual choice on God's part, radically identifying God with the marginalized — a child whose parentage is questionable by his society's norms and values. The resurrection of Jesus from the dead is a dramatic reversal, but too late and not fully clear. Would not a show of power have been more effective before Jesus died, especially if it had ushered out the old regime and brought in a new, perfected regime? Would not God have been wiser to produce a clear vision of what ac-tually happened in the resurrection and what it meant? These are not questions of mockery, but of common sense. Christmas and Easter mark God-events that were not governed by common sense; they were governed by reversals.

For Christians accustomed to the Christian story, the scent of reversal may be faint; the story is told as a familiar formula rather than a parable or paradox. Christmas and Easter are happy, even dramatic, events, but they are not reversals. Such "taming" and moralizing of the Christian story was already taking place in the early church. We see in Acts the attempt to use the resurrection of Jesus as an argument to the Jews that Jesus is Messiah, spoken in the same address in which Peter accuses his fellow Jews of killing Jesus (Acts 2:22–24, 29–36, esp. 36). Peter sharply contrasts God's raising Jesus from the dead with a human wrongdoing. In so doing, Peter sets up a dichotomy in which God's wondrous work is contrasted with sinful, mistaken people, more particularly with sinful, mistaken Jewish people. Herein, we lose some of the parabolic subversion of the world. The parabolic moment of blowing wind and tongues like fire that touch all the people (2:1–4) is exchanged for a morality tale that singles out one people.

These associations have fed anti-Jewish thinking within Christianity for cen-turies. The reversal of resurrection was converted into a less powerful reversal that could be used by one people against others. Peter's intent (and the intent of Luke in writing Acts) may have been quite different; after all, Peter was a Jew himself and was addressing his Jewish brothers and sisters. On the other hand, Christians have used Peter's words to support the scapegoating of Jews and to deny reversals of a more dramatic kind.

How difficult it is to grasp paradox! This may be one reason why Christmas and Easter are commercialized. Commercialization subtly reduces their reversal power. Ironically, preaching against the commercialization of Christmas may be another way to detract from the season's reversal power. This approach, well intended and appropriate at times, contributes to dichotomizing: Christmas is either religious (putting Jesus back into Christmas) or commercial (focused on gifts, parties, and so forth). The dichotomy hides a more central question — whether people encounter the reversals of Christmas. Likewise, for Easter, how can twenty-first century people grasp the power of that reversal, which empowered radical faith in a shamed group of disciples and created a Jesus movement that continues to this day? These are continuing challenges of Christmas and Easter.

Sacraments

The sacraments are marked by bold reversals as well. Consider one occasion of celebrating eucharist with a young child: *A few years ago, I was worshiping with my extended family. In my aunt's church, we went to the altar to receive the bread and grape juice. I walked forward with my six-year-old cousin, Beth, and helped her receive the wafer and juice.*[5] *When we returned to our seats, she looked up at me and said, "M.E., that was yummy," as she rubbed her tummy and licked her lips. One of our aunts heard Beth's comment and said, "Shame on you; this is Jesus' body and it is not supposed to taste good." Quietly, I whispered to Beth, "It tastes good to me too!"*

I have thought of that moment many times since. If this is Jesus' meal and Jesus' body, it should indeed taste good. When it delights the taste buds, it invokes bodily power — a power to be celebrated within the context of Jesus' life, which was one of flesh and blood, walking and talking, living fully within a body. It also invokes the power of sweetness, associated with the sweetness of God's grace. This story, of course, reveals reversals: *tragedy and grace co-exist in the eucharist, as do the serious power and welcoming pleasure of the eucharistic meal.* That which was tragic is transformed into an act of grace, and that which bears serious power does so by welcoming people to the table and offering the pleasure of bread and wine (or juice).

One could say that eucharist is God's shocking table, for tragic death is transformed into a celebration of life, and an act of spiritual seriousness brings joy. Similarly, baptism holds together the world's sin and sorrow with the promise of new life, and the seriousness of being born into Christ's Body with the ecstatic joy of the event and its promises. These reversals are difficult to grasp. Returning to my story, I doubt that anyone in the congregation that day (including me) understood the reversals. Our aunt seemed incapable (on that day at least) to reconcile the tragic and gracious qualities of the meal. Her response reveals how difficult it is for people to grasp and cherish reversals, and how difficult for the church to teach them.

Reversals continue in the biblical origins of baptism. John the Baptist recognized the reversals when Jesus asked him to baptize him. He responded with shock: "I need to be baptized by you, and do you come to me?" (Matt. 3:14) The reversal here calls forth humility as *ordinary human beings touch God and the things of God.* It is no wonder that the church has debated whether baptism can be performed by a person in an unholy state, and whether persons need to be purified before they are baptized. Yet, as discussed earlier, holiness is not a necessity. The principle of *ex opere operato* (from the act done) affirms that the holiness of

---

5. Beth is a fictitious name; the story is real.

presiders and congregants does not determine the effectiveness of the sacraments; they are effective by God's act.[6]

This discussion quickly opens into another form of reversal in baptism, namely, that *the sacrament, while practiced by ordinary people with ordinary water, reflects God's cosmic act in Jesus Christ.* Not only does the sacrament include remembering the baptism of Jesus, but it also reveals Jesus as God's primary sacrament, for Christ reveals and mediates God's grace to the world. Eucharist, too, is practiced with ordinary gifts of the earth, offered by the people with accompanying prayers for acceptance. The humble offerings are transformed into a holy meal, again with cosmic significance.

The reversals revealed in baptism and eucharist are related to the theological reversals of incarnation and resurrection. In my family's story, Beth was physically aware of this; she could *taste* the significance of the holy meal. Susan Ross gives words to Beth's experience, and to our aunt's experience as well: "The radical and, to some, scandalous conjunction of divine and human in the Incarnation is at the root of sacramental theology."[7] This means that God's incarnation in human flesh is related to the bodiliness of ordinary life. In the story, this delighted Beth and scandalized our aunt. Like Beth, much feminist theology delights in these connections, encouraging people to celebrate the sacraments with more explicit reference to ordinary experience (as birth and daily meals).[8] Theologies of incarnation and resurrection also challenge people to *live* differently, giving reverence to the Holy in these daily, bodily experiences.

One more sacramental reversal is that *God breaks fully into the present while also promising what is to come.* Matthew begins his baptism story with John's announcement as he baptized people along the Jordan: "I baptize you with water for repentance, but one who is more powerful than I is coming after me; I am not worthy to carry his sandals. He will baptize you with the Holy Spirit and fire" (Matt. 3:11). This pronouncement is future-oriented. Matthew's story concludes with Jesus' baptism, after which the Spirit descends and God speaks, "This is my Son, the Beloved, with whom I am well pleased" (17). We discussed earlier that immanence and transcendence are intermingled in Matthew's narrative of Jesus' baptism.[9] In this exchange, we see also that God's in-breaking is both present and future.

I have identified four reversals in the sacraments, and others could be named. What is most important is to recognize how thoroughly infused the sacraments

---

6. In chapter 2, we recognized that, in most Christian theology, the validity of the sacraments is not understood as contingent on the state of mind or soul of those who preside or gather.

7. Susan A. Ross, "God's Embodiment and Women: Sacraments," in *Freeing Theology: The Essentials of Theology in Feminist Perspective,* ed. Catherine Mowry LaCugna (San Francisco: Harper, 1993), 198; cf. 206.

8. Ibid., 185–209, esp., 200, 204–5.

9. See also Mark 1:9–11; Luke 3:21–22; John 1:31–34; and the more extensive discussion in chapter 3.

are with reversals. Reversals are present in the sacramental events themselves, in the events to which they point, and in the transformative power they communicate to the human community. The sacraments point beyond themselves to the paradoxical, parabolic nature of God and God's creation.

Theology of Paradox and Parable

The theology of paradox and parable that emerged in analyzing church practice leads to questions about God and the world that have haunted Christians for generations. Jesus' birth, life, death, and resurrection were so filled with mystery that controversies of interpretation erupted early, and doctrinal debates led to a series of ecumenical councils. The first ecumenical council in Nicaea (325-27 C.E.) insisted that Jesus was fully divine, of like substance with the Father. The third and fourth ecumenical councils in Ephesus (431 C.E.) and Chalcedon (451 C.E.) explained the paradox further by identifying Jesus as one person with divine and human natures. The paradox was named, but controversy did not end. People continued to ask whether Jesus was human or divine, and, if both, how. Questions about God and creation still begged for answers, creating East-West divisions and pointing to the chaos exposed in Catherine Keller's theology of becoming.[10] Thus, we turn to theological affirmations expressed in terms of paradox and complexity.

1. God Is More Than Meets the Eye

The first theological affirmation is that *God is more than meets the eye — present and visible, yet mysterious and invisible; part of daily life, yet pulling life toward eschatological hope; caring for the smallest and humblest parts of creation, yet seeing in them more than others see.* We have already seen that sacraments, practiced by ordinary people with ordinary water and wine, reveal God's cosmic action in history, and chapter 3 stresses God's transcendent immanence and immanent transcendence. Now, we return to Matthew to reflect further on God's "moreness" as regards present and future.

Theologically, Matthew's story speaks to realized and future eschatology — a promise of God's New Creation, made real in Jesus Christ, but not yet fully present. Since the original hearers of Matthew's Gospel lived in a tension between the end of Jesus' life on earth and the hope for God's final fulfillment, this tension plays a major role in Matthew's Gospel. The Gospel opens with Jesus' genealogy, demonstrating his historical origins from the root of Jesse and line of David (1:1–17) and his birth according to prophecy (18–25). Matthew thus connects Jesus' birth with the *fulfillment* of God's promises. The Gospel closes with

---

10. Keller, *Face of the Deep*, xv-7. Note: Even the ecumenical councils reveal underlying chaos. The Orthodox Church does not recognize the ecumenicity of councils after the second ecumenical council in Nicaea in 787.

Jesus' postresurrection appearance to the disciples, commissioning them to go into the world and "make disciples of all nations, baptizing them . . . , and teaching them to obey everything that I have commanded you" (28:19–20). Here Jesus projects the future, for which the disciples are to make the world ready.

In Matthew's baptism narrative, John's baptizing of Jesus marks a realized eschatology. Jesus is baptized, the sky opens, and God speaks. This is followed immediately by the reminder that eschatological hope is future as well. Emphasizing the future dimensions, the baptism narrative is followed by temptations of Jesus in the wilderness; Jesus refuses three times to give an immediate show of power (4:1–11). The promises of Jesus' life appear to be slowly unfolding ones. The baptism takes place in the beginning of Jesus' ministry, and the full story of his ministry, death, and resurrection is yet to follow. Similarly, when people are baptized into the Body of Christ, they stand at the beginning of their ministries, and much is yet to come. This present-future paradox has strong parallels in the eucharist. Consider the familiar words of the eucharistic liturgy that represent the past, present, and future dimensions of Jesus' revelation: "Christ has died, Christ is risen, Christ will come again." In these words, we see the paradox of Christ being both dead and risen, both present and not yet.

God's "moreness" is also revealed in Jesus' blessing of the children in Mark's Gospel (10:13–16). This is a different kind of revelation. Jesus' moreness is expressed in his greater compassion for children (in comparison with the disciples) and his ability to see the sacrality of children's lives. Similarly, in Luke's Gospel, we see Jesus' ministry beginning in reversal, again related to childhood. We are told only one story of Jesus' childhood years and it upsets family norms, for Jesus left the crowd traveling home after Passover, giving no notice (Luke 2:41–52). After three days of searching, Jesus' parents found their twelve-year-old son in the temple, "sitting among the teachers, listening to them and asking them questions" (46). People were amazed at Jesus' understanding. His parents also were astonished, but they admonished his disappearance. Jesus responded: "Did you not know that I must be in my Father's house? (49). We see Jesus, a child himself, already pronouncing reversals and being more than social norms would expect.

We can expand this analysis of moreness by reflecting on children in the ancient world. When Jesus blessed the children, who were marginalized in his society, he pointed to a reversal world in which marginalized persons could flourish.[11] The familiar story in Mark 10 is preceded by other reversal stories. Jesus had healed a boy with an unclean spirit after rebuking the disciples for their inability

---

11. James L. Bailey, "Experiencing the Kingdom as a Little Child: A Rereading of Mark 10:13–16," *Word and World* 15, no. 1 (Winter 1995): 58–67. Susanne Johnson draws from this same work in reflecting on the urgency of responding to children and poverty. See Susanne Johnson, "Women, Children, Poverty, and the Church: A Faith-Based Community Revitalization Approach to Addressing Poverty," paper presented to the International Academy of Practical Theology, Stellenbosch, South Africa, April 2001, 1–3.

to do so (Mark 9:14–29). The boy was not only a child, but also possessed with a debilitating spirit that people neither understood nor knew how to treat. Jesus' mission to the marginalized was again visible.

Shortly after this incident in Mark's crafting of the story, Jesus responded to a heated discussion among the disciples about who was the greatest. To the disciples, he spoke strong reversal words, "Whoever wants to be first must be last of all and servant of all" (Mark 9:35). Then Jesus placed a child among them, took the child in his arms, and said, "Whoever welcomes one such child in my name welcomes me, and whoever welcomes me welcomes not me but the one who sent me" (37). This series of events in just two chapters of Mark reveals reversals in abundance. In a few actions, described in close succession, Jesus upset the normal ways of responding to the world. He evoked reversals in acts of rebuking, healing, explaining, challenging his disciples' competition, uplifting children, and announcing children as revealers of Jesus and the kingdom of God. He also revealed himself as seeing sacrality in the world that others could not see.

2. People Are Easily Deceived

In chapter 2 we discussed biblical traditions of reversal, noting ways in which traditions sometimes upset comfortable beliefs, values, and social structures, as well as the parabolic model of Jesus' life and teaching. Traditions can anchor people and provide cause for celebration, but they can also upset the status quo. When this happens, people often do not recognize it. They are *deceived — dismissing ideas that do not fit with their existing constructs or squeezing the new ideas into familiar constructs where they do not fit.* This was evident in the third story with which this chapter began, for Nermina's teachers had no categories to explain Nermina's behavior in school other than misbehaving. They were deceived into thinking that copying from someone else's paper is a bad behavior in any circumstances, and that Nermina's shaking her head ("like a wild animal") signified a personal problem rather than a limited academic background and well-founded exasperation. People are easily deceived into preserving their familiar categories of explanation, long after the categories cease to work.

Further, people are easily deceived into thinking that the status quo is the ideal state of affairs. The youth counselor in the second case study understood that this is not always true. He believed that the youth needed to probe beneath their assumptions and easy answers; they needed to probe issues from new angles. In a similar way, whenever we become comfortable with the status quo, we need to ask ourselves hard questions. On the surface, this appears to undermine harmony, and it *does* undermine cheap harmony. It does more, however; probing the depths of ideas and issues and encouraging people to work toward a harmony in which every person and every part of God's creation can be considered. This is not a harmony conformed to superficial expectations of the world, but one in which our deceptions are challenged and we can expect to be transformed by the renewing of our minds (Rom. 12:2) — transformed in the spirit of Christ.

3. *Imagination and Risk Are Twin Gifts from God*

Another theological affirmation is the *twin gifts of imagination and risk — the vision to see new possibilities and the inevitable demand that accompanies such vision.* Consider Rosa Parks, who refused to yield her bus seat to a white person on December 1, 1955, in Montgomery, Alabama. That was a reversal, but it arose from her life of vision and action. Parks's seemingly small act became a major incident, leading to the Montgomery bus boycott, sparking national publicity and fueling the civil rights movement. That too was a reversal, emerging from a *community's* vision and action. Today Rosa Parks still imagines a better world. She writes that her goal is for a unified world with "everyone living together in peace and harmony and love."[12] This is not idle dreaming for Parks. She says, "I still believe there can be a day when we will have true freedom.... A day when we can all get along regardless of our race. This is not a dream. It is alive within the ability of us all."[13] That too would be a reversal and would require further risks. In light of Rosa Parks's past, why not?

This chapter will be false if the cost of seeking reversals is ignored. Most Christians know the price Jesus paid for living a life of reversals; it cost him his life. Less attention is paid to the risks of others who have given themselves to reversal living. When Oscar Romero was first named archbishop of El Salvador, he was chosen because of his conservatism and caution. This was not to last. In relating pastorally with his people, the archbishop came to know their oppression; his imagination was stirred. From them, he also learned radicality and risk — seeking reversals, naming reversals, and living reversals. In his biography, James R. Brockman describes a critical moment when Archbishop Romero presided at the funeral mass of his friend's mother:

> Romero spoke of Sarita's simple dedication to building the kingdom of God, the encouragement she gave to her children. "You just heard in Christ's gospel that one must not love oneself so much as to avoid getting involved in the risks of life that history demands of us, ... But whoever out of love for Christ give themselves to the service of others will live, like the grain of wheat that dies, but only apparently.... Only in dying itself does it produce the harvest."
>
> He exhorted all to follow Dona Sarita's example, each one undertaking the task in his or her own way, with hope, with faith, with love for God....
> [He then introduced the mass]: 'So let us join together intimately in faith

---

12. Rosa Parks, *Rosa Parks: My Story* (New York: Puffin Books, 1992), 187–88.
13. Rosa Parks, with Gregory J. Reed, *Quiet Strength: The Faith, the Hope, and the Heart of a Woman Who Changed a Nation* (Grand Rapids, Mich.: Zondervan, 1994), 88; cf. 88–89.

and hope at this moment of prayer for Dona Sarita and ourselves.' At that moment a shot rang out.[14]

In this decisive moment, Romero's life was snuffed out, and the church, for a moment, was awakened to the imagination and risk of reversals. Still today, Romero is celebrated around the world as a martyr for Jesus Christ and the cause of his people. His martyrdom was rooted in the reversals he discovered in ministering with his people; they stirred his imagination for a more just world and inspired his risk-taking. Both the imagination and the risk are gifts of God, irrevocably intertwined.

4. God Is Present through Paradox and Parable

This discussion leads back to God, *present in the world through paradox and parable. Paradox is the co-existence of two or more realities that are generally thought to be mutually exclusive* (from the Greek *paradoxos* and Latin *paradoxus*, meaning "contrary to all expectation"). *Parables are comparative stories, images, or metaphors that liken a deep truth to something ordinary* (from the Greek *parabole*, meaning "a comparing"). In the tradition of John Dominic Crossan, I refer to parables as comparative narratives that *turn the world upside down*, or subvert expectation and conventionality.[15]

We have already considered several paradoxes in this chapter. For example, the sacraments are *fully* serious and *fully* delightful, *fully* representative of tragedy and *fully* representative of grace. No either/or dichotomy can do justice to the complex character of these reversals-in-relationship, nor can a "mix and stir" formula. Concepts of parable and paradox are necessary to understand God and God's relation with the world. They are also necessary for understanding Jesus — God and human, gentle and revolutionary. Years ago, Donald Baillie sought to resolve the debate between the Jesus of History and Christ of Faith, concluding that Jesus was not simply an extraordinary figure in history, nor simply the messianic center of faith. Jesus must be understood paradoxically — as both, and more.[16] Likewise, God is by nature paradoxical, and we need to welcome complexities if we are to respect the elegant complexity of God and God's world.

We discussed the subject of dichotomies in relation to Christmas and Easter; the subject also rises in relation to God (as in chapter 3's discussion of immanence and transcendence). The ease of imaging God in dichotomies has fed schisms in

---

14. James R. Brockman, *Romero: A Life* (Maryknoll, N.Y.: Orbis, 1989), 244–45.

15. John Dominic Crossan, *The Dark Interval: Towards a Theology of Story* (Sonoma, Calif.: Polebridge, 1988).

16. Donald McPherson Baillie, *God Was in Christ: An Essay on Incarnation and Atonement* (New York: Charles Scribner's Sons, 1948). Baillie drew upon paradox to describe human life as well. The paradox of grace is the conviction that "every good thing in [a person], every good thing he does, is somehow not wrought by himself but by God" (114). This paradox — ascribing everything to God without disclaiming human personality and responsibility — is, in Baillie's view, at the heart of Christian life.

church history, as it feeds either/or thinking among Christians today. Modern church assemblies vivify these dichotomies. People divide over "high" and "low" Christologies, Trinitarian and non-Trinitarian theologies, and social justice dualities. They assume that "there are two sides to every issue" and "everything in between." They image issues in a spectrum with two ends and a middle. The only way to resolve an issue when it falls on a spectrum is for one end or the other to "win," or for a compromise to be reached in the middle.

The parabolic nature of God defies easy description in terms of two alternatives and a middle. Biblically, the God of history is revealed as involved in the world and not identical with the world — present and distant; effecting change but not controlling every event; immanent and transcendent. Even these ways of describing God are inadequate because they rely on pairs of words. God is actually present in thousands of ways and distant in many ways as well; thus, the easy pair of present and distant is not really a pair at all. Further, a Trinitarian perspective speaks of God as three, and as one and many — many in one and one in many. The relations within God, and God's relation to the world, are more like a dance (*perichoresis*) in which the different dimensions co-inhere and move in relation to one another, or a kaleidoscopic image of many colors in a circle, changing configurations with passing time.

Living with reversals puts people face to face with the paradoxical, parabolic nature of God. God, as paradox, is revealed to the world in uncountable ways but still defies definition. To speak of Jesus as the sacrament of God is to recognize that Jesus incarnates and points to God, yet Jesus is a paradox — human and divine; past, present, and future; simple in his teaching to love God and neighbor, yet mystifying and question-posing from the beginning to the end of his life. Jesus thus reveals God *paradoxically;* the more we know Jesus, the more we know that we do not know. Jesus also reveals God *parabolically.* Jesus, as the parable of God, reveals and raises questions about who God is and how God works, and subverts the world that people think they know. The revelation is indefinable and subversive, but not simple confusion. Confusion would be a safe place to hide; God's revelation begs a response.

Hermeneutic of Suspicion

This discussion leads to a hermeneutic of suspicion — *critiquing received traditions and assumed values, posing questions, and seeking sources and perspectives to help reconstruct interpretation.* In a hermeneutic of suspicion, one poses questions to texts and life situations — what do they communicate to the poor and oppressed, how are dominant interpretations distorted, and what is their good news for people and lands on the margins. Liberation theologians have employed such questions to rediscover and interpret the subversiveness of biblical texts. I employ the hermeneutic here in relation to biblical, historical, and living texts, which themselves include written texts, art and artifacts, and life situations.

The opening stories of this chapter raise suspicion in themselves. The young family raises suspicions about commonsense practices of ignoring people by the side of the road. The youth counselor raises suspicions every Sunday night. Sonya Wu raises suspicion of the teachers' conclusions about Nermina's behavior. These people stand in a long tradition — reflected in Jesus stories, Rosa Parks's decision on the bus, and Oscar Romero's standing with the poor. Reflecting further on Rosa Parks, we can see the complexity of a hermeneutic of suspicion. She did not reach her bus decision in a vacuum, but had studied nonviolence for several years and practiced suspicion in interpreting racist social patterns and exploring alternatives.[17] She had been fine-tuning her hermeneutic of suspicion, preparing herself for that fateful moment on the bus.

Suspicion is vital in liberation theologies. Gustavo Gutiérrez uses the hermeneutic to interpret diverse texts — reading Job from the standpoint of the poor, and drawing wisdom from oppressed peoples to interpret spiritual traditions and beliefs about God.[18] Ada María Isasi-Díaz, likewise, reads the Bible and Christian tradition from the standpoint of *mujeristas* — Hispanic and Latina women who have told her their faith stories and described their struggles for liberation.[19] She gives theological priority to the struggles of ordinary women. Similarly, Elsa Tamez attends to voices of women and oppressed peoples of Latin America, engaging women in public theological discourse and reading the Bible from the perspective of the oppressed.[20] Other theologians scrutinize classical Christian theologies with suspicion. Jacquelyn Grant critiques traditional and white women's Christologies as she constructs a womanist view, while Hyun Kyung Chung's Christological and theological images draw upon Asian women's perspectives.[21] Delores Williams reclaims and reinterprets the story of Hagar from the perspective of African

---

17. Parks, *Rosa Parks: My Story*, 55–124. Among other things, Parks served as secretary of the Montgomery NAACP and attended a workshop on desegregation at the Highlander Folk School in Monteagle, Tennessee.

18. Gustavo Gutiérrez, *On Job: God-Talk and the Suffering of the Innocent*, trans. Matthew J. O'Connell (Maryknoll, N.Y.: Orbis, 1987). See also Gutiérrez, *We Drink from Our Own Wells: The Spiritual Journey of a People*, trans. Matthew J. O'Connell (Maryknoll, N.Y.: Orbis, 1984); *The God of Life*, trans. Matthew J. O'Connell (Maryknoll, N.Y.: Orbis, 1991).

19. Ada María Isasi-Díaz, *Mujerista Theology: A Theology for the Twenty-first Century* (Maryknoll, N.Y.: Orbis, 1996); Isasi-Díaz, *En la Lucha: In the Struggle: A Hispanic Women's Liberation Theology* (Minneapolis: Fortress, 1993).

20. Elsa Tamez, *The Amnesty of Grace: Justification by Faith from a Latin American Perspective*, trans. Sharon H. Ringe (Nashville: Abingdon, 1993); Elsa Tamez, ed., *Through Her Eyes: Women's Theology from Latin America* (Maryknoll, N.Y.: Orbis, 1989); Elsa Tamez, *Bible of the Oppressed*, trans. Matthew J. O'Connell (Maryknoll, N.Y.: Orbis, 1982).

21. Jacquelyn Grant, *White Women's Christ and Black Women's Jesus: Feminist Christology and Womanist Response* (Atlanta: Scholars Press, 1989); Hyun Kyung Chung, *Struggle to Be the Sun Again: Introducing Asian Women's Theology* (Maryknoll, N.Y.: Orbis, 1990).

American women and the experience of slavery.[22] Even this brief review reveals that reading texts, doctrines, worldviews, and ethical values from the stance of people who are oppressed or marginalized can pose critical questions and alternate perspectives.

A hermeneutic of suspicion has compelling and frightening qualities. Elisabeth Schüssler-Fiorenza uncovers three of these qualities. First, *a hermeneutic of suspicion is a public and influential act* — a society-shaping quality that motivates many scholars to engage in a lifetime of suspicion. This quality resounds in Schüssler-Fiorenza's feminist critical hermeneutics. In her work on Christology, she enters a struggle against kyriarchal oppression and seeks a path toward transformation for women and all people.[23] She also does an explicit political reading of Revelation, arguing that such a reading is compatible with Revelation itself and its "utopian vision of justice and well-being for all."[24]

Second, *a hermeneutic of suspicion uncovers lost and neglected histories.* Schüssler-Fiorenza introduces *In Memory of Her* with the struggle to remember a forgotten woman.[25] She recalls the woman who anointed Jesus as well as his response: "And truly I say to you, wherever the gospel is preached in the whole world, what she has done will be told in memory of her" (Mark 14:9). A hermeneutic of suspicion leads her to this woman's story and raises questions regarding why the woman has *not* been remembered, and was not named in the text. Her hermeneutics of suspicion yields a bountiful harvest — uncovering untold, neglected, or distorted stories.

Third, *a hermeneutic of suspicion is emancipatory.* When a community applies suspicion to ordinary texts or practices, the results are not predetermined; yet the act of seeking reversals is likely to unseat dominant assumptions, freeing people to encounter the world in a new way. What people encounter may resonate with diverse theological and political perspectives, but suspicion typically opens a text to emancipatory interpretations. Schüssler-Fiorenza's approach to biblical interpretation includes historical-critical method, hermeneutics of suspicion, and construction of a feminist heuristic model. The result is what she describes as a

---

22. Delores S. Williams, *Sisters in the Wilderness: The Challenge of Womanist God-Talk* (Maryknoll, N.Y.: Orbis, 1993).

23. Elisabeth Schüssler-Fiorenza, *Jesus: Miriam's Child, Sophia's Prophet — Critical Issues in Feminist Christology* (New York: Continuum, 1994), 31. She describes this work as both critical and public: "My critical discourses seek to stage a critical conversation and public debate among those gathered around the christological table set by Divine Wisdom. In this way I hope to contribute to the refiguration and rearticulation of both feminist and hegemonic christological discourses within the social-political contexts of struggle in the global village under the radical democratic horizon of the ekklesia of wo/men."

24. Elisabeth Schüssler-Fiorenza, *The Book of Revelation: Justice and Judgment* (Minneapolis: Augsburg/Fortress, 1998), 229; cf. 207–15.

25. Elisabeth Schüssler-Fiorenza, *In Memory of Her: A Feminist Theological Reconstruction of Christian Origins* (New York: Crossroad, 1994, 1983).

feminist critical hermeneutics for liberation.[26] This is more than a retrieval process and more than critique. Schüssler-Fiorenza is struggling to identify texts in which women and men struggle against patriarchal domination. She reads with suspicion, seeking emancipatory elements and more complete descriptions of Christian origins that include the lowly and rejected.[27] In her quest, she uncovers evidence about the women who gathered around Jesus and in early Jesus communities — an "ekklesia of wo/men."[28] This evidence counteracts more hegemonic and patriarchal readings of early communities; it fuels critique of dominant interpretations, reconstructs history, and stirs emancipatory vision for the future.

The work of seeking reversals has political consequences, usually directed toward social change in the church and beyond. The hope is to uncover lost and neglected histories, and to encourage emancipatory readings. This work of seeking reversals is not fantasy, in the sense of untrue, but it employs imagination. For Schüssler-Fiorenza, imagination plays a role in the reconstruction process, but only in filling gaps that are grounded in the texts themselves and in careful study of biblical literature and social-historical-political context. Reversals, therefore, cannot be whatever we want them to be. They *are* informed by the critical questions we bring to traditions and social realities (as all interpretations are), and they often lead to radical critique and reshaping of those traditions and realities. Traditions and dominant structures can be quite wrong, and a hermeneutic of suspicion serves to pose questions and uncover alternate interpretations.

Educational Practices:
Teaching through Reversals

The conclusion of the previous section begs the question of how people discern what is wrong in traditions and dominant structures, and by what standards they make judgments. The reversal tradition of Christianity raises another question, however: what are the dangers of *not* engaging in such discernment? The risk of discerning and judging is real, and the standards are sometimes elusive; however, Christians cannot be true to their reversal tradition without vigorously searching for reversals. Teaching through reversals is *uncovering hidden and underinterpreted sources, posing questions, and seeking fresh insight into the beliefs and practices of Christian faith in the world.*

To seek reversals is to walk along the edge of a frightening precipice. This precipice is where we teach, engaging in the struggle to discern and live with reversals. Precipice-walking is filled with fear; yet, education is inherently frightening

---

26. Ibid., xlv–liv, 3–40.

27. Ibid., xxvi–xxxv. Schüssler-Fiorenza introduces these themes in the first edition, but engages in an expanded dialogue with methodological questioners in this "Introduction to the Tenth Anniversary Edition."

28. Schüssler-Fiorenza, *Jesus: Miriam's Child, Sophia's Prophet*, 27.

for teachers and learners. I have worked for more than thirty years now with people in local churches and other religious communities, seminary students, doctoral students, and teaching colleagues. I have heard cries from all of them regarding their experiences of fear: vulnerability in exploring new territory, resistance when facing new questions or ideas, and nervousness when entering an activity that threatens to change themselves and others. I have also experienced the fear that Parker Palmer describes in himself and others whenever they walk into a class or face a new venture.[29] This fear can be psychologically debilitating, leading people to disconnect from the educational process. It can also block people from knowing, and the fear of knowing can overwhelm the desire to know.[30]

Seeking reversals is grounded in a theology of paradox and parable. It involves struggle and also stirs hope, evident in Paulo Freire's thirty-year influence on educational imagination. For Freire, teaching through problem-posing is radical, dangerous, and promising. His ideas are sufficiently radical that, at one time in his life, he had to leave his native Brazil and seek refuge in another country. His *Pedagogy of the Oppressed* — with its critical social analysis and conscientizing approach to education — was popular across the world, but the powers of his country saw it as dangerous.[31] Freire's own motivation was his hope that education could contribute to social transformation, led by and for oppressed people. Henry Giroux says that Freire combined "the language of critique with the language of possibility." His theory of education thus "takes seriously the relationship between radical critical theory and the imperatives of radical commitment and struggle."[32] For Freire, critique and collective struggle combine with a philosophy of hope, yielding prophetic vision and a pedagogy of struggle. His own exercise of suspicion and search for liberative insight are akin to the practices proposed below.

1. Practice Undercover Investigation

One approach to teaching through reversals is the practice of undercover investigation — *discovering and reclaiming lost traditions, including texts, rituals, theological ideas, and other expressions of faith.* The undercover investigator asks what is missing or minimized in the tradition (like the names and presence of many women), what is missing or condemned by dominant interpretations, what biases persist in

---

29. Parker J. Palmer, *The Courage to Teach: Exploring the Inner Landscape of a Teacher's Life* (San Francisco: Jossey-Bass, 1998), 35–60.

30. Mary Elizabeth Mullino Moore, "Teaching Justice and Reconciliation in a Wounding World," in *The Other Side of Sin: Woundedness from the Perspective of the Sinned-Against,* ed. Andrew Sung Park and Susan L. Nelson (Albany: State University of New York Press, 2001), 143–64; Moore, "Wisdom, Sophia, and the Fear of Knowing," *Religious Education* 92, no. 2 (Spring 1997): 227–43.

31. Paulo Freire, *Pedagogy of the Oppressed,* trans. Myra Bergman Ramos (New York: Continuum, 2000, 1970); Paulo Freire, address to Religious Education Association, November 1982. An overview of Freire's biography is also recorded in Alice Frazer Evans, Robert A. Evans, and William Bean Kennedy, *Pedagogy for the Non-Poor* (Maryknoll, N.Y.: Orbis, 1987), 1–10, 219–31.

32. Henry A. Giroux, "Introduction," in Paulo Freire, *The Politics of Education: Culture, Power, and Liberation,* trans. Donaldo Macedo (Westport, Conn.: Bergin & Garvey, 1985), xii; cf. xvii.

the tradition and common interpretations of it. Then the investigator seeks possible responses, including responses from within the tradition. Such investigative work is critical to Christianity, for God is always more than meets the eye.

Consider a common example: Why do good things happen to bad people, and bad things to good people? Biblical and historical traditions do not have easy answers to this question; however, on close investigation, one can discover some interesting responses. First, distinctions between good and bad people quickly break down in the Bible. Crafty Jacob, who cheated his brother Esau from his birthright, was blessed to carry on the lineage of Israel. Hot-tempered Moses, who murdered an Egyptian, was called by God to lead the people of Israel out of their bondage in Egypt. Adulterous David, who slept with Bethsheba and sent her husband to the front line of battle to be killed, was the great king of Israel. A woman caught in adultery was the person who anointed Jesus. Paul, who was often hard on women and people who disagreed with him, guided young Christian communities to discover how to live together as followers of Jesus.

People could add other examples, but what is important in undercover investigation is to ask hard questions and then to search in unexpected places for lost and neglected traditions. What is more common in church teaching, and even in school teaching, is to ignore offensive or countercultural parts of tradition, such as shortcomings of great heroes and heroines, or to explain them away. In one recent Bible study group, the leader explained what a good person Paul was and what a hero he was in the early Christian community. The teacher's focus was on celebrating the accomplishments of Paul rather than his full humanness; further, he accented what Paul had done for the Christian community at Corinth, ignoring the complexity, humanness, and giftedness of the Corinthian people. This approach is not only selective heroism; it is also individualistic and leader-centered (even male-centered in this case). Reclaiming lost traditions is different. It *does* involve searching for Paul's heroics, but also for his yearnings, and failings, and for the community's heroics, yearnings and failings.[33] Consider Paul's admonitions to the women of Corinth. His words imply that women were formidable spiritual leaders, troublesome to Paul.[34] Such insights arise when people search beneath dominant interpretations to discover new perspectives in Paul's letters.

People do not need to be biblical scholars to do undercover investigation. Carol Lakey Hess, in religious education, investigates missing pictures of women's

---

33. Two examples of scholarship on the Corinthian letters reveal how scholars can uncover missing traditions and thereby discover reversals in interpretation. These are Vincent Wimbush, *Paul, the Worldly Ascetic: Response to the World and Self-Understanding according to 1 Corinthians 7* (Macon, Ga.: Mercer University Press, 1987); Antoinette Clark Wire, *The Corinthian Women Prophets: A Reconstruction through Paul's Rhetoric* (Minneapolis: Fortress, 1990). One can also find examples in writing for broad audiences, such as Philip and Sally Scharper, *The Gospel in Art by the Peasants of Solentiname* (Maryknoll, N.Y.: Orbis, 1982).

34. Wire, *The Corinthian Women Prophets*, 37–38. Wire develops this idea throughout her book, reading through Paul's words to his context.

agency and women's development in Christian communities. Awakened by daily experiences, she pursues her concerns in systematic research.[35] Hess and other scholars model what people everywhere can do — to search religious traditions for missing strands, fresh questions, and insights. Our educational task is to invite *all* people into that search.

2. Pose Questions

Akin to undercover investigation is the practice of posing questions — *inviting people to approach traditions and contemporary situations with questions that grasp their existential interest, raise their suspicions, and promise emancipation for themselves and others.* The popularity of mysteries in novels, movies, and television suggests a human yearning to solve puzzles — a yearning that resembles theological investigation, with its question-posing and endless searching. This is promising work, but challenging because people (ourselves included) are easily deceived, willing to settle for premature answers. On the other hand, people are naturally inclined to ask questions, a capacity developed at a young age. The youth counselor described in the opening story knew that. He stirred reversal thinking by encouraging the natural questioning of youth.

Cultivate Interest

Cultivating interest is a form of question-posing — *ask people how a subject of study intersects with their lives and affects the well-being of themselves and others.* Interest is a commonly expressed value in education, easier to espouse than practice. Consider a local church case, as shared by the church's educator: *"I have a woman who has been teaching our primary Sunday school for years — except that she doesn't teach or actually use the materials; she thinks the kids 'just need to have a good time.' "*[36] *The educator explained that one primary child had complained to her mother, saying that she does not want to go to class the Sundays this woman is there (every other week) because* "they don't DO anything." I do not know details of this particular situation, but the scenario occurs frequently in varied forms. It reveals several possible issues in conflict — teachers' desire to entertain, children's desire to learn, teachers' desire to minimize preparations, children's desire to receive the best that teachers can offer, everyone's desire to be interesting and interested.

Teachers often express concern about students' boredom. In a recent visit, a professional colleague inquired about my writing. I gave an enthusiastic response, to which he replied, "What about boredom? Are you responding to teachers'

---

35. Carol Lakey Hess, *Caretakers of Our Common House: Women's Development in Communities of Faith* (Nashville: Abingdon, 1997). Another example of undercover investigation is the search for women scholars of the past, often less known and appreciated than male colleagues. See Barbara Anne Keely, ed., *Faith of Our Foremothers: Women Changing Religious Education* (Louisville: Westminster John Knox, 1997).

36. E-mail exchange, August 21, 2001. The quote is used with permission, but details of names and places are confidential.

experiences of boredom and the reality that teaching is often routine?" In truth, my book *does* focus on many high and low moments of human life, but most moments are neither; most are routine. This is challenging in a world that thrives on novelty. No student complaint is more condemnatory than "boring!" Youth counselors, schoolteachers, church teachers, parish visitors, and retreat leaders fear this verdict. Yet the natural response — to provide a more entertaining and dramatic experience — may be the opposite of what needs to happen. What may be needed is for teachers and learners to probe into boredom — to dive into the middle of a routine and discover the big questions that loom there.

Some aspects of study are inevitably tedious, even when important to learning; however, reversal questions are a better antidote to boredom than the latest gimmicks in technique and technology. Some practices are suggested by cases of this chapter:

- *Ask people what responses they have to a particular text, belief, or practice* — How do they interpret it at first glance? How do they imagine others' interpreting it? What do they hope it does *not* mean? This approach cultivates a sense of being an active subject; it also poses questions for rigorous investigation and analysis.

- *Ask people what they really believe about God and why* — What beliefs would be the hardest to let go? What Christian practices are most central? What difference does any of this make in a torn-apart world?

These practices are only suggestive, but cultivating interest is critical to honest engagement with faith. Also, interest inevitably surfaces surprising reversals.

Cultivate Suspicion

A second way to pose questions is to cultivate suspicion — *invite people to ask difficult, even heretical, questions of the Christian tradition and Christian community.* This is a work to be done within religious communities, across traditions, and in the public square. I was part of a two-year trialogue, in which Jews, Christians, and Muslims met monthly to reflect on our faiths. We began with life stories and easy questions and then moved to more difficult ones. Our conversations deepened when we reflected together on "problem texts" in our diverse traditions. Alternately, a person from one faith brought a text to study, offering a brief reflection on the text and its common interpretations and then inviting dialogue. In the discussions, we entered fear-ridden territory. We reflected on texts that some of us thought problematic in our own traditions, and inescapably problematic in an interreligious context. The group had built respectful relationships over time, enabling us to probe hard questions. Interestingly, our relationships deepened even more during the months of discussing suspicions within and among our three traditions.

Another example of cultivating suspicion fits a more school-like setting. History is a subject that engenders boredom in many students and a sense of irrelevancy in others; actually, it is rich with reversals. Christopher Columbus's "discovery" of the New World in 1492 was really not the discovery of a new world; Native people had lived here for thousands of years. Further, Leif Ericson may well have been the first European to set foot in the New World, nearly five hundred years earlier. Likewise, the arrival of English settlers in Jamestown in 1607, popularly known as the first permanent European settlement in the United States, was preceded by the permanent establishment of St. Augustine by Don Pedro Menéndez de Aviles in 1565, which was preceded by Ponce de León's landing in the same area in 1513. Analyzing such realities reverses the language of history.

Add to this analysis the encounters between European settlers and Native Americans. Even now, legends persist of Indians wreaking havoc on European settlements; yet these same Europeans took away Indian land, converted them to Christianity (often to subdue their antagonism), disparaged Native traditions, and spread European diseases.[37] The Timucuan people, who lived in northern Florida for more than a thousand years, were obliterated within a few decades of Europeans' arrival, devastated first by diseases for which they had no immunity and later by forced labor and battles. Indian attacks on white settlements were sometimes the only recourse that Native people could imagine for defending themselves against European power. Meanwhile, Christian missionaries were sometimes complicit in creating these conditions, intentionally or not.

This peep into United States history is cursory, but it reveals many reversals. These have been uncovered over time by historians using a hermeneutic of suspicion, studying history from the perspective of the oppressed, seeking overlooked historical accounts, analyzing distortions in dominant interpretations, and searching for good news to those who are marginalized, even persecuted, by dominant histories. Such reversal history belongs in churches as well as schools, cultivating suspicion for the sake of a deep and honest understanding of the past. Such is the practice of cultivating suspicion.

Seek Sources of Emancipation

A third way of posing questions is to *encourage and equip people to search for sources of emancipation.* Just as reversals permeate Jewish and Christian traditions, so does the longing for emancipation. As the Israelites crossed the Red Sea and wandered in the wilderness, God repeatedly promised emancipation. Jesus continually challenged people to be emancipated from their shackles — shackles of yearning to be

---

37. George Tinker, *Missionary Conquest: The Gospel and Native American Cultural Genocide* (Minneapolis: Fortress, 1993).

first; desiring to exclude children and marginalized folks from the Jesus community (Mark 9:33–37; 10:13–16); or dependence on possessions (10:17–22). Paul also stressed emancipation, urging people to be transformed by the renewing of their minds so they "may discern what is the will of God — what is good and acceptable and perfect" (Rom. 12:2).

Seeking sources of emancipation feeds political activism, if not insurrection. This may seem wrong-headed to some people. On the other hand, education can never be neutral, as Paulo Freire frequently reminded. Educators either support the status quo or teach people for freedom.[38] Freire himself was particularly concerned with those who are oppressed economically, socially, and politically, but emancipation comes in many forms. People may be oppressed because of their learning ability, gender, race, nationality, beliefs, sexual orientation, or age. People may also be oppressed in one area, and oppressors in others. The situation is complex, but not so complex as to justify inaction.

People are naturally torn between aligning themselves with dominating forces and committing themselves to the oppressed; it is safer to be teamed with oppressors. When people commit themselves to the oppressed, however, they experience Easter: "they die as elitists so as to be resurrected on the side of the oppressed." Freire acknowledges how difficult it is to overcome an education identified with the dominating class, which dichotomizes "theory and practice, the transcendent and the mundane, intellectual work and manual work."[39] Conversely, he links the search for emancipation with the rebirth of Easter, reflection with action, and transcendence with the mundane (incarnation).

The vision here is prophetic education that prepares people to seek and practice emancipation, and to work toward the freedom and well-being of creation. Freire, like Groome and Moore, emphasized education that was "a political praxis at the service of permanent human liberation," thus emphasizing the ongoing process that does not end with one or two changes.[40] The educational search also needs to be expansive toward all God's creation, concerned with people, creatures, and land beyond one's own community. This pushes beyond Freire's emphases, but it is urgent. Consider the ease with which white feminist women, protesting the oppression of patriarchal society, could ignore and dominate women of color. Feminism is gradually being born into a larger consciousness, but only through the emancipatory question-posing of women of color. Such examples abound, awaking people to the possibility of many Easters as they seek emancipation and

---

38. Freire, *Pedagogy of the Oppressed*; Paulo Freire and Antonio Faundez, *Learning to Question: A Pedagogy of Liberation*, trans. Tony Coates (New York: Continuum, 1989); Freire, "Education, Liberation and the Church," in *The Politics of Education*, 121–42.

39. Freire, "Education, Liberation and the Church," 122–23, 130, 142 n. 17.

40. Ibid., 140; cf. Thomas H. Groome, *Sharing Faith: A Comprehensive Approach to Religious Education* (San Francisco: HarperSanFrancisco, 1991), 133–54, 379–406; Mary Elizabeth Mullino Moore, *Teaching from the Heart: Theology and Educational Method* (Harrisburg, Pa.: Trinity Press International, 1998, 1993), 163–95.

die again and again to those beliefs and attitudes that imprison them and oppress others.

This discussion suggests that sources for emancipation can be found through many particular practices: searching for emancipatory traditions, like Fiorenza's "ekklesia of wo/men"; acting and reflecting on action; seeking emancipatory interpretations of tradition; and joining with others in analyzing the world. Seeking sources for emancipation involves critical retrieval, as well as imagination, to which we now turn.

3. Practice Imagination

This discussion leads naturally to the practice of imagination. Imagination takes many forms, but two practices are particularly important to seeking reversals: *imagining oneself in the place of others and imagining alternative futures.* These practices are important psychologically, building human relations, self-understanding, and a sense of future possibility. They also echo the incarnation and resurrection emphases of this chapter, encouraging empathic identification with others and hope toward New Creation.

Maria Harris has been a bold leader in designing educational approaches to stir religious imagination. As noted earlier, her approach consists of steps, like steps in a dance: contemplation, engaging, form-giving, emergence, and release.[41] The names of these steps suggest images of education: openness to transcendence (contemplation); active engagement with other people, the natural world, texts and issues (engaging); seeking to express oneself or one's community in music, clay, painting, program design, and so forth (form-giving); allowing new forms to emerge (emergence); and letting go of one's creations so they can be received by others (release). These images encourage teachers to draw upon imagination at every step.

Take the Role of Others

Incarnation is enfleshment, or entering into the life of the world. Through Jesus — incarnate in a living, breathing person — the world can see the throbbing presence of God. What people have known in countless ways through time is manifest in Jesus — God identified fully with the world. Yet through the ages people have touched God's presence in Jesus *and* in creation. Indeed, this sense of presence deepens as people seek God-in-the-other. Theologically, the imaginative act of taking the role of another is an imitation of Christ, identifying

---

41. Maria Harris, *Teaching and Religious Imagination: An Essay in the Theology of Teaching* (San Francisco: HarperSanFrancisco, 1991, 1987). Harris names these steps differently in later writing, but her basic approach is constant, whether reflecting on teaching or women's spirituality. See Maria Harris, *Women and Teaching: Themes for a Spirituality of Pedagogy* (New York: Paulist, 1988); Maria Harris, *Dance of the Spirit: The Seven Steps of Women's Spirituality* (New York: Bantam Doubleday Dell, 1989).

with others as Jesus did and discerning God in the other. Psychologically, this is how people learn social rules and values and grow in humanness. According to George Herbert Mead, people develop by taking the role of others, integrating them in an inner conversation, and making decisions about how to respond.[42] By "walking in others' shoes," people *develop the capacity to imagine the feelings, views, and values of others,* which is critical to human relations and to seeking reversals.

The act of taking the role of others is also spiritually significant. By identifying with others or discerning what is important to them, people can reverse fixed patterns of thinking and open themselves to something new. Howard Thurman identified this as a spiritual discipline, which rocks people to their foundations, frees them from self-preoccupation, and enables them to participate in acts of redemption. He makes a bold claim: "The place where the imagination shows its greatest powers as the *angelos* of God is in the miracle which it creates when one man, standing in his place, is able, while remaining there, to put himself in another man's place."[43] In this miraculous act, people are freed to see the world more fully and participate in the work of angels.

Taking the role of others is not necessarily agreeing with the other person or community. It is important, however, for learning ways of the world (Mead's point), for seeing beneath the surface (Thurman's point), and for discerning new possibilities. I frequently engage students in role-taking in the process of interpreting written texts and movies. I invite them to stand in the creator's shoes and present the creator's view. Only later do we step back to evaluate the work from *our* perspectives. Teachers can engage people in many kinds of role-play and simulation games, inviting them to take the roles of a creator, an enthusiast, a critic, characters in a story, or people in a conflict situation. Role-taking can also be enhanced in dialogue about creative works, asking such questions as: What is the creator saying and why? To what forces is he or she reacting? What difference does the creator hope to make? How might different audiences receive this? One can use this approach in analyzing biblical and historical texts, as well as contemporary texts, movies, or works of art. One can also research details about creators, communities, and contexts to enhance the accuracy and fullness of role-taking.

Imagine Alternative Futures

Another aspect of practicing imagination is imagining alternative futures. This is resurrection work — *preparing a community to die to the old and be reborn to God's*

---

42. George H. Mead, *The Social Psychology of George Herbert Mead* (Chicago: University of Chicago, 1956), 37–38, 241–42; George H. Mead, *The Philosophy of the Present* (LaSalle, Ill.: Open Court, 1932), xxv.

43. Howard Thurman, *The Inward Journey* (Richmond, Ind.: Friends United Press, 1961), 121.

New Creation. Inspirational leaders in history have been able to imagine new possibilities and stir others' imagination. Martin Luther King's "I Have a Dream" speech stirred a people and a nation.[44] Even now, it is often quoted, stirring people to hope and action yet again.

Imagining new alternatives is the stuff out of which utopian novels are made. It is also a current deep in Jewish and Christian history; God is the ultimate Promise-Maker. God makes and fulfills promises, only to make more promises.[45] The human search for God's promises stirs imagination, which brings the promises closer to fulfillment. Yet imagining alternative futures goes beyond inspiration; it also generates courage and hard work. Unfortunately, disillusionment can easily follow; therefore, imagining alternative futures is not an innocuous game. It carries a mandate for people to build toward the future they imagine and to remain open to critique and reformation. People are asked to give abundant effort along with hope, while also recognizing the New Creation of God that transcends and chastens the very best alternative futures they can imagine.

4. Practice Parabolic-Paradoxical Thinking

This leads to the last act of reversal teaching — the practice of parabolic and paradoxical thinking. Parables are variously known as wise sayings or proverbs, communicated in such diverse forms as allegories and metaphors.[46] As noted earlier, they also subvert accepted ways of thinking about the world. Both parabolic and paradoxical thinking are necessary for an incarnational-resurrection theology; both center on dramatic reversals in God's relation to the world. Such thinking is also necessary for people living in confusing times. Parable is grounded in a "last shall be first" theology, and paradox, in "both/and" patterns of thinking. Both recognize the small and large reversals that pull upon every routine moment of living. Parabolic and paradoxical thinking invite people to *search for meaning and direction beyond obvious and "taken for granted" realities.*

Empower People to Encounter Parables and Paradox

The searching quality of parabolic thinking leads people beyond information into an active search for reversals. It requires people to *gather information, comprehend*

---

44. Martin Luther King Jr., *I Have a Dream: Writings and Speeches That Changed the World,* ed. James Melvin Washington (San Francisco: HarperSanFrancisco, 1992).

45. Jürgen Moltmann, *Theology of Hope: On the Ground and the Implications of a Christian Eschatology* (New York: Harper & Row, 1975); cf. Jürgen Moltmann, *Hope for the Church* (Nashville: Abingdon, 1979).

46. F. L. Cross, ed. (E. A. Livingstone, ed. 3rd ed.), *The Oxford Dictionary of the Christian Church* (Oxford: Oxford University Press, 1997, 1957), 1217–18; Alan Richardson, ed., *A Theological Word Book of the Bible* (New York: Macmillan, 1966, 1950), 162–63. Note that the Hebrew word translated as "parable" is *mashal,* which means proverb. John Dominic Crossan has emphasized the challenge of parable; see his *In Parables: The Challenge of the Historical Jesus* (Sonoma, Calif.: Polebridge, 1992, 1973).

common patterns of thinking, and then seek subversive reversals in God's life with creation. This might involve any of the practices already discussed. It might also involve the study of parables and paradoxes in religious texts and daily life.

Consider Luke 14:1–14 as a text for parabolic, paradoxical study. Luke abounds with parables. It also flows with paradox — statements that run contrary to common thinking, or statements that seem contradictory and absurd but overflow with truth. The book centers on reversal traditions, such as "the last shall be first." In Luke 14, we see Jesus watched closely at a sabbath meal in the home of a leading Pharisee. A series of three parabolic actions take place within the context of that meal. In the first action (1–6), Jesus challenges the people with a question about healing on the sabbath, then Jesus heals a man with dropsy, and finally Jesus asks another challenging question about rescuing a child or an ox from a well on the sabbath. In the second action (7–11), Jesus notices that the people are choosing places of honor at the table, so he tells them a parable:

> When you are invited by someone to a wedding banquet, do not sit down at the place of honor, in case someone more distinguished than you has been invited by your host; and the host who invited both of you may come and say to you, "Give this person your place," and then in disgrace you would start to take the lowest place. But when you are invited, go and sit down at the lowest place, so that when your host comes, he may say to you, "Friend, move up higher"; then you will be honored in the presence of all who sit at the table with you. (14:8–10)

In this action, Jesus is referring people to Proverbs 25:6–7, and also reiterating the "first shall be last and last shall be first" theology that resounds in Luke.[47] In the third action (12–14), Jesus instructs his host, when inviting people to a meal, not to invite friends, brothers, relatives, or rich neighbors, for they may repay you; the host should invite the poor, the crippled, the lame, and the blind because "they cannot repay you" (12–14).

Each of these actions in Luke 14 is parabolic. Taken together, they unearth another parable — that the requirements of justice and mercy call forth different responses from different people. The man with dropsy was healed and sent on his way, with no requirements before or after the healing. The guests were told to seek the lowest places at table, and the host was told to invite outcasts. Simply stated, the healing of the man suffering with dropsy was to reverse his "outcast"

---

47. Many scholars develop these themes. One example is R. Alan Culpepper, "The Gospel of Luke," *The New Interpreter's Bible* 9 (Nashville: Abingdon, 1995): 283–88. Jesus' radicality is vivid in relation to the limiting social practices of his day, found in extreme form in the Qumran community, which would not have allowed a man with dropsy to participate in assemblies or in the congregation (287).

status. The healing of people suffering from arrogance was to reverse their honor-loving ways. The healing of the host was to propose a more difficult ethical path and offer hospitality to outcasts.

Paradox also pervades Luke's account. In the opening verses, the people are watching Jesus, and then he is watching them. Jesus is seen and seeing. In the opening verses, Jesus challenges the people with difficult questions and has compassion on a man with dropsy. He confronts the lawyers and Pharisees, and is confronted by the suffering man. Later, Jesus challenges people to choose the lowest places at the table for the sake of not being embarrassed if they choose a higher place and the host asks them to move down. Jesus is giving clever, practical advice, which at the same time conveys radical reversals regarding social position. Further, he uncovers paradoxes regarding what is acceptable behavior at a meal, what are appropriate structures of human honor, and what are rewards for human behavior (sitting in places of honor or receiving honor from others and from God). These represent more reversals than Jesus' dinner companions were prepared to hear, and probably more reversals than modern readers can grasp. Modern Christian readers can point out Pharisaic legalism but rarely see the reversals demanded of us. Despite the difficulty, however, encountering the reversals of parable and paradox is important in teaching and learning. We need not look far to find them, and then to equip people to meet them in religious texts and contemporary encounters.

Engage People with Artistry and Metaphor

Parabolic thinking is not only generated from parables; it is also generated as people *exercise artistry and metaphor to express depths of religious meaning*. The power of analogical imagination for David Tracy and metaphorical theology for Sally McFague reveals the urgency of thinking beyond the boundaries of existing texts and theological frameworks. In her early work on metaphorical theology, McFague pointed out that people often long to express their religious experience, but they have no way to express it fully or adequately; therefore, they express it though images and metaphors.[48] The sheer impossibility of defining God and the human experience of God leads people to speak in metaphors. We might say, for example, that "God is like a tree." Hyun Kyung Chung names many metaphors for Jesus, such as shaman, worker, and grain.[49] Each metaphor opens new possibilities for grasping the meaning of Jesus' life, death, and resurrection; each opens new possibilities for experiencing Jesus in our lives.

Analogies and metaphors convey realities that are inexpressible in direct language. They uncover truths that transcend language altogether. McFague argues

---

48. Sallie McFague, *Metaphorical Theology: Models of God in Religious Language* (Philadelphia: Fortress, 1985, 1982).

49. Chung, *Struggle to Be the Sun Again*, 62–73.

that metaphors have a quality of saying both "yes" and "no."[50] Thus, the language of metaphor is both true language and doubting language. David Tracy emphasizes knowing and expressing God through analogies, an affirmation grounded in natural theology. He asserts that we can know God through the natural world, even if not fully, but an act of imagination is necessary.[51] The human act of analogical imagination points to the sublime. The similarities of these two views are more important here than the distinctions. Both McFague and Tracy suggest that artistry and metaphor are necessary to describe God, creation, and ineffable religious experience.

I have asked students on several occasions to express their understanding of God and creation in a story, metaphor, or other artistic medium. I have made several discoveries in the process. First, this is difficult, and some people have had dramatic religious experiences in the course of preparing themselves to do it. Second, it draws out theological wisdom that people do not think they possess. Third, the results are awe-inspiring. This simple educational practice of parabolic thinking generates new insights and opens the way for continued alertness to parables and paradoxes in the course of living. Like the other practices described in this chapter, parabolic thinking opens the way to discover reversals and more reversals.

Concluding Reflections

This chapter calls forth a pattern of thinking and acting that is not common in most contemporary cultures. It fits with postmodern ways of thinking, but the term "postmodernism" is used in such divergent and complex ways that it cannot be identified as a clear cultural pattern. The purpose of this chapter has been to uncover the riches laden in reversal thinking and reversal living. At the same time, the paradox of the entire chapter is that the very reversals identified here will be reversed further as people continue to ponder and wrestle. As in liturgical and educational practice, the journey is the goal, not the destination. We will never arrive at a final set of reversals that are beyond being overturned. We will hopefully continue this journey, seeking reversals as an act of faithfulness to the God who transcends our narrow thought frames and awakens us to the unacceptability of our accepted ways of life.

---

50. Sallie McFague TeSelle, *Speaking in Parables: A Study in Metaphor and Theology* (Philadelphia: Fortress, 1975). In this early book, McFague laid foundations for later work in metaphorical theology, which emphasize that metaphors for God communicate "is" and "is not" simultaneously. When more extensively developed, metaphors become models. See McFague, *Metaphorical Theology*, 13; Sallie McFague, *Models of God: Theology for an Ecological, Nuclear Age* (Philadelphia: Fortress, 1987); Sallie McFague, *The Body of God: An Ecological Theology* (Minneapolis: Augsburg Fortress, 1993).

51. David Tracy, *The Analogical Imagination: Christian Theology and the Culture of Pluralism* (New York: Crossroad, 1981). See also Gordon D. Kaufman, *The Theological Imagination: Constructing the Concept of God* (Philadelphia: Westminster Press, 1981).

Reflecting Further

To continue reflecting, consider some of the possibilities below:

1. *Ponder the seasons of Christmas and Easter as celebrated in your church or community.* In what ways do the celebrations enhance reversal faith? How might they invite a deeper encounter with the radicality of incarnation and resurrection? How would your lives change if you identified yourselves as "resurrection people"?

2. *Seek reversals in popular movies.* How does the movie embody reversals, and how does it reinforce stereotypes and dominant ways of thinking and acting?

3. *Choose one or two promising educational practices from this chapter, and ponder how you might develop that practice for your context.* Use the practice to reflect upon familiar hymns or other texts of tradition, to reflect on a recent public event, or to ponder theological perspectives that diverge from views of your community.

Chapter Six

Giving Thanks

✡

How does one follow a chapter on reversals, especially faced with the subversive nature of reversal-thinking and reversal-action? In the practical thinking of North America and many parts of the world, discerning reversals should lead to transformative action, especially when reversals uncover existential heartache. Yet we turn now to thanksgiving, an act of transformation in its own surprising ways. We will leave the more obvious acts of transformation — reconstruction and repair — for chapter 8. This may seem odd. Thanksgiving is commonly associated with happy, carefree times or high holy days, such as Christmas, Epiphany, and Easter in Christian tradition and Passover or Succoth in Judaism. Thanksgiving is more than this, however; it is an expression of gratitude to the One who creates, liberates, redeems, reconciles, and abides, even in the most troubling times. To consider the complex qualities of such gratitude, we turn to stories.

Nothing prepared Steve for the news of his disease, Amyotrophic Lateral Sclerosis (Lou Gehrig's Disease), or for doctors' explanations; Steve's muscles would degenerate slowly until he could no longer work, eat, drink, talk, walk, sit, or express love to his family in familiar ways. Steve had two teenage girls and a spouse, and their close family life had long inspired others. Yet for five years they were to live with this escalating disease. When it had destroyed most of Steve's movement, he dictated these words:

I believe that life is not always fair. It has certainly been true in my case. It is not fair that I should have wonderful, caring, supportive parents who raised me right, and brothers and sisters that are there when I need them, not to mention the aunts, uncles, cousins, nieces, and nephews who are all so special. It's not fair that I should be blessed with a beautiful, talented wife and together we should have two equally beautiful, talented daughters who make us proud daily. No, life is not fair. Why should I have had so many years of good health and the energy and good friends to camp and backpack with through the years, and how could I

*be so fortunate to be accepted into such a giving, loving congregation as we found
at Aldersgate? ALS is a terrible disease, but it does not negate the rest of my life.*[1]

Shortly after expressing these sentiments, Steve celebrated his forty-ninth
birthday with his family at his bedside. A month later, he died.

Another man, Al, has learned that he has early-onset Alzheimer's disease. *Al is
a husband, father of two teenagers, pastor, musician, and composer. Well known for his
creative genius, he now faces the loss of his anchors. Shortly before retiring from his
pastorate, he offered a communion meditation in a circle of friends. He began by noting
that everything has a name — places, people, ideas. Then, he invited people to imagine:*

> *But what would happen if one of these names just drops out of your head. I bet
> a lot of us have experienced this. You see something or somebody that you know
> well, but the name does not come to you. It's like there is a little light bulb in your
> head, and it made a little pop and a little bitty puff of smoke came up, and after
> that it never worked again. And you continue to see this familiar thing, but the
> name . . . the name is nowhere to be found. That's what Alzheimer's disease is.*

*Al continued the sermon by describing how he now manuscripts each detail of Sunday
worship, including his greeting: "It all goes into the manuscript because, because I am
afraid that that word might be the one whose light bulb is about to go out." He added:*

> *All of these things could be given a name such as a "real bummer." At today's
> breakfast I wrote this out on a napkin. "Question: Have I been feeling sorry for
> myself? The answer is 'yes!' At times I've given my self-pity a good strong effort.
> It was an exercise that was very understandable, but not very productive."*[2]

*At this point, Al paused while someone read the text for the day: "When Jesus saw the
crowds, he went up the mountain, and after he sat down, his disciples came to him.
Then he began to speak and taught them, saying: Blessed are the poor in spirit, for theirs
is the kingdom of heaven . . ." (Matt. 5:1–9). After the reading, Al continued:*

> *I am learning that, when difficult things come into our lives, there are other things
> that come with it. People who are poor in spirit are brought to the kingdom of
> heaven. Those who mourn are comforted. . . . In every setback, in every tragedy,
> there are wonderful people who come to us. . . . And in their love, we discover that
> there are opportunities for coming closer to the struggles of others. When I call*

---

1. Steven Allen Fiske dictated these words to his wife Debra Britt-Fiske. They were printed in the Aldersgate United Methodist Church bulletin and in the "California-Pacific Annual Conference Memorial Service," Redlands, Calif., June 15, 2001. Steve was born September 28, 1951, and died October 29, 2000.

2. Al Rhodes Wickett, sermon preached in Methodist Federation for Social Action Service of Eucharist, California-Pacific Annual Conference, Redlands, Calif., June 17, 2001.

upon someone who is struggling with memory, I can use the word "we" rather than "you." That's a gift for which to be thankful.

When I draw a blank, I can't bring the name back by swearing at it. . . . Healing comes from calmness and understanding . . . , the gifts that are continually offered to us. We call it the Holy Spirit. The name we call it is God's love. . . . Indeed, throughout our lives we are guided and challenged by a river of love, older and stronger and more beautiful than any of us can imagine. Thanks be to God.

This chapter builds upon the sentiments of Steve and Al. They know something that many people miss — the power of living thankfully, even in times of distress. Thanksgiving is a gift, and also a decisive act — a choice that can be encouraged and cultivated; thus, it is not grounded in external circumstances. When I have interviewed youth and young adults, asking their hopes for the future, the most commonly recurring word is "happiness."[3] Most interviewees have meant more than momentary pleasure, but most associate happiness with good relationships, jobs, and lifestyles. These wishes are natural, but a spirit of thanksgiving is more. *Thanksgiving is a spirit of gratitude even when life is tough; an ability to see God's gifts even when they are not obvious; and an ability to give thanks as a discipline of appreciation for the bounties of life.* The sacramental practice of giving thanks has real power, expressed in the church's praise and in a theology of bounty. In this book's descriptions of sacramental spirituality, we have already reflected on a spirituality of expectation, tragic memory, and reversals. Now we turn to a spirituality of thanksgiving, focusing on sacramental practice *that inspires thanksgiving, seeks reasons to be thankful, and guides people toward thankful living.*

Power in Giving Thanks

In the stories of this chapter, thanksgiving overshadows the burdens of human illness and loss. These stories echo the stories of Edinburgh, Nairobi, and Rome discussed in chapter 2. They also echo church traditions of doxology (giving praise to God) and eucharist (thanksgiving). Such traditions often rise from the world's pathos, but they offer the pathos to a caring, transforming God.[4] Thanksgiving thus comes in many forms. It can be individual, familial, or communal on a grand scale. And people who share in the act of gratitude are inevitably blessed by it, even as they bless others.

The tradition of showing gratitude is deep in human history. Consider Jewish, Christian, and Muslim traditions of building altars to God. Noah built an altar to

---

3. This is a tentative conclusion, based on the first ten interviews in a longer series, Children in Religion, Law and Society Project, sponsored by the Center for the Interdisciplinary Study of Religion, Spring 2004.

4. Don E. Saliers, *Worship as Theology: Foretaste of Glory Divine* (Nashville: Abingdon, 1994), 25–33, 39–48.

thank God for the end of flooding (Gen. 8:20); Abram built an altar to Yahweh, "who had appeared to him" (Gen. 12:7; cf. 13:3–4, 18). Still today, people build altars to thank God for miracles, tucking a shrine beside an Austrian village church or Mexican highway. People also build shrines to give thanks for the life of a saint or family member, marking the place of burial or a place of special meaning in that person's life. This tradition typifies many religious traditions, but, for Judaism, Christianity, and Islam, places of thanksgiving are often shared and sometimes contested, such as the site of Rachel's tomb outside Bethlehem, or the tombs of Abraham, Sarah, and others in Hebron. Thanksgiving is a powerful impulse of the human spirit; as such, it can lead to dispute as well as to shared joy.

Power of Shaping a Grateful Spirit

The practice of thanksgiving has *power to shape a grateful spirit — a way of being that is not fully determined by external circumstances.* I discovered that power forcefully when a woman, recently fired from her church position, told me her story. The pastor said she was no longer needed in the congregation where she had served effectively for more than a decade. She was to be replaced by another. Having given much of herself, and having a family that depended on her, she was devastated. For some days she cried and talked with friends about her plight. Then she decided to approach the situation differently; she began a gratitude journal. Her discipline was to record five things for which she was thankful every night before she went to bed. The discipline was difficult at first, but it became easier over time, even enjoyable. Soon she discovered that her own feelings were shifting; more surprising to her, she was finding strength from deep inside to face the difficult days and begin searching for another position.

A spirituality of thankfulness encourages people to practice thankfulness, even when they do not feel it. As I said earlier about expectation, this is not a "positive thinking" veneer, but a deep sense that goodness dwells under the rancor and devastation of daily life. It is the force that allowed Julian of Norwich, in the midst of plague and war, to discern God's assurances: "I [God] may make all things well, and I can make all things well, and I shall make all things well, and I will make all things well; and you will see yourself that every kind of thing will be well."[5] When people practice thankfulness, they are able to commune with the God of promise and the created world of possibility. To live in hope is to face that world, even its horrors, and to choose a spirit of grateful communion. Such thankfulness was manifest when people gave thanks for New York firefighters and

---

5. Julian of Norwich, *Showings,* in Classics of Western Spirituality, trans. Edmund Colledge, O.S.A., and James Walsh, S.J. (Mahwah, N.J.: Paulist, 1978), 229, cf. 229–33 (Long Text), 151–53 (Short Text). The different auxiliary verbs (may, can,...) refer to the Trinity's work, God's acts through time, and the future of those saved into union with God. Julian offers complex gratitude to a complex God, who relates with the world in many ways. The more familiar quote, also found in the thirteenth revelation, is: "Sin is necessary, but all will be well, and all will be well, and every kind of thing will be well" (225, Long Text).

police officers who, on September 11, 2001, gave their lives to help people escape the crumbling World Trade Center, and for people who risked their lives to carry a wheelchair-bound stranger down the stairs. A spirituality of thanksgiving shapes a spirit that can see sparks of beauty in tragedy. Such spirituality does not avoid or deny tragedy but strengthens human courage to face it, whether by protest or acceptance.

Power of Drawing Goodness from Tragedy and Despair

This discussion leads then to a second form of power — the *power to draw goodness from tragedy and despair.* In times of disaster — such as hurricanes in Florida, an earthquake in India, or devastations of war — people are often moved to acts of heroism, and also to overflowing gratitude for the heroism and generosity of others. In times of personal tragedy, such as those shared by Steve and Al in the opening stories, people awaken so sharply to loss that they also awaken to gratitude. When Steve and Al, living with ALS and Alzheimer's disease, were asked to share with their communities, they took quiet moments to reflect on what they most wanted to say; both decided on gratitude. In times of personal failure, people can be similarly awakened to gratitude, as I have experienced more than once in my life. I remember a moment of great failing, when I did not think I could face my best friend. I can still remember her running across the parking lot to hug me, letting me know that she still loved me. In that moment, my gratitude was more than I could hold. I cried with joy, and so did she.

One sees such a moment in Jesus' story of the woman who was forgiven much. The woman comes to Jesus while he dines in the home of a Pharisee, and she lavishly covers his feet with ointment, tears, and kisses (Luke 7:36–40). The Pharisee was apparently insulted at Jesus' receiving such a gesture from a known sinner. When he protested, however, Jesus responded with a question: "A certain creditor had two debtors; one owed five hundred denarii, and the other fifty. When they could not pay, he canceled the debts for both of them. Now which of them will love him more?" (41–42). The Pharisee, Jesus' host, responded that the man who owed five hundred denarii (about five hundred days' wages) would love him more; Jesus agreed (43–44). Jesus turned to the woman and declared that her sins were forgiven, thus arousing *more* suspicion regarding his claims of divine authority. For the woman, however, the despair of her life had seemingly enhanced her gratitude for Jesus and her desire to express thankfulness by lavishly anointing his feet.

Power of Mutuality with God and God's Bounty

As for this woman, gratitude has *power to nourish a mutual relationship with God and God's bounty — power to receive from and respond to God's acts of love, and thus to open to God's ongoing work of love.* In the biblical texts of Noah, Abram, and this unnamed woman, a cyclical pattern of gratitude appears. In each, the person or community acted in response to God. Noah built and filled an ark to help creatures survive a great flood; Abram moved with his family and household across the countryside to a new land; the woman anointed Jesus. In each, divine action continues, leading to a grateful response. According to the texts, Noah and Abram first responded to God's instructions, and the woman responded to news that Jesus was in town; they all acted decisively. In each story, the human actions culminated in thanksgiving, whether in building an altar or anointing Jesus. Then, in each story, God responded to the person with further promises. Smelling the pleasing odor of Noah's sacrifice, God promised never again to destroy every living creature (Gen. 8:21–22). In the reiterating stories of Abram, God's pronouncements generally precede Abram's building an altar — promising land to Abram's offspring (12:7) and promising that Abram will have many offspring (13:14–18). The pattern is cyclical, however, because God makes promises again and again, and Abram returns to the place where he built the first altar (3–4) and he builds new altars in critical moments of interaction with God (e.g., 13:14–18; 15:7–21; 22:1–19). These many moments involve revelation, mutual response between God and a person, and human acts of devotion.

Looking more closely at the woman who anointed Jesus, we see the patterns of revelation and mutual response in bold relief. The Pharisee is told that the woman's "sins, which were many, *have been* forgiven; *hence* she has shown great love" (emphasis added). Then Jesus said to her, "Your sins are forgiven." We see here the cyclical nature of forgiveness; it is neither a gift earned by human effort nor an act of God independent of human response. Jesus declares it in the past tense, "her sins...have been forgiven" (Luke 7:47) and in the present, "Your sins are forgiven" (48). The former is the apparent reason she is acting with such gratitude; the announcement of forgiveness in the present tense is seemingly a response to her act. God's actions go before *and* after human responses; the human act of thanksgiving is a response to God, and God then responds again to the human outpouring of gratitude.

Power of Being Washed in Divine Presence

Mutuality leads to a fourth power of thankfulness — the *power of being washed in God's presence*. The cyclical relationship described above suggests that people respond to God, and God to people. By why would thanksgiving arise from people laden with troubles, like Steve and Al? I suggest that *thanksgiving emerges from the relationship itself* — from prayer, worship, study, and other practices of building relationship with God. Thomas Merton had a sense of how powerful this relationship was, urging novices to begin prayer with a sense of union with God. He believed that the relation with God would then guide their words.[6] Inspired by these instructions, I long ago initiated a spiritual discipline that I practice

---

6. Thomas Merton, *What Is Contemplation?* (Springfield, Ill.: Templegate, 1978).

to this day. At the beginning of prayer, I quiet my body and focus on God's presence at the center of my being. In the very moment when my senses are overwhelmed with the presence of God, the words that almost always come to me are, "Thank you, God." The act of focusing is, for me, an intentional discipline. On agitated or distracted days, it requires some effort and time. The response of "thank you, God," is not intentional; it simply flows from being washed in divine presence.

Roots of Thanksgiving in Church Practice

In addition to the cases of this chapter, thanksgiving is deeply rooted in the church's historic practice. Church practice cannot manufacture thanksgiving, but it can reveal glimpses of God's work and stir gratitude. Indeed, *doxa* refers to divine glory, and *ortho-doxa* is the practice of rightfully giving glory or praise to the One to whom glory is due.[7] Orthodoxy, thus, has more to do with praise than belief. Church practice, at its best, enhances this praise, but it can also obscure it, stirring images of a world in which people have to live by hard work and fear, rather than grace and thanksgiving. When church leaders urge people to suffer for the sake of the Gospel, work hard to escape damnation, or issue harsh judgments on others, they damage gratitude. When leaders communicate God's bounties and the human vocation of grateful response, the picture of God's relationship with creation is permeated with thanksgiving

Thanksgiving is embodied in the seasons of Epiphany and Eastertide — seasons of celebrating good news and sharing that news abroad. A community can hardly contain its joy when singing the spiritual, "Go Tell It on the Mountain," announcing that "Jesus Christ is born."[8] This is not a solemn hymn announcing that Jesus is the only way to new life and drawing lines between believers and nonbelievers. Sung often during Epiphany, it is an outpouring of thanksgiving from one community to another. Similarly bountiful is the Easter hymn "Christ the Lord is Risen Today."[9] Both hymns reveal the spirit of thanksgiving indwelling the seasons of Epiphany and Eastertide, seasons that follow upon Christmas and Easter respectfully, and carry forth the good news of those high holy days.

Similarly, both baptism and eucharist have thanksgiving at their core, and both include prayers of thanksgiving. The sheer physicality of the sacraments invites gratitude, whether in the delight of water or the touch and taste of bread and wine. This does not mean that the water, bread, and wine are always delightful; some persons are frightened of the water and dislike the bread and wine.

---

7. Saliers, *Worship as Theology*, 40–42.

8. African American Spiritual, "Go, Tell It on the Mountain," words adapt. John W. Work Jr., music adapt. William Farley Smith, *The United Methodist Hymnal* (Nashville: Abingdon, 1989), 251.

9. Charles Wesley, "Christ the Lord Is Risen Today," *The United Methodist Hymnal*, 302.

These physical symbols are gifts of creation, however, and intended for enjoyment. Whenever the senses are allowed full play in sacramental celebration, the potential delight is magnified. This powerful sensate experience is celebrated and encouraged by people as diverse as Baron Friedrich von Hügel (Evelyn Underhill's mentor) and June O'Connor. For von Hügel, the body and senses have "an inalienable place and function" in religion; in O'Connor's feminist analysis, the sensual aspects of the eucharist foster a reclaiming of sensual gifts in daily life.[10] For both, the embodied practice of thanksgiving is critical to sacramental theology.

Epiphany and Eastertide

Epiphany and Eastertide both have a revelatory quality. The word "epiphany" literally means "manifestation," and it refers to the divine manifestation of Christ. This manifestation follows Christmas (January 6) and is associated in the Eastern church (since the third century C.E.) with the baptism of Christ. In the Western church, the primary association is with the arrival of the three wise men (or sages), representing the gentile people to whom the baby Jesus was manifested alongside his own Jewish people. Some attention is also given in Western liturgies to Christ's baptism and the miracle at Cana when Jesus turned water into wine (John 12:1–11).

With multiple meanings, the feast of Epiphany has endured through the centuries, traditionally celebrated on the Sunday falling between January 2 and 8. In some countries, such as Spain, this is a larger celebration than Christmas, and people give gifts as they remember the sages' gifts to Jesus. In the early church, from the fourth century, Epiphany was one of three major feasts, along with Easter and Pentecost. It continues to be important, especially in the Eastern church, where associations with the blessing of water continue to be strong. *The multiple associations interweave sacraments (baptism), sacramental elements (water), and sacramental moments (like Jesus' miracle in Cana).*

Eastertide, likewise, is a festival season, extending the celebration of Jesus' resurrection and God's victory over death. The revelation of Easter is the manifestation of God's refusal to let forces of destruction be final; new life comes out of the worst horrors. Whether one attests to the literal or symbolic resurrection of Jesus, the power of Easter faith is that God lives beyond death and destruction, and hope is not quenched. Feminist and womanist theologians (myself included) raise sharp questions regarding the death of Jesus, interpreting the crucifixion as

---

10. Baron Friedrich von Hügel, "On Certain Central Needs of Religion, and the Difficulties of Liberal Movements in Face of the Needs: As Experienced within the Roman Catholic Church during the Last Forty Years," *Essays and Addresses on the Philosophy of Religion, Second Series* (London: J. M. Dent & Sons, 1930, 1926), address delivered in Edinburgh, July 7, 1914, 91–131, esp. 100; June O'Connor, "Sensuality, Spirituality, Sacramentality," *Union Seminary Quarterly Review* 40, nos. 1–2 (1985): 59–70; cf. Don E. Saliers, *Worship Come to Its Senses* (Nashville: Abingdon, 1996).

the consequence of Jesus' radical way of life and self-giving ministry rather than a choice by God to sacrifice Jesus or to enact violence for the sake of redemption.[11] These interpretations upset the idea that Jesus' suffering was *necessary* for saving humankind, or that God somehow planned the suffering. The interpretations still lead, however, to the conclusion that Easter is a victory day, pointing to a world beyond suffering. The world to which these voices speak does not glorify suffering by describing it as a divinely intended act; rather, it reveals that *God will journey through the suffering of this world and rise from its ashes so that new life can come again and again.* Such acts of God evoke thanksgiving.

Although interpretations of God's actions vary considerably, the power of new life celebrated in Easter points to the possibility of new life in the present moment and in years to come. This new life is promised even when the Christian community is unstable, unjust, or unloving in a given moment of time. The church, however imperfect, is invited to *dwell* in the hope of Easter. The season continues for forty days; thus, Easter is not a brief moment to celebrate before returning to life as normal; it is a moment to savor and live fully, so that the community's life can be forever transformed.

The fact that Eastertide continues until Pentecost is significant. The post-resurrection days were not easy for Jesus' disciples. The disciples, confused by the death and resurrection of Jesus, did not know what to do with their lives. They missed the daily guidance of Jesus' walking and talking with them, and they awaited God's help (Acts 2:1–13). They moved awkwardly into the post-resurrection era; thus, Pentecost was an unexpected gush of God's Spirit, marking a radically new life in the Spirit. In the Christian calendar, Pentecost is the culmination of Eastertide. Easter hope upholds people in a sense of wonder while they await the continuing revelation and guidance that will sustain them. Eastertide is like the sun's reflection on the sky when the sun is rising. Even when you cannot see the sun, you see pinks and purples play across the horizon, windows aglow with sunlight, and clouds changing hue as the earth makes its daily rotation. The celebration of Easter similarly points to the movements of God, never fully revealing God's grace, but coloring the horizon with brilliant color and hope. Seen in this way, Eastertide is a time of thanksgiving! Like Epiphany, it is a season for sharing God's blessing with the world — in good times and bad, happy times and sad — spreading the spirit of thanksgiving for God's bounties.

---

11. Rita Nakashima Brock, *Journeys by Heart: A Christology of Erotic Power* (New York: Crossroad, 1988); Rita Nakashima Brock and Rebecca Ann Parker, *Proverbs of Ashes: Violence, Redemptive Suffering, and the Search for What Saves Us* (Boston: Beacon, 2001); Delores S. Williams, *Sisters in the Wilderness: The Challenge of Womanist God-Talk* (Maryknoll, N.Y.: Orbis, 1993); Rosemary Radford Ruether, *Women and Redemption: A Theological History* (Minneapolis: Fortress, 1998); Isabel Carter Heyward, *The Redemption of God: A Theology of Mutual Relation* (Washington, D.C.: University Press of America, 1982); Carter Heyward, *God in the Balance: Christian Spirituality in Times of Terror* (Cleveland: Pilgrim, 2002).

Sacraments

The spirit of thanksgiving stirred by Epiphany and Easter is at the heart of the sacraments, which give thanks for God's gifts and strengthen the community with hope. Recall the African American slaves who walked many miles to celebrate a baptism — to thank God for the wonder of Jesus and for wonders in the lives of those to be baptized.

In this chapter, I focus particularly on thanksgiving in the eucharist. The Greek word *eucharistia* translates as "giving thanks to God." The tradition relating the Lord's supper with eucharist derives, in part, from Jesus' prayer of thanksgiving at the last meal with his disciples (Matt. 26:26–29; Mark 14:22–25; Luke 22:14–20; 1 Cor. 11:23–26). In the early church, thanksgiving was at the heart of many shared meals (Acts 2:46–47); the Lord's supper was particularly identified with "joyful thanksgiving."[12] As Jesus followed the Jewish prayer tradition in giving thanks to God before breaking the bread and sharing the meal, so eucharistic prayers today follow the form of the Hebrew *berakah* or "the act of blessing God."[13] Hebrew prayer traditions, according to Don Saliers, have to do with blessing God, not making things holy by asking God to bless them but by *offering them to God* and *blessing God's name for them.* The eucharistic prayers of the early church consecrated the bread and wine in this way, enabling the community "to discern the power and presence of God in Christ."[14] Similarly, James White accents "thankful commemoration of God's works and prayer for their continuance," rather than human gratitude per se.[15] In sacraments, people gratefully *remember God's works from the dawn of creation and anticipate God's works to come.*

The emphasis on thanking God in the Lord's supper is enduring, seen in the early teachings of the second-century *Didache* and throughout the history of Christian tradition.[16] James White notes that the Eastern church has always focused its prayers on giving thanks for *all* of God's works through time, whereas the Western church (both Roman Catholic and Protestant) has focused on the work of Christ, particularly on the death and resurrection. This distinction is beginning to shift, however; recent liturgical reforms in the West have reintroduced an emphasis on giving thanks for all God's work in creation.[17] Most eucharistic services of the current day tend to focus thanksgiving on the wholeness of God's work past and present, with abiding hope for God's future.

---

12. James F. White, *Sacraments as God's Self-Giving* (Nashville: Abingdon, 1983), 54; cf. James F. White, *The Sacraments in Protestant Practice and Faith* (Nashville: Abingdon, 1999), 100–104.

13. Don E. Saliers, *Worship and Spirituality* (Akron, Ohio: OSL Publications, 1996, 1984), 22.

14. Ibid., 65–66; cf. Saliers, *Worship as Theology*, 93–97.

15. White, *Sacraments as God's Self-Giving*, 54.

16. Saliers, *Worship as Theology*, 90–97; *Didache,* trans. Willie Rordorf et al., in *The Eucharist of the Early Christians,* trans. Matthew J. O'Connell (New York: Pueblo, 1978), 1–23.

17. White, *Sacraments as God's Self-Giving*, 56.

Eucharistic thanksgiving does more than reiterate historic patterns; it shapes human life. According to Don Saliers, "Life is consecrated and brought to holiness by giving thanks to God for it."[18] Further, the eucharistic practices of "take, bless, break, and share" represent a pattern for human life — receiving God's gifts, giving thanks, and breaking our lives open to share with others. Thanksgiving is at the heart of these actions, from receiving to breaking. We are further asked to "offer ourselves as a 'living sacrifice of praise and thanksgiving,' " to give our lives in praise. In the words of Don Saliers, "the great thanksgiving is what our lives are meant to be."[19] This claim is bold. The act of thanksgiving is not a way to earn God's rewards or plead for new favors; it is like opening a window to God's light and God's illumination of human purpose. As we give thanks, we see the world and the human vocation more clearly. As we give thanks, we come to know what it means to be created in the image of God. And living in the image of God means that we share with God in praise — looking at the world through the window of thanksgiving and declaring it to be good (Gen. 1:4, 10, 12, 18, 21, 25, 31).

Historic liturgies and prayers of the church have carried this spirit of thanksgiving through time, and modern ones carry the spirit still. Thus, I conclude these ruminations with a eucharistic prayer that expresses the ancient spirit of gratitude in new words:

> In gratitude we come to this Table at the invitation of our Lord.
> We come not knowing why we are so loved
>> by the One who set the stars in the skies
>> by the one who sent the child Jesus into the world
>> by the One who watched as darkness had its day.
> In gratitude we come to this Table to find food for our souls.
> We come not knowing why we are so graced
>> to receive the bread of heaven
>> to touch the holy in our midst
>> to taste Christ upon our lips.
> In gratitude we come to this Table to receive drink for our spirits.
> We come not knowing why we are so blessed
>> with this sign of God's new covenant
>> with life-giving refreshment
>> with the real presence of Christ.
> Still we pray, as those who cannot fully comprehend this mystery,
>> that the Spirit of love and grace and blessing
>> might be upon us as we open our hearts in thanksgiving.

---

18. Saliers, *Worship and Spirituality*, 22.
19. Ibid., 66–67; cf. 61–68.

Fashion us ever more into a faithful people
   known by our love for one another
   captured by the grace of Christ
   compelled to be a blessing to others. Amen.[20]

Theology of Bounty

The practice of the church points to a reality beyond itself. Thanksgiving is much more than a human or ecclesial act. It is, first, a practice of God — the same God who declared creation good, who lives among us, and brings life from death. Thanksgiving is rooted in *the abundance of God's being and God's creation*. This theme is emphasized in theologies rooted in sacramental practice. In Don Saliers, for example, worship arises from the glory of God: "Liturgical worship therefore begins and ends in praising, thanking, and blessing the reality of God."[21] Similarly, thanksgiving begins and ends in God's abundance. In the sacraments, and I would argue in sacramental living, these bounties are revealed and celebrated.

Another theological tradition linked with sacramental practice gives similar emphasis to the glory of God. Von Hügel identified seven truths about God that he considered important for shaping prayer and spiritual life — God's richness, natural and supernatural action, perfect freedom, delightfulness, otherness, adorableness, and prevenience.[22] His theological position varies in many respects from that presented here (particularly regarding the otherness of God); however, I join von Hügel in two central assumptions: that tenets about God can deepen and broaden human prayer, and that people are drawn to different tenets at different moments of their spiritual lives. In short, theological formulations make a difference in spiritual life. Further, I affirm von Hügel's sense of God as "a stupendously rich Reality." This view inspires a rich spirituality and reveals why people with different theological perspectives can come together in thanksgiving. It also prepares the way for theological affirmations I make here.

---

20. Mark Richardson, "Eucharistic Prayer," Trinity United Methodist Church, Los Osos, California, Palm/Passion Sunday, April 8, 2001 (used with permission).

21. Saliers, *Worship as Theology*, 85–86.

22. Baron Friedrich von Hügel, "The Facts and Truths Concerning God and the Soul Which Are of Most Importance in the Life of Prayer," *Essays and Addresses on the Philosophy of Religion, Second Series* (London: J. M. Dent & Sons, 1930, 1926), 217–26. The original address was delivered in Beaconsfield, October 26, 1921. The seven theological positions are (1) "God is a stupendously rich Reality"; (2) God is author of, and reflected in, all of Nature and Supernature; (3) God is fully free; (4) God is the Supreme Good; (5) God is other, not human; (6) people need God more than God needs people; and (7) God is prevenient, meaning that God's love precedes and makes possible human love for God and others. Von Hügel drew these positions from Scripture, dogmatics, theologians of the church, and his own work.

1. God and God's Creation Are Bountiful

The first theological affirmation is that *God and God's creation are bountiful —
surpassing our imagination in plenitude and overflowing love.* During one of the most
difficult times in my life, my family lived on a bluff in our desert community. On
nights when storms raged in the desert, lightning bolted across the sky, thunder
rocked our house, and I sat with my children and watched. Those storms were
strangely comforting. They stirred a strong sense of God's greatness — not *distant* greatness, but the awesome power of God and God's creation. The storms
revealed a vastness that made my life problems seem small by comparison. I was
conscious in those moments of the bounteous world, but not of bounties in gentle,
pleasant forms. I experienced distance and greatness, but these qualities belonged
to God *and* the universe, and I was interwoven with both. God's creation was
throbbing in my soul, transforming my perspectives and spirits. Even my young
children, hugged tightly against me, seemed to sense their oneness with the universe, quelling their fear and stirring gratitude for God's wonders. On one such
night, my young son whispered, "God is really big!"

My mountaintop experiences in the desert echo the opening stories of this
chapter. Steve and Al faced unimaginable loss, but chose to dwell on the bounties of their family and church relationships, the bounties of God's love, and
the continuing opportunities to give themselves to living. The everyday gifts of
tenderness and love are the God-gifts they treasured. Drawing from their stories,
and from communities faced with poverty, displacement, and isolation, one finds
remarkable witnesses to the bounties of God's creation amid deprivation. Yet two
questions emerge.

The first question is *whether God is obscured or absent in times of severe and
persistent hardship.* Is thanksgiving possible in situations that magnify the yearning
for, and seeming impossibility of, encountering God's bounty? If that were so, the
struggling people of Peru could not have addressed Pope John Paul II in God's
name; they would have abandoned their struggle and abandoned God long before.
However, Victor and Irene Chero, of the Christian Workers' Movement, spoke
for their communities in 1979:

> "We suffer affliction, we lack work, we are sick. Our hearts are crushed by
> suffering as we see our tubercular wives giving birth, our children dying,
> our sons and daughters growing up weak and without a future...." "But,
> despite all this, *we believe in the God of life....*" Holy Father, may your
> visit once again make the words of Jesus effective among us: "Today, the
> prophecy you have just heard is fulfilled...." "Our *hunger for God* and our
> *hunger for bread* will both be heeded."[23]

---

23. Quoted, with emphases, in Gustavo Gutiérrez, *The God of Life,* trans. Matthew J. O'Connell
(Maryknoll, N.Y.: Orbis, 1996), xi–xii.

Sometimes people know God's presence, and are thus encouraged to hunger for more of the life that God promises. Sometimes people cannot *know* God's presence; they can only *yearn* for it. Even so, people in great need are often profoundly grateful for small blessings that touch their lives.

My interviews with people in South Africa confirm the insight of the Cheros: the people who radiated gratitude for changes in South Africa were often those who live close to the bone of hardship, either by necessity or by a choice to walk in solidarity with people who struggle.[24] When we asked people to reflect on postapartheid life, people still threatened by poverty and oppression offered hope-filled replies. Seemingly, *the act of yearning and giving thanks for the God of Life enhances people's discernment of and plea for God's bounties, even amid deprivation.*

A second question is *whether gratitude requires a sense of God's overwhelming distinction and distance from creation.* Much theology that emphasizes God's majesty and generosity, as that of von Hügel (above), also emphasizes God's otherness. This raises a fundamental theological issue. Certainly in the opening stories, Steve and Al experienced God as *both* awesome and present in the minutes of their days. When God spoke to Moses from the burning bush, the experience was awesome and strange, but also *present* to Moses in an earthy way (Exod. 3:1–6). As awe-inspiring as God is, God's Spirit flows *in and through* creation. This assertion reiterates the discussion of immanence and transcendence in chapter 3, and joins with Ada María Isasi-Díaz in describing God's transcendence as radically immanent.[25] *Divine movements flow under, over, within and beside God's creation, thoroughly present, even when surpassing human abilities to sense and name them.* These God-movements propel many feminist theologians to rethink God-language and concepts, uncovering the mystery that is shrouded by dominant metaphors and conceptualizations for God.[26] Divine presence is so full that it bursts *all* theological descriptions and dwells among us in mystery.

2. People Need Thanksgiving

We have focused thus far on the reality of God's bounties and those of creation, but another reality presses on human life; that is the *human need for thanksgiving.* Theologies of distance — assuming that God is great, powerful, and far away — place emphasis on correct belief (in the greatness of God) and action (humble service). Theologies of closeness call forth a different emphasis, one of God-awareness, world-awareness, and self-awareness. Such awareness evokes

---

24. This study, conducted in Spring 2001, was too partial to draw extensive conclusions; however, I interviewed, or listened to interviews (some lasting several hours) and presentations, of nine people working in Cape Town townships and settings of social challenge. I also have drawn on several academic analyses.

25. Ada María Isasi-Díaz, *En la Lucha: In the Struggle: A Hispanic Women's Liberation Theology* (Minneapolis: Fortress, 1993), 154–56, 178–79.

26. Elizabeth A. Johnson, *She Who Is: The Mystery of God in Feminist Theological Discourse* (New York: Crossroad, 1992).

gratitude too deep for words, sometimes too deep to sense in the more conscious range of human feeling. This truism is evidenced in reflecting on contemplative life, psychology, and education. David Steindl-Rast, monk and psychologist, sees gratefulness as the heart of prayer, binding the giver and receiver of thanks into a relationship of interdependence.[27] Psychological studies reveal a relation among a person's environment (warmth, encouragement, and affection), their ways of seeing the world (more positively or negatively), and their participation in altruistic behavior.[28] These studies suggest that a spirit of gratitude for life might emerge from and contribute to a positive relationship with the world. Educator Steven Levy makes similar connections. He argues that an absence of gratitude represents impoverishment: "I have come to see that if the blessings in life do not awaken a sense of gratitude and compassion, they actually work like a curse."[29]

This affirmation also leads to questions. First, *what are the effects of gratitude?* Countless religious experiences testify to the power of thanksgiving in uplifting and empowering people. Consider one — the testimony of Zilpha Elaw, an African American preacher of the early nineteenth century. Elaw was a traveling preacher when women were clearly not encouraged to travel; further, her calling led her into slave-holding states to proclaim the Gospel. Elaw's courage for ministry was nourished in camp meetings. In her memoirs about these meetings, she expressed an overwhelming spirit of gratitude.

[In the camp meetings] many thousands assemble in the open air, and beneath the overspreading bowers, to own and worship our common Lord, the Proprietor of the Universe; there all arise and sing the solemn praises of the King of majesty and glory. It is like heaven descended upon an earthly soil, when all unite to "Praise God, from whom all blessings flow."

---

27. David Steindl-Rast, *Gratefulness, the Heart of Prayer: An Approach to Life in Fullness* (New York: Paulist, 1984). For Steindl-Rast, gratitude engenders vulnerability and belonging — a repeating theme in his writing. He says: "In giving gifts, we give what we can spare, but in giving thanks we give ourselves. One who says 'Thank you' to another really says, 'We belong together'" (17). See also David Steindl-Rast, *A Listening Heart: The Spirituality of Sacred Sensuousness* (New York: Crossroad, 1999, 1983), 112–25.

28. Reviews can be found in Pearl M. Oliner and Samuel P. Oliner, "Promoting Extensive Altruistic Bonds: A Conceptual Elaboration and Some Pragmatic Implications," in *Embracing the Other: Philosophical, Psychological, and Historical Perspectives on Altruism*, ed. Pearl M. Oliner, Samuel P. Oliner, Lawrence Baron, Lawrence A. Blum, Dennis L. Krebs, and M. Zuzanna Smolenska (New York: New York University Press, 1992), 369–89; Ervin Staub, "The Origins of Caring, Helping, and Nonaggression: Parental Socialization, the Family System, Schools, and Cultural Influence," in ibid., 390–412.

29. Steven Levy, *Starting from Scratch: One Classroom Builds Its Own Curriculum* (Portsmouth, N.H.: Heinemann, 1996), 98–116. In this chapter, Levy describes gratitude issues in fourth grade classrooms. In the book, he draws from twenty plus years of studying and practicing teaching. Levy has taught all grade levels; has designed award-winning curricula; and has been awarded Teacher of the Year for Massachusetts, John F. Kennedy prize for teaching history, and Outstanding General Elementary Teacher by Walt Disney Company. His approach to gratitude is to involve students in action learning regarding how things are produced, and in historical study of communities' origins and ways of life over time.

In this passage, Zilpha Elaw implicitly describes the human need for praise, likening the community's singing of "Praise God..." to the descending of heaven. Elaw further elaborates on effects of the community's praise: "The hardest hearts are melted into tenderness, the driest eyes overflow with tears, and the loftiest spirits bow down: the Creator's works are gazed upon, and His near presence felt around."[30]

Here we see a power imbued to the "hardest hearts," "driest eyes," and "loftiest spirits." People are *softened, moved,* and *humbled* in the act of praise. Elaw's testimony uncovers the transformative power of thanksgiving. When linked with the woman who kept a gratitude journal, Elaw's testimony reveals a God who responds to human praise with overflowing generosity. In the face of harshness, God responds to human needs with presence — offering peace and confidence (the woman who recorded daily blessings after losing her job) or a softened heart and humbled spirit (camp meetings). In all of these cases, an internal impulse led people to express thanksgiving; the act of expressing thanks was further rewarded by what the people themselves interpreted as a divine response. *The act of thanksgiving awakens people to their need and others' need to express gratitude, and to God's grateful response to them.*

The discussion leads to another question: *To what extent does conscious feeling motivate gratitude?* The cases of this chapter suggest a complex interplay between the conscious and unconscious. Thanksgiving is more than feeling. It is *knowing* that God moves in the world, even when our senses and feelings of devotion and praise are dull. Thanksgiving runs deep, like a vein of strong stone running through rock and soil. It is not always visible, but it provides the solid ground upon which life can be built.

Evelyn Underhill wrote similar ideas to a worried correspondent (M.R.) in 1909: "If by losing the spirit of prayer you mean losing the heavenly sensations of deep devotion I am afraid that does not matter a scrap." She proceeded to speak of prayer as a part of spiritual routine:

> I think you are really getting on all right: but you must be prepared for a steady dying down of glamour and a throwing of you more and more on the normal resources of life. If your prayers really do the day's work for you — what more do you want?[31]

---

30. Zilpha Elaw, "Conversion and Call," in *Can I Get a Witness? Prophetic Religious Voices of African American Women — An Anthology,* ed. Marcia Y. Riggs (Maryknoll, N.Y.: Orbis, 1997), 11; cf. Zilpha Elaw, "Memoirs of the Life, Religious Experience, Ministerial Travels, and Labours of Mrs. Zilpha Elaw, an American Female of Colour; Together with Some Account of the Great Religious Revivals in America [Written by Herself] (1846)," in *Sisters of the Spirit: Three Black Women's Autobiographies of the Nineteenth Century,* ed. William L. Andrews (Bloomington: Indiana University Press, 1986), 64–67.

31. Evelyn Underhill, "To M.R. (Thursday night, 1909)," in *The Letters of Evelyn Underhill,* ed. Charles Williams (London: Longmans, Green, 1943), 103–4.

Here we see the possibility of daily thankfulness — a spirit that occasionally flares in dramatic sensation, but is mostly routine and modest in tone. This gratitude does not rely on dramatic feeling, but on the bounties of God and God's creation, daily given. *The act of giving thanks is marked by the ability to express praise and gratitude, even when one feels little or nothing to inspire those expressions.*

The first two theological affirmations are intertwined. The bounties of God and creation are interwoven with human needs. Plentitude inspires people to practice thanksgiving, as in the opening cases and biblical accounts of Noah, Abram, and the woman who anointed Jesus. Likewise, the human need to express gratitude turns people to spiritual practices (even routine prayer), which awaken them to God's gifts. This is what Underhill wanted M.R. to understand, rather than fretting about undramatic religious feelings. Together, God's generous actions and the human exercise of gratitude establish a root system to support the continuing growth of thanksgiving

3. God Is Generous and Calls Creation to Generosity

The third affirmation is an extension of the other two — that *God is generous and calls creation to generous living.* To say that thanksgiving is rooted in the bounties of God and God's creation is to emphasize God's generosity rather than human needs and desires. Indeed, those who hoard the bounties of this earth or deny bounty to others, are abandoning the spirituality of thanksgiving for a spirituality of materialism, placing their trust in possessing *things* rather than praising the Creator and giving thanks for creation. *Thanksgiving is marked by such appreciation for God's generous gifts that people seek to share those gifts generously with others.*

Divine generosity is a reality to appreciate but neither to possess nor control. Temptations to possess and control God's gifts are great, akin to Jesus' temptations in the wilderness at the beginning of his ministry (Matt. 4:1–11; Luke 4:1–13). Temptations can be so subtle that they emerge gradually and people do not recognize them as temptations, or they develop rationalizations. People may identify God's generosity as deserved blessings, or as special privileges and responsibilities that God has given to them or to their community or nation. When that happens, thanksgiving is narrowed to that which serves oneself and one's own, yielding a spirit of selfishness (sometimes called enlightened self-interest or *noblesse oblige*) that damages others.

Societies sometimes elaborate the spirit of selfishness into a comprehensive worldview with far-reaching effects. Such a worldview allows many of us in the United States to thank God for wealth, good fortune, or good health, while conducting ourselves in ways that oppress others. One can find this ideology in railroad barons and water barons of the nineteenth century, who were sometimes convinced that the privileges they enjoyed were gifts of God to be enjoyed and shared (but only from the overflow of vast accumulation). Such a worldview has allowed the United States at times to pursue international policies that hurt some countries while supporting those that support us. In so doing, the assumptive worldview is often abundantly clear — we are a blessed nation that must protect the blessings we have been given. This view takes many forms; one of the most common is claiming to be blessed as a beacon of freedom, which we must protect for others and ourselves. We fail to recognize that our own practices of freedom sometimes fail, or we protect national interests while obstructing the freedom of others.

Returning to the generosity of God is one of the most effective antidotes to selfish preoccupation. God's generosity inspires thanksgiving, and thanksgiving inspires generous living. Generosity is thus born in gratitude and expansive love, not in guilt and shame.[32] Guilt is appropriate when people destroy the ability of others to receive and enjoy God's gifts. Shame is appropriate when people hoard God's bounties from others and focus their lives on human-constructed goods (that which is less than good) and on human-constructed images of the good life (that which is less than the image of God). Both guilt and shame appropriately evoke confession. God's generosity evokes gratitude and generosity — the hallmarks of a spirituality of thanksgiving.

Hermeneutic of Thanksgiving

The hermeneutic of thanksgiving is a way to *search for bounties for which to be thankful* and to *respond with gratitude to gifts in the present and past*. In the cases with which this chapter began, thanksgiving was not the first response of the two men confronted with devastating news about their health; yet both men yearned for hope. In their search, they found much for which they were thankful. This is the heart of a hermeneutic of thanksgiving — the search for hope, even in desolation, and the yearning to find that which fills life with joy, even in moments of great sadness.

The hermeneutic of thanksgiving is grounded in a sense of God's powerful love, expressed well by Evelyn Underhill, who herself knew struggles:

> Not to me
> The Unmoved Mover of philosophy
> And absolute still sum of all that is,
> The God whom I adore — not this!
> Nay, rather a great moving wave of bliss,
> A surging torrent of dynamic love
> In passionate swift career,

---

32. See Steindl-Rast, *Gratefulness*, 163–89; Oliner and Oliner, *Embracing the Other*, 370–86. Both direct and indirect evidence exists for these claims; an extensive review of the social-psychological literature is needed in the future.

> That down the sheer
> And fathomless abyss
> Of Being ever pours, his ecstasy to prove.[33]

This poem reveals more than a theory of God; it reveals the *movement* of God's love. Underhill is not moved by "the Unmoved Mover of philosophy" but by "a great moving wave of bliss" — the God who stirs in her soul and pours over creation. In this spirit, Underhill echoes Julian of Norwich, who also focused on bliss — Jesus as "supreme bliss," people as Jesus' bliss, and Jesus' work as drawing people "into his bliss."[34]

I have turned to Underhill to reflect on thanksgiving because she had the unusual experience of writing systematic works in theology while participating actively in spiritual direction, speaking, and mentoring people who were active seekers and teachers. The very breadth of her experience — and the struggles of her life as an early academic woman, a person faced with debilitating illness, and an ardent pacifist during World War II — honed her spirituality of thanksgiving. Hers was not a simplistic thankfulness, but one painted with the rich colors that come from wrestling with oneself and others. She was thus able to express her spirituality in many different forms and venues. Underhill was a fellow of King's College, London; translated and edited critical editions of classic spiritual works; wrote extensive studies of mysticism and worship; participated actively in the church; corresponded with spiritual friends; and reflected with teachers about their distinctive roles in teaching the young. In short, she functioned as a practical theologian, and her works ranged from the systematic to the concretely practical.

I am struck that Underhill's communication with teachers is even permeated with what I am calling a hermeneutic of thanksgiving. She describes this as a "spirit of worship." The purpose of education is thus "to set up a full, true relation between pupil and environment; and for Christians, the ultimate fact about that environment is, that it is the work of God, indwelt by God, and a means of serving, knowing and glorifying God." Thankfulness, then, is more than believing in God or adoring God at a distance. It is alertness to the world: "Few people look, most of them only glance: but looking is the first step to worship." This leads to a God-centered educational process — "conscious of mystery, coloured by worship" — as opposed to a human-centered process that focuses on human interests and opportunities, material progress and exploitation.[35]

---

33. Evelyn Underhill, *Theophanies: A Book of Verses* (London: J. M. Dent & Sons, 1916), 3, cf. 3–4.

34. Julian, *Showings*, 230–31; cf. 216–20.

35. Evelyn Underhill, "Education and the Spirit of Worship," in *Collected Papers of Evelyn Underhill*, ed. Lucy Menzies (London: Longmans, Green, 1946), 190–92; cf. 188–207. This essay was originally the Winifred Mercier Memorial Lecture, Whitelands College, Putney, November 1937.

I quibble with Underhill's sharp distinction between God-centered and human-centered education, for human life can itself reveal God. Further, focusing on human concerns (whether poverty, alienation, depression, or political oppression) can illumine God's will for the world. On the other hand, Underhill is advocating, as I am, for teachers to practice a hermeneutic of thanksgiving, searching for that which awakens hope and stirs awe. This does not require a particular set of Christian or religious beliefs; it simply requires an openness to wonder and a yearning for hope, even when troubles weigh heavily on oneself or one's community.

Educational Practices:
Teaching through Thanksgiving

The presentation thus far might be summarized simply. Thanksgiving is a great and glorious practice that begins with God, is made possible by God, and is really a lot of fun (rewarding). Thanksgiving finds expression in the gathered worship of the church, particularly in seasons of Epiphany and Eastertide, and is embodied in baptism and eucharist. The discussion draws from sources often kept separate — from life situations and from systematic and liturgical theology. Such integrative analysis illumines spiritual life, but continues some separations, focusing largely on worship (service to God) in the gathered community. If we stop here, we obscure the sacramentality of all of life and the community's service to God in the larger world. If worship is done by the scattered community as much as the gathered one, and if sacramental living is as important to Christian vocation as celebrating the formal sacraments, then giving thanks is a sacramental practice for *all* aspects of life. It is part of the human vocation and is simply revealed and intensified by gathered worship and the celebration of sacraments.

To prepare and support people in this vocation, we need teaching that *inspires people to Holy awe — trusting God's love, celebrating God's gifts, and sharing those gifts with generous spirits.* Over twenty-five years of teaching, I have asked students to recall a significant teacher in their lives and then to describe that person and analyze the values in his or her teaching. Whenever I have done this (at least a dozen times), the most frequently named characteristic is that the teacher *appreciated,* or *cared about,* me or us. Students said: "the teacher loved us," "enjoyed our company," "saw the good in us that we could not see ourselves," "encouraged us to appreciate ourselves and to be the people we could be."[36] These words express thanksgiving — teachers' being thankful for their students and helping them be thankful for themselves and the world. Interestingly, this takes many

---

36. Quotes taken from transcripts of student reports, drawn from the eight sets of reports (totaling 221 students) that were gathered and tabulated according to themes. One chapter reader, Debra Fiske Gara, also asks children's teachers to recall outstanding teachers; she receives similar responses. She further draws analogies: that people learn God "from teachers who believe in them and honor who they are."

forms — gentle encouragement, bold challenge, or refusing to help students do something they can better do themselves. Whatever the form, teachers' gratitude for students endures, as does their encouragement of gratitude in the learning community. One of my friends models this spirit. She has taught kindergarten for thirty years, and she giggles when she tells stories about the amazing moments she experiences with children in her classroom. The wonder she experiences is fresh each day. This is thanksgiving!

Not only can teaching be an act of thanksgiving, but the church's liturgies of thanks and praise are also acts of teaching and learning. We find this accent in liturgical theology, as when Don Saliers claims that "praise, thanksgiving, and 'blessing God' are themselves forms of knowing God." He builds on this idea by drawing an explicit connection between acts of worship and teaching, claiming that liturgical acts teach people to pray. He refers particularly to passional knowing — or forming one's life according to God's ways; this is "a process of being formed in specific affections and dispositions...that manifests 'what is known about God.'" For Saliers, this includes forming affections of gratitude and praise through ritual gesture, which eventually leads to "a capacity for sustained gratitude, in season and out of season" and a greater sense of truth regarding "how things are." This leads further to the reshaping of our lives and relationships, as modeled in the eucharistic prayers — the most intense and inclusive thanksgiving in Christian tradition — with their focus on God's self-giving.[37]

Thanksgiving thus takes place in rituals, both in those most often associated with teaching (when teachers and students gather in a classroom, camp, or retreat center) and in rituals of worship. Both form our ways of knowing and relating with God and the world. Rather than focus on the diverse settings themselves, we turn now to three educational practices that can be enacted in many different settings: practices of trust, gratitude, and generosity. Each of these is grounded in the praise practices of the church and a deep sense of God's bounties and the bounties of God's world.

1. Practice Trust

Teaching trust is *inspiring and guiding people to trust that God will act and God will call forth, empower, and be thankful for our action.* Practicing trust thus begins with a sense of the ever flowing, overflowing gush of God's love. Unfortunately, we often turn to this divine spring with low expectations, or with expectations only for ourselves and those we love. We can also be debilitated when we realize that God does not have all the power in this world. Indeed, real evil exists and tragic events occur without God's blessing. What is often missed is that God's persuasive power can still transform the world. This reality can creep up on us in unexpected times, however, when we find ourselves trusting God spontaneously

---

37. Saliers, *Worship as Theology*, 86–89; cf. 85–105.

in vulnerable moments. Stories told by people escaping hurricanes, earthquakes, or human-made disasters attest to this wonder. People are unexpectedly overcome with trust in God.

Trust in God can also be a way of life, as it was for Al and Steve in the opening cases. Trust allowed their spirits to thrive under debilitating circumstances, trusting in the ever-moving, ever-working love of God for strength. Trust is not passive, however. It calls forth the active participation of people and other creatures in the work of God. We saw this even in Steve's active decision to trust God's goodness when his body would no longer function.

Trusting God also involves acting toward God's future, even when possibilities of abundant love, justice, and peace seem remote. Many years ago, Carter Heyward wrote *The Redemption of God*, arguing that God *needs* human beings to do the work of redemption in this torn apart world.[38] She argued that God, whose power is in relation, needs people to exercise their power for the good of creation. With her, I affirm that human beings are actors in the drama of human and cosmic history. What we do will unearth hidden possibilities, clear pathways for God's fullness, and contribute, however modestly, to the future. What we do not do will be left undone, at least until God finds another way. Trusting God involves high expectation of God, and expectation for human life lived in and with God. On the rush of a mighty river or the trickle of a threatened stream, transformation can come!

What does this suggest for the practical art of teaching? It suggests the urgency of cultivating a trusting spirit in community life and encouraging people to live boldly for justice and peace, even when risks are high. Such action can inspire trust in divine reality and in eschatological visions that transcend immediate and tangible results (or the lack thereof). The practical arts of teaching require much from teachers, especially cultivating their own practices of trust and building trust relations within the learning community. Evelyn Underhill speaks of the "three great marks" of a teacher's life: regular and humble worship of God, self-giving to God, and service to and cooperation with God. She adds that an "even more important" quality is a " 'right attitude' to God." These are all marks of trust. In Underhill's view, they are qualities critical for teachers and for "the little growing spirits for whom you are responsible to God."[39] The educational practices that emerge are important to teachers and students alike, whether "little growing spirits" or wise old adults.

---

38. Isabel Carter Heyward, *The Redemption of God: A Theology of Mutual Relation* (Washington, D.C.: University Press of America, 1982).

39. Underhill, "The Spiritual Life of the Teacher," in *Collected Papers of Evelyn Underhill*, ed. Lucy Menzies (London: Longmans, Green, 1946), 172–73. This address was originally delivered to the South London Centre of the Guild of the Epiphany. Underhill appended a note explaining that the address, including material from other addresses, was not written for publication.

Cultivate Trust in God

Teaching first *awakens people to the trustworthiness of God.* Such practices are more often taken for granted than consciously developed, and teachers often focus more on spiritual-moral formation than on cultivating trust. Marsha Woodard accents trust in African American faith experience, however. She urges people to "develop our legacy of faith" — a legacy grounded in thanksgiving to God, and growing through acts of trust.[40] Woodard closes one sermon with her hope that children will be blessed with the legacy of trust sung in the gospel song: "Through it all, through it all, Oh I've learned to trust in Jesus, I've learned to trust in God."[41] Yolanda Smith similarly accents the spirituals, which support trust in God through the interplay of African, African American, and Christian heritage.[42] David Steindl-Rast heralds similar ideas, affirming that learning to trust God is a foundation for gratitude.[43] Drawing from these theories, and from cases of this chapter, we are urged *to speak trust, sing trust, live trust, and thereby to teach trust.*

These ruminations lead back to the importance of cultivating teachers' trust, which can be done in many ways — through hiking, study, music, dance, prayer, and contemplation. Evelyn Underhill urged teachers to nourish their sense of God through a "secret life of prayer" and participation "in the great life of the Church." She identified a "deep, wide and steady devotional life" as the essential foundation for teaching and for trust. Although Underhill was less critical of the "great life of the Church" than many people today would be, she urged a trust in God that was not bounded by the institutional church. She was more concerned with movements that "make up the full life of our souls": (1) unconditional and trustful self-giving to God; (2) communing with God in meditation and silence; and (3) co-operation with God as tools and channels.[44]

Cultivating trust in God involves attending to God and probing one's doubts and faith. In turn, trust offers hope in moments of despair. In a sequel to one of the opening cases, Al describes a session when he and his Alzheimer's support group shared stories. Two people shared "how crummy it was to have this disease." Al agreed. He recalled how he had begun with denial, finally concluding that "having the disease had something to do with me being a bad person." Others could identify with his story. With guidance from the group and its leaders, however,

---

40. Marsha Woodard, "No Greater Legacy," in *Can I Get a Witness? Prophetic Religious Voices of African American Women — An Anthology,* ed. Marcia Y. Riggs (Maryknoll, N.Y.: Orbis, 1997), 102; cf. Ella Pearson Mitchell, ed., *Those Preachin' Women: More Sermons by Black Women Preachers,* vol. 2 (Valley Forge, Pa.: Judson, 1988), 35–39. Woodard's work focused in Baptist congregations and the Division of Church Education of the American Baptist Churches in the U.S.A.

41. Woodard, "No Greater Legacy," 102.

42. Yolanda Y. Smith, *Reclaiming the Spirituals: New Possibilities for African American Christian Education* (Cleveland: Pilgrim, 2004).

43. Steindl-Rast, *Gratefulness,* 84–122, 163–64.

44. Underhill, "The Spiritual Life of the Teacher," 173, 176.

Al discovered that the fault is the *disease,* not the person. Al also had another thought building inside; this had to do with trusting God. For the first time, he shared his faith explicitly with the group: "Being sick, but knowing God's love, is a far better thing than being in perfect health but neither seeing nor caring about the wonder of God's love and guidance."[45] Such trust in God does not arise instantaneously; it is cultivated over time. This is the work of sacred teaching.

Cultivate Trust in Community

Just as cultivating trust in God is important, so is cultivating trust in community — *building communities that practice and nourish trust, even when they fail and have to try again.* God's life is thoroughly interwoven with human and natural communities; thus, to trust the Creator is to trust the sacredness of creation. Although people and other creatures are not so trustworthy as God, their earthy lives are intertwined with the life of God, as threads are interwoven in a rug or vines twist together on the forest floor. Evelyn Underhill compares this relationship with a fabric woven with golden threads. She encourages people to develop inward and outward lives "like one of those beautiful shot materials in which the gold thread runs one way and the coloured thread runs the other way, and both together make a fabric more beautiful than each would make alone."[46] The accent here is on divine-human communion: God and humanity are interwoven. According to Underhill, spiritual education helps people weave the threads evenly throughout the fabric. I take this further; spiritual education helps people weave threads from *all* God's creation into the fabric; thus, *communing with other people, with animals and plants, with wind and soil cultivates trust in God and in God's creation.*

In light of this discussion, sacred teaching is God-centered and simultaneously grounded in community. The practice of trust invites trust in creation — attuning with one's community and the rhythms of nature so as to relate respectfully, caringly, and collaboratively. Such trust is not naïve, but is real and respectful, while also pointing to what God's creation can yet be. Teaching is an act of appreciating a community, seeing possibilities, and encouraging people to live toward those possibilities.

Nowhere is this view of teaching more evident than in the quintessential teacher, Mary McLeod Bethune, who founded Bethune-Cookman College and the National Council of Negro Women. At the age of seventy-six, she pondered the legacy she wanted to leave her people — faith, racial dignity, a desire to live harmoniously with others, love, hope, the challenge of developing confidence in one another, a thirst for education, a respect for the use of power, and a responsibility to her people. These qualities speak of gratitude; they do so by encouraging trust in God, oneself, one's community, and the larger global community. Bethune

---

45. Al Rhodes-Wickett, Letter to Mary Elizabeth Moore, January 20, 2002.
46. Underhill, "The Spiritual Life of the Teacher," 178; cf. 178–79.

says, "God is the greatest power, but great too, is faith in oneself." She also emphasizes that the black community must be "interracial, interreligious, and international," while offering practical help to one another (as in Negro banks, insurance companies, and so forth), not allowing economic separatism, but helping one another even as the community spreads.[47] In this view, building trust is essential to education, and it takes the form of eschatological vision and practical proposals regarding how people can work together.

Educational practices of cultivating trust in God and community will take many forms, but will surely include prayer and meditation, collaborative learning, working together on shared projects, peer mentoring, building partnerships with the larger community, and building relations with communities different from one's own. This is a tall order, but these various practices interweave with one another. The result will surely be greater trust in the Creator and created community, whose mutual respect and cooperation are essential for the whole community's quality of life.

2. Search for Creation's Bounties and Spread Gratitude

The second teaching practice is *to search actively for creation's bounties, and to spread a spirit of gratitude*. To do this is to embody a hermeneutic of thanksgiving, looking at the world with gratitude in one's soul and inviting others to do the same. The story of the woman who kept a gratitude journal is but one example. The woman knew that her life was grim at that moment; what she wanted and needed was to know that life was still good. The search for gratitude eventually led her to *feel* gratitude.

Searching for gratitude is enacted in disciplines of discerning and appreciating creation's bounties; spreading gratitude is enacted by engaging others in celebration. Such disciplines evoke respect for the thinness of everyday moments and places. In Celtic tradition, certain holy places are known as "thin," meaning that God touches close to the earth in these places. I join with Evelyn Underhill, however, who said: "I am far from denying that from our human point of view, some places are a great deal thinner than others: but to the eyes of worship, the whole of the visible world, even its most unlikely patches, is rather thin.[48] I have surprised myself in dialoguing so actively with Underhill in this book. I earlier judged her work as overly conventional and out of date; however, her emphasis on the spirit of worship returned me to her. In teaching, this spirit involves discerning the preciousness of the world and celebrating that world with others.

---

47. Mary McLeod Bethune, "My Last Will and Testament," in *Can I Get a Witness? Prophetic Religious Voices of African American Women — An Anthology*, ed. Marcia Y. Riggs (Maryknoll, N.Y.: Orbis, 1997), 83–84; cf. 82–85. Excerpt is taken from the original mimeographed version distributed by the National Council of Negro Women, Inc.

48. Underhill, "Education and the Spirit of Worship," 196; cf. 194. This was first delivered as the Winifred Mercier Memorial Lecture, Whitelands College, Putney, November 1937.

Thus teachers respond to the human need for thanksgiving through disciplines of searching and spreading.

Search — Discern and Treasure Creation's Bounties

Sacred teaching requires teachers to *search — to discover, treasure, and build upon the sacred moments that arise in life and in the act of teaching.* These are glimpses of the Holy. Gratitude begins with treasuring the sensuous universe in which one lives.[49] It also takes very practical forms. When television star Victoria Rowell recently visited the David and Margaret Home, she spent most of the day with girls whose families are not able to care for them and girls embroiled in various legal and social problems. Rowell — known for roles in *The Young and the Restless, The Cosby Show,* and *Diagnosis Murder* — listened intently as she walked through the campus of David and Margaret and heard the girls' stories. When she spoke after lunch, she described her own experiences as a foster child and some life-changing opportunities; she challenged the youth not to allow "their traumatic life experiences to hold them back from pursuing their dreams." She urged them "to take advantage of every opportunity that was available, to accept help when it was offered, and to be thankful for the gifts that they have received."[50] Rowell has herself learned to seek and express gratitude and to encourage others to do the same.

Teachers are like travel guides, inspiring people to treasure the world and to dive into opportunities on their life journeys. Teachers can be tempted to take people "on a cheap personally conducted tour ... eliminating risk and fatigue, taking all the short cuts, and covering as much ground as possible in the shortest possible time." For Underhill, the alternative is love and freshness: "If you are really to lead your pupils to the mountains, it must be because you love the mountains; and every time you go there it is a fresh adventure."[51] To teach in this way is a privilege. Although we do not need Victoria Rowell and Evelyn Underhill to point the way, the striking similarity of their messages — drawn from different times, places, and life experiences — reveals the power of teachers to guide faith travelers into the joys of discerning and treasuring.

Spread — Engage People in Celebrating the Sacred

How do we cultivate a spirituality of thankfulness in others? For this, we need also to *spread gratitude — to engage others in celebrating the holiness of life.* As noted earlier, the Eucharist conveys grace whether we feel it or not. This is true of ordinary life as well. Teachers can thus encourage folks to celebrate even when they

---

49. Steindl-Rast, *A Listening Heart,* 8–81.

50. "A Tradition of New Beginnings," La Verne, Calif.: The David and Margaret Home, Fall 2001, 3

51. Underhill, "Education and the Spirit of Worship," 199, 201. She quotes Gerard Manley Hopkins to describe: "this world 'charged with the grandeur of God' which you are privileged to show to those you teach" (201).

do not feel joyful. This can involve ritual celebrations of birthdays, anniversaries, life changes (such as retirements and graduations), movements of peace, and moments of justice. It can also involve quieter forms of celebration, as embodied in Evelyn Underhill's story of Mother Janet Stuart. When a student was ill, Mother Stuart brought flowers to her every day:

> She only brought one of each kind, and about each she had something beautiful to reveal and interesting to say. But what the child remembered most vividly was the reverence and gentleness, the delighted love with which her visitor touched the flowers: that gave to her, as no words could ever have done, a sense of the wonder and holiness of living things.

Mother Stuart did not like nature study that pulled plants to pieces to study them; she felt that such an approach communicated only information. She wanted to communicate "the sense of the beauty and sacred character of all life."[52] This is the work of sacred teaching — to teach in such a way that people are inspired to appreciate the sacredness of life. Such thankfulness awakens people to creation's fullness — to thin moments and thin places where people can commune with God and one another.

3. Practice Generosity

Gratitude often leads to educational practices of generosity — *giving of oneself to the learning community and engaging with the community in generous action within and beyond itself.* When a teacher takes time to listen to someone's problem or discern dis-ease or excitement within the learning community, that is generosity. When teachers are so impassioned about their subject matter that they cannot wait to share it, that is generosity. When a community is impassioned by their study and collaborative projects, when they seek to share these bounties with others, that too is generosity.

The practice of generosity is intertwined with practices already identified — trusting and spreading gratitude. If one trusts that God provides, that God's creation is good, and that human community can thrive by sharing, then one is freer to share with others. A teacher who trusts the goodness of God and God's creation beneath the rabble of destruction is freed to practice generosity in acts of compassion that are like baptizing others.[53] A teacher who practices thankfulness is one who *wants* to be generous and encourage others' generosity.

The failure of trust and gratitude can impede generosity. Fear, for example, can destroy the spirit of generosity, especially fears that the supply of money or food is insufficient for everyone to share. On the other hand, generosity can be

---

52. Ibid., 195.

53. Simone Weil, *Waiting for God* (New York: Harper Colophon, 1973, 1951), 146. Weil emphasizes the relation among gratitude, compassion, and generosity, making sacramental connections in the process: "To treat our neighbor who is in affliction with love is something like baptizing him" (ibid.).

stirred by a spirit of trust and gratitude for what people *do* have, even if it is small by external measures. This is why wealthy people can sometimes be slower in generosity than the poor; they may be governed by internal attitudes of fear (turned at times to greed) rather than by the actual dollar figures in their bank accounts and the worth of their holdings. I do not suggest that people never face real reasons for fear, or that generosity should be naïve. Neither do I suggest that generosity will always emerge naturally from the practices of trusting and giving thanks. The central point is that trust and gratitude are attitudes toward the world that make a difference. They are attitudes shaped by realism about what the world *is*, but they allow people not to be fully determined by the size of their bank accounts or the amount of free time they have. Practices of trust and gratitude cultivate the soul so generosity can grow; likewise, the practice of generosity inspires trust and gratitude. The three practices are thus inseparable in teaching and learning. With that relationship in mind, we focus on generosity practices.

Encourage Response to God's Generosity

Remember the woman who anointed Jesus! According to the story in Luke 7, the woman was aglow with generosity, stirred by the generosity of God who had forgiven her so much. Extrapolating from this text, God's generosity inspires and requires human generosity in response. Such generosity encourages generous giving (as in the woman's giving), but also generous receiving. Jesus, in Luke's story, gave to the woman by generously receiving her anointing. Without assuming simplistic mandates to imitate Jesus' particular actions, one might conclude that teachers and learning communities are called to *practice generosity in giving, receiving, listening, sharing, collaborating, and engaging compassionately with others.*

What is being suggested here involves charity, but it also involves justice-making, protesting, tearing down, and rebuilding. The woman in Jesus' story was breaking social conventions — causing a stir — as was Jesus. The generosity practiced by each of them was unconventional and their actions threatened to upset the social order, encouraging the larger society also to be more generous. Jesus in this text reveals the depth and complexity of God's generosity — the ability to see the woman for who she was, to ignore social and religious conventions that would deny her access, to receive her gift, to declare that she was forgiven. The woman similarly reveals the depth and complexity of human generosity — the ability to see Jesus for who he was, to ignore social and religious conventions in order to minister to him, to give what she had to give, and to appreciate God's gift of forgiveness. We see here a multifaceted generosity. It has to do with attitudes toward others, engaging in concrete acts of giving and receiving, and delighting in the restoration of relationships (as in the acts of giving and receiving forgiveness).

Multiply the Generosity of Creation

As generosity is grounded in the God-human relationship, so it is nourished by the generosity of God's creation. Teachers and learners are challenged to *respect and multiply creation's goodness,* not simply to bask in it. They are called to understand the significance of what Jesus did when he fed five thousand and four thousand hungry people — taking what small gifts could be found, giving thanks, and multiplying them for others (Mark 6:30–44; Matt. 14:13–21; Luke 9:10–17; John 6:1–13; Mark 8:1–10; Matt. 15:32–39).[54] These feeding stories reveal a multiplication of creation's gifts similar to my friend's gratitude journal, which allowed her to focus on the small gifts of creation and, thus, to multiply and share them with others.

Such generosity is born of respect for God's creation, as proclaimed in the Psalms: "The heavens are telling the glory of God; and the firmament proclaims [God's] handiwork" (19:1) or "I lift up my eyes to the hills" (121:1).[55] The second of these psalms has complex interpretations, but Evelyn Underhill reads it as I often do — as a devotional mantra of appreciation for God's presence in creation. She says that we do not look to the hills because of the science of geology, the rich flora, the possibility of mining operations, or even their contribution to good health. Rather, we look to the hills "in a spirit of humble contemplation, delighting in the solemn beauty, the independent reality of that which lies beyond myself."[56]

Such contemplative practices are difficult, requiring time and discipline, but they foster respect for creation. Without the capacity for worship, Underhill believes that people "starve their real teaching power at its source; and therefore risk starving their pupils, just at that point where they most need to be fed." Generous teaching requires grateful participation in the "living, growing universe" and in Christianity as a living religion. This is responsibility and sacred trust, for "a bit of this creative work is given to every teacher."[57] Respect for God's creation deepens relations in the natural world and in learning communities, thus magnifying generosity in daily living.

Generosity is also born of respect for the larger community, as revealed in the lives of many justice advocates through history. Fannie Barrier Williams, a persistent advocate for women's rights in the late nineteenth and early twentieth centuries, urged African American women to work for the social betterment of their whole race. She emphasized the necessity of duty, action, and sympathy for that work, but she insisted that sympathy must include respect for the dignity of other persons. In the words of this chapter, we could say that sympathy needs to

---

54. More detailed analysis of these texts and their connection with multiplying God's gifts is found in Mary Elizabeth Moore, *Ministering with the Earth* (St. Louis, Mo.: Chalice, 1998), 40–44.

55. The role of psalms in celebrating God's creation is developed in ibid., 23–26, 97–99.

56. Underhill, "Education and the Spirit of Worship," 197–98.

57. Ibid., 198, 207.

be infused with trust and gratitude. In Williams's words, sympathy is a spirit of being *with* others:

> By sympathy is not meant that far-away, kid-gloved and formal something that enables women merely to know of those who need them, but that deeper and more spiritual impulse to helpfulness that will enable them to find delight in working *with*, rather than *for*, the unfortunate of their sex. In social reforms we must see but one thing, and that is the vivid soul of humanity — that divinity which neither rags, dirt nor immoralities can entirely obscure.[58]

Williams knew that much would have to be unlearned in order for this vision to be made real. This would require understanding social questions in new ways, not based in congeniality, but in love — a "sisterhood and brotherhood based on something deeper than selfish preferences."[59] Such generosity is akin to the educational vision of Paulo Freire, who criticized the "false generosity" of people in power toward those who are oppressed.[60] Williams and Freire both call for a generosity of solidarity, recognizing and multiplying the goodness of others rather than giving them leftovers.

Being in solidarity with others comes naturally when people see the divine nature of others, akin to Jesus' ability to see the sacred nature of the woman's anointing act. Divine energy awakens people to others' needs and to their own yearning to respond as attested by Fannie Barrier Williams: "If we can so expand our hearts to this divine energy, we shall discover all the needs of the human heart and be able to apply the remedies to every secret cause of misfortune." This means that people need to unlearn ingrained patterns and attune to divine energy, but they also need to study and prepare for social reform, which requires "not only aroused hearts, but an aroused and penetrating intelligence."[61] The whole self and the whole community are needed to attune to God's generosity and to multiply the generosity of God's creation.

Concluding Reflections

The danger of a chapter on giving thanks is that it could encourage naiveté and positive thinking that ignore tragedy. The stories of this chapter, and the very history of church practices — Epiphany, Eastertide, eucharist, and baptism — are

---

58. Fannie Barrier Williams, "The Awakening of Women," in *Can I Get a Witness? Prophetic Religious Voices of African American Women — An Anthology*, ed. Marcia Y. Riggs (Maryknoll, N.Y.: Orbis, 1997), 114, emphasis added; cf. *A.M.E. Church Review* 13 (1896–97): 392–98.

59. Williams, "The Awakening of Women," 115.

60. Paulo Freire, *Pedagogy of the Oppressed*, trans. Myra Bergman Ramos (New York: Continuum, 2000, 1970), 26–27.

61. Williams, "The Awakening of Women," 115–16.

far from naïve. They are genuinely celebrative, as is the praise of God in ordinary days. At the same time, they are grounded in the verity that true thanksgiving arises from realities of the world, which all too often include tragedy. The challenge of this chapter is to see thanksgiving as a vital part of sacramental living and teaching. Thanksgiving complements the acts of expecting the unexpected, remembering the dismembered, and seeking reversals. It grows from and feeds these acts, while grounding sacramental living in the bounties of God and God's creation, which make it possible. Awaking people to God's gifts, thanksgiving prepares the way for another sacramental act, nourishing life.

Reflecting Further

The reflection opportunities described below include one set on Epiphany as it interplays with human life journeys, and one on the practice of thanksgiving.

1. The season of Epiphany is a season of spreading the light of Christ. It is also the season when Christians remember Jesus' baptism, marking the beginning of his ministry. Epiphany is thus a time for remembering Jesus' journey and reflecting on our journeys. You might reflect on Epiphany in three different ways:

    (a) Reflect on the gospel song, "Go Tell It on the Mountain," and on Isaiah 42, esp. verses 5–12. What do these reveal about God and the world, Epiphany, and the spirit of thanksgiving? What do they ask of me (us)?

    (b) Meditate in silence on the poem "Epiphany Journey":

    > Epiphany — the season of spreading light,
    >   and remembering three sages who followed a star
    >   to the foot of a manger;
    > Epiphany — the season of Jesus' baptism
    >   and descending doves,
    > Epiphany — the season of Jesus' ministry begun —
    >   Blessed by the gifts of wise men from the East,
    >   Blessed by the waters of baptism, and
    >   Blessing others by turning water into wine,
    >   Setting out to teach and preach and heal,
    >   to befriend and be befriended,
    >   to live in holy relationship with God
    >   and God's world.
    > Epiphany — the season to reflect on our journeys —
    >   Journeys to the manger
    >   guided, like the sages, by a star,

Journeys to the ends of the earth
to spread the light of Jesus' life
and the gift of God's grace,
Journeys marked not by the miles we travel,
but by the way we live our lives.

(c) What does this poem communicate about Jesus' life and the life journeys to which *we* are called?

2. Reflect on educational practices discussed in this chapter — trust, gratitude, and generosity. How does your community engage in these practices? How else does your community practice thanksgiving? How could your community enhance its thanksgiving? Consider practices of this chapter and others that you imagine.

Chapter Seven

Nourishing Life

✡

"Where you go, I will go; where you lodge, I will lodge; your people shall be my people, and your God my God" (Ruth 1:16b).

These words from Ruth have become a symbol of human commitment. Ruth commits herself to be present with Naomi in traveling and lodging, to belong to her people, and to be faithful to her God. The commitment is personal, between Ruth and Naomi; it is also communal and political. Ruth commits herself to Naomi and also to her people. At the end of the narrative (Ruth 4:13–22), we see that the commitment will be significant for Israel as well. Ruth will be the great grandmother of Israel's King David, and an ancestor to Jesus, one of two women identified in Matthew's genealogy (1:5). In Ruth's life, we see the power of nourishing life — sharing in presence, community, and faithfulness to God.

To say that teaching has to do with nourishing life is to emphasize the commitment of teachers and learners to live in community. Such teaching draws from promises of life in Ruth's story, which are anything but glib. Naomi (Pleasant) calls herself Mara (Bitter) when she returns to Bethlehem (1:20). Her life has been torn to shreds through the years in Moab. Naomi's efforts to nourish life are feeble and bitter, first encouraging her daughters-in-law to remain with their people and begin a new life (1:8–15), and then traveling with Ruth to Bethlehem. In Bethlehem, despite Ruth's loyalty, Naomi declares that she has returned home empty (1:21). As the story unfolds, however, we see Ruth and Naomi taking hold of promises and exerting themselves in bold acts of seeking and nourishing life — caring for one another, gleaning in the fields, and appealing to Boaz in unconventional ways. Finally, Boaz and Ruth marry and have a son, Obed, who will be the father of Jesse and grandfather of David, king of Israel.

The acts of Naomi and Ruth, then of Boaz, ensure their survival, and also the survival of their family and the flourishing of Israel. Similarly, our present acts of nourishing life are bold claims on life, even when death and bitterness surround us. Further, our acts are important to personal well-being, to our people, and to the larger human community. Like Naomi and Ruth, our efforts to nourish life are personal, communal, and political. Like them, some of our efforts will cross

religious communities and traditions. Unlike Ruth, some of our nourishing of
religious crossings will be as *partners* with others rather than as full participants
in their communities; we now live in a world that cries out for interreligious
understanding and respect.

The theme of nurture is found in the story of Ruth, in the nourishing sacraments of baptism and eucharist, and in religious education literature. Nurture,
however, is not always conventional and sweet. It is often prophetic and controversial, as when a congregation offers succor to people who are outcast in the
larger community, or when parents refuse to give up hope for their child, even
when the child persists in self-destructive and other-destructive behavior. *Nourishing life involves searching for life in the most difficult situations and encouraging even
the tiniest seeds of life to grow. In this chapter, we probe the importance of discerning
God's life in every situation and nourishing that life in every possible way.* First, we
turn to stories.

I recently had two experiences that brought me back to myself. The first was a visit
to my hometown in Louisiana for my fortieth high school reunion. *I was nervous
during the preceding week, recognizing that my path had taken different directions from
most of my high school friends. I feared that I would experience the visit as a journey
from another planet. I had also lost touch with some of my close friends; I dreaded their
anger and my guilt. The visit, in actuality, was pure delight. We talked until we were
hoarse, shared our life stories, and recalled funny moments of our youth. We laughed as
if we were fifteen, but with mellowness that comes with age. I apologized to two friends
for my poor communication; they apologized for theirs. For a few hours, we were friends
without walls; our lives were interwoven and we cared deeply (and still care) for one
another.*

In reflecting later on the power of this reunion for me, I came to one central
conclusion: These were my people! We had been through many trials and joys
together. We did not choose one another; we simply grew up together. Of course,
the situation was more complex. Although we were mostly middle class, straight,
white Southern folks, we did represent some economic difference, as well as ethnic
variations (including Italian, Cajun, British, and other origins). We had widely
different interests and dreams, different sexual orientations, family experiences,
and personalities. None of these differences seemed as acute now as they did forty
years ago, however. Why?

The other personal experience took place later at the California-Pacific Annual
Conference (United Methodist Church). Having been part of the conference
almost thirty years, it is home to me. It is not home because I grew up there,
although I did grow in countless ways over the years. It is not home because of
homogeneity, for this is one of the most diverse conferences in the denomination.
On a typical Sunday morning, more than thirty languages are preached within

the Conference bounds (Southern California, Hawaii, Guam, and Saipan). The theological and social perspectives are countless, and the disagreements are vivid. At the same time, we are bound together.

Conference opened with a memorial service and a sermon resounding with the message, "All I have is you!"[1] *The congregation remembered clergy and spouses who had died during the previous year as a family member lit a candle for each one. As a name was read, friends and family of the deceased stood in place, expressing gratitude for the person's life. Eucharist followed, and people moved to stations to receive the bread and grape juice. Some people walked with bowed heads; others quietly greeted friends they had not seen since the previous conference. The community glowed. When people then passed the peace, they said words of blessing, shook hands, hugged, and smiled — chaotic movement and a joyful buzz of voices. This was the first night of Conference.*

Conference proceeded with the usual: plenary sessions, reports, discernment, and decision-making; prayer, Bible study, and worship; commissioning-ordination; group meals; retirement; and a concluding service of baptism renewal and appointment-reading. Throughout the time, people greeted friends and colleagues, and built relationships — sharing life stories, laughing, crying, grousing, discussing, and playing together.

In many years past, this conference has wrestled with difficult and divisive issues. This was not such a year. The calm of most sessions evoked delight, along with some nervousness that something was being "covered up." We did hear strong words about just-peacemaking, and we acted on resolutions regarding peace, environmental protection, and other critical issues. We did not discuss at length the issues that divide us most strongly, however. Those issues would return more forcefully in years to come, but the memory of their earlier force lingered pungently in our memories. At the same time, this conference was a time for building upon what had been established previously in regard to decisions, commitments, and structures. This was a conference for building relationships and solidarity, preparing for the wrestling to come.

The opening stories pose the possibility of being a people. Sometimes people are bound by familial relationships (Naomi and Ruth); sometimes, by the happenstance of geographic and political boundaries (my high school). Sometimes they are bound by mixed factors, such as the annual conference's bonding by geographic and political boundaries, suffused with people's active choices to be part of a particular denomination in a particular location. Whatever the bonds, people often come to know themselves as "a people," and individuals, to know themselves *through* their people. Their experiences of traveling together often strengthen the bonds and nourish life. This process is nurture.

In this chapter, we pursue the qualities of community life and the role of nurture in feeding people's hungers. Ruth's story reveals decisions, risks, and loyalty.

---

1. Cheol Kwak, "All I Have Is You," sermon preached at California-Pacific Annual Conference, United Methodist Church, University of Redlands, California, June 18, 2002. The sermon was based on the Ruth 1.

The high school reunion reveals a formative culture based on constancy and belonging. The annual conference reveals a formative culture that often stands against dominant culture, pointing toward an alternative way of life, grounded in faith and pervaded with diversity, discernment, and proactive community-building. All of these focus on birth. All are possible because people dare to search for life in their particular situations and to seek and offer nourishment in every way they can imagine. The focus in all of these communities is on birthing and supporting life, pointing to themes at the center of Christianity — the birth of Christ, the possibilities of new birth for people who are hurting, and the birth of new opportunities for communities that are oppressed or discouraged.

The stress on *life* in Christian tradition encourages people to consider educational practices that support life. With its theological preoccupation with sin and redemption, the Christian Church has often neglected themes of birth and life or subsumed them under redemption, seeing life only as a consequence of God's redemptive work. Such an accent distorts God's gift of life and obscures the role of human communities in nourishing life, or practicing *a spirituality of nurture*. To this sacramental role we now turn.

Power in Nourishing Life

In the previous chapter, we explored how thanksgiving awakens people to life's potential and opens the way to nourish life. Many religious symbols, such as the Madonna in Christianity, underscore the significance of nourishing life. The mother and Christ child symbolize new beginnings from an ordinary woman's womb. Curiously, this icon has given hope to multitudes of people over centuries and throughout the world. Surely its power arises, in part, from God's giving and nourishing of life through ordinary people. The birthing mother gifts the world with God's progeny; the nursing mother cares for the Child of God. Artists sometimes portray Jesus' Mother as having special influence on Jesus in heaven. Mary is portrayed, surrounded by people in need, with an imploring glance at Jesus, even with a gesture of pressing her milk to remind her son that she once nursed him. In such paintings, Mary calls upon her personal relationship with Jesus to advocate for others. The personal is political, to quote a familiar feminist aphorism. What one does in the personal sphere influences the body politic.

Such logic becomes even clearer when we look at the ways in which certain people become cultural icons of nurture. Consider Mother Teresa and princess Diana — not as perfect human beings but as symbolic nurturers. Each of these women became larger than life in public imagination. Elevated through rituals of honor, memorials, and books, they inspired and encouraged others, even in their humanness. As you consider these persons, however, you discover their own experiences of being nurtured, longing for nurture, and nurturing others, all of which shaped their work in the body politic.

Mother Teresa, born as Agnes Bojaxhiu, was nurtured by her family in the Serbian-dominated Skopje, Albania, of 1910. In her home, the Roman Catholic faith was central, and, although her family was poor after her father died, they offered hospitality to people who were poorer. Young Agnes shared the responsibilities, such as washing the sores of one woman and visiting another in her dying days.[2] Later, Sister Teresa was nurtured in her religious order (Loreto Sisters) in India. Still later, on a train ride, she received a call from God to "help the poor by living among them."[3]

Princess Diana grew up in a family broken and sometimes tormented. She longed for nurture that was not always forthcoming; yet she experienced tenderness from a few key people in her life. Her early experiences of longing for love and being loved helped shape her care of her sons and, later, her care of people with AIDS, landmine victims, and many other suffering souls. Like Mother Teresa, but more tragic, her life symbolized a blend of personal and public nurture. When these two women died within a month of one another in 1997, the world compared them, struck by the loss of two nurturing souls — both symbolic and real. The press coverage of the two women, popular responses to their deaths, and comparisons made through the previous decade reveal something of the fascination, and perhaps longing, that people have for nurture and for guiding symbols of nurture. To tease out the possibilities, we return to the stories with which this chapter began.

Power of Gleaning Hope in Times of Despair

Nourishing life yields first the *power to glean hope in times of despair — seeking and gathering the seeds or remnants of hope that can be found.* The book of Ruth is about nourishment and faithfulness, permeating the narrative in an uneasy dance with famine, death, and desolation. A famine had driven Elimelech, Naomi, and their two sons to Moab. After some years, however, the men died, leaving Naomi without husband or sons (1:1–5). The biblical story opens with this tragic context and Naomi's decision to return home. A subtle promise of nourishment underlies Naomi's decision; Bethlehem (the House of Bread) awaits her. As she departs, Naomi entreats her daughters-in-law to return to their families, to begin a new life among their own people. Orpah consents, but Ruth insists on traveling with Naomi — to join her people and worship her God. She aligns her destiny with Naomi's, taking on the same hardships and promises, though the promises seem very dim at this point of the story.

Jewish Bibles place Ruth among the Five Scrolls of the Writings, for it prepares people to celebrate life. Reading Ruth on the festival of Shavuoth (Festival of Weeks, Pentecost), the community celebrates the end of barley harvest and

---

2. Anne Sebba, *Mother Teresa: Beyond the Image* (New York: Doubleday, 1997), 16.
3. Ibid., 46.

beginning of wheat. It also celebrates the promise of new life arising from death.[4]
Ruth thus offers clues for a spirituality of nurture — gleaning leftovers in the
fields and acting resourcefully, if not conventionally, to preserve life. Ruth reminds people of desolate times when God's promises are dim. Naomi and Ruth
do not initially live by nourishment, but by gleaning and vague hope. Similarly,
Mother Teresa reminded people of the preciousness of life, as she tended those
dying on the streets of Calcutta, and Diana, Princess of Wales, reminded people
that compassion for others surpasses human foibles and disappointments. All of
these characters, in different ways, were gleaners of hope from destruction.

Power of Being a People

The opening stories of this chapter also point to the *power of being a people.*
The high school reunion was undoubtedly not joyful for everyone present or
for everyone who longed to be there; some did not even want to attend. Some
qualities marked that high school class, however. We had been blessed (even
spoiled) by our circumstances. When we were in the seventh and eighth grades,
city leaders built a new high school in our neighborhood. For practical reasons,
the high school began with ninth grade, and one grade was added each year;
thus, my class was the oldest each year. People frequently told us that we were
helping to build the school. In truth, one small class of seniors was added the
year we were juniors. This meant that one class graduated before ours; however,
these people blended with us and we thought of the two classes as one.

Our experience highlights qualities of nurture. We studied with several teachers for six years (since many middle school teachers moved with us to the new
high school). They knew us and encouraged our gifts while prodding us to face
our shortcomings. We also knew one another over time; in those years, people
were less mobile than now. Most important, we were given leadership opportunities throughout our high school years, and encouragement to exercise leadership
for the benefit of the school and future generations. With teachers and admin-
istrators, we invented the school's alma mater, organizations, and traditions.
We received attention equivalent to many private schools, and people placed
confidence in us to excel and help the school to excel. We did!

This kind of nurture has parallels in magnet schools, private schools, Native Survival Schools in Canada, and black colleges throughout the U.S.[5] Such

---

4. Adele Berlin, "Ruth: Introduction," in *The HarperCollins Study Bible,* ed. Wayne A. Meeks
(New York: HarperCollins, 1993), 409.

5. Black schools and colleges have strong records of academic achievement and mentoring, using
measures of graduation, future study, and work. See United States Congress, *The Unique Role and Mission of Historically Black Colleges and Universities* (Washington, D.C.: U.S.G.P.O., 1988). This document
reports a hearing before the Subcommittee on Postsecondary Education, Committee on Education
and Labor, House of Representatives, 100th Congress, Durham, N.C., September 12, 1988. Similarly,
an extensive ethnography of an indigenous Canadian school reveals its educational effectiveness by
way of teaching traditional school subjects, Native traditions, and respect for self and community.

schools are held together with a central mission and focus, and also by some form of homogeneity (common interests, culture, or specialization); intentional commitment of leaders; special attention to students by teachers over time; and encouragement of students to take responsibility and leadership for the sake of the larger community. These are qualities that need *not* be reserved for elite schools, but they often are. These are qualities that can be part of diverse schools, public agencies, and faith communities.

Power of Shared Mission and Sense of Belonging

Turning to the annual conference session, we see another power in nourishing life — the *power to bind people with a shared mission and sense of belonging*. The conference is marked by diversity of social class, ethnicity, sexual orientation, theological perspectives, religious practices, and social passions. It is also shaped by immigration patterns of the Pacific Rim, and by the clothing, rituals, and traditions of many peoples. In the conference session, a Native American pastor, United Methodist Liaison in Jerusalem, and Kenyan scholar led in reflection; music came from Latin America, the Philippines, Africa, contemporary praise bands, African American choirs, and others. Conference mission teams described their upcoming journeys to the Philippines and Vietnam, led by people native to those countries. When issues arise in this conference, divisions of opinion do not follow dependable patterns. With multiple perspectives on most issues, the "liberal-conservative" split does not fit. Groups divide among themselves, and a given group may vote on the so-called liberal side of one issue and the so-called conservative side of another. Though people hold stereotypes of one another, surprises continually emerge, breaking stereotypes yet again. Thus, prejudice persists, but is severely weakened; inclusion persists, and is continually strengthened.

Much strength in this community comes from shared mission — the experience of living and working purposefully over time. Much also comes from intentional acts of community building — a Festival of the Spirit, basketball games, communal discernment, and worship. These efforts anchor the community's mission, binding people with shared vision, common work, and communal relationships for large purposes.

Power of Birth, New Birth, and Nurture

In all of these cases, the *power of birth, new birth, and nurture* is evident. Communities that deepen over time are ones in which people are born again and again. Thus, the theological accent falls on birth and rebirth, rather than on death and redemption. Consider the powerful roles of birth and nurture in stories of this chapter. In seeking to begin life anew, Ruth and Naomi sought nurture wherever

See Celia Haig-Brown, Kathy L. Hodgson-Smith, Robert Regnier, and Jo-ann Archibald, *Making the Spirit Dance Within: Joe Duquette High School and an Aboriginal Community* (Toronto: James Lorimer & Company, 1997).

they could find it. Their decisions led to physical survival, marriage, and parent-
hood; they also left a legacy of descendants, including David and Jesus. Birth and
nurture are evident in the high school story as well; a group of ordinary teenagers
and their teachers birthed a school. With responsibility and encouragement, the
youth became leaders, and a high school blossomed. In the annual conference session, nurture included remembering the dead, celebrating communion, praying,
playing, and deliberating; mutuality was the key. Acknowledging these multiple
forms of nurture leads to a sense of power to endure, create, and sustain community. Such power grows from roots in church practice and inspires theological
affirmations, both powerful in shaping the future.

Roots of Nurture in Church Practice

Nurture is almost taken for granted in church life, but debates between conversion
and nurture predate the writings of Horace Bushnell (1802–76) on Christian
nurture. The subject is more controversial than many think.[6] It raises questions
about the role of God in relation to the role of human beings, the suddenness and
gradualness of God's work in human lives, the relationship between the dramatic
and the everyday, and more.

Nurture is rooted in the church's celebrations of Christmas and Pentecost
and in the nourishing qualities of baptism and eucharist. Christmas is a time for
celebrating the birth of Jesus, and Pentecost, a time for celebrating the church's
birth. The whole of the sacraments embody nurture, represented visibly in prayers
over ordinary water, bread, and wine. Nurture is also visible in historic practices
of care — caring for and guiding the young, caring for the infirm and elderly, and
feeding people within and outside the community. Such practices are often most
intense in the nurturing seasons of Christmas and Pentecost and in baptism and
eucharist. On the other hand, church practice confounds nurture when it focuses
largely on human sin, the atoning work of God, and the centrality of redemption,
especially when it discounts human goodness, the creative work of God, and the
significance of natality. In this section, we will focus on the shape of nurture in
church practice, heralding the presence and work of God in nourishing life.

Christmas and Pentecost

Nurture is represented by every season of the Christian year, but particularly by
Christmas and Pentecost. At Christmas, we celebrate both the birth and care of

---

6. Horace Bushnell, *Christian Nurture*, intro. Luther A. Weigle (New Haven: Yale University Press,
1960, 1916). Parts of this book were published in 1847 as *Views of Christian Nurture*. The present form
was published in 1860; the new edition was published by Scribner in 1916, and continued by Yale
University since 1947. This trajectory of publication reveals something of the power of Bushnell's
ideas.

new life; at Pentecost, we celebrate the gift of God's Spirit and God's accompanying promise to abide with the people forever. Interpretations of God's actions in Christmas and Pentecost vary, but both events mark an in-breaking of life, and both stir people to awe and action. Further, both convey power, from early times to the present — the birth of Jesus, incarnating God's power and God's reality in a baby, and the birth of the church, incarnating God's spiritual power in a rag-tag band of would-be followers.

Christmas is a time of new birth, taking place amid difficult economic and political circumstances, and circumstances of physical hardship. This birth symbolizes hope, for no circumstances could stop it, and no political power (e.g., Herod) could destroy it. Christmas is a celebration of birth *and* caregiving. As birth is celebrated in Christian iconography, so is the care of children. Mary and Joseph are pictured beside their small child Jesus, as are shepherds, angels, and wise travelers from the East. Care is thus embedded in a nuclear family, but also in the human family and in relations with the transcendent (angels). Care is also embedded in the narratives, art, and sites that mark the tending of Jesus: the Milk Grotto outside of Bethlehem where tradition says Mary nursed Jesus; the stories of Joseph's being warned in a dream to flee with his family to protect Jesus (Matt. 2:13–15; cf. 16–23); and paintings portraying their flight to Egypt.

As discussed in the past chapter, Eastertide continues until Pentecost. During this season, the disciples encountered Jesus, gathered, prayed, and were generally confused. Although the postresurrection days were not easy for the disciples, sparks of life were kindling. Even in their gathering, they showed signs of hope that consolation or guidance would come. Just as Pentecost marked the birth of the church and the beginning of a new way of life with the Spirit, so also it brought to practical, everyday fruition the promises of Eastertide. Easter hope upholds the people in a sense of wonder and expectation while they await the continuing revelation and guidance of Pentecost, which will sustain them through ordinary times. As the church year unfolds, ordinary times then yield to Advent, and the expectant waiting for new life that it represents. Thus, all of the seasons point to God's life, which is starkly present and boldly celebrated in Christmastide and Pentecost.

Sacraments

Echoing the life-oriented celebrations of Christmas and Pentecost, the sacraments also nourish community. Baptism announces new life in God; eucharist renews life at God's table through acts of blessing, feeding, and receiving. I earlier said that the physicality of sacraments evokes thanksgiving; it also awakens people to nurture — washing and feeding. With sacramental nourishment come renewed promises for daily sustenance, as found in Ruth and biblical tradition. Sacraments also reveal God's faithful nourishment of creation, which we encounter as we live sacramentally day by day.

The celebration of new life in baptism is often the theme of Christian iconography. In early centuries, churches sometimes had a special building or section for the baptistery. Constantine constructed an octagonal baptistery within St. John Lateran Church in Rome (rebuilt in 432–40 c.e.) Also in the early fifth century, the separate Orthodox baptistery was erected in Ravenna, the political hub of Italy at the time. Later, the cathedral of Pisa was built with an elaborate baptistery, a separate building dating from 1153.[7] Baptismal fonts also embody the significance of baptism, whether in parish churches or cathedrals. Consider the Black Tournai Fonts imported from Belgium for major English churches in the late twelfth century. Not only are these fonts important for their age, imported artistry, and role in church life; they also bear symbolic carvings of death and life, evil and good. The font of Winchester Cathedral depicts the legendary murder of three boys and St. Nicholas's raising the boys from the dead. The font of Lincoln Minster is surrounded with symbolic griffons, fanciful animals, the lion of St. Mark, and the ox of St. Luke, together representing evil and divine power.[8] For most medieval churches, as for much of church history, the font is critical to Christian faith and community life. Fonts are thus often placed at the entrance of a church or cathedral to symbolize entrance into new life and entrance into the Body of Christ.

Nurture is also at the center of the eucharistic meal: "Take, eat; this is my body which is given for you. . . . Drink from this cup, all of you; this is my blood of the new covenant."[9] In these words, the memory of Jesus is linked to nurturing in the present community. The question of who is invited to the table is a contested one; however, all traditions keep their invitation open to rich and poor, young and old, disturbed and joyful, and ordinary people with all of their flaws, idiosyncrasies, and sins. In some churches, the invitation goes only to those baptized or confirmed within its own tradition. In other churches, the invitation goes to those baptized or confirmed in *any* Christian tradition. In still other churches, the invitation is open to *all*, symbolizing free, unmerited, unearned grace. Questions of invitation are important to contemplate and debate; however, the larger point is that all churches have some form and degree of openness in the invitation. Despite theological and practical differences in regards to presiding and receiving, the feast is for the *community*, not a small elite group. Further, eucharist culminates

7. George Zarnecki, *Art of the Medieval World: Architecture, Sculpture, Painting, the Sacred Arts* (Englewood Cliffs, N.J.: Prentice-Hall, 1975), 35–39, 274–78.

8. Cecil H. Eden, *Black Tournai Fonts in England: The Group of Seven Late Norman Fonts from Belgium* (London: Elliot Stock, 1909), esp. 9–13; 22–23.

9. *The United Methodist Book of Worship* (Nashville: United Methodist Publishing House, 1992), 37; cf. 48. See also *The Book of Common Worship* (Louisville: Westminster John Knox, 1993), 69; cf. 71, 74. *Lutheran Book of Worship* (Minneapolis: Augsburg Publishing House, 1978), 69–70; cf. 89–90, 110–11. *The Book of Common Prayer* (New York: Seabury Press, 1979), 335; cf. also 362.

in the giving and receiving of bread and wine — a holy feast for the people.[10] The bread and wine are not simply tokens, even symbols; they are sources of genuine nourishment.

Neither baptism nor eucharist is an individualistic sacrament of nurture. In both, the individual participants are important, but the sacraments focus on the community's communion with one another. The ritual action embodies God's gifts to the community as a whole (grace, new life, nourishing food); God's expectations of the people; and the community's mutual participation and accountability. The sacraments also represent God's generosity and the renewal of life. Thus, people who are extravagant in their own self-giving over time, such as Mother Teresa and Princess Diana, find frequent communion to be essential for renewing their ministries. Baptism and eucharist are sources of nourishment for the community, for each individual, and for the world beyond.

Theology of Life

Underneath the sacramental practice of nurture is a theology of life, grounded in the nurturing movements of God — the source of all life. This nurture is God's active response to longings in creation for nourishment. The longings include the most basic human needs for food, physical comfort, and physical exercise, and the more subtle human yearnings for sense stimulation — seeing, hearing, touching, smelling, and eating. People also yearn for knowledge of what, why, and how to, and for opportunities to express and give themselves to the larger community. Many of these yearnings extend to all creation. Certainly, all living things need nourishment, even beyond the obvious needs for food, water, and shelter. Even rivers and seas need to be fed with water from rain, snow, and aquifers, and animals need sensory variety in order to enjoy maximum social and intellectual growth and contentment. All of these yearnings call out for nurture, and the origins of this nurture are in the life-giving God.

The life of God endures in the face of death and destruction; it breathes life into creation, even when creation is flailing and failing. No wonder that symbols of life flow so energetically through Christian tradition. God breathed life into the first humans in the second creation story; Jesus was born from an ordinary woman's womb; the Madonna and child and the empty tomb are central symbols in Christian art. The empty tomb visually reiterates the empty womb and points

---

10. Alexander Schmemann, *For the Life of the World: Sacraments and Orthodoxy* (Crestwood, N.Y.: St. Vladimir's Seminary Press, 1973, 1963), 42–43. This theme pervades the literature discussed in other chapters. Schmemann, in these pages, describes the communion among Christ, the bread, and the world: "And now when we receive this bread from His hands, we know that he has taken up all life, filled it with Himself, made it what it was meant to be: communion with God, sacrament of His presence and love" (43).

to new life all over again, also revealing how intertwined are the symbols and themes of a Christian theology of life.

1. God Is Life

Certainly death and destruction are real, but even the most hateful, destructive moments of life on this planet hold seeds of life to be nurtured. Thus, my first affirmation is that *God is Life, breathing new life into the world even amid death and destruction.* Saying this is neither naïve optimism nor stubborn denial of sin and evil; it is simply shifting the figure and ground, focusing on God's presence and gifts amid death and destruction rather than on the death and destruction itself.

In her autobiography, Donna Meehan shares her life as a stolen child in Australia.[11] In early years, she lived with her Aboriginal family and community. At five, her mother boarded her on a train for what she expected to be a great adventure; however, her mother never boarded. Later she realized that she had left her mother and whole life behind; at the end of her train journey, she met new parents. Donna was to carry years of resentment toward her natural mother for giving her away, not realizing until much later that her family were victims of a government policy to remove Aboriginal children from their homes so as to assimilate Aboriginal people into white Australia.

Donna was more fortunate than some stolen children, as she was fostered and adopted by loving parents, who nurtured and walked with her, even encouraged her as a young adult to search for her natural mother and rebuild relationships with her Aboriginal family. What sustained Donna and helped her repeatedly to reframe her life was trust in God's active presence in her life. She titled her autobiography *It Is No Secret,* drawing from the gospel song, "It Is No Secret — What God Can Do."[12] This is the wellspring from which she drew hope to reshape her life. It is the well from which she drew courage to reclaim her Aboriginal heritage and work tirelessly for Aboriginal rights and respect.

2. God Can Open Eyes That See and Ears That Hear

As for Donna Meehan, God's life is not always obvious, yet *God can open eyes that see and ears that hear.* Glimpsing divine life in a hard-hearted world requires a hermeneutic of nurture — seeking and nurturing seeds of life, even when they are tiny and vulnerable. Unfortunately, nurture can be tamed to mean care and guidance of the most superficial kinds; the implicit hermeneutic is to ignore evil and pain and to see only the uplifting and comforting. A hermeneutic of nurture is much more radical and transformative. Consider the transformative move of people imprisoned by apartheid leadership in South Africa; they chose to transform their prison experience through a hermeneutic that transformed the horrors of that experience into a source of hope.

---

11. Donna Meehan, *It Is No Secret* (Milsons Point, NSW: Random House Australia, 2000).
12. Ibid., 143.

Robben Island is where Nelson Mandela was imprisoned for twenty years off the coast of Cape Town, South Africa. When I visited there, the guide was a former prisoner, Sipho Nkosi, who quoted Mandela: "We no longer call this Robben Island Maximum Security Prison, but Robben Island University, because we turned what we learned here into good, not into bad as the apartheid government expected." Another former prisoner, Dan Cetywayo, added these words: "Robben Island has become a symbol of the triumph of the human spirit." Following the words and example of Mandela and imprisoned teachers, these two men have chosen to reshape their memory of Robben Island so it can be a force for good rather than evil. They have chosen to look for life in the midst of death and to build upon it.[13]

3. Life Is a Choice

This discussion leads to a third affirmation, that *life is a choice people can make even in the face of death*. Sipho Nkosi and Dan Cetywayo have chosen to trust life. Similarly, Ruth and Naomi chose life, even when God's promises were dim. These stories reveal an important aspect of the human vocation — to choose life again and again. In South Africa, the choice for life has been transformative for individuals, for the nation, and for people around the world. I had the privilege to visit Robben Island with an international group of theologians. At one point we sat on hard benches and heard stories of the torture and punishments at Robben Island during apartheid years. I sat beside a German colleague whose eyes filled with tears. He leaned toward me and said, "This is what my people did to the Jews; I am overcome that these men at Robben Island could now love the people who did these terrible things." My colleague made connections between what he heard and the history of his own country; simultaneously, I made connections with racism in the Unites States. We were all being challenged to choose life.

4. Life Is Mediated through God's People

In light of the stories and case studies of this chapter, we can affirm that *life is mediated through God's people*. In Ruth, life is mediated through traveling, dwelling, being, and worshiping together: "Where you go, I will go; where you lodge, I will lodge; your people shall be my people, and your God my God" (Ruth 1:16b). In my high school, life was mediated in building a new school, dwelling with a diverse crowd of friends, and simply *being* with one another. Worship did not bind us, but a common mission did. Our visions were limited in those last years of segregated schools, and we infused the school traditions with Civil War symbols (building on the school's name, chosen by the school board to honor a Civil War general). The choices we made reveal the narrow perspectives that exist among God's people. Human legacies are always a mix of God's work and human finitude; thus, the creations of our 1960s generation need to be transformed by later generations.

---

13. Nelson Mandela, *Long Walk to Freedom* (Boston: Little, Brown, 1994), 467.

On the other hand, the story points to the power of people to create a school of excellence. Though the school was far from perfect, it provided a ground on which later generations could grow and build.

5. People Are Called to Sustain Life

People are not only given life; *people are called to sustain life and pass it on.* In Ruth, we see the human vocation unfolding as Ruth, Naomi, and Boaz act to sustain life. In the annual conference session, people build a life-giving community through worship, play, and political debate, negotiation, and decision-making. In the session described in the case, each day was suffused with prayer and worship. One evening was a Festival of the Spirit — a time of feasting, sharing at table, and worshiping. One afternoon was for play, including a basketball game with rowdy cheerleaders and the bishop playing on both teams. Over time, our conference has also restructured its political community, having developed a process of communal discernment, which has now been used several times in negotiating the swirling waters of controversy.[14] The Conference now has a response team that previews controversial actions related to homosexuality and encourages open, respectful dialogue among people with diverse life experiences and points of view. This is the stuff that mediates God's life and God's call to a vocation of sustaining life. It is intentional; it is hard work; it is finally a gift of God.

6. God Creates Spaces for New Birth

In the cases I have shared, the theological accent falls more strongly on birth and nurture than on death and redemption. What is needed if we are to nurture the option for life is a theology grounded in natality, fecundity, and life, recognizing that *God continually creates spaces for new birth.* Here I am in harmony with Elisabeth Moltmann-Wendel, who argues that the Christian emphasis on death needs to be replaced with an emphasis on birth — natality.[15] She further encourages a theological shift from a focus on Christ's sacrifice to a focus on his friendship toward others — eating with sinners, celebrating over meals, giving himself for his friends.[16]

To develop these ideas, we turn to biblical narratives of birth and nurture, vividly represented in Jesus' birth when God sent a child to an aching world. One also sees birth and nurture in texts related to children, such as: the actions of Hebrew midwives, Shiphrah and Puah, to disobey the king of Egypt and save the

---

14. I analyze one of the early moments in this annual conference process in Mary Elizabeth Moore, "Richness in Religious Education: Ethnic, Religious and Biodiversity," in *The Fourth R for the Third Millennium: Education in Religion and Values for the Global Future,* ed. Leslie J. Francis, Jeff Astley, and Mandy Robbins (Dublin: Lindisfarne Books, 2001), 115–35; "Ethnic Diversity and Biodiversity: Richness at the Center of Education," *Interchange* 31, nos. 2 and 3 (2000): 259–78.

15. Elisabeth Moltmann-Wendel, "How My Mind Has Changed," paper presented in Annual Women's Forum, Candler School of Theology, Emory University, Atlanta, April 8, 2002. See also Elisabeth Moltmann-Wendel, *Rediscovering Friendship* (London: SCM, 2000), 32–52.

16. Moltmann-Wendel, *Rediscovering Friendship,* 32–52.

Hebrew boy children at birth (Exod. 1:15–22); the actions of Moses' mother and sister and Pharaoh's daughter to save the baby Moses (Exod. 2:1–10); and Jesus' blessing of the children (Matt. 19:13–15; Mark 9:33–37; 10:13–16; Luke 18:15–17). In all of these texts, God creates space for life to flourish. And God does this through people who *play* around with the orders of kings and the rules of their community. These are not isolated acts of care for children by one individual for the sake of one child. These are acts of individuals on behalf of the community for the sake of the child *and* the community.

Themes of birth and nurture also appears in less obvious ways. Consider the biblical texts studied in the previous chapter. The woman who came to Jesus with lavish ointment for his feet (Luke 7:36–50) was known as a sinner, but Jesus looked through her sinfulness to see the spark of life in her soul. Perhaps he saw the spark in her acts of generosity or in her deep emotions (covering his feet with tears and kisses). Perhaps he saw the spark in some other way. Whatever he saw, as Luke tells the story, Jesus knew the woman better than his critics did. They saw her only as a sinner, lumping her into a category and dismissing her better attributes. Jesus saw her love for him and that was enough. Naming that love, he declared that her sins were forgiven.

As noted in chapter 6, Noah, Abram, and the woman who anointed Jesus were responding to God. Noah built and filled an ark to help creatures survive a flood (Gen. 6:9–7:22); Abram moved his family and household to a new land (Gen. 12:1–9); the woman anointed Jesus (Luke 7:36–50). In each case, people responded to signs of life as they were given; they did what they knew to do, either because of God's instructions (as in the case of Noah and Abram) or because of a passion to serve Jesus (as in the case of the woman). All of these people were nurturing life. Noah tended to the well-being of God's creation by loading two animals of every kind into the ark. Abram tended to the well-being of his family and household by following God's directions to move to another land. The woman tended to the well-being of Jesus and herself by washing Jesus' feet.

These were all acts of nurture, and each was working within their limited circumstances — a pending flood for Noah, a call to move for Abram, and a dinner in a Pharisee's home for the woman. The acts all involved ridicule and risk as well. Noah was asked to do a ridiculous task in building an ark and gathering the animals (Gen. 6:9–7:5). Abram had only God's vague promises and instructions as guides, but no guarantees; further, the so-called promised land was already occupied by other people. The unnamed woman had no access to Jesus without entering the Pharisee's house, and she was neither invited nor wanted. In spite of limited circumstances, risk, and ridicule, all of these characters acted in a way that responded to God with generosity and constancy.

These narratives reveal challenges for nurture, but also possibilities. The fact that people transmitted the stories across generations reveals their power to communicate God's ability to make space for new birth. Further, new birth happens in many ways and often takes the form of eccentric responses to God in ambiguous circumstances. *Nurture is caring for that which we have been given with whatever guidance we receive from God (however sketchy) within whatever circumstances we find ourselves (however limited) and in the face of whatever risks present themselves.*

Hermeneutic of Nurture

Focusing on the power of nurture and a theology of life demands a hermeneutic of nurture — *seeking and analyzing seeds of life in sacred texts and ordinary life events.* Such a hermeneutic digs through the rubble of sorrow and tragedy for signs of life, however dim. Such a hermeneutic grows from Jewish and Christian traditions, however easily it is obscured or overshadowed by less hopeful elements.[17] Jewish and Christian traditions have always recognized the value of life — teaching the importance of basic human nurture (Deut. 6:1–9); mourning oppression and loss (Gen. 4:1–16; 21:8–21; 23; Exod. 3:1–12, esp. 7–10); celebrating the deliverance of people from bondage (Exod. 15:1–21); remembering God's provision of manna in the wilderness (Exod. 16); and calling people to respond to the givens of their lives with the giving of their lives (Gen. 32:3–33:17).

Even in this sample of texts, we see glimmers of life in messy circumstances. Yet Christian theology has often focused so heavily on sin and sinfulness that it has attended minimally to *life.* Even redemption is more often understood as the forgiveness of sin — the forgiveness of a negative — than as a positive reality that can be envisioned and received and lived. To practice the hermeneutic of nurture is to seek seeds of life in every situation and to nourish these seeds with further reflection and interpretation.

Unfortunately, nurture is sometimes tamed to mean superficial forms of care and guidance; the implicit hermeneutic is to ignore evil and pain, to see only the uplifting and comforting. Consider popular lists of comforting biblical texts, Christian movements of positive thinking, or the wide range of self-help books in local bookstores. These testify to the human longing for nurture, but also to the longing for easy answers to perplexing problems. A hermeneutic of nurture is much more radical and transformative than this.

Consider the transformative move that was made when people like Nelson Mandela, Sipho Nkosi, and Dan Cetywayo chose to transform their prison experience on Robben Island through a hermeneutic of nurture. They neither ignored nor smoothed over the horrors of apartheid and imprisonment, but they transformed their worst horrors into a source of hope. Such a spirit is at the heart

---

17. Here, as in other places, I follow the challenge of Mary C. Boys and Padraic O'Hare to reflect on Christian tradition and Christian education from the perspectives and wisdom of Jewish tradition. See Boys, *Has God Only One Blessing? Judaism as a Source of Christian Self-Understanding* (New York: Paulist, 2000); O'Hare, *The Enduring Covenant: The Education of Christians and the End of Antisemitism* (Valley Forge, Pa.: Trinity Press International, 1997).

of sacramental living — mediating God's grace through the ordinary stuff of creation (even prison life) for the sanctification of human life and the well-being of all creation. To live sacramentally, for these former prisoners, is to champion justice — to build a just society in the New South Africa.

Dreaming of New Creation is foolish when you reflect on human history. Surveying the history of war, oppression, and abuse is sufficient reminder that optimism is impossible in the face of human tragedy — even more so when human abuse of the cosmos is taken into account. The dream of New Creation is possible only if you trust a power greater than your own. For most Christian theology, that power is God, and a hermeneutic of nurture is grounded in God's persistent gift of life.

Educational Practices:
Teaching through Nurture

Nurture — *discerning God's life in every situation and nourishing that life in every possible way* — has always been central to teaching, from the earliest days of the church until the present time. In Acts, we read of early Christians studying, gathering in fellowship, breaking bread, praying, and sharing worldly goods with one another and others according to need (Acts 2:41–47). According to the Acts text, these practices are permeated with praise to God; thus nurture and thanksgiving are interconnected.

The many practices of nurture described in Acts and elsewhere in the New Testament have continued through history. Medieval parish churches and cathedrals had elaborate art crafted in stone, wood, and stained glass, communicating images and stories of Christian faith to edify the people (including the large number of nonreaders). For Orthodox churches, icons played a primary role in relating people with the Divine. Important to the Reformation period were hymns and catechisms, both used for nurturing people into a Christian culture of beliefs, attitudes, and practices. Martin Luther (1483–1546) composed the Long and Short Catechisms for purposes of nurture, asking families to teach from the catechisms in their homes, and pastors to examine people on the catechisms in the churches.[18] Later Charles Wesley (1707–88) composed more than six hundred hymns to express, spread, and guide Christian faith.[19]

---

18. Martin Luther, *A Catechism for the People, Pastor, and Preacher* (Manchester: A. Brothers, for the Holbein Society, 1892, 1553); Martin Luther, *Doctor Martin Luther's Small Catechism: Explained for Children and Adults,* ed. C. Gausewitz (Milwaukee: Northwestern Pub. House, 1956, 1941); Martin Luther, *Getting into Luther's Large Catechism: A Guide for Popular Study,* ed. F. Samuel Janzow (St. Louis: Concordia, 1978).

19. John Wesley, *A Collection of Hymns, for the Use of the People Called Methodists* (London: John Mason, 1864); Charles Wesley, *Hymns for the Nativity of our Lord,* intro. and notes, Frank Baker (Madison, N.J.: Charles Wesley Society, 1991); Charles Wesley, *Hymns on the Trinity,* preface, S. T. Kimbrough Jr., intro., Wilma J. Quantrille (Madison, N.J.: Charles Wesley Society, 1998); John and Charles

Still later and extending into modern times, African Americans in the United States practiced nurture within contexts of slavery, servitude, and freedom. For them, as for early Christians, nurture combined with thanksgiving; people gathered "to offer thanks and praise to God . . . and to be spiritually fed by the Word of God!"[20] Also like early Christians, African American nurture took many forms. Melva Costen describes how the "uninhibited enthusiasm" of early Methodist worship appealed to the African American community, as did Methodist piety, rituals without service books, and small class meetings, which "were helpful in shaping spiritual directions and discipline, and in promoting corporate prayer."[21] These are all acts of nurture.

In light of this history, how can communities today develop nurture that will guide them in the present moment? In a sense, the prophet Micah summarizes many dimensions of nurture in his instructions to the people of Israel. He poses the question: What does the Lord require of you? Then, he responds: to do justice, love mercy, and walk humbly with your God (Mic. 6:8). Micah's instructions could be developed in many ways for the contemporary practice of nurture, and some have attended to this development.[22] The practice of justice nurtures one's own life as it nurtures the world, for justice is a way of life — living with equity toward all peoples, both within and beyond one's community. Also important to nurture is the practice of mercy, or kindness. Mercy is a practice of self-giving that transcends the worthiness of the other or the goodness of oneself; it transforms the giver, the gift, and the receiver. Finally, nurture includes the practice of humility — walking as your true self with God. This is the daily walk with God that nourishes everyone along the way. In its many forms, humility reshapes attitudes and removes barriers so people can relate more fully with God and God's creation.

Building on the texts and analyses of this chapter, we turn now to educational practices. The practices may be enacted in different settings and in different ways, shaped by the culture and personalities of a community, but each is grounded in a deep sense of God's life-giving presence in the world.

1. Offer Care

In response to the God who continually breathes new life into the world, people are called to *offer care — to nourish people's bodies, minds, and spirits in the learning community and larger world.*[23] This practice, though prominent in educational

---

Wesley, *A Selection of Hymns on the Lord's Supper,* preface, Donald G. Rogers (Exeter: Methodist Sacramental Fellowship, 1995).

20. Melva Wilson Costen, *African American Christian Worship* (Nashville: Abingdon, 1993), 13.

21. Ibid., 109.

22. Walter Brueggemann, Sharon Parks, and Thomas H. Groome, *To Act Justly, Love Tenderly, Walk Humbly: An Agenda for Ministers* (Eugene, Ore.: Wipf & Stock, 1992, 1986).

23. Examples are Norma Cook Everist, *The Church as Learning Community: A Comprehensive Guide to Christian Education* (Nashville: Abingdon, 2002); Anne E. Streaty Wimberly and Evelyn L. Parker,

literature, is easily underestimated. Care is more than a simple act toward in-dividuals or small communities; it is transformative. Recall the close, loving communities (aboriginal and white) that cared for Donna Meehan, and the transformations that were possible for her.

Consider the case of Le Chambon-sur-Lignon, a village in the Cévennes Moun-tains of France, known internationally for radical acts of care during World War II.[24] The villagers, mostly peasants, lived in relative solitude from global movements, though they had self-consciously chosen a Protestant minister fo-cused on peace a few years before. Over time, the pastor and pastor's spouse — André and Magda Trocmé — influenced the spirit of the community, as did others in the congregation. When anti-Jewish feelings began to stir in France during the late 1930s, Jewish families increasingly came to Le Chambon as paying guests (a longtime practice for holiday-makers when townspeople opened their homes for extra income). In the early days of World War II, the practices began to shift. A German Jewish woman knocked on the pastor's door and asked for refuge; she was received. News of this caring act spread to villagers and, also, to the resistance network; more Jews came. More people in Le Chambon opened their homes, and more Jews came. In time, the whole town was engaged in the re-sistance movement, housing refugees, and taking increasing risks. The refugees stayed one night or several weeks if they were awaiting the birth of a child or facing illness or pressing need. The villagers worked together — religious and non-religious — offering sanctuary to at least five thousand people fleeing death camps and persecution during the course of the War.

As a case study, this community offers clues for care giving. First, *the practice of care can bind a community, even when people are diverse in belief and values, and even when their acts of care arise from different motivations.* Care giving does not require doctrinal agreement or common religious affiliation. It requires simply that people see needs and respond. People of Le Chambon, when interviewed, said things like, "It was the Christian thing to do," or "it just seemed like the right thing." Most did not see their actions as extraordinary. Even the Trocmé family saw their actions as

---

eds., *In Search of Wisdom: Faith Formation in the Black Church* (Nashville: Abingdon, 2002); Isa Aron, Sara L. Lee, and Seymour Rossel, eds., *A Congregation of Learners: Transforming the Syna-gogue into a Learning Community* (New York: UAHC Press, 1995); Thomas H. Groome, *Sharing Faith: A Comprehensive Approach to Religious Education* (San Francisco: HarperSanFrancisco, 1991); John H. Westerhoff, III, *Will Our Children Have Faith?* rev. ed. (Harrisburg, Pa.: Morehouse, 2000); John Dykstra Eusden and John H. Westerhoff, III, *Sensing Beauty: Aesthetics, the Human Spirit, and the Church* (Cleveland: United Church Press, 1998); and John H. Westerhoff, *Building God's People in a Materialistic Society* (New York: Seabury, 1983).

24. Carol Rittner and Sondra Myers, eds., *The Courage to Care: Rescuers of Jews during the Holocaust* (New York: New York University Press, 1986); Philip P. Hallie, *Lest Innocent Blood Be Shed: The Story of the Village of Le Chambon, and How Goodness Happened There,* 1st Harper Colophon ed. (New York: Harper Colophon, 1980, 1979); Pierre Bolle, *Le Plateau Vivarais-Lignon: Accueil et Résistance, 1939–1946: Actes du Colloque du Chambon-sur-Lignon* (Le Chambon-sur-Lignon: Société d'Histoire de la Montagne, 1992); Pierre Sauvage, *Weapons of the Spirit,* videorecording (New York: First Run/Icarus Films, 1987).

"what we thought had to be done — nothing more complicated." More startling still, the German Governor of Haute-Loire, Julius Schmahling, who protected the village actions against Gestapo and auxiliary troop invasion, claimed simply that decency is "the normal thing to do."[25]

Second, *the practice of care can begin with one or two caregivers, one or two immediate needs, and spread.* In Le Chambon, a Jewish woman sought refuge in the pastor's home. Magda Trocmé describes the moment as rather ordinary: "And I said, 'Come in.' And so it started. I did not know that it would be dangerous. Nobody thought of that."[26] The decision of André and Magda Trocmé to offer refuge was based on years of reflecting on and teaching the Christian vocation of peacemaking. Though that decision was cultivated over time, the initial act of hospitality was a simple response to a person in need at a particular moment in time. Their act led others to seek help with the pastor's family, and inspired others in Le Chambon to follow their example. A community that nourishes life is often inspired by the acts of one or two people, addressing immediate needs; then, a larger community becomes aware of needs and begins to respond.[27] Even if the movement never spreads beyond the original caregiver, however, seeds may sprout in unexpected places in the future. The practice of care is thus a practice of *looking for opportunities wherever they are found within the immediate community, responding, and inviting others to respond.* The transformative effects of care-giving ministries (as pastoral care teams and mission trips) reveal the power of one person or group to begin a movement.[28]

A third clue is that *the practice of offering care has power to attribute value and dignity to people who have been rejected, and to inspire larger responses and solutions to major political and structural problems.* Though care is often associated with the status quo, care giving with marginalized people (political refugees, elderly people, homeless people, people with AIDS) can turn structures upside down. The people of Le Chambon became increasingly aware of the tense political-military situation in Europe, actively choosing to resist; thus, their individual acts of care escalated into risky political action and influenced others in their region. The people of

25. Magda Trocmé, "Le Chambon," in *The Courage to Care*, ed. Rittner and Myers, 102; Philip Hallie, "Major Julius Schmahling," ibid., 114–15; cf. Pierre Sauvage, "Ten Questions," ibid., 139–40; Robert McAfee Brown, "They Could Do No Other," ibid., 146. Philip Hallie recognized that Schmahling was a spontaneous man who responded to immediate needs. "He was no hero, no declared enemy of Nazism or of any other 'ism. . . . ' But seen up close, and seen from the point of view of the hundreds, possibly thousands, of people he protected from the Gestapo and from his own vicious auxiliary troops in the Haute-Loire, he was a good man. He compromised with evil, and helped defenseless people as much as he could" (114). See also Hallie, *Lest Innocent Blood Be Shed*.

26. Magda Trocmé, "Le Chambon," 101–2.

27. Brown, "They Could Do No Other," 146–47; Mary Elizabeth Moore, "Congregations Struggling with Hope: Embodied Knowing," in *People of a Compassionate God: Creating Welcoming Congregations*, ed. Janet F. Fishburn (Nashville: Abingdon, 2003), 131–57

28. This power is also documented in congregational case studies. Alice Frazer Evans, Robert A. Evans, and William Bean Kennedy, *Pedagogy for the Non-Poor* (Maryknoll, N.Y.: Orbis, 1987); Fishburn, *People of a Compassionate God*.

Denmark actually saved ninety-five percent of their Jewish population by offering care in a full-scale way; they were able to resist the German domination of their country that many European countries could not do. Many attribute their efforts to acts of care that expanded to political resistance, including broad citizen effort and collaboration by a key German official.[29]

Building from these clues is a fourth: *the practice of care involves tending and deepening relationships with God and others, thus reflecting Divine compassion.*[30] Such tending took place in Le Chambon, even among the children and youth, who helped hide their friends. This particular clue has often been named in religious education literature, which recognizes care as both spiritual and human. Sondra Matthaei argues that God is present in the "'in-between' of personal relation-ships," and she recognizes that active care and advocacy emerge in that context.[31] In a more patriarchal spirit, Evelyn Underhill compares teachers with sheep dogs, helping the shepherd tend the sheep:

> The best dog that I saw never barked once; and he spent an astonishing amount of his time sitting perfectly still, looking at the shepherd. The com-munion of spirit between them was perfect. They worked as a unit.... The dog went steadily on with it; and his tail never ceased to wag."[32]

Underhill's analogy underscores the relationship between caring for students and communing with God.[33] In the case of Le Chambon, the Trocmé family embodied these ideals of Matthaei and Underhill, living God-centered lives and caring for people as they came. Indeed, they recognized each person who came to them as "a unique and living spirit infinitely dear to God."[34] Others in Le Chambon followed their lead with diverse motivations, but the originating power was deeply spiritual and deeply human.

Inspired by the people of Le Chambon, as well as theorists of teaching, teach-ers everywhere are left with a challenge: to care for the spiritual, physical, and psychological health of each person within their purview and for the well-being of the whole community. This is a huge responsibility, but it does have rewards.

---

29. Moshe Bejski, "Examples of Heroism," in *The Courage to Care*, ed. Rittner and Myers, 130–32.

30. Robert W. Pazmino, *God Our Teacher: Theological Basics in Christian Education* (Grand Rapids, Mich.: Baker, 2001).

31. Sondra Higgins Matthaei, *Faith Matters: Faith-Mentoring in the Faith Community* (Valley Forge, Pa.: Trinity Press International, 1996), 1. Matthaei links care with the guarantor's role of being present with and advocating for another (66–70).

32. Evelyn Underhill, "The Teacher's Vocation: An Address to Teachers of Religion," in *Collected Papers of Evelyn Underhill,* ed. Lucy Menzies (London: Longmans, Green, 1946, 1928), 157–58. This essay was delivered at the annual meeting of the Southwark Diocesan Sunday School Association in Church House, 1927. Underhill observes that the sheep dogs work without barking, fuss, ostentatious authority, or busy-ness. I think she overplays the dogs' docility and sheep's tiresomeness, but the analogy is a good one.

33. Ibid., 159–60; cf. 158–59. See also Underhill, "The Spiritual Life of the Teacher," in *Collected Papers,* 172–87. This address was delivered to the South London Centre of the Guild of the Epiphany.

34. Underhill, "The Teacher's Vocation," 164; cf. 169.

Drawing upon the biblical story of feeding the five thousand, Evelyn Underhill insists that teachers have responsibility to feed hungry souls; yet, they are also fed. In the feeding miracle, the disciples served and ate, but the twelve baskets of leftovers would feed each of them on the following day.[35] Thus, the practice of offering care often yields unexpected nourishment for teachers.

2. Seek and Reflect on Life Wherever It Is Found

The second practice is to *seek and reflect on life wherever it is found*. This is the challenging enactment of a hermeneutic of nurture. People can usually decry evil with ease; to perceive life in the midst of evil is more difficult. Discerning and appreciating seeds of new life is particularly difficult in a world that pushes for quick, easy answers to problems. The challenge is well told in Anthony de Mello's story:

> A woman dreamed she walked into a brand new shop in the marketplace and, to her surprise, found God behind the counter. "What do you sell here?" she asked. "Everything your heart desires," said God.... "I want peace of mind and love and happiness and wisdom and freedom from fear," she said. Then, as an afterthought, she added, "Not just for me. For everyone on earth." God smiled, "I think you've got me wrong, dear. We don't sell fruits here. Only seeds."[36]

This story is a splendid metaphor for nourishing life, but it calls attention to the natural human desire for ready-made solutions to the world's ills. To seek and reflect on life is to look farther and deeper, seeking seeds of life that have not yet grown to fullness. To do this is to trust that God really can open eyes that see and ears that hear — to develop insight beyond sight, and understanding beyond hearing.[37]

Nowhere is this style of searching better embodied than in Julian of Norwich (1342–c. 1416), discussed briefly in chapter 6. Having lived through wars and plagues, she became ill around the age of thirty, and the priest was called to administer Last Rites. During this illness, however, Julian experienced sixteen "revelations of divine love," and saw glimmers of God's compassion that nourished her the rest of her life.[38] When Julian became well, she committed her life to God as an anchoress and lived her remaining years in a cell attached to a parish church. Within the cell, she prayed, ate and slept, worshiped, received eucharist, wrote

---

35. Underhill, "The Spiritual Life of the Teacher," 181–82.

36. Anthony de Mello, S.J., *Taking Flight: A Book of Story Meditations* (New York: Doubleday, 1988), 103.

37. John M. Hull, *On Sight and Insight: A Journey into the World of Blindness* (Oxford: Oneworld Publications, 1997, 1990); Kathy Black, *A Healing Homiletic: Preaching and Disability* (Nashville: Abingdon, 1996).

38. Julian of Norwich, *Showings*, in Classics of Western Spirituality, trans. Edmund Colledge, O.S.A., and James Walsh, S.J. (Mahwah, N.J.: Paulist, 1978).

about God's revelations (a long and short version), and offered spiritual counsel to people who came to her. Meanwhile, war and plague wreaked torment on her medieval world, and Julian sensed the traumas, even in the solitude of her cell.[39] She reiterated her diagnosis of the world: "Sin is necessary, but all will be well, and all will be well, and every kind of thing will be well."[40]

Within her context, Julian developed a theology that accounted for sin and for God's providence. She saw God's generosity offered through the Trinity — Father, Son, and Holy Spirit; or Father (Creator), Mother (Christ as nourishment for our lives), and Lover (intimate Spirit). Julian's persistent hermeneutic was not naïve optimism, but an intentional choice to seek seeds of life in all life situations, trusting in the presence and provision of God. Julian's life story suggests several specific educational practices:

- *seeking for God within tragedy;*
- *expecting and opening to God's revelations, even in times of danger and death;*
- *revisiting revelatory experiences and probing them for deeper meanings;*
- *engaging in regular spiritual practices (eucharist, silence, prayer), expecting them to hone one's alertness to God and the ways of God.*

To do this is a life vocation, but it is also a practice that can be exercised in a Bible study group, Sunday school class, or work camp, where experiences of tragedy and revelation often emerge and invite deep engagement. It is a practice of opening to God again and again, never being satisfied with edicts and answers, but always encouraging more questions and more searching for the seeds of life that God uncovers in unlikely places.

3. Participate in Forces of Good

The practices of seeking and reflecting lead naturally to a third set of practices, *participating in forces of good — discerning and responding to forces of good within a particular context.* In ambiguous contexts, people might be seeking the forces of most good or least evil. The first challenge is to discern, to build courage, and to equip the community to respond. When a youth group visits people who are unable to leave their homes, they share a gift of presence that transcends the single act. When the youth group further volunteers to do "fix-it" jobs for the people

---

39. Grace M. Jantzen, *Julian of Norwich: Mystic and Theologian*, new ed. (New York: Paulist Press, 2000); Grace M. Jantzen, *Power, Gender and Christian Mysticism* (New York: Cambridge University, 1995); Jane Frances Maynard, "Finding Religious and Spiritual Meaning in AIDS-Related Multiple Loss: A Comparative and Constructive Theological Analysis of Communal Bereavement," Ph.D. diss., Claremont School of Theology, 2001. Maynard draws parallels between traumas in a contemporary parish and those of Julian's world, doing comparative analysis between a contemporary ethnography and a historical-textual study.

40. Julian, *Showings*, 225 (Long Text).

they visit, they give both physical help and psychological comfort. When a children's class creates a peace mural to remind their congregation to pray for peace, they participate in a movement for peace. The same is true for acts of charity and justice performed by Sunday school classes, outreach groups, and mission teams. These are the bricks and mortar out of which large movements grow, grounded in Micah's call to justice, mercy, and humility. Habitat for Humanity began as a small effort, as did the Heifer Project, as did the civil rights movement. One effort led to another until vast numbers of people were involved, and vast effects were felt.

Such practices confirm the theological affirmation that people can choose life, even in the face of death. Sometimes the efforts, even extensive well-chosen efforts, will seem fruitless. Sometimes they will bear fruit beyond imagination. The efforts of countless people in South Africa reveal that some justice efforts take decades and involve death and discouragement along the way; yet, they do bear fruit. When we visited South Africa, we asked many people if frustration is mounting about the slowness of change. The people most involved in grassroots building movements said to us, "Yes, people get frustrated, but we can see changes from month to month, and we can see people working hard for change. That is enough to keep us hopeful." One man told us that he is inspired by the poorest of the poor — people without homes, jobs, or food, who find a way to gather a few boards to build a crude home, sell vegetables, cut people's hair, or start a bed and breakfast in their township. They survive and inspire others to survive by their hope — the fruit of participating in the good. They also point to educational practices of *protest, building and equipping,* and *participating in acts of kindness and justice.*

Protest

In South Africa, many acts of *protest* were carried out over a period of decades, particularly by black and colored South Africans, but by many white South Africans as well. The protests included mass movements, small communities' insisting on justice for themselves or others, underground theater, and individual refusals to participate in oppressive actions. Taken together, these and other acts created a climate for change. Such protests in dangerous circumstances inspire church communities to engage in protest wherever they are. Indeed, many congregations have refused to close their eyes to injustice and destruction in their communities. One church gathers a group of seniors to protest reductions in health care; another protests the treatment of prisoners in a nearby prison; another protests the treatment of Muslims in their city. These are educational acts that sometimes emanate from a small group within a congregation; they may also emanate from one or two people who encourage others in their church to study a particular issue.[41]

---

41. Evans, Evans, and Kennedy, *Pedagogy for the Non-Poor*; Fishburn, *People of a Compassionate God.*

Build and Equip

Many acts of protest become acts of *building and equipping*, as people become involved in the lives of others, whether seniors in the congregation, prisoners down the road, or gay and lesbian people in the community. The movement to create welcoming congregations for gay, lesbian, bisexual, and transgendered folk began largely to protest church actions, especially actions that marginalized gay people and fed other social abuses with anti-gay rhetoric. Some protest grew from ideology, some from personal compassion. Whatever the initial motivation, congregational protest often moved toward deeper understanding, stronger human relationships, and increased hospitality.[42] In South Africa, practices of building and equipping included many elements — educational expansion, job training for unemployed workers, efforts by the Malay community to rebuild their cultural riches, work to educate families and rebuild healthy family relationships after years of social oppression and family separations, and work by religious and community groups to defuse racial prejudice. These are only a few examples, but they spark imagination about how local communities might reflect on unique needs in their settings and then contribute to building and equipping.

Practice Kindness and Justice

Practices of kindness and justice are fundamental to participating in forces of good. Important to rebuilding South Africa were the multiple efforts of kindness and justice that marked daily life. These included (and include) personal niceties on the street, social services, job-creation, home-building for people living in camps far from family, a new South African Constitution, reshaped legal structures, and efforts to encourage businesses to return after the international embargo lifted. Practices of kindness and justice also include education: university studies of South African cultures and religions; expanded educational offerings (including technical, arts, localized, cultural, and continuing education options); expanded efforts to provide education for all peoples; and education for teachers in South African cultures. These few examples represent the bricks and mortar for a new nation. They are similar to the small-scale efforts of my high school class to build a school, or the effort of our annual conference to build a welcoming community that engages in disagreement with compassion and respect.

These practices are important to small communities and institutions, as well as nations. National and local efforts support one another, as do practices of learning communities in churches, schools, and other bodies. As one might expect, the purposive, development-oriented educational theories of John Dewey and other progressives are still relevant to education that seeks to participate in forces of good.[43] People are nurtured in faith as they practice faith in a community that,

---

42. Fishburn, *People of a Compassionate God.*

43. Dewey's accent on the social and purposive nature of education is particularly important here. See John Dewey, *Experience and Education* (New York: Collier Books, 1977, 1938), esp. 58–60, 67–72;

at least roughly, embodies and instills its values, and keeps the windows open for lively critique, protest, and re-formation.

4. Engage in Story and Ritual

Now we turn to educational practices that support an ethos of nurture: to *engage in story and ritual with a community of God's people — to nurture life through narrative and performative relationships.* This includes remembering, reflecting upon, rehearsing, or creating relationships, and it takes place in worship, classes, prayer groups, work teams, or fellowship events. Whatever the form and wherever the engagement, narratives and liturgical action have the power to nurture and transform a community.

Stories are narrative embodiments of experience, involving characters, movement, and interactions over time. Whether mythic or parabolic, stories evoke perspectives and questions about God and the world; whether fictitious, documentary, reconstructed, or surreal, stories stir relational images of the Creator and creation. For all of these reasons and more, teaching through story is relational, connecting people with the relationships in their lives, in the cosmos, and in the divine encounter.[44]

Ritual, on the other hand, is *the community's reenactment of central events or meanings in their encounter with God and the world.* Rituals can take historic forms or be created in the moment. Some Protestant churches, for example, celebrate eucharist according to their denomination's most recently developed liturgy, but celebrate an older liturgy during certain seasons, like Lent. The same churches often create new rituals that fit their community as well, such as inviting children to lead a contemporary benediction at the close of each Sunday's worship. Such rituals are performative embodiments of experience, involving the community in repetitive actions with and for one another. To teach through ritual (as through story) is to teach relationally, but in ritual the accent is on dynamic interactions within human community and divine relationships.

Engage in Story

Engaging with story is more than storytelling. True engagement involves *living, telling, dramatizing, dancing, analyzing, singing, critiquing, meditating on, and reshaping stories.* Consider this chapter's stories from South Africa. They capture, in a small way, the spirit of South Africa. However partial and incomplete (even distorted), such stories invite people to experience a slice of reality with some degree of

---

John Dewey and Evelyn Dewey, *Schools of Tomorrow* (New York: E. P. Dutton, 1962, 1915), 121–31; cf. Martha Snyder, Ross Snyder, and Ross Snyder Jr., *The Young Child as Person: Toward the Development of Healthy Conscience* (New York: Human Sciences, 1980).

44. See Susan M. Shaw, *Storytelling in Religious Education* (Birmingham: Religious Education Press, 1999); Anne Streaty Wimberly, *Soul Stories* (Nashville: Abingdon, 1994); Mary Elizabeth Moore, *Teaching from the Heart: Theology and Educational Method* (Valley Forge, Pa.: Trinity Press International, 1998, 1991), 131–62.

fullness. This does not mean that all stories are historically accurate (or even intend to be); stories simply invite people to experience a world of images, events, ideas, or movements. They invite people into stories of faith, social context, and imagination.

Stories serve many functions in a community of faith. First, *they communicate the passions of a people,* whether they are personal, biographical, or symbolic. Consider the annual conference story. Conference members often retell the story of our ten-year journey into new patterns of relationship, telling the story for strength and vision during times of fear or antagonism. Indeed the process by which we moved into new ways of doing business was infused with story sharing. One gay man, after sharing his faith journey in a conference session some years ago, said to me, "I feel so honored to be asked to tell my story. This is the first time the church has ever been interested." I expressed surprise at his response because people had said some strong things against homosexuality in the discussion; the man responded that he could deal with strong views if he felt people were genuinely sharing and listening. Two lesbian women said almost the same thing. One might say that storytelling communicates passions and often helps people respect disagreements, at least enough to honor the passions of others.

Second, *stories open windows into the cultures in which people live.* The news media, for example, tell stories of the world, stories that people want to hear, and stories that will increase their viewers or readers. Studying stories of the media (e.g., minimal coverage of religion, maximal coverage of violent crime, skewed coverage of international events, and so forth) illumines the world, but requires complex interpretive frameworks. Without critical analysis and comparative research, the picture of culture is distorted. Thus, people seeking to understand culture do well to ask: What stories do people tell one another? What stories are missing? What movies, books and magazines are popular? Why?

Third, *stories enable people to cross boundaries into worlds quite different from their own.*[45] In religious education, this boundary-crossing function involves crossing boundaries of time (traveling into biblical and historical stories), as well as space (exploring stories from diverse parts of the world, diverse ethnicities, and diverse life situations). It also involves crossing religious traditions, coming to know others through their sacred stories and life sagas, and crossing into imaginary worlds, such as utopian or dystopian worlds. Such boundary-crossing nurtures empathy toward others and raises important existential questions in encounters with similarities and differences.

Another function of stories is to *open windows into the natural world.* Modernity is largely bankrupt in its dearth of natural world stories, but indigenous cultures, and the cultures out of which biblical texts emerged, are rich with earth stories.

---

45. "Telling Stories and Crossing Boundaries," in *Unitarian Universalism, 1988,* ed. Charles A. Howe (Boston: Unitarian Universality Ministers Association, 1989), 25–41.

These illumine the textures and interactions of diverse parts of the creation, as well as the relations that human beings have with the rest of creation. Some ecologists have created a genre of earth stories to stir modern imagination regarding the immensity, complexity, and wonder of the cosmos.[46] Others have recovered stories from Christian tradition, such as tales of St. Francis, early Celtic Christians, or later indigenous Christians.[47] Still others tell descriptive stories of environmental crises, movements and responses.[48] These diverse narratives open windows to the wonder and trauma of the natural world.

One other function of stories is to *open windows into the workings of God in the world*. This function is served by stories from religious communities and texts. It is also served by stories from diverse cultural traditions, especially when analyzed in dialogue with religious narratives. C. S. Song's paradigm guides such theological work: discerning God's action in life stories; exploring issues, questions, and connections among diverse stories; developing empathy toward others; and uncovering meaning.[49] Song encourages people to seek the transcendent in all life stories, thus to stretch and deepen theology. This view resonates with Anne Wimberly's educational process of story-linking — linking biblical, historical, cultural, and personal stories.[50] In both, stories reveal and guide.

Engage in Ritual

The spirit of faith is also carried by a *community's actions, expressed most succinctly and powerfully in its performance of memory and meaning*. Rituals include the sacraments, but also the traditional and not-so-traditional liturgies of the community. Engagement is strongest when people participate in the rituals, and also when they study and grow into deeper understandings over time. With or

---

46. Thomas Berry, "The New Story: Comments on the Origin, Identification, and Transmission of Values," *CrossCurrents* (Summer/Fall 1987): 184–99.

47. E. M. Blaiklock and A. C. Keys, trans., *The Little Flowers of St. Francis: The Acts of St. Francis and His Companions* (London: Hodder and Stoughton, 1985); Esther De Waal, comp. and ed., *The Celtic Vision* (London: Darton, Longman & Todd, 1988); Nora Chadwick, *The Celts* (London: Penguin, 1991, 1971); Chadwick, *The Age of the Saints in the Early Celtic Church* (Oxford: Oxford University Press, 1961); Gregory Cajete, *Look to the Mountain: An Ecology of Indigenous Education* (Durango, Colo.: Kivaki, 1994).

48. See, for example: Robert D. Bullard, "Anatomy of Environmental Racism and the Environmental Justice Movement," in *Confronting Environmental Racism: Voices from the Grassroots*, ed. Robert D. Bullard (Boston: South End, 1993), 7–39; Steven C. Rockefeller, "The Earth Charter Process," *Earth Ethics: Evolving Values for an Earth Community* 8, nos. 2 and 3 (Winter/Spring 1997): 3–8. These various efforts to recover, create, and share narratives are important educationally. See, for example, Mary Elizabeth Moore, *Ministering with the Earth* (St. Louis: Chalice, 1998); C. A. Bowers, *Educating for an Ecologically Sustainable Culture: Rethinking Moral Education, Creativity, Intelligence, and Other Modern Orthodoxies* (Albany: State University of New York Press, 1995); and C. A. Bowers and David J. Flinders, *Responsive Teaching: An Ecological Approach to Classroom Patterns of Language, Culture, and Thought* (New York: Teachers College, 1990).

49. Choan-Seng Song, *The Believing Heart: An Invitation to Story Theology* (Minneapolis: Fortress, 1999); Choan-Seng Song, *Tell Us Our Names: Story Theology from an Asian Perspective* (Maryknoll, N.Y.: Orbis, 1984).

50. Wimberly, *Soul Stories*.

without our understanding, however, rituals have potential to mediate God's transformative grace.

The multiple dimensions of ritual participation dazzled me one Sunday when I served the cup in our church's service of eucharist. Some of our church leaders had decided to encourage young children to participate in the sacrament and to reorient our Sunday worship to enhance their participation. The pastor talked with the congregation and parents, and altered the Sunday schedule. Another pastor taught the children for several weeks about the meaning and practice of eucharist (communicating in various ways with the various ages). At the end of the study, the pastor enthusiastically interpreted it to the congregation. When the children came to the chancel that day, they knelt or were carried by a parent. Each child held his or her hands up to receive the bread, then dipped the bread into the cup. As I watched their smiles and eager postures, I was moved to a tearful smile myself. Never had I seen such eagerness to receive; never had I encountered the meaning of eucharist more deeply. Reflecting on this later, I became aware that the combination of physical preparation, study, and participation enhanced the celebration for the entire congregation, and most especially for the children.

Ritual participation is the center of worship, but it is also important in study and fellowship settings, taking diverse forms. Ritual can involve the rhythmic patterns of a class session, special room arrangements, the formal lighting of a candle at the beginning of a session, prayers, music, the sharing of joys and concerns, and so forth. Such ritual actions are richer when reflectively planned. For example, some groups have special ways to celebrate birthdays, but do not communicate to newcomers how they too might be included. Other groups have practiced the same rituals for years, and have not reflected to see if they still have life. Other groups have special ways of saying goodbye to people who are moving or congratulating those who are graduating, but do not practice these rituals consistently; thus, they celebrate some and neglect others. These are just a few tangible examples, but the value of intentional care is larger than the examples.

The significance of ritual is perhaps best described through a particular case. In a large downtown church, an adult Sunday school class had dwindled to four members, all past eighty years of age and often unable to attend church. The class had shared decades of life together, however, and did not want to disband or forfeit their room and funds. To close would seem like death, which none was prepared to face. The church council worried about how to respond to the class. A younger group in the church was looking for meeting space, but no one wanted to close the older class to make room for others. Finally, the council decided to invite the older group to reflect on the issues and to decide what kind of legacy they wanted to leave the church: to continue to meet as a class (a real option), to pass their space to a new group, or to make some other contribution to the church that fit their hopes for the congregation. They did meet, and they chose to close their class, to pass their space to a new group, and to create an endowment fund for the church. The church council then planned a church party to honor the group that had been the backbone of the church for so many decades. They invited the group to present their endowment and to commission the new group. The ritual was planned as carefully as a Christmas Eve service. The resulting transition delighted all concerned. The ritual itself nurtured the passing of a legacy, honoring the past and welcoming the future.

5. Mentor

The final practice — *mentoring* — *is supporting the relational, vocational, and spiritual life of others.*[51] It involves all of the practices named thus far. In mentoring, people become partners, usually with one older partner and another who is sponsored or nurtured by that person. Partnership can, however, be a peer relationship, with mentoring moving both ways. It may also be communal; a community can mentor its members or one community can mentor another. In all of its forms, the mentoring relationship has potential to guide, inspire, and encourage people in their life journeys. Reflecting back on the texts from Acts and Micah, we find important guides for contemporary Christian communities; however, the texts give only thin outlines of faithful life. To mentor is to embody these texts. To mentor is to recognize, develop, and use one's gifts and to recognize, develop, and encourage others' gifts. Thus, mentoring involves many particular actions, five of which I will develop here.

Walk with Others

Most fundamentally, mentoring is *walking with others.* In her interviews with seventy-eight churched and unchurched adults, Sondra Matthaei discovered how influential these relationships are. She identified four primary roles of mentors — guide, model, guarantor, and mediator. All of these roles involve *spending time, taking an interest in another's life, seeking ways to enhance the quality of the other's life, responding to the other's needs and yearnings, and praying and caring for the other,* all without promise of reward. This is the heart of mentoring — simply walking with others.

---

51. Matthaei, *Faith Matters*, 20; cf. 20–29. This definition echoes that of Matthaei: "A faith mentor is a co-creator with God who, as a living representative of God's grace, participates in the relational, vocational, and spiritual growth of others" (ibid.). Matthaei's definition also resonates with the sacramental theme of this book, particularly in her accent on co-creating, and representing God's grace. Diverse perspectives on mentoring can be found in Michael Zeldin and Sara L. Lee, eds., *Touching the Future: Mentoring and the Jewish Professional* (Los Angeles: Rhea Hirsch School of Education, Hebrew Union College–Jewish Institute of Religion, 1995); Sharon Daloz Parks, *Big Questions, Worthy Dreams: Mentoring Young Adults in their Search for Meaning, Purpose, and Faith* (San Francisco: Jossey-Bass, 2000); J. Furlong and T. Maynard, *Mentoring Student Teachers* (London: Routledge, 1995).

Listen and Explain

A second practice of mentoring is *listening to questions and explaining.* One of the masters of this kind of mentoring was Howard Thurman, who left his prominent position as chaplain of Howard University to become pastor of the Church for the Fellowship of all Peoples in San Francisco — an intercultural, international congregation in the 1940s and 1950s. While serving the church, he was called to visit a parishioner at Stanford University Hospital. Thurman was African American and his parishioner was white, as were all of the doctors and nurses in the hospital at that time. When Thurman arrived at the nursing station, the nurse said, "What are you doing here?" He explained, but she was indignant and insisted that she could not give him Miss L.'s room number. She asked him if he were sure he was a minister. Thurman replied:

> Before I answer your question, I must explain to you why you are reacting to my presence as you are. There is nothing in the total experience of your young years that would prepare you for such an occasion as this. Miss L. is a member of the Church for the Fellowship of All Peoples — an integrated church in the San Francisco community. I am her minister and have the minister's privilege of visiting her.[52]

This story reveals the power of listening to questions and explaining. Thurman grasped the nurse's questions and resistance (even when unexpressed). By responding to her questions, he honored her and invited her to broader understandings. He dove into the middle of a tense situation, neither avoiding the conversation nor Miss L. Like Thurman, *a mentor walks into difficult situations and seeks ways to nurture people into growth.*

Modeling

A third practice of mentoring is *modeling and calling other people to faithful acts.* This does not require a perfect life or perfect world; mentors guide and inspire others by living well in adversity. Gershon Baskin described this in the life of his friend Isaac Saada, a teacher involved in peace education in Israel and Palestine.[53] Isaac had once told him how difficult it was to teach his children to love and hope for peace, for they had seen many terrible things. They asked their father how he could possibly work with the Israelis. He urged them to believe in peace and insisted that peace will eventually come: "the worst thing that could happen to them and to the Palestinian people would be if they filled their hearts with hatred." Soon after saying these words, Isaac Saada died in a shelling meant for terrorists. Saada, however, had been faithful to his call, modeling for his children

---

52. Howard Thurman, *With Head and Heart: The Autobiography of Howard Thurman* (New York: Harcourt Brace Jovanovich, 1979), 154.

53. Gershon Baskin, Co-Director of Israel/Palestine Center for Research and Information, letter of July 18, 2001.

and many others. Saada's decision to *live toward a vision of peace and love amid realities of destruction and hate* was a decision to mentor others. If he could do this with shells flying, others can do it as well.

Share Opportunities and Responsibilities

A fourth practice of mentoring is *sharing opportunities and responsibilities*. Mentoring involves people once again in acts of justice and kindness, but this time the focus is on the mentor or mentoring community, called to let go of control and allow others to seize opportunities and assume responsibilities. Returning once again to the woman who anointed Jesus, note that Jesus showed no sign of being offended at the woman's serving him, even in a tense situation at the end of his life; neither was he offended at her breach of social convention. He left space for her to respond to the opportunity and responsibility that beckoned her. We can see similar mentoring in a Norwegian Lutheran congregation in rural Minnesota.[54] In the church, adults gradually give responsibilities to children and youth, according to their ages and abilities. Young people care for the nursery, help tend the churchyard and mend the church building, co-teach children's classes, and cook church suppers. Children look forward to new roles, especially those associated with older children or youth. The adults mentor by *inviting, teaching, and guiding* them as they assume these roles and contribute to the community.

Guide

One other practice of mentoring is *guiding people to discern and use their gifts*. Mentoring is embodied in godly acts of seeing and encouraging the gifts of others. This may be done in formal processes of discerning spiritual gifts (talents, personality traits, and so forth) or in informal discernment in daily life and in encouragement to give of oneself. In some churches, every person in the congregation has a calling, and elders of the congregation meet with each person each year to discern that call, whether singing in the choir, engaging in social service, or teaching a class. The church thus guides by *affirming that every person has gifts that are valued and needed in the community*.

6. Play

Just as mentoring is important, so is the *practice of play*. It is a part of walking humbly with God, for play is the avenue by which people explore faith and experiment with spiritual practices, reinforcing their sense of God's ongoing creation, especially God's *creation of space for new birth*. Play is a way by which space is cleared for thinking new thoughts (through imagination or thought experiments); engaging new practices (trying new spiritual practices in a retreat or other setting); developing new forms of expression (through diverse arts and media); and

---

54. The congregation was one of six ethogenic studies of youth ministry conducted 1986–98.

practicing new ways of being (spiritual disciplines or attitudes). Paul Ricoeur recognizes the power of play in human life, as did John Dewey, for whom play was an important part of the educational process.

We need not turn to theoreticians to make a case for play, however. One Sunday morning, I watched a group of children during the Children's Moments in worship. The leader was reading a children's story about the birth of Jesus and had beside her a manger scene with a stable, animals, people, and a star. As she introduced the story, the children looked at her, but as soon as she turned her face to read from the book, the children jumped up from their quiet seated poses to play with the wooden figures. They continued playing throughout the story. I do not know if they were listening to the story or what they learned as they played with the wooden figures; however, a few weeks later, the same leader asked the children to recall the characters' names and characteristics, which they did readily. This vignette exemplifies the importance of multidimensional play for nurture. The children were fully engaged with their hands, eyes, and ears. Some may have heard more, and others may have touched more, but all of their senses were being summoned to attention during the children's moment. This is playful nurture.

Without play, the note of grace is lost, and the focus of nurture falls into narrow forms of teaching correct answers or burdensome practices of works-righteousness. Indeed, the liberal theological movement that heralded nurture in religious education was often critiqued for trusting overly much in human action. Play is a practice by which the forms and rules of a community are passed down, as well as a practice by which those same forms and rules are transformed by the practice of alternative forms of life.

This brief excursus suggests that play should be an intentional part of Christian educational practice, not reserved for children or for breaks interspersed amid the "real lessons." Play should be woven into the fabric of a community, enabling people to dive more deeply into the subject at hand, to experiment more radically with alternative patterns of living, and to exert agency that will empower them for the future.

Concluding Reflections

A brief word is sufficient to conclude. Nurture — taken for granted in educational ministry — is a way to mediate God's Life through ordinary relationships and interactions in community. This work nurtures fullness of life — acknowledging the preciousness of all persons and communities and calling them to live as God has created and called them. This work also nurtures God's creation by calling forth empathy, compassion, and reverent relationships with self, other people, and the earth. This work is sacramental!

Reflecting Further

1. Reflect on what people want and need to learn in your community. Take time for silence; then write individually or share in a group what you have discerned. Consider the poem below and reflect on how your insights relate, amplify, or contradict visions of the poem.

> We want to learn that God is with us —
> God cares,
> That we are together as we travel
> and bumble along,
> That life does have meaning
> and we can know it,
> if even for a moment,
> and live it,
> even if it takes a lifetime
> of learning
> and longing
> and loving.
>
> We want to learn that God cares
> for the hurts of the world
> That we can be together with God
> and one another
> in the repair of the world,
> That Jesus Christ showed us,
> shows us,
> will always show us the Way,
> That Faith is a bursting light,
> a deep darkness,
> a wild energy,
> that comes from God,
> and makes all the difference!

2. Reflect on how your community or family presently nurture one another and others. Considering the educational practices discussed in this chapter, what nurture is particularly strong in your community? What is needed? How could you expand your practices in the near and distant future?

Chapter Eight

Reconstructing Community and Repairing the World

✡

If we will look to God and work together — not only here but everywhere — then others will see this world too and help to make it a reality. (Rosa Parks)[1]

For if you keep silence at such a time as this, relief and deliverance will rise for the Jews, but you and your father's family will perish. Who knows? Perhaps you have come to royal dignity for such a time as this. (Esther 4:14)

As Rosa Parks reached her sixties and seventies, she spoke a lot about human unity. She concluded one of her pleas for unity with the words quoted here, expressing a vision that had guided much of her life. Parks's determined hope began early in life, leading her to step after step of work for racial justice, eventually leading her to refuse to yield her seat for a white man on a Montgomery bus and, beyond that, to years of continuing work for civil rights, racial justice, and human unity. We have already seen how dearly Rosa Parks paid for the just and whole world that she envisioned (chapter 5). Now we turn to a vision of sacramental living in which that kind of self-giving is advocated as a human calling.

Turning to a time some three thousand years ago, we can also see determined hope in the biblical account of Esther. Esther married the king whose administration was oppressing her people and was readying to enslave them. Having been convinced by her uncle Mordecai that marrying the king and working from inside his palace was the only hope for her people, Esther responded. Both she and Mordecai risked their lives, and also failure, but they were pulled by necessity and vision to take those risks.

These two narratives set the stage for a chapter in which the challenges and hopes that guided Rosa Parks, Esther, and Mordecai are seen as touchstones for teaching ministry. The focus of the chapter is *the human calling to mediate*

---

1. Rosa Parks, with Gregory J. Reed, *Quiet Strength: The Faith, the Hope, and the Heart of a Woman Who Changed a Nation* (Grand Rapids, Mich.: Zondervan, 1994), 89.

187

God's prophetic, redemptive work through the sacramental practice of reconstructing community and repairing the world. The challenge of such sacramental living is to address destructive prejudices and oppression over time, and also as they arise. Whether engaging in a step-by-step commitment, like Rosa Parks, or being called by the urgency of a particular time, like Esther, the call for prophetic action and redemptive work resounds. These women exemplify a *spirituality of reconstruction and repair — walking and working with God for the repair of the world.* How can teaching inspire and support such a spirituality?

This chapter focus upsets many common assumptions, such as: who is powerful (Rosa Parks and Esther); how change takes place (sometimes through decisions made in the moment without full awareness of their consequences); what influences social change (sometimes grassroots movements, such as the civil rights movement that trained Rosa Parks and hundreds of others for action); and what is the role of people behind the scenes (such as Mordecai behind Esther). Another common assumption is unseated in this chapter, namely, the seeming dichotomy between building community and engaging in prophetic action in the world. Rosa Parks's words, with which the chapter began, reveal how false that dichotomy is. The building of community, according to Parks, is one central way by which people actually change the world. She echoes Paul's image of the church as the Body of Christ (Corinthians and Romans) and John Wesley's plea that the Christian community practice "keep the unity of the Spirit in the bond of peace."[2] Parks is speaking of global human unity; Paul is writing to the Corinthians and Romans about Christian unity; and Wesley is addressing "the people called Methodists." All of them recognize, however, that unity and community are essential if people are to make a difference in the throes of the world.

As signaled in chapter 2, prophecy is an action of God to be received and enacted by *all* God's people; thus, sacramental living and teaching are prophetic acts of the community. Sacramental teaching will call, encourage, equip, and support the prophetic action of all God's people, individually and collectively. This chapter thus centers on education that equips people to participate in God's redemptive work, reconstructing local communities and repairing the larger world. First the stories.

A few years ago, I attended the graduation ceremony of the University of Judaism.[3] *A Jewish rabbinic student was graduating with a master's degree in Hebrew literature*

---

2. John Wesley, Sermon 74: "Of the Church," *The Bicentennial Edition of the Works of John Wesley* (Nashville: Abingdon, 1984–), 3:50, 55; "The Character of a Methodist," *Works* 9:32–46. Wesley adds: "Whoever they are that have 'one Spirit, one hope, one Lord, one faith, one God and Father of all,' I can easily bear with their holding wrong opinions, yea, and superstitious modes of worship. Nor would I on these accounts scruple still to include them within the pale of the catholic church" ("Of the Church," 52).

3. This story is also included, without details about Rabbi ben Zakkai, in Mary Elizabeth Moore, "Sacramental Teaching: Mediating the Holy," in *Forging a Better Religious Education for the Third Millennium*, ed. James Michael Lee (Birmingham: Religious Education Press, 2000), 41–68.

before proceeding to the next step in her education to become a rabbi. She told a story about her first day at the University of Judaism. All of the new students gathered to meet one another and learn about the University of Judaism. A person was present who had just conducted a vast demographic study of Judaism in the United States, discovering for example that the rate of Jewish intermarriage with persons in other religions is more than 50 percent. He presented some of his findings on that day and concluded by saying, "I have good news and bad news." The good news was that in two generations Jews would still exist; the bad news was that they probably would not exist in any recognizable form. Judaism would be different from the traditions that the students and their parents had known.

The graduate went on to tell of first-century Jewish people in the years before the Temple was destroyed. The Romans were closing in, and the Jews experienced much fear. This was the same period when Matthew's early Christian community was in unrest, waiting for the Kingdom of God to come. The only worship they knew was going to the Temple to make sacrifices three times a day. At that time, they practiced no other form of prayer, and they had no synagogues or houses of study. Further, they lived in a Mediterranean world where all peoples thought that destroying a temple was the same as destroying a people's God.

One of the religious leaders in that world, Rabbi Yohanan ben Zakkai, gained favor with one of the Roman authorities, who offered to grant him one request. Ben Zakkai's request was for a safe place where he could gather Jews together to study and pray. The request was granted, and he gathered a few Pharisees outside of Jerusalem in Gabara (Lower Galilee) to pray and read Torah together. Over time, with the leadership of Rabbi ben Zakkai, they formed Jewish law and new patterns of worship and study.[4] Meanwhile, most Jews stayed in Jerusalem to defend the Temple and, with it, their God and their faith. They finally lost their struggle, however; the Temple was destroyed.

Rabbi ben Zakkai and his community of Pharisees had, in the meantime, been reconstructing Judaism — building a new form of Judaism in which faith was not centered in the Temple but in small groups of people who gathered together to study Torah. These people did not worship God through sacrifices three times a day, but through three times of prayer — a practice that has continued. Beginning with Rabbi ben Zakkai, and continued by Rabbi Gamaliel II, Jewish practices shifted from the Temple to synagogues and Jewish law was elaborated in a form that still guides Jewish practice.

The graduate summarized this story about ben Zakkai and then made a connection with modern Judaism. She explained that Judaism today finds itself in a situation similar to the first century C.E. — on the verge of destruction in all recognizable forms. Modern Jews are faced with a choice of trying to preserve the tradition exactly as it is for its own

---

4. For a more complete description of the context, see H. H. Ben-Sasson, ed., A History of the Jewish People (Cambridge, Mass.: Harvard University Press, 1976, 1969), 245–81. For further discussion of Yohanan ben Zakkai, see Jacob Neusner, First Century Judaism in Crisis: Yohanan ben Zakkai and the Renaissance of Torah, augmented ed. (New York: KTAV, 1982, 1975); Jacob Neusner, Development of a Legend: Studies on the Traditions Concerning Yohanan ben Zakkai (Leiden: Brill, 1970).

sake, or to reconstruct the tradition and carry it on. She concluded, "We are the people faced with that choice."

Like the first- and twenty-first-century Jews, Christians today are religious people whose hearts burn with a love for God and a calling to serve God in the world. We too are faced with changes that threaten to destroy Christian faith, the church, and church practices as we know them. How will we respond? Will we defend the temple, or will we seek to reconstruct our communities and repair the world? How can our teaching empower prophetic communities in such a church and such a world?

The second case is told in the form of free verse, based as it is in the life of a particular community in Los Angeles:

> *I remember a base community in South Central Los Angeles*
> *Where five women gather every week*
> *To read the Bible, to pray, to reflect on their lives.*
> *One night they were gathered,*
> > *And the youngest woman in the group read the text*
> > > *Because the oldest woman could not read.*
> *The story was about Jesus walking on water*
> > *and Peter trying to follow,*
> > > *just moments before he sank;*
> *As she listened, the oldest woman cried out,*
> > *"That story is about us, we are like Peter,*
> > > *only we are not afraid of walking on water;*
> > *We are afraid of walking out of our doors,*
> > > *where gang members hang out*
> > > > *and threaten us."*
> *The five women talked and prayed;*
> > *they all agreed with this wise old woman,*
> > > *they knew their fear.*
> *And so, these women decided on that fateful night*
> > *that they would walk into their fears,*
> > > *open their doors to their neighbors,*
> > > > *stand outside to chat.*
> *For one whole week, they stood on their doorsteps,*
> > *chatting with each other,*
> > > *facing their fears,*
> > > > *until they gathered the next week for their study.*
> *They read the Bible, prayed, and reflected on their lives;*
> *They were proud of walking on water . . .*
> > *yet they knew their step was only tiny.*

> They vowed that during the next week,
>   they would sit outside on the lawn,
>   reading magazines, walking into the deep.
> And so they did,
>   and each week was like the one before, but better;
> Each week, these women took another step,
>   until they sponsored a barbecue for the gang members,
>   and a reaching-out plan for parents of these youth,
>   and a coordinated effort with other base communities
>   that continues even to this day.
> All of this began with one quiet night when five women
>   gathered to read the Bible,
>   where the youngest woman read aloud
>   because the oldest woman could not read,
>   but the oldest woman could see visions
>   and the whole community was transformed![5]

When I first heard the story of these women, I was struck by the daring ways of God, and the subversive power of scripture and courageous readers. In a setting of study and prayer, a community of women was willing to engage biblical texts and their own lives with honesty and courage. Their story is echoed by base communities in South and Central America as well, contributing to new visions of the church.[6] Their story embodies the heart of this chapter — reconstructing community and repairing the world.

The opening stories pose both challenges and possibilities. Opening to God and to the possibility of prophetic action is an almost overwhelming challenge. It is even more so when external forces pressure religious communities onto the margins of society, or when forces of violence threaten the safety of people in their own homes. Many other kinds of threat could be named; yet the possibility suggested in the opening stories is that new life, or New Creation, can rise from threat and fear. Further, new life depends, in part, on individuals and communities that are willing to open to God and take a new road. What kind of road might that be for communities in the world today?

Sacramental teaching is teaching in which the church's conflicts and the world's turmoil are not cause to defend what has always been and to escape into some other world, but to gather with others for study and prayer. This is particularly challenging for Christian communities where conflicts exist within the

---

5. Mary Elizabeth Moore, "Five Women," Los Angeles, 1997.
6. Leonardo Boff, *Ecclesiogenesis: The Base Communities Reinvent the Church,* trans. Robert R. Barr (Maryknoll, N.Y.: Orbis, 1986).

community, as well as without. Even without visible conflict, people in most congregations differ widely in values and faith experiences. The Baby Boomers and the Busters generations, for example, are much more likely than the generations who preceded them to think that people can be religious without the church, or that the church is really not very important to spiritual life at all.[7] Differences in social class, ethnicity, gender, age, abilities, or denominational background compound the variety within a community of faith. Sacramental teaching is not about uniformity, however, or even about church participation; it is about mediating God's grace through the ordinary stuff of creation, which may be quite different for diverse people within a community.

Sacramental teaching takes place when a community responds to the drama in their particular place and time in history. Sacramental teaching requires courage — courage to seek new life, even in the midst of conflict and turmoil. The sacraments of baptism and eucharist, after all, are a promise of what is to come — a foretaste of God's New Creation. Sacramental teaching represents a movement of hoping for God's future by seeking to reconstruct the community and repair the world.

Power in Reconstructing and Repairing

The power of reconstructing and repairing is revealed throughout scripture and Jewish and Christian history, as in other religious traditions. Likewise, it is revealed in the stories with which this chapter opened. Here we will take a closer look at the story of Esther, interpreting it as a prototypical tale or case study, which it has often been in the history of biblical interpretation. Then we will consider this biblical text in dialogue with the opening stories, seeking to understand the power of reconstructing and repairing.

The story of Esther begins with oppression of Hebrew people by a power "from India to Ethiopia" (Esther 1:1). In one of the opening scenes, we already see the dynamics of power at work, suppressing the Hebrews and also others in social positions of lesser power. Queen Vashti, in spite of being a queen, is asked by the king to come out as an object of display for his guests (1:10–22). She refuses and is cast out of the king's favor and into prison, after which she disappears from the story. When the king begins looking for another wife, Mordecai has the idea of arranging a marriage with his cousin Esther. In this way, the Hebrew Esther will be in the inner circle and can exercise influence on the king to save her people. Obscuring her own Jewish heritage, Esther agrees to the plan and eventually weds

---

7. Jackson W. Carroll and Wade Clark Roof, *Bridging Divided Worlds: Generational Cultures in Congregations* (San Francisco: Jossey-Bass, 2002); Wade Clark Roof, *Spiritual Marketplace. Baby Boomers and the Remaking of American Religion* (Princeton, N.J.: Princeton University Press, 1999); Wade Clark Roof, Jackson W. Carroll, and David A. Roozen, eds., *The Post-War Generation and Establishment Religion: Cross-Cultural Perspectives* (Boulder, Colo.: Westview, 1995).

the king. With this, a risky tale begins. Esther and Mordecai send secret messages to one another, plotting to divert plans to destroy their people. Finally, their efforts work, and the king guarantees the Hebrews' safety at the behest of Esther. What we see here is a powerful tale, in which seemingly powerless people — the enslaved Mordecai and the woman Esther — turn the world upside down for the sake of their people. Several forms of power are embodied in this tale, including the power to read a situation, envision an alternative, become deeply involved with others, break the rules, protest, and take risks.

To these many forms of power we now turn, drawing insights from the biblical narrative and the opening cases. One could identify other dimensions of power, but the ones named here reveal the transformative influence of reconstruction and repair.

Power of Communal Discernment

First is the *power of communal discernment — searching together for the movements and call of God.* In the saga of Esther and Mordecai, communal discernment was an urgent practice. Members of the community secretly shared with one another in order to discern what was happening and what alternatives were conceivable. Indeed, the future of the Jewish community depended on their discernment. Similarly in the first-century Jewish community, Rabbi ben Zakkai actively discerned his frightened community's plight as he lived in their midst. He conceived the possibility of gathering others with him to study and pray, seeking to discern God's movements in this new time. He was inventing new possibilities for communal discernment. Likewise, the women in the Los Angeles base community discovered the power of communal gathering as they met each week to study scripture, pray, and share their life stories and struggles.

In all of these cases, communal gathering was critical, sometimes done in opportunistic, secretive ways and sometimes in regular patterns. In all of the cases, discernment was also critical — reading the immediate situation and reading the traditions of their people, whether the traditions were of survival (Esther and Mordecai), daily prayer (ben Zakkai), or scripture (the women). The stories reveal the power of sacramental teaching. Conflict and turmoil in the world were not, for these people, a reason to give up, defend the past, or hide. In spite of their dangerous situations, they chose to gather together and discern the movements of God as best they could.

Power of Visioning Alternatives

The three case studies also reveal the power of *visioning alternatives,* but in different ways. For Esther and Mordecai, alternatives were urgent, and the people did not have much time for deliberation. Communication was limited as well; thus, responsibility for visioning alternatives fell initially with Mordecai, and increasingly with Esther. The fact that Jewish people have continually retold this story and included it in their scriptures, and that Christians also included it in their canon, suggests that the unorthodox ways of visioning alternatives, and the primary role of a woman in that process, were considered to be somehow important for Jewish and Christian peoples.

Turning to the first-century Jewish community, we see a different approach to visioning alternatives. Rabbi ben Zakkai had a vision of a small group gathering to study Torah and pray three times a day, but apparently did not know where that would lead. He did not predict a reformation of Jewish practice that would endure for many centuries. Similarly, the women of the Los Angeles base community only envisioned one step at a time. Each week, they reflected self-consciously on their actions and the results of their actions, but they did not envision the far-reaching changes that would take place in themselves and others over time. In light of these cases, one could conclude that the power of envisioning alternatives is not a magic that transforms everything at once; it often requires many steps, and slowly spreads across communities and generations.

Power of Becoming Deeply Involved with Others

A third dimension of *power* in constructing and repairing is *becoming deeply involved with others — engaging with others in the fullness of their lives.* Esther and Mordecai were involved in their own people's plight, but the situation also required their becoming involved with the Persian people. They found themselves trusting one another and others in their community out of necessity; this was the only way to accomplish what they set out to do. Further, they became involved in a dangerous political situation in order to help their community. Their actions challenge modern individualism to be sure; they also challenge the notion of separating religion and politics.

For the first-century Jews around Rabbi ben Zakkai, the primary involvement was with God and one another. Gathering to study and pray three times a day, their close communion was probably burdensome at times. Yet something new arose from their growing relationship with God, the Torah, and one another. For the five women of the base community, the involvement was similarly intense and multifaceted, both with one another and with God. Soon it included others — gang members, friends in the barrio, other base communities, parents of gang members, and police. Their involvement with one another led them to reach out, and each involvement expanded the circle. Like the first-century Jews, they did not know what would grow from their experiment of standing in their doorways to chat; neither could they predict how the circles of relationship would spread. They simply knew that they were committed to God and one another.

Power of Breaking the Rules

Another form of power in these cases is *breaking the rules,* or subverting the normal conventions of behavior in their communities. When you look closely at these three narratives, you see an obvious flaunting of rules, but a deep commitment to the larger purposes and principles of their respective traditions. Esther determined to marry the king without revealing her Jewish identity, and she secretly passed information to Mordecai. Mordecai planned to outwit King Ahasuerus and his plotting commander Haman, and thereby prevent the destruction of his people. Both Esther and Mordecai were committed to their people and to the relation of their people with Yahweh. In the interest of these larger purposes, they were willing to break the conventions of honesty and marriage relationships. They did not glibly neglect social convention, but they discerned a direction that transcended narrow and absolute interpretations of social rules. Similarly, King Ahasuerus granted the requests of Esther with extravagance (6:14–8:17).[8]

As for Rabbi ben Zakkai, the longtime practices of his people were to pray at the Temple three times a day. The people were spiritually focused on the Temple, and both their religious practice and a growing fear and anger regarding threats to the Temple dominated their self-understandings. Rabbi ben Zakkai developed an alternative that separated him somewhat from those familiar spiritual practices and social alienations of the first century. The alternative was to continue daily prayer and study while breaking out of the religious and social conventions of his time. Ben Zakkai's work with others to elaborate Jewish law and develop the synagogue as a house of prayer and worship involved more than shifting *away* from social conventions; it also involved developing *new* conventions for a new time.

Similarly, the base community women challenged their *own* conventions in reflecting on Peter's attempt to walk on water and his experience of becoming frightened and sinking. They were familiar with fear and its conventions, as were most people they knew. Further, their reluctance to walk out of their homes was a commonsense practice of safety. When they decided to stand in their doorways, and later to sit on the lawn, they unseated their fears and violated the normal safety practices of their community. They persisted in breaking rules when they reached out to gang members in their community, and later to their families, and still later to the police. Their rule breaking finally made it possible for them to *change* social conventions, and thereby to change the larger community. Given the conservative nature of institutions, and particularly of religious institutions, the practice of breaking rules is one of the most revolutionary that I have identified, pointing once again to the disruptive potential of sacramental living.

Power of Taking Risks

Continuing the revolutionary tone of breaking rules is the power of *taking risks,* or engaging in practices that may have difficult consequences for oneself or others. The cases of this chapter involve genuine danger, but of different kinds. In the

---

8. Kristin De Troyer, *The End of the Alpha Text of Esther: Translation and Narrative Technique in MT 8:1–17, LXX 8:1–17, and AT 7:14–41,* trans. Brian Doyle (Atlanta: Society of Biblical Literature, 2000).

biblical account of Esther and Mordecai, we see a time of great peril for the Hebrew people. Yet Esther and Mordecai planned together and risked their lives to save their people from slavery and death at the hands of the king and his leaders, especially Haman. For Rabbi ben Zakkai, danger lurked outside the community; the Temple *was* destroyed, marking the end of the spiritual center that bound the Jewish people. Danger also abided *within* the rabbi's community, where his novel approach to spiritual practice was suspect. Yet ben Zakkai found it necessary to risk creating a spiritual alternative, diverting focus from protecting the Temple to another way of relating with God and studying God's ways.

Turning to the base community, the five women took both physical and social risks. They risked intimidation and physical harm from gang members who hung outside their doors; they risked ridicule and anger from their neighbors, for whom the status quo of leaving the youth alone was seen as necessary for everyone's survival. Yet the women sensed a call from God to take the risks of doing daily life differently, not unlike Peter's stepping out of his safe boat and attempting to walk on water toward Jesus.

To think of reconstruction and repair as powerful practices is somewhat shocking, for they are often meager and ineffective. Indeed, they are often counteracted by powers of destruction in the church and society. Even so, power does arise from reconstruction and repair, revealing divine movement beneath human action, often mixed in a struggle against real evil. Esther and Mordecai, for example, were not reacting to a mood swing, but to oppressive forces that threatened their people. Rabbi ben Zakkai could see the evil threatening the Temple, as well as the inadequacy of his people's fear to change the situation. Further, the women of Los Angeles were not naïve about the threat of gangs in their community. The threats were real, and people died every week as a result of gang activity and gangs' competing with one another. Many of the murdered were innocent bystanders who were in the wrong place at the wrong time; many were children. The three cases reveal what we already know, that sin and evil are real in this world; yet, also real are God's tender heart and bold redemptive work in a hurting creation. We thus need a theology that embraces the God of mystery, who dwells within and beyond the complexities of this world. Much existing theology is simply inadequate to that task.

Roots of Reconstruction and Repair
in Church Practice

From the earliest time, Christians have been concerned with reconstruction and repair. Paul's letters are filled with advice regarding Christian life in community. The Corinthian letters are particularly good examples, but advice flows also in Galatians, Ephesians, and others. Similarly, the pastoral epistles (Titus and

Timothy) are filled with advice for living. From the beginning of the church, people have disagreed about how to organize Christian community and how to live in the world. Many conflicts in the early church, such as those reported in Acts (11:1–18; 15:1–21; 19:21–41; 21:17–26:32), reveal disagreements about the laws, values, and actions of Christian communities. These conflicts reflect sharp differences, to be sure, but they also reveal how serious people have been about Christian living, from the early days until today.

The church's elongated celebration of Pentecost, or what is sometimes de-scribed as Ordinary Time, is a time for focusing on the time-consuming but urgent work of reconstruction and repair. The sacraments of baptism and eucharist sup-port this work, as they re-present and invite participation in the transformative work of Christ in the world.

Ordinary Time

Christians are called to engage in transformative work throughout the church year. No time is more important, however, than the elongated season of Pen-tecost, or Ordinary Time. This is a time to focus on the daily and continuing challenges of Christian life. The season stretches from Pentecost (the rush of God's spirit) to Advent (the awaiting of Jesus' birth and New Creation); thus, the church has several months for *self-examination and daily living with the trans-formative Spirit of God*. The rush of Spirit at Pentecost was the beginning of life-changing, community-changing, world-changing movements. The disciples had their lives turned upside down, and we can expect the same. The Pente-cost drama is impressive; however, *living in the Spirit of Pentecost* is demanding. It inevitably shatters the status quo, yet gives no clear, universally accepted guide-lines for belief and practice. This is a perennial challenge, for every generation and situation makes distinctive demands for faithful change; churches today are challenged to find their way in much the same way as the early churches.

In recent history, some churches added a season of Kingdomtide during this long period. The practice did not endure, but the eschatological emphasis is appropriately part of Ordinary Time. Reconstruction and repair are indeed acts that anticipate God's Kingdom, Kin-dom, or New Creation. The focus of the season is not on indiscriminate change, but on participating in, and contributing to, God's future. Thus, the accent is on reconstruction and repair, guided by God and lured by visions of New Creation.

Sacraments

The sacraments of baptism and eucharist are themselves a promise of what is to come — a *foretaste of New Creation*. They have to do with *re-creating the world*. Much recent reflection on the eucharist reminds Christians that the eucharist is a source of human liberation and a gift of bread for the hunger of the world.[9] If baptism and eucharist do not contribute to the well-being of the world, then, how have Christians distorted and misunderstood and domesticated them? Likewise, if our teaching does not contribute to the well-being of the world, can we call it sacramental teaching?

Promises permeate the sacraments. Eucharist anticipates the heavenly banquet, and also the feeding of all who are hungry. John's water baptisms anticipated the One who would baptize with the Spirit (Matt. 3:11; Mark 1:7–8; Luke 3:15–17; John 1:24–28). And Jesus' last meal with the disciples pointed to the future, both distant and immediate (Matt. 26:17–35; Mark 14:12–31; Luke 22:7–34; John 13:1–38). Further, Jesus' life was permeated with promises; even at the end, his resurrection appearances pointed to the future (Matt. 28:9–20; Mark 16:7–8, 14–18; Luke 24:44–49; John 20:11–23; 21:1–19). The eschatological nature of the sacraments — and of Jesus Christ, the sacrament of God — stirs the Christian community to vision, encourages it to live in hope, and strengthens it to participate in God's work.

Even with this emphasis on New Creation, the sacraments can themselves be distorted; thus, a *critique of sacramental theology is part of the work of reconstruction and repair.* One distortion of the eucharist arises from its multiple meanings. Some of those meanings — thanksgiving, sacrifice, and transformation — have sometimes been fused and confused into a theology that praises suffering as a pathway for transformation. When Jesus' death is taken to be a necessary act of God to save human beings, we are left with a God who glorifies suffering, and in some views causes suffering to happen for the sake of a larger good, namely, the salvation of the world. Likewise, these views tend to encourage human suffering for the sake of God's will, even as a necessary pathway to transformation. Carrying this view, people sometimes seek opportunities to suffer or to accept their suffering joyfully, as in abusive family or work relationships. Church leaders sometimes encourage people to suffer willingly for the sake of the Gospel, often encouraging women to accept suffering in their families and church for the sake of harmony or support to others. Such practice is common in the U.S., Korea, and other parts of the world, a practice with long history. In eighteenth- and nineteenth-century European epitaphs, women were often praised for being "long-suffering," revealing values attached to women that continue today, albeit in more subtle forms.

Another distortion of eucharist arises from the fused traditions of God's free grace, human responsibility, and God's judgment. This fusion can lead to works-righteousness, which easily permeates baptism and eucharist, especially when people think of the sacraments as something to earn or deserve. The sacraments

---

9. Tissa Balasuriya, O.M.I., *The Eucharist and Human Liberation* (Maryknoll, N.Y.: Orbis, 1979); Monika K. Hellwig, *The Eucharist and the Hunger of the World* (New York: Paulist, 1976). Balasuriya writes from the context of Sri Lanka, and Monika Hellwig, of the United States, but their emphases are similar.

are, rather, transforming gifts of God that are freely *given*, even when they are not deserved, earned or felt. Common sense, and United States civil religion, dictate that "people get what they deserve." In truth, we usually do not get what we deserve; we are often not rewarded for the good we do, nor punished for the bad. The world is filled with harsh realities (a child killed by a drunk driver, children killed in war or inducted as soldiers, people forced from their homes and villages because armed forces take their land). The eucharist speaks to these realities, just as the last meal with Jesus and his disciples was surrounded with promising words of life *and* threats of impending death. On the other hand, the eucharist does not require that we set the world or ourselves straight before celebrating at the table. The disciples came to the table just as they were, and Judas came to the table as well, having already betrayed Jesus. The table was transformative for the disciples, who remembered and recorded it for posterity. Perhaps the table was also transformative in some way for Judas; certainly he was included (Matt. 27:3–5).

Because the gift of eucharist is free, neither the heart of the celebrant nor that of the communicant needs to be in good relationship with God and the world for the eucharist to be powerful. Augustine (354–430 c.e.) made this point more than fifteen hundred years ago, and it has been carried forward in Christian tradition, despite the frequent movement toward stringent requirements of holiness for celebrants and participants in eucharist. Evelyn Underhill echoes Augustine's emphasis in a letter to M.R. With characteristic emphasis on humility, she warns against the danger of thinking "more of your own imperfection than of the Perfection which you approach." She emphasizes instead the necessity of faith, hope, and charity, concluding:

> To rely utterly on God and be in charity with the world — this is essential. What you happen to be *feeling* at the moment, does not matter in the least. Do — *do* try and be more objective in your religion. Try to see yourself less as a complex individual, and more as a quite ordinary scrap of the universe [emphasis hers].[10]

The Eucharist is efficacious because it is God's table. The mix of thanksgiving, responsibility, and judgment is a testimony to God's ability to hold all reality in tension; it is not a moral lesson regarding how people should feel and act.

Theology of Prophetic Redemption

The sacramental practice of reconstructing community and repairing the world is grounded in a theology of prophetic redemption and shaped from the soils of tragedy and hope. Such theology is realistic about brokenness in the world (tragedy)

---

10. Evelyn Underhill, "To M.R. (St. Patrick's Day, 1909)," in *The Letters of Evelyn Underhill,* ed. Charles Williams (London: Longmans, Green, 1943), 95–96.

and trusting in God's promises and faithfulness (hope). Prophetic redemption is *God's pull on a broken world toward wholeness — toward New Creation.*

Such theology centers on the reiteration of God's grace in the messiness of the world, promising prophetic redemption in a world that cries and languishes in its brokenness. A theology of prophetic redemption builds upon insights of earlier chapters regarding: the wonder of God and God's creation, God's suffering with creation, the revelation of God in paradox and parable, the bounties of God and God's creation, and the life-giving work of God in the middle of the world. God's wonder offers hope amid tragedy; God's suffering offers compassion; and God's paradoxes and parables point to mystery — touchable but not fully knowable. Further, God's bounties and life-giving work open possibilities for New Creation to grow. In response, people can live with hope and compassion in their lives, but they cannot expect to control outcomes. Similarly, people can receive and appreciate the bounties of God and can build upon God's life-giving work, but cannot expect God, or anyone or anything, to take full care of them. People are given much, but finally they are also given responsibility to receive and magnify the promises, compassion, mystery, bounties, and seeds of life that God has given, and to do so for the sake of their own lives and the larger world.

In the previous chapter, I pointed to Christian depictions of the Madonna and Child to reveal the power of birth and natality in Christian consciousness. Here I point to Christian depictions of the crucifixion to reveal the power of God's entry into brokenness for Christian consciousness. We can also turn to artistic renderings of the pietà, resurrection, and ascension. Unlike the crucifixion, depictions of Jesus' being held by his mother after death, or rising from death or ascending into heaven, usually include other people. The community is present to care for Jesus' body in death or to wonder at the empty tomb or to gasp at the ascending of Jesus. This art points to the theological heart of chapter 8 — *that God gifts the community with compassion and vision toward a hurting creation, so they may be partners in the work that God began long ago and will continue eternally.* Arising from this central affirmation are six theological themes, all pointing to God's prophetic redemption of the world. In this chapter, more than the others, the themes (and the educational practices that follow) overlap with other chapters. None of the chapter themes is fully discrete, flowing as they do from the same source and toward the same ends; however, this chapter builds boldly on the others, so the discussion is briefer and the interweaving is more explicit.

1. God Created the Cosmos for Community

The first affirmation is that *God and creation are relational through and through, and God creates the cosmos for covenantal relationship.* This accent is strong in the creation stories of Genesis 1 and 2; indeed, it runs throughout scripture.[11]

---

11. Mary Elizabeth Moore, *Ministering with the Earth* (St. Louis: Chalice, 1998), esp. 23–44.

We find interdependence between gardens and rivers, creatures and vegetation, and human beings with the whole of creation; relationships permeate creation before human beings are even created. God thus makes covenant with the whole creation. A common biblical pattern reveals God coming to individuals as a way of entering covenant with a whole people. Abraham and Sarah are called to become father and mother of a great nation; Moses and David are called to lead the Israelites in times of trouble; and Jesus is called to point people — Jews and Gentiles alike — to the ways of God and God's future. Certain qualities persist in all of these covenants: *God's gracious act establishes the covenant relationship — binding God with creation, establishing a relationship of mutual expectation between God and humanity, and planting vision in God's people.*[12] The actual forms of covenant vary from time to time and place to place, including the formal sacraments and more ordinary sacramental acts.

The significance of creation, community, and covenant in Christian tradition is paired with the value placed on reconciliation. Reconciliation is a bringing together of diverse aspects of reality into a life-giving whole, to nourish all parties of the relationship. Reconciliation cannot be identified with agreement or homogeneity, or with the absence of conflict; it establishes community from the diversity, tension, and gritty reality of creation. For this reason, reconciliation cannot be forced. Force will only create "false harmony," or a one-sided agreement that masquerades as reconciliation. In fact, reconciliation is perhaps most authentic when it arises out of conflict. One revealing moment was when the Reverend Karen Dammann was tried by a United Methodist Church court on charges of violating *The Book of Discipline of the United Methodist Church* by living in a committed lesbian relationship. Controversy rocked the denomination in the wake of this decision. People differed as to whether they believed that the decision was or was not faithful to God, and was or was not made according to the church's discipline. Suspicion and anger grew among people with diverse views. In response, Bishop Mary Ann Swenson wrote:

> I am confident that God is pressing on before us, calling us to become more completely the community of God. The trial of the Reverend Karen Dammann and the decisions of the jury are not a cause for fear or celebration or division: they are the result of our struggling to grow in faith, to move into God's future.[13]

12. This theme is elaborated in Mary Elizabeth Moore, *Covenant and Call: Mission of the Future Church* (Nashville: Discipleship Resources, UMC, 2000), 14–24. An expression of covenant that is similar to this one, without the emphasis on all creation, is found in Thomas D. Parker, "Covenant," in *A New Handbook of Christian Theology*, ed. Donald W. Musser and Joseph L. Price (Nashville: Abingdon, 1992), 106; cf. 105–7. See also Mary Elizabeth Moore, *Ministering with the Earth* (St. Louis: Chalice, 1998), 49–68.

13. Mary Ann Swenson, "Statement by Bishop Mary Ann Swenson re: Dammann Trial," in *Cal-Pac Update*, lhygh@cal-pac.org, March 24, 2004.

Bishop Swenson chose to focus on Christian community and the value of its struggles in relation to God and God's future, recognizing that the relationship itself transcends the most wrenching and heartfelt human conflicts. Community includes struggle, but is always larger than the struggle.

2. We Live in a Broken World

A focus on community and covenant shines light on another reality. *The world in which we live is badly broken.* The more common depiction of the world in Christian theology is "fallen," focusing on the sinful actions of human beings, which led to the fall of God's idyllic creation and continues to diminish the world. To speak of the world as broken is not antithetical to fallenness, but it is larger.[14] It takes full account of human sinfulness, while recognizing the multitude of ways that destruction and diminishment abide in creation, some arising from human sin and some from other causes. It also accents restoration and renewal more than guilt for human sin.

A focus on brokenness can lead to radical reconstruction of theology. In the wake of the Holocaust, Irvin Greenberg said that no theology can be considered adequate if it does not make sense in the presence of burning children.[15] Such a test of theology opens our eyes to the anti-Jewish threads in Christian theologies, and it stirs Christians today to reshape their perspectives and actions. In a parallel way, we can say that no theology is worthy that does not make sense in the presence of the most abused and oppressed people and places of the world. To make sense in the presence of hurting people and places, theology needs a robust understanding of the broken world.

3. God Is Compassionate toward the Groaning Creation

God is not only great and good, but *God is compassionate — feeling the pain and tragedy of creation, and responding.* Saying this reiterates themes elaborated in chapters 2 and 4. As earlier discussed, God came to Moses in the burning bush, saying, "I have observed the misery of my people who are in Egypt; I have heard their cry. . . . Indeed, I know their sufferings" (Exod. 3:7). To mediate the love of God is to mediate the empathy of the Holy One who knows the suffering of creation and feels our pain.

God's compassion is sometimes directly expressed by God, and sometimes through people, as in the story of Esther. Esther and Mordecai were the beacons of compassion in that narrative, and they were able to effect deliverance for

---

14. Andrew Sung Park, *The Wounded Heart of God: The Asian Concept of Han and the Christian Doctrine of Sin* (Nashville: Abingdon, 1993); Andrew Sung Park and Susan L. Nelson, eds., *The Other Side of Sin: Woundedness from the Perspective of the Sinned-Against* (Albany: State University of New York Press, 2001).

15. Irvin Greenberg "Cloud of Smoke, Pillar of Fire: Judaism, Christianity and Modernity after the Holocaust," in *Auschwitz: Beginning of a New Era?* ed. Eva Fleischner (New York: KTAV, 1977), 23.

the Hebrew people because they heard their groans. Esther was also able to help King Ahasuerus to hear her people's groans, thus ensuring their safety. These several characters underwent marked change in the course of the narrative. Esther allowed Mordecai to convince her to marry the king, thus to intervene for her people. Mordecai faced increasing risks to his life as the plot thickened. And the king seemingly underwent a transformation. This was the same king who had imprisoned his other wife, Queen Vashti, for refusing to come out for his friends. He was now willing for Esther to influence him into granting safety for her people.

4. God Is a Promise-Maker

God, according to the biblical texts, does not end with mourning. God is also *a Promise-Maker, offering hope into situations that seem totally bereft of hope.* God's redemptive work has no end, and God's ultimate promise is New Creation. To say this is not to identify God as a magician who fixes all of creation's problems as they arise. It is, rather, to identify God as one who makes and keeps promises, however broken is the world, however loud are creation's groans, and however inadequate are people in responding to God's call.

The promises sometimes arise or unfold gradually. Neither Rabbi ben Zakkai nor the five women in Los Angeles knew where their relation with God would lead. They simply took one step at a time. Ben Zakkai initiated a new way of praying and studying Torah, which became vital to the Jewish community over time. The five women reflected on their fears and reformed their daily actions in response to the biblical story of Peter's failed attempt to walk on water. The Promise-Maker played prominently in both stories, but neither narrative involved a dramatic, clear communication from God with a blueprint for action. Both involved many steps of faithfulness over a long period of time.

5. God's Work Is Transformative and Countercultural

This discussion leads further to the idea that God's work is transformative and countercultural. Consider the mixed pictures of reality painted in the Psalms, which are colorfully honest about a full range of human situations and emotions. The Psalms are a valuable genre of expression through which people seek to construct or reconstruct the world. Walter Brueggemann explains that the Psalms can be used to make *and* unmake a world. The Psalms of recital construct a world that is "intergenerational, covenantly shaped, morally serious, dialogically open, and politically demanding"; simultaneously, they unmake a world that is "one-generational," "devoid of authoritative covenanting," morally indifferent, "monologically closed," and politically indifferent.[16] The world they create could be called a "counterworld."[17]

---

16. Walter Brueggemann, *Abiding Astonishment: Psalms, Modernity, and the Making of History* (Louisville: Westminster John Knox, 1991), 21; cf. 21–28.

17. Ibid., 28.

The Psalms are neither univocal nor gentle in their poetic messages, but they are penetrating in their honesty about human experiences of God and the world. They are also bold in their work of making and unmaking the world; thus, they serve well in the sacramental practice of reconstruction and repair. In light of the Psalms, and similarly bold religious literature, one can see how diverse religious impulses can be interwoven, and how important the work of construction, deconstruction, and reconstruction can be for people who seek to walk with the transformative Spirit of God.

6. God Depends on the Faithful Action of God's People

How does God's transformative, countercultural work take place? I earlier made a case that God exercises power in unexpected ways. We need also to recognize that *God depends on the faithful action of God's people.* Human beings have a vital role in the work of God, and diverse aspects of that vocation have been identified throughout this book, especially in chapters 4, 6, and 7. Humans were actually created for responsibility — created in the image of the creating God, according to Genesis 1. People are thus living into that image as they participate in repairing the world (in Hebrew, *tikkun olam*).

The opening stories accent this point. Rosa Parks, a seamstress, readied herself for great work by participating actively in her church, freedom organizations, and nonviolent training. She did not wait for others to organize a freedom movement. She learned as much from others as she could, she supported others' work as much as she could, and she acted as faithfully as she knew how. In the end, a movement arose, in part from her own bold decision not to give up her seat on a Montgomery bus. In her mind, this decision was simply an act of faithfulness to God. Similarly, the five women in Los Angeles were not making a dramatic stand to change the world in an instant. They began their long journey when they read the Bible and prayed together; they continued it when they analyzed their fears of gang members. Discerning guidance from God, they developed genuinely helpful responses; thus they were faithful, one step at a time.

Hermeneutic of Reconstruction

Focusing on a theology of prophetic redemption requires a hermeneutic of reconstruction — *discerning Holy nudges, analyzing sacred texts and life events, and then reconstructing community life, theology, and action in light of the emerging visions and insights.* Such a hermeneutic seeks fresh insight to guide the structures and practices of human life; thus, it requires many kinds of interpretation, as well as imagination and a spirit of openness.

All of the approaches to interpretation discussed in this book are important for reconstruction and repair. *Wonder* evokes expectation of God's movement in the present world and the possibility of new vision emerging, even in destructive situations. *Tragic memory* evokes compassion for those who are hurting or oppressed, and *suspicion* engages people in critique of the world, religious texts, and dominant theologies. These three approaches to interpretation weave together spiritual expectation and social analysis, as well as discernment of God, realism about global problems, and suspicion toward *all* interpretations, including the most obvious, comfortable, and popular ones. Complementing this curious mix of approaches are thanksgiving and nurture. *Thanksgiving* seeks to discover and delight in God's many gifts in creation, thus encouraging people to see the world in relation to God and to see the traumas of life within a perspective of God's bounty. A hermeneutic of *nurture* builds upon these gifts by exploring the potential for new life — new possibilities for thinking and action.

Drawing upon these various approaches to interpretation, people can probe deeply into themselves, their communities, and their cultures, seeking the roots of evil or discord and the genuine possibilities of good. The character Adam in John Grisham's *The Chamber* asked his grandfather, "Why do you hate?" His grandfather had grown up in the Klu Klux Klan and was living on death row, convicted of bombing a law office in which two young children were killed and their father seriously injured. He replied, "I don't know; I suppose it was a way of life."[18] Probing such "ways of life" is the work of a hermeneutic of reconstruction. This is what Eric Law calls "iceberg work," for it involves probing beneath the surface of a situation.[19] In situations of conflict, the probing requires people to give sustained attention to passions evoked by the situation, to identify forces that contribute to those passions, and to seek resolutions that contribute to larger resolutions. This is not individualistic work; it uncovers deep connections. It is, thus, most effective when done in community and for the sake of community.

Evident in this discussion is the intimate relation between the personal and social. Paulo Freire holds the personal and social together in a dialectical way. He argues that "knowing presumes a dialectical situation: not strictly an 'I think,' but a 'we think.' "[20] He adds that "the 'we think'... makes it possible for me to think."[21] People are imbedded in society, but not determined by it. The future of the individual *and* society is always open to be reenvisioned and reshaped. This is why conscientization is so vital, for clarifying "what remains hidden within us

18. John Grisham, *The Chamber* (New York: Doubleday, 1994), 206–7.

19. Eric H. F. Law, *Sacred Acts, Holy Change: Faithful Diversity and Practical Transformation* (St. Louis: Chalice, 2002), 33–45; cf. Eric H. F. Law, *Inclusion: Making Room for Grace* (St. Louis: Chalice, 2000); Eric H. F. Law, *The Bush Was Blazing but Not Consumed: Developing a Multicultural Community through Dialogue Liturgy* (St. Louis: Chalice, 1996).

20. Paulo Freire, "The Process of Political Literacy," in *The Politics of Education: Culture, Power, and Liberation*, ed. Paulo Freire, trans. Donaldo Macedo (Westport, Conn.: Bergin & Garvey, 1985), 99.

21. Ibid., 100.

while we move about in the world."[22] This is the hermeneutic work of understanding and re-creating reality, knowing that what we create will be critiqued and recreated by future generations, maybe even by ourselves.

What is needed is a kind of social psychoanalysis, to use William Pinar's term, for personal and social analyses are intertwined. Pinar proposes that educational curriculum be viewed as texts permeated with social views, which can be discovered, critiqued, and reshaped. Pinar first developed these ideas in relation to "curriculum as racial text," urging people to analyze their cultures socially and psychoanalytically.[23] He exemplified the idea with a proposal for Southern studies in the Southeastern United States. This would involve several elements: the recovery of memory, the study of many disciplines in relation to one another (literature, history, social sciences, the arts, and so forth), and a critical analysis of race and class. Such a study, according to Pinar, would empower the South and contribute to "horizontal social and economic relations."[24]

This discussion suggests an approach to hermeneutics that focuses on relationships — relationships with the past, with the many communities and cultures of the present world, with forces within ourselves, and with God. Adding to this interpretive work is the exercise of imagination — seeing the world from new perspectives and stirring new vision about what could be. Building on the imaginative work is the equally vital role of opening to the future — to whatever future people discern in their walk with God and their analysis of the world. This can be radically different from the present or radically similar; people need to be open both to the new and to the old, for neither can be a trusted blanket to guide every decision. A hermeneutic of reconstruction is a multifaceted process of discernment, prayerfully and courageously engaged.

Educational Practices:
Teaching through Reconstruction and Repair

The educational challenge of this chapter is to foster holy living that builds communities and works prophetically for a better world. This involves reconstructing the communities in which we live and working together to repair the world — mediating God's redemptive work throughout creation. When problems arise today in our nations and churches, people often bemoan the lack of leaders and

---

22. Ibid., 107.
23. William F. Pinar, "Notes on Understanding Curriculum as a Racial Text," in *Race and Identity in Education*, ed. C. McCarthy and W. Crichlow (New York: Routledge, 1994), 60–70; Louis A. Castenell Jr. and William F. Pinar, eds., *Understanding Curriculum as Racial Text: Representations of Identity and Difference in Education* (Albany: State University of New York Press, 1993); Pinar and William M. Reynolds, eds., *Understanding Curriculum as Phenomenological and Deconstructed Text* (New York: Teachers College, 1992); Joe L. Kincheloe and William F. Pinar, eds., *Curriculum as Social Psychoanalysis: The Significance of Place* (Albany: State University of New York Press, 1991).
24. William F. Pinar, "Notes on Understanding Curriculum," 67.

recall the "good old days" of strong leadership. What would happen if, instead, educators built communities of hospitality and prophetic communities for children, for people wounded by our society, for people struggling to survive, for people who are eager to live more fully, for the well-being of land and trees and seas?[25]

This educational work is like reconstructing and repairing a building. The building may still be strong in many ways, but it is not quite the building that we need right now. Also, it is not quite the building that meets the earthquake codes of God. This is a playful metaphor, but it is not as far-fetched as it seems. The Greek word *oikos*, which means household (and also the whole earth), is the root for all of our "eco" words, such as ecumenical, ecological, economic, and so forth. Imagine how we might act if we thought of ourselves as repairing and tending to God's *oikos* — God's household, or the whole earth. Education would have a role in tending ecumenical relationships across Christian and religious traditions, the ecological balance of the earth and sky and sea, the economic disparities of our neighborhoods and nations. In addressing homelessness, people would ask: How would I respond to these persons if they were my daughters or brothers? The educational challenge is to inspire and equip people for such reconstruction and repair. I will identify seven educational practices, informed by the theological affirmations of this chapter and themes developed throughout this book and elsewhere.[26]

1. Commune

The first educational practice is to *commune — to build covenantal relationships in which people commune with God and the gathered community for the sake of those who gather and the larger world.* Communing is critical in light of God's covenantal relationship with creation; it is also a critical pathway by which human communities are transformed in the directions of God's future.

---

25. Some models and embodiments have been developed in the past. See, for example, Janet F. Fishburn, ed., *People of a Compassionate God: Creating Welcoming Congregations* (Nashville: Abingdon, 2003); Evelyn L. Parker, "Hungry for Honor: Children in Violent Youth Gangs," *Interpretation: A Journal of Bible and Theology* 55, no. 2 (April 2001): 148–60; David D. Mitchell, *Black Theology and Youths at Risk* (New York: Peter Lang, 2001); Moore, *Ministering with the Earth*; Herbert Anderson and Susan B. W. Johnson, *Regarding Children: A New Respect for Childhood and Families* (Louisville: Westminster John Knox, 1994); Celia Haig-Brown, Kathy L. Hodgson-Smith, Robert Regnier, Jo-ann Archibald, *Making the Spirit Dance Within: Joe Duquette High School and an Aboriginal Community* (Toronto: James Lorimer, 1997); Gregory Cajete, *Look to the Mountain: An Ecology of Indigenous Education* (Durango, Colo.: Kivaki, 1994); T. Andree, C. Bakker, and P. Schreiner, eds., *Crossing Boundaries: Contributions to Inter-religious and Intercultural Education* (Münster: Comenius-Institut, 1997).

26. The educational practices of this section build on earlier work, reported in Mary Elizabeth Moore, "Beyond Poverty and Violence: An Eschatological Vision," *International Journal of Practical Theology* 7, no. 1 (Summer 2003): 39–59; Mary Elizabeth Moore, "Teaching Justice and Reconciliation in a Wounding World," in *The Other Side of Sin: Woundedness from the Perspective of the Sinned-Against*, ed. Andrew Sung Park and Susan L. Nelson (Albany: State University of New York Press, 2001), 143–64.

An important aspect of communing is *building prophetic community — developing relationships based in God's love and God's call to repair the world*. Such relationships do not depend on common background, belief, or interest, but on God's gift of community and hard work in community building. People often think of community-builders as people who are not willing to take risks or take a stand, and we think of prophets as people who are divisive. I challenge both of those assumptions. Community building can be a boldly prophetic act. Marc Gopin is a Jew who works hard on building relations between Israel and Palestine. He is constantly trying to understand the various positions held by Israelis and Palestinians, to understand the reasons for those positions (including the most emotional and painful reasons), and to evoke the best from both sets of leaders.[27] Some people criticize him for betraying the Jews; others criticize him for being too mild in his critique of Israel's treatment of the Palestinians. His concern, however, is to build lasting relationships that move beyond the typical "winner-loser" ways of disputation. He believes that it is necessary to uncover the deep pain of Jews in Israel, particularly the Holocaust pain that still pervades consciousness; likewise, it is necessary to uncover the deep pain of Palestinians and the unjust treatment they have experienced at the hands of Israelis. His very efforts to build human relationships across great chasms of difference represent a brave and prophetic act.

Similarly, prophetic acts of protest or social critique can actually contribute to community building. People are bound into stronger relations through common cause, working together for the well-being of the world. As noted in chapter 2, Christians have tended to see prophecy as the work of individual prophets, rather than an action of God through the community. To encourage the development of prophetic communities seems contradictory, but prophecy is an act of God to be received and enacted by *all* God's people; prophetic leaders simply call the people into their common vocation. The challenge for every group that gathers in Christian community is to *ask what God's prophetic call is to your community, and how you can best embody that call*. The five women in the Los Angeles base community did just that, and their actions have continued to effect transformation far beyond what they dreamed was possible when they began.

2. Cry and Listen to Cries of Others

A second educational act is to *cry and listen to the cries of others — to mourn the destruction and brokenness of the world*. The practice of lament is an honest, sometimes terror-filled recognition that problems *do* exist in the world; in fact, they are deep and pervasive. As they wreak havoc in the modern world, neither modernist nor postmodernist thought is adequate to stir and support an adequate

---

27. Marc Gopin, *Holy War, Holy Peace: How Religion Can Bring Peace to the Middle East* (New York: Oxford University Press, 2002); Marc Gopin, *Between Eden and Armageddon: The Future of World Religions, Violence, and Peacemaking* (New York: Oxford University Press, 2000).

human response. We need to turn instead to the primal cries of pain, indignation, and horror that come from our brothers and sisters around the world.[28]

Just as religious educators have often not been in the forefront of social justice movements, so they have not been in the forefront of crying. This is understandable in light of education's central role in formation, focused on equipping and guiding. On the other hand, transformation is also a vital role of education, and transformation comes, in part, through a hermeneutic of reconstruction, for which crying is foundational. To discern pain and the God-nudges that come through hurts in the world is essential to discerning what needs to be reconstructed and repaired. As developed in chapter 4, we need to take up the challenge of Maria Harris to include mourning in the steps of religious education. This will include many dimensions, but for reconstructing community and repairing the world, we need particularly to listen to cries, participate in crying, and discern what kinds of repair are necessary as a result of the cries. The challenge for learning communities is to ask *what cries of pain are calling out for your attention; to attend to those cries through listening, study, and active mourning; and to seek ways to respond with reconstruction and repair.*

3. Confess

The discussion of crying leads naturally to a third educational practice, *confession — to speak with God, oneself, and others about failings in oneself and one's communities.* Brokenness is not something that is "out there"; we live in the middle of it. Thus, we need to confess our participation in broken lives, broken relationships, broken political and international relations, and a broken ecology. God's compassion toward the groaning creation can evoke this human compassion. To have com-passion is to *feel with* the creation, thus, to repent — repenting what we have failed to do that we should have done, and what we have done that we should not have done. Repenting is more than "I am sorry." It is *turning toward shalom — toward wholeness — made possible by the touch of God.* This includes turning *away from* sin and oppression; it includes turning *toward* God's promises for life. It is an act of one's whole body — with the whole body of the church — toward shalom. The role of education is critical because it can awaken people to community and to pain (as the first two practices of this chapter suggest). It can also contribute to people's confessing sins and shortcomings that deny brokenness in the world or resist reconstruction and repair.

Individually, we could probably confess many different ways of violating God's creation and falling short of God's call on our lives (*harmartia*). In educational communities, we might need most to confess our failure to engage sufficiently in practices and reflections that address the most hurting in this world. The

---

28. This theme is developed further in Moore, *Ministering with the Earth*, 119–27; Moore, "Teaching Justice and Reconciliation."

challenge for learning communities is to *ask what problems have gone unaddressed or what destruction has been actively caused or permitted by the action or inaction of your community and the members thereof.* Teachers need to create opportunities to reflect on such shortcomings and failings, to name them in community, to lift them in prayer and to discern directions for future attitudes and action. Consider the five women in the Los Angeles base community once again. The simple act of confessing their fears of gangs led them into further study and prayer, and into active confession and repentance (turning around), one step after another.

4. Celebrate — Celebrate the God of Hope

Honesty about cries and confession stir a yearning for hope; and we have already said that God is a Promise-Maker. To respond to the human need for hope and the hope-filled actions of the Promise-Maker requires the educational practice of celebrating. Celebration is the act of *giving thanks to the God of hope,* who offers ever-new possibilities of transformation for the sake of creation's flourishing. This act of thanksgiving, as noted in the extensive discussion of chapter 6, enables people to see life in the context of God's graciousness. It also brings people together to praise God, thereby diminishing their preoccupation with human affinities. Further, it stirs genuine hope that the world, by God's grace, has potential for transformation. Celebration thus inspires and supports efforts to reconstruct community and repair the world.

Celebration can be challenging for religious educators, especially given the seriousness of educational responsibilities and expectations. However, celebration is that which gives us eyes to see the movements of God and the joys of human community amid our deepest struggles. Celebration is thanksgiving for life, even when life-destruction is everywhere present. Celebration is honoring that which is good in our midst, even when struggles sap our energies. Celebration is the nest that nourishes our capacities to cry and confess, and to be transformed. In light of this affirmation, learning communities need to *ask when you last celebrated and how that affected your community; then to ask what causes for celebration, what possibilities for celebration, and what plans for celebration you discover.* Further, you need to take the time to be joyful with others, either in small groups or with the entire community. Celebration is, after all, a vital source of nourishment, a refreshing change from other patterns of church life, and a space-maker, creating spaces for people to play together (chapter 5) and be renewed.

5. Convert — Envision Alternate Futures

Celebration, or giving praise to God, is an end in itself, but it is much more than that, for God's work is transformative and countercultural. God's work is not only to be admired and appreciated, but also to be effective in human lives. Thus, we need a fifth educational practice, *to convert — to turn together into a new way of life.* This is an obvious practice for reconstruction and repair, as it focuses on envisioning alternate futures (what forms of life are good and possible) and actively moving toward them. This practice well describes the characters of Esther, Mordecai, and King Ahasuerus. Each was converted from comfortable assumptions about normal personal and ethnic relations, especially between King Ahasuerus's people and the Hebrews. Each also began to act differently when they were converted to another view.

This discussion raises interesting questions for religious educators, who are expected to help people grow in faith from an early age (nurture). This role is often seen as being in tension with conversion. The tension is especially apparent when conversionists emphasize the sinfulness of individuals to prepare them to be converted to faith in Jesus Christ, or to be converted to a new form of Christianity or another religion. The most nuanced understandings of conversion emphasize the full-bodied, radical nature of conversion while recognizing that it arises from many influences and takes many forms; such a view is thoroughly compatible with the goals of religious education. Another tension arises when people claim postmodernist reasons to dismiss religion altogether. The best of postmodernism is open to more than simple rejection, even as it engages in real struggle. The best of postmodernism is critical of reigning thought patterns, cultural patterns, and practices that hold human beings hostage. The best of religious education does the same.

Conversion, then, is an important goal of religious education. It is a change of a particular kind. It is not adequately described as a simple transformation from sin to grace, or a transformation from nonfaith to faith, from one faith to another, or from a set of clear beliefs to a more doubting view. These views of conversion have an either-or cast to them. Conversion can be more adequately described as a turn toward God and God's calling to reconstruct community and repair the world. It will sometimes be welcome, and sometimes traumatic, but its possibilities are real. Thus, learning communities need to *ask what God is doing in your lives, what alternate futures are possible for the communities in which you live and for the larger society and ecology, and also what actions you need to take in order to make those futures a reality.*

Engage in Transformative Action

The community that wrestles with these questions will be challenged to transformative action. This is the work of reconciliation — *restoring relationships between and among God, human beings, and all of God's creation.*[29] In chapter 4, we discussed reconciliation with the past, which is critical for transformative action. We need also to consider reconciliation within the present contexts of our communities

---

29. The definitions for repentance, reparation, and reconciliation are developed and elaborated in Mary Elizabeth Mullino Moore, "New Creation: Repentance, Reparation, and Reconciliation," in *Wesleyan Perspectives on the New Creation,* ed. Douglas M. Meeks (Nashville: Abingdon, Kingswood, 2004).

and world. Educationally, this means that we need to study those situations and seek ways to participate actively in bringing all parties into life-giving relations with one another. It also means that we need to encourage deepened relations with God. As Emilie Townes describes womanist spirituality, for example, "It is the deep kneading of humanity and divinity into one breath, one hope, one vision."[30] Such a spirituality, as embodied in Christian tradition, "is not only a way of living, it is a style of witness that seeks to cross the yawning chasm of hatreds and prejudices and oppressions into a deeper and richer love of God as we experience Jesus in our lives."[31] This is the witness that finally leads people toward transformation.

Townes's metaphor of kneading is apt, for it points to the deep connections among spiritual practice, social witness, and vision, as to the deep connections between God and humanity. One finds a similar view in Gustavo Gutiérrez: "God is first contemplated when we do God's will and allow God to reign; only after that do we think about God. To use familiar categories: contemplation and practice together make up a *first act;* theologizing is a *second act.*"[32] Both Townes and Gutiérrez pose a view similar to that of this book, namely, that spiritual life, social witness, and the grist of daily life are all one in the human walk with God. These take precedence over reflective or intellectual work, which ironically is often elevated above the rest. Thus, education for transformative action includes attention to spiritual practices, social analysis, and ethical living, all of which is held together in the God-human relationship.

Because religious educators work closely with people in multiple settings of daily life, they are often profoundly conscious of their communities' failures to embody the highest values of their traditions. For the same reason, they are also conscious of possibilities and hopes that reside within reach of religious people. These possibilities and hopes are discovered as people walk with the God of history, especially as they walk and learn with others. In the walk, people discover a tug to trust God's transforming power. Educators equip people for that walk and support them as they grow in living their daily lives in God's Spirit.

Build Transformative Leadership

In addition to transformative action, religious educators need to attend to *building transformative leadership — equipping people to use their unique gifts to transform whatever situations are within their reach.* One Episcopal priest in Los Angeles convinced some city churches to buy Skid Row hotels in order to prevent their being

---

30. Emilie M. Townes, *In a Blaze of Glory: Womanist Spirituality as Social Witness* (Nashville: Abingdon, 1995), 11.

31. Ibid.

32. Gustavo Gutiérrez, *On Job: God-Talk and the Suffering of the Innocent,* trans. Matthew J. O'Connell (Maryknoll, N.Y.: Orbis, 1988), xiii. "The mystery of God comes to life in contemplation and in the practice of God's plan for human history; only in a second phase can this life inspire appropriate reasoning and relevant speech" (ibid.)

destroyed for high rises. She did this by convincing churches that they had a mission to the homeless, and near-homeless, in the city. Further, action was urgent ("for such a time as this"), and could not be delayed until all problems and questions had been resolved. This kind of mobilizing exemplifies the power of posing alternatives, as well as the possibility of developing transformative leadership by inviting people to participate in a critical movement. Other forms also exist. Some local churches pride themselves in the number of people they have called into ordained ministry over twenty or thirty years; others give great attention to equipping children and youth for compassionate service and justice ministries, both in their young lives and in the future.[33] Social science evidence has been building regarding the human need to be involved in transformative leadership, as well as the experiences of empathy and service that contribute to people's ability to give such leadership.[34] Thus, we see the dual need to invite people into leadership and to help them develop their abilities.

Reflecting on biblical texts, Paul frequently addresses issues of unity between Jewish and Gentile Christians and expresses concern when rivalry or tensions intervene. Paul offers an alternative in Ephesians, "For he is our peace; in his flesh he has made both groups into one and has broken down the dividing wall, that is, the hostility between us" (Eph. 2:14–16). Like the exemplars already named, Paul's approach is to stir imagination regarding how people might live together as one; he is posing alternatives and hoping to build transformative leadership throughout the early Christian communities with whom he ministers.

6. Construct — Practice Holiness

In the last movement of this chapter, we turn to constructing, the slow, painstaking work of constructing a new world from the ashes of the former one. This is an urgent practice because God does indeed require the faithful to act on behalf of creation. Holy living includes a community's structures and practices, as much as individual ones.

My last word to educators is that religious education is important to life. Whether one is an activist educator, or a reflector on action, the measure of our work is its contribution to holy living and to the quality of life in all God's creation. Some of us will speak directly of action, and others will develop theories; both are important. The point here is that the sacramental practice of constructing is a discipline of discerning hope, reflecting on it deeply, and mediating hope through your own life work. If we do that faithfully, our work just *may* contribute

---

33. Two schools are exemplars of such efforts. See James Youniss and Miranda Yates, *Community Service and Social Responsibility in Youth* (Chicago: University of Chicago Press, 1997); Haig-Brown et al., *Making the Spirit Dance Within.*

34. Miranda Yates and James Youniss, eds., *Roots of Civic Identity: International Perspectives on Community Service and Activism in Youth* (Cambridge: Cambridge University Press, 1999); Samuel Oliner and Pearl Oliner, *Embracing the Other* (New York: New York University Press, 1995), 375–76, 386.

to constructing a more just and merciful world. The practice of constructing calls on learning communities to *ask what kind of New Creation you discern in God's future and what kinds of holy living are necessary for you to contribute to that future.*

Practice Risk-Taking and Self-Giving

An important part of constructing is the *practice of taking risks and giving ourselves.* Some years ago, I was asked by one organization on our campus if I were willing to talk with the National U.M. Native American Center to co-sponsor a conference. Because I had been eager to have the Center on our campus and wanted to support and collaborate with them, I said yes, although the timing was very bad for me and I was very busy. The conference came after careful collaboration and hard work on my part. But the conference blew up, and the blame was cast on me by Native American students who attended from across the country. I was crushed, exhausted, and glad that I was leaving the next week for my sabbatical; I needed space to heal.

This story did not end here, however. Immediately, at the close of the conference, I wrote letters of support on behalf of two of the students who were having difficulties within church structures. Also, when I returned from sabbatical leave, I went out of my way to attend a conference sponsored by the Native American organization. Further, I worked closely with Native American students in my classes and some with colleagues at General Conference. In time, the Native American community began to trust me, at least as much as Native people can trust a white person. They know now that I am a partner with them, and this has been possible only because they and I have been willing to stay in this relationship over a long period of time. This story introduces possibilities of constructing new patterns of life through risk-taking and self-giving over time. These are vital ingredients in constructing, though the results are never guaranteed.

Practice Hospitality

Another important part of constructing is to *practice hospitality — welcome the stranger and outcast as a part of the community.* In the story about the Native American organization and my initial failures to relate well, I realize that the key ingredient bringing us through that difficult time was the offer of hospitality on both sides. The Native American leaders continued to be hospitable to me, and I to them. The relationship grew, not from little niceties, but from meeting over conversations and meals, discussing issues with intense honesty, offering respect to one another in every setting, and offering trust and acceptance when attempts at respect were misguided. I have seen similar hospitality in a Native American congregation where everyone is made to feel welcome, and where the congregation offers a meal each Sunday for the poor.[35] Unlike benevolent services

---

35. This intertribal Protestant congregation is in the Los Angeles region and was part of the Youth and Culture ethogenic studies, sponsored by the Association of Theological Schools, 1986–98.

in some other setting, this entire congregation sits to eat the meal; the poor are seen as being fully part of the congregation, as much as the church leaders.

7. Commission

Rather than offer a concluding reflection to this chapter, I will add one more educational practice, namely, commissioning. Commissioning derives from its root — *co-missio* — or sending out together. Thus, commissioning has to do with *sending people out together to do God's will (or God's work) in the church and world.* In this sense, it is similar to God's commissioning Abram and his family to leave the land of Haran and go to a new land, or God's commissioning Noah and his family to build an ark, or God's commissioning Esther to help save her people, or Jesus' commissioning his disciples to go out two-by-two to proclaim the good news, or Jesus' final commissioning of the disciples to make disciples and feed God's sheep. We already see in these brief references that the work of commissioning can be challenging and multifaceted. As described in other chapters, it can involve traveling and making home in a new place (Abram and Sarai); building a safe ark for people facing threat (Noah and his family); working for the salvation of people in danger (spiritual, physical, and social salvation as represented by Esther and Mordecai); proclaiming the good news of Jesus (the traditional twelve disciples and women followers of Jesus); or caring for others (making disciples or feeding Jesus' sheep).

The challenge for learning communities is to practice commissioning, creating rituals for individuals and groups, sending people out for small and large ministries, and valuing the life vocations of each and every one. Learning communities can *ask what God is calling your community and each individual to contribute to the New Creation and how people might be sent forth to do those ministries with the blessings of God and support of the community.* Commissioning is the ending of Matthew's Gospel, but the beginning of the Christian story. Likewise, commissioning is a new beginning every time, but it points to a vocation of living with God that has no end.

Reflecting Further

1. Review the questions identified in italics at the end of each practice of this chapter. Consider these questions in relation to your learning community. Conclude your reflections by asking how your answers lead your community into the future.

2. Engage in writing poetry, drawing, or using other art forms to express your visions of reconstructing community and repairing the world within your context. You might even find an opportunity to share these in a special event.

Chapter Nine

Sacramental Saga

✧

I had to conclude the revisions and editing of this chapter while caring for my mother, initially helping her to recover, and later helping her to die. I was struck in those six weeks with her that our encounter with life and death revealed much about sacramental living. Spending three months with my mother during her last year, I was aware of how precious life is, and how small kindnesses magnify life a hundredfold. In my mother's first illness of the year, one of her friends brought me lunch in the hospital, the first meal I had had in two days. Another friend came to visit when I was doing a difficult task for my mother. She took me aside and said that she had done the same for her family members and she appreciated what I was doing. She was praying for me. I felt no self-pity in either instance because I was doing what I wanted to do; however, I was touched by the gestures of kindness. That is sacramental living.

In this chapter, I will explore how the many aspects of sacramental living are interwoven in ordinary life situations and biblical narratives. I will also draw conclusions about the transformation of religious education and propose a planning process for church bodies that long to live sacramentally in the world.

Treasuring the Holy in the Midst of Life

Through the sacraments, people are touched by God's grace, and they respond by offering themselves to God. Through sacramental living, they do the same. In this final chapter, I return once again to connections between the church's sacraments and the sacrament of life. According to Alexander Schmemann, the eucharistic liturgy is a time of offering God the totality of our lives and the world in which we live, represented by our bringing food to the altar.[1] The liturgy does not end at the table, however; it continues into all of life. People are "created as *celebrants* of the

---

1. Alexander Schmemann, *For the Life of the World: Sacraments and Orthodoxy* (Crestwood, N.Y.: St. Vladimir's Seminary Press, 1973, 1963), 34. Schmemann proposes that we do this, knowing that "food is life, that it is the very principle of life." Underscoring the importance of this liturgical act, he claims that this offering is the "initial 'eucharistic' function" of human beings; it is both a responsibility and a fulfillment of life.

sacrament of life, of its transformation into life in God, communion with God." In fact, for Schmemann, "real life is 'eucharist,' a movement of love and adoration toward God."[2] This view from the Orthodox tradition expresses well the *central affirmations of this book — that all of life is sacramental, that the church's sacraments make visible the sacramentality of God's creation, and that the human calling is to participate in the sacrament of life.* To vivify the power of sacramentality and its interrelated movements, we turn to two narratives, one personal and the other biblical. Both reveal holy presence in the rhythms of life.

Sacramental Living in a Time of Dying

I began this chapter with reference to my mother's death. I return now to that time as a season of epiphany, revealing God and realities of sacramental living. My mother lived her last six weeks in the hospital. During most of that time, I slept in her room — awaking when she cried out, performing minor nursing roles, relating to her nurses and doctors, and holding my mother's hand. What a precious time that was! As I reflect on them now, I realize how those days were soaked in sacramental living. I was daily encountered with the sacramental movements discussed in this book. My mother and I *expected the unexpected.* On some days, we both prayed for her restored health; on other days, we prayed for a peaceful death; on most days, we prayed simply for God's will to be done. We expected something, but we knew not what.

Together my mother and I also *remembered the dismembered.* Mother recalled many joyful moments of her life and her family's, but she also recalled sadness and tragedy, some of which I had never heard. She and I both confessed how much we would miss each other when she died. No soft words wiped away that pain. Several days after Mother had resolved to give up her home and move near us in another state, away from her beloved church and friends, she experienced major setbacks. She realized then that she probably would not live to move at all. She looked at me intensely one morning, "I can do all of the rest, but I am going to miss you so much." This was a day of reckoning for my mother — reckoning with losses too great to imagine. That moment marked the beginning of *seeking reversals,* most especially seeking to let go of permanence and to treasure every simple moment. That particular reversal led both of us, surprisingly, into *giving thanks.* I am now shocked to realize that those six weeks were among the happiest of my life. Rarely have I been so intensely in love with life and so grateful to God for the gifts of family, love, and friendship.

The sacramental act of *nourishing life* was among the more obvious and the more surprising experiences of those six weeks. Nurture was obvious; my mother was in a hospital receiving medical care from a fine team of doctors, nurses, technicians, and therapists, all pouring energy into nourishing her life. The surprise,

---

2. Ibid.

however, was in the turning point when my mother announced she was ready to die and the doctors agreed. Everything in the care plan changed at that point, but the spirit of nurture was just as intense. The team nurtured my mother's life toward death as they had earlier nurtured her life toward recovery. Some people were better at one than the other, but nurture was fully present in both parts of my mother's journey. My mother's nurture of us also persisted to the very end, bringing us together around her bed and telling us funny stories of the past. Indeed, she was not going to depart this life without giving her only child one last blessing. On her last day, when everyone else had left, she called out to me, looked directly into my eyes, and breathed her last breath.

An experience of living with death is like an experience of giving birth — intensely real, emotion-stirring, and hope-filled. Relationships can be built and broken during such times. One of my mother's friends gave me an unexpected tongue-lashing; another gave me unexpected support. What was clear, however, was the deepening of many relationships — through time and tears, honesty and appreciation, empathy and working together. Those relationships will never return to what they were. Our family and friendship circles made strides toward recon-structing community and repairing the world, and we parted with promises not to wait for the next funeral. Of course, such promises are easily broken, but, quite often, families and close communities do *change* — relationships are strengthened or weakened, resentments are removed or intensified, roles shifted — as do per-spectives and relations in the larger world. Even the act of promise-making can strengthen bonds of love and reshape people's way of being in the world. Many families and individuals are forever changed by a sacramental experience of death, as are institutions and local communities for which death marks a "passing of the mantle" or a dramatic shift in power and relationships. These experiences, perme-ated with the sacramental presence of God, can lead to life-giving transformation (rather than destruction), especially when people are open to receiving God's blessings and responding, sometimes even when they are not.

This reflection reveals how easily the dimensions of sacramental living inter-twine in ordinary life moments. The intention is not to say that every moment or every season will always have, or should always have, all six sacramental move-ments. The intention is simply to reveal the presence of the sacred in all life, to be cherished and nourished.

Sacramental Living in Biblical Narratives

Sacramental living is also part of biblical accounts, which point repeatedly to God's movements in unexpected times and to the potential human response of mediating God's grace. Here we return to Ruth's story as an exemplar of sacramental living and its several movements, again revealing God's grace in ordinary life. We thus extend the discussion of chapter 7.

Naomi, devastated by the circumstances of her life, continued in bitterness, even after returning to Bethlehem, where she named herself Mara (Ruth 1). She did not hesitate to *remember the dismembered.* Settling in Bethlehem, Naomi sent Ruth to the fields of Boaz to glean; Ruth went (2). Both women were, in that act, *expecting the unexpected,* at least expecting to glean what the workers would leave behind for the poor and sojourners according to Jewish practice. In time, Naomi sent Ruth to Boaz to do more — to perform a ritual of lying at his feet (3). Here we see a courageous act of *seeking reversals.* Neither Naomi nor Ruth was passive in this narrative. They actively mourned, expected, and sought to reverse their situation. Naomi sought to survive and guarantee Ruth's survival; Ruth followed Naomi's directions, hoping to reverse their circumstances.

Boaz did respond. He promised Ruth to arrange for her provision, to return the field of her husband's family to her through the next of kin or, if that person said no, through himself (3:8–4:12). Boaz was *nourishing life,* as were Ruth and Naomi in seeking a way to survive when their lives were devastated. When Boaz and Ruth later married, they had a child, and Naomi took the child to her bosom and nursed it, again nourishing life (Ruth 4:13–16). Both Boaz's marriage to Ruth and the birth of their child were miracles, as was the irony of Bitter (Mara) Naomi's having milk to feed the child. These acts represent another narrative shift toward birthing and tending life. The child was to be "a restorer of life and a nourisher of [Naomi's] old age" (4:15). Further, Naomi and the women of Naomi's community celebrated, *giving thanks* for new birth (4:13–17). The story then closes with one more set of promises. The narrator reminds readers that this child was to carry on the life of Israel; indeed, the child was to become an ancestor of Jesse, the father of David (17–22). Here, we see the hope of a child, who renews life in the present and into the future — *reconstructing community and repairing the world.* The immediate promise is the joy of birth and the assurances of nourishment and lineage that attended birth in the ancient Middle Eastern world. For Christians, the story also points to the messianic promise of God's repairing the world, for Jesus is born into the line of David, which is also the line of Boaz and Ruth.

Reading Ruth from the perspective of sacramental living is not intended to be glib or to squeeze the narrative into an artificial framework. The book is far richer than the description given here. What is astounding, however, is that the narrative really does uncover the elements of sacramentality developed in this book. While the elements do not exhaust the meanings of the text, they do reveal how such elements are embraced and interwoven in biblical narrative.

Transforming Religious Education

In some ways, this book pushes the edges of educational theory and practice. For those who teach in schools and churches, the book poses a challenge to revere every act of teaching, and every act of living, as a sacred act. Such a view is in-timidating, for it transforms the comfortable ordinariness and neat categorization of human practice. Teaching, in this view, is more than a defined body of subject matter and practices. Like worship, preaching, administration, pastoral care, and social action, it is *a holy practice in response to the Holy One who gifts the world with grace and power beyond imagination.*

This idea is easier to say than to implement. Even within Christian education theory, a split exists between those who draw more heavily on theology and those who draw primarily on general educational theory. The split is often expressed in debates regarding disciplinary definition: Is Christian education a subdiscipline of practical theology or of education?[3] More pointedly for this book, subtle differ-ences exist even in reflections on teaching and the sacraments. James Michael Lee takes a social science approach, drawing upon educational theory and the human sciences; Robert Browning and Roy Reed draw more heavily on theo-logical traditions and analysis.[4] Sometimes the divide described here is expressed in Christian communities as a divide between Christian education and religious education or, more explicitly, a divide between those who see the purpose of educational ministry as the particularized formation of persons in Christian faith, and those who see the purpose as the spiritual formation and transformation of all aspects of human life in the world, as shaped by Christian faith traditions, or by other traditions, as found in Muslim, Jewish, and other communities.

These distinctions are oversimplified, for many people combine these disci-plines and use the terms in diverse combinations. For example, many people who identify themselves as Christian educators draw heavily on the social sciences and educational theory, and John Hull, who teaches religious education in a "secular" university, also writes in practical theology. Further, the works of James Michael Lee, Robert Browning, and Roy Reed overlap and complement one another. Such complexity is not the primary issue, however. The issue is that *the divide between theology and educational theory is a false one, as is the divide between sacrality and secularity.*[5]

An underlying purpose of this book is to reflect on the holiness in everyday life and in teaching, further to underscore the relation between the church's sacraments and the sacramentality of life. Distinctions do exist, but they are distinctions of function and form, rather than ontological difference. The church's sacraments serve to symbolize, re-present, and make present God's work in Jesus Christ and throughout time, for the sanctification of humanity and the well-being

---

3. One discussion of this is found in Allen J. Moore, "Religious Education as a Discipline," in *Changing Patterns of Religious Education,* ed. Marvin J. Taylor (Nashville: Abingdon, 1984).

4. James Michael Lee, *The Sacrament of Teaching: A Social Science Approach* (Birmingham: Re-ligious Education Press, 2000); Robert L. Browning and Roy A. Reed, *The Sacraments in Religious Education and Liturgy: An Ecumenical Model* (Birmingham: Religious Education Press, 1985).

5. This view is further developed in Mary Elizabeth Mullino Moore, *Teaching from the Heart: Theology and Educational Method* (Harrisburg, Pa.: Trinity Press International, 1998, 1993).

of the world. In so doing, they awaken people to sacred presence in all of life; thus, the sacramentality of ordinary life serves to symbolize, re-present, and make present God's work within a particular time and place, for the sanctification and well-being of God's creation. Each magnifies the other.

This perspective pushes the edges of contemporary theory in religious education and liturgical theology. It also critiques the common church practices of drawing sharp distinctions between teaching and worship, and between the sacraments and rest of ministry. Yet, it has historical precedents. Adding to the historical discussions of this book, I will name two precedents in Augustine for identifying sacramentality with a wide range of life events and church practices. In the first, Augustine described the conversion to Christianity of the great Roman teacher Victorinus, who first made private affirmations of Christian faith. When Victorinus then decided to enter the church, he was "granted the initial sacraments of instruction," the early period of instruction for baptism.[6] In telling this story, Augustine explicitly associated the sacraments with instruction. In later writing, Augustine also included the Creed and Lord's Prayer as sacraments. In both instances, his view was compatible with the wide-ranging identification of sacraments that typified the first thousand years of church history.[7]

For Christians today, the analysis of this book also suggests a broad view. Thus, we can affirm that *faithful living is a response to God's sacramental presence in all times and places and God's calling for people to mediate divine grace through the ordinary stuff of creation for the sanctification of human life and the well-being of all creation.* Such a perspective transforms spirituality into a life lived, in every detail, in response to the Holy; it transforms religious education into a teaching-learning process that is constantly formed and transformed in relation to the Holy. Such ministry draws upon every available theological and educational resource to inform its purposes and practices, and seeks God to be the primary guide, luring people toward discernment, decision-making, and action.

Planning for the Future

One challenge of sacramental education is to create space for sacramental practices and perspectives in community ministries. To that end, I have developed a planning process to help communities move in fresh directions without decrying

---

6. Augustine, *The Confessions of St. Augustine*, Book 8, chapter 2, trans. John K. Ryan (New York: Image Books, Doubleday, 1960), 184. Augustine was following the convention of considering the different aspects of baptismal preparation as sacraments of instruments. Ordinands also received instruments.

7. E. A. Livingstone, *The Oxford Dictionary of the Christian Church* (Oxford: Oxford University Press, 1997), 1435; Peter Taylor Forsyth, *The Church and the Sacraments* (London: Independent Press, 1953, 1917), 130–70; Oliver Chase Quick, *The Christian Sacraments* (London: Nisbet, 1929, 1927), 1–5, 104–10; John William Charles Wand, *The Development of Sacramentalism* (London: Methuen, 1928), 110–23.

all that is past. In common practice, planning begins with needs and then moves to measurable goals and objectives, reinforcing the sense that education and ministry exist to address human needs, even more narrowly to address the needs of a particular community. While this is a worthy goal, it is insufficient. In God's presence, need is real, but goodness is already happening, providing foundations for further building. In God's redemptive work, the cries of all creation, not just human communities or local communities, are heeded. In God's creativity, all things are possible, and sometimes far more is possible than people imagine or measure. In God's vast cosmos and eternal time, each sacramental act is small, yet each is precious, vital to the well-being of a broken creation.

Here I propose a planning process of nine steps. A community may choose to do fewer steps, to mix them in a different order, to dwell longer on some than others, or to move back and forth among the steps. "Steps" connote the movements of a dance, as described by Maria Harris, rather than steps on a staircase to a higher plane.[8] Some of these steps may be done in the context of worship, some in the context of study, and some in traditional planning sessions. In one setting, I developed Steps 1–5 into an extended worship service, followed by a planning session with Steps 6–8; in another group, I invited people to engage Step 6 as a time of meditative silence in the middle of the planning process. My way of presenting and ordering the steps does follow a logical progression, but life situations may require another logic, responsive to God's movements in a particular time and place. I have used this planning process with small and large groups and have discovered the fruitfulness; however, the real test is its life in the hands of others. Thus, I offer the process as one way to enlarge the possibility of sacramental visioning and sacramental living within the raw realities of life in the world.

1. Where Are We?
Where is our congregation or community now?

Reflect on the present situation of the community for which you are planning. Take time to meditate in silence, to share stories from the community, to gather demographic data about the community and its larger context, to do truth-telling, and to listen carefully to one another. A small group can do some of this research, but much needs to take place within the full body, either gathered as a whole or divided into small groups, or both. Sometimes this step needs to be extensive, taking a fresh look at the situation. Sometimes it can be done simply and briefly as a prelude to further work. Whether extensive or brief, this step needs to be done with conscientious listening to others and genuine openness to fresh insight.

---

8. Maria Harris, *Teaching and Religious Imagination: An Essay in the Theology of Teaching* (San Francisco: HarperSanFrancisco, 1991, 1987).

2. God's Blessings and Surprises:
Where do you see signs of God's blessings or surprises in the community?

Reflect on signs of God's movement in your community and its larger context. This is a time to focus on blessings, discerning what God is already doing and how your community might participate in these holy movements. Again, this step can be done in many ways, inviting silence, creative expression (through the arts or storytelling), and litanies of blessing. This is not a step for debate about which events are blessings and which are not, lest the focus be diverted. It is a time, rather, for attuning to God's movements and seeking the Holy — *expecting the unexpected* in the dramatic and ordinary movements of life, even in moments of tragedy. What one person sees as a blessing may be a curse in the eyes of another. Being honest about that is important for probing beneath the surface; however, debating about what is and is not a blessing is rarely fruitful in this step of the process. One might say, instead, "That event seemed less hopeful to me than to you, but I do see blessing in. . . . "

This step of seeking God's blessings and surprises is well served by the educational practices associated with *expecting the unexpected*: engaging with God and creation, searching for wonder, expecting, and hoping.[9] A community might be creative with the practices: taking time for an exploratory stroll through God's wonders within their context, naming wonders of their distant and recent past, identifying wonders in ritual or worship, expressing their blessings through the arts, or interviewing one another to discover blessings that diverse people have seen or experienced.

3. Destruction, Danger, and Threats:
What destruction, danger, or threats do you see in the present situation, or on the horizon?

Identify elements of destruction, danger, or threat that you see in or around your community. Like the previous step, the practice of identifying destruction, danger, and threats needs to be done in a safe way so that all contributions are respected and received, even when people see the situation differently. Also like the previous step, it can be done within ritual, worship, diverse art forms, interviews, or simple discussion. This step is an opportunity to *remember the dismembered,* drawing on educational practices of chapter 4: loving, truth-telling, mourning and repenting, and reconciling with the past.

Moving beyond stubborn impasses in a congregation, small group, local community or global situation requires honest acknowledgment of pain and problems;

---

9. This sacramental theme was developed in chapter 3. Indeed, the entire planning process of chapter 9 builds on sacramental themes of this book. People may wish to review earlier chapters to expand on the planning proposals; however, returning to earlier chapters is not necessary for the planning process. It can stand on its own.

it also requires moving beyond them.[10] I thus propose this step for the middle of a planning process. If it were the first step, it would imply that planning exists primarily to fix problems; if last, it would invite people to dwell in pain as an end in itself. The purpose of this step is, however, to dwell in pain as part of a larger movement of God's Spirit. Some communities need to dwell for some time, and some can move through this step rather quickly. Yet all communities need to be honest about destruction, danger, and threats — both from inside and from outside the community — and then move toward new moments of hope beyond pain.

4. Wild Imagination:
What wild imagination do you have for your community's future?

Create space for your imagination to elaborate, subvert, or redirect the present values and practices of your community. This is not a moment for planning details, but a time for meditating with openness to the God of reversals, who often does a new thing. Include times of silence in this movement, particularly at the beginning, so that people can empty themselves of their favorite agendas and wait upon God. Also, record the imaginings of the community during this movement, knowing that you can return to these ideas later for lingering reflection.

During this movement, the focus is on *seeking reversals*, not on deciding what does and does not work. Thus, several educational practices (elaborated in chapter 5) are helpful: undercover investigation, posing questions, imagination, parabolic thinking. This is a time in which people might gather in small groups to *brainstorm, building upon other's insights and refraining from evaluation or fine-tuning details,* which will come later. This is a time when people might read stories of other churches and communities to stir imagination, when they might remind themselves constantly to think beyond what they have known in the past. It is a time to prod the community with such challenges as: "Imagine!"; "What if?"; or "In what new directions is God's New Creation pointing?"

5. Gifts and Strengths:
Upon what gifts or strengths could you build?

Identify gifts in the community and its context that might contribute to the future. Consider gifts that are obvious and often celebrated, as well as gifts that people have overlooked in the past. The gifts may be in individuals, or in the community as a whole. For example, a faith community may be blessed with many artists or musicians; a congregation may have a history of effecting social change; it may have journeyed through tragedy and emerged with a strong sense of community; a small group may have spent time in personal sharing, enabling them to support

---

10. Marc Gopin, *Holy War, Holy Peace: How Religion Can Bring Peace to the Middle East* (New York: Oxford University Press, 2002); Marc Gopin, *Between Eden and Armageddon: The Future of World Religions, Violence, and Peacemaking* (New York: Oxford University Press, 2000).

one another in hard times or unite around a common mission; a large church body may have learned how to wrestle respectfully with controversial issues, thus preparing it to face new controversies.

In this movement of the planning process, a time of meditation and thanksgiving can be helpful, perhaps at the beginning of the movement or at the end. Pause for a time of silence in which people meditate on the gifts and strengths of the community. In this way, the practice of *giving thanks* can permeate the inner life of the planning community, as well as the conversation. The educational practices of chapter 6 suggest ways to celebrate gifts and strengths: trust, gratitude, and generosity. The planning process might include these practices, clearing space for people with diverse views to express themselves and listen respectfully to one another, to identify gifts and give thanks for them, and to invite generous sharing of gifts in ministry with others.

6. Yearnings and Hopes:
What yearnings and hopes do you have for your congregation or community? Of the ideas identified earlier, which seem most important for the community to consider?

This step is really a *pause for free-form reflection.* It is a time for people to stop and share their deepest yearnings and hopes for the community — to reflect on what is most vital in the group's work through earlier steps. Here, the community is discerning without pressure to make decisions or debate options. Full participation and respectful listening are critical, for what seems superficial or tangential to one group might be centrally important to another. To focus on yearnings and hopes is to identify seeds of life that can later be selected and nourished into fullness. This step thus draws upon the sacramental practice of *nourishing life,* particularly on the educational practices of seeking and reflecting on life, participating in forces of good, and playing. When this step concludes, people will hopefully have a clearer sense of values; thus, the community is poised to make decisions regarding priorities and future actions.

7. Choosing Priorities for the Future:
What priorities will we set for the future of this community — for the immediate or long-range future?

Here the planning group is encouraged to *identify central purposes and directions for the community's future ministry.* At this point, a community will often develop or reshape their mission or vision statement. They may, instead, revisit their mission statement (or central metaphor, symbol, or motto) and develop a list of priorities for the future that reflect their existing mission, informed by the discernment of the present process.

The questions below invite a community to *choose priorities for future ministry* — to decide how they will respond to God's nudges toward New Creation. Here, and in Step 8, the educational practices of *reconstructing community and repairing the world* are critical: communing, crying and listening to cries of others, confessing, celebrating, converting, constructing, and commissioning. Leaders may, of course, select or shape the questions according to unique needs, intentions, and hopes within their community.

- Prioritize blessings and surprises (identified in Step 2): *Which of God's blessings and surprises will* most likely *strengthen the future ministry of this community?* This does not mean that others are unimportant, but only that certain ones will get particular attention in the near future.

- Prioritize destruction, danger, and threats (from Step 3): *What cries are* most *urgent, demanding immediate and long-term attention?*

- Prioritize the community's wild imagination (from Step 4): *Which of our imaginings do we discern to be* most *compelling, God-ordained, and possible for our future?* Here, the community seeks to discern and refine its earlier imagination list by a process of grouping, revising, and deleting. Other questions can be helpful in this process as well: Which imaginings do we block because of our failure in vision or faithfulness? Which stir our sense of joy and commitment?

Depending on the size and communication styles of your community, these questions might be asked in many ways — by response cards, small group reflections, or silent times of meditation. The purpose is to prioritize. Whether the questioning is done in groups or in the whole body, however, a smaller planning team will probably need to compile the results in preparation for the next step of making decisions and commitments.

8. Making Decisions and Commitments: What, how, and who?

The practice of prioritizing prepares the way for a community to *decide on future action, develop detailed plans, and make commitments for action:*

- Build upon gifts and strengths (from Step 5): *How specifically will we draw upon the gifts of our community* to move in these new directions?

- Decide among yearnings and hopes (from Step 6): In light of our yearnings and hopes, *which plans of action will we adopt* in order to follow God's call in this time and place?

- *How will we develop these plans?* What will be our *specific goals?* How will we *design* the community's common work — its prayer, study, direct action, fellowship, and reflection? What will be the *timeline* for next steps? How will we build *ongoing reflection and re-formation* into the plans?

- *Who will take responsibility* for developing and implementing the different aspects of our design? What groups and individuals will give leadership? Who will be major participants? Who will provide additional support through prayer, consultation, advocacy, or occasional assistance?

- *What commitments will people make for next steps?* If people are not ready to make these commitments, consider whether a change in design is needed to respond to unresolved issues. What encouragement, inspiration, or removal of barriers is needed?

- *Commission the community* into service. As fitting to the particular community and its plans, commissioning might take place in a service of worship, a formal announcement, a grand celebration, or a mix of events.

9. *Reflecting and Beginning Again*

Planning is a process that never ends. Thus, a community needs to *engage in periodic times of beginning again — reflecting, evaluating, making new decisions, and reshaping ministry.* This is more than evaluating what was good, bad, or indifferent about a previous design and its implementation. It is a time to think deeply about the community and its mission — longer and deeper reflection than the ongoing reflection and re-formation process mentioned above. The following questions are helpful:

- *How has the design (purposes, structures, processes, and events) shaped our community? What has been especially meaningful, powerful, and transformative?*

- *How has the design affected others' lives?* This could include people's personal lives; their families; the larger congregation or denomination; the city, town, or neighborhood; or other parts of the global village.

- *What in this design does the community need to continue into the future, and what needs to be changed?*

Reflecting on such questions leads back into the first movement of the planning process, thus beginning the process all over again.

With the approach I have described here, no plan can be a failure because the very practice of planning, developing, and implementing a design contributes to the wisdom of a community. Plans may indeed lead to problems; however, even problems can stir a community to reflect, repent (turn around), and begin again. What is important is to continue praying and reflecting so as to be open to God's never-ending pull to the future.

Concluding Reflections

The sacramentality of God's creation surpasses the ideas and proposals of this book. My concluding hope is, however, that the book will contribute to sacramental living and the flourishing of God's creation. With eagerness to join with others in this common work, I close with a litany for the road:

Leader: As this journey of life continues, we give thanks to the God of journeys!

All: We give thanks for fellow travelers, for earth and sky and seas, and for God's abiding presence:

Leader: God's presence wherever we go, whatever wrongs we commit, however unfaithful we are, whatever wonderful dreams we dream.

All: We give thanks for visions planted in our souls, courage in our hearts, and strength in our bodies.

Leader: For everything God has done, thanks!

All: For the simple joy of hoping for tomorrow, thanks!

Leader: We pray that we will have courage and strength to discern and follow God's visions into the future, whatever the risks!

All: We pray that God will wake us up, energize and inspire us. We yearn to mediate God's grace in this world. May it be so! Amen.

Appendix

Overview of Teaching
as a Sacramental Act

Expecting the Unexpected

Power — Surprise, engaging with God, God's response

Roots in Church Practice — Advent; Unexpected blessings of baptism and eucharist

Theology of Wonder — Wonder of God and creation, transcendent immanence and immanent transcendence, incarnation, God's sacramental presence

Hermeneutic of Wonder

Educational Practices — Engaging with God and creation, searching for wonder, expectancy, practicing hope

Remembering the Dismembered

Power — Releasing, uncovering, taking time, preparing for repentance and reconstruction

Roots in Church Practice — Lent and Holy Week; Remembrance in baptism and eucharist — remembrance of Jesus' suffering and death and remembrance of brokenness in God's creation

Theology of Suffering — God's suffering, God's receiving and transforming, power of human grief, God's reconciling and call to reconciliation

Hermeneutic of Tragic Memory

Educational Practices — Loving, truth-telling, mourning and repenting, reconciling with the past

229

Seeking Reversals

Power — Reshaping relations with the past, transformed living, transformed thinking

Roots in Church Practice — Christmas and Easter; baptism as God's breaking into the world and welcoming the world into Christ's Body; eucharist as God's table of reversals

Theology of Parable and Paradox — God's "moreness," people easily deceived, God's twin gifts of imagination and risk, God's communication through parable and paradox

Hermeneutic of Suspicion

Educational Practices — Undercover investigation, posing questions, imagination, parabolic thinking

Giving Thanks

Power — Shaping a grateful spirit, drawing goodness from tragedy and despair, mutuality with God and God's bounty, being washed with God's presence

Roots in Church Practice — Epiphany and Eastertide; baptism and eucharist centered on thanksgiving for Jesus' life and God's gifts

Theology of Bounty — Bounties of God and creation; human need for thanksgiving, God's generosity, and creation's vocation of generosity

Hermeneutic of Thanksgiving

Educational Practices — Trust, gratitude, generosity

Nourishing New Life

Power — Gleaning hope from despair; being a people; shared mission and sense of belonging; birth, new birth, and nurture

Roots in Church Practice — Christmas and Pentecost; baptism as entrance into new life; eucharist as renewing of life through blessing, feeding, and receiving in community

Theology of Life — God as Life, God's opening of eyes and ears, life as a choice, life as mediated through others, human vocation to sustain life, God's creation of spaces for new birth

Hermeneutic of Nurture

Educational Practices — Care giving, seeking and reflecting on life, participating in forces of good, engaging in story and ritual, mentoring, playing

Reconstructing Community and Repairing the World

Power — Communal discernment, visioning alternatives, becoming involved with others, breaking the rules, taking risks

Roots in Church Practice — Ordinary Time; baptism and eucharist as transformative acts

Theology of Prophetic Redemption — God's creating the cosmos for community; brokenness of the world; God's compassion for groaning creation; God as Promise-Maker; God's work as transformative and countercultural; God's need for faithful human action

Hermeneutic of Reconstruction

Educational Practices — Communing, crying and listening to cries of others, confessing, celebrating, converting, constructing, commissioning

Bibliography

Alexander, Hanan A. "A Jewish View of Human Learning." *International Journal of Children's Spirituality* 4, no. 2 (1999).

————. *Reclaiming Goodness: Education and the Spiritual Quest*. Notre Dame, Ind.: University of Notre Dame, 2001.

Anderson, Herbert, and Susan B. W. Johnson. *Regarding Children: A New Respect for Childhood and Families*. Louisville: Westminster John Knox, 1994.

Andree, T., C. Bakker, and P. Schreiner, eds. *Crossing Boundaries: Contributions to Interreligious and Intercultural Education*. Münster: Comenius-Institut, 1997.

Aron, Isa, Sara L. Lee, and Seymour Rossel, eds. *A Congregation of Learners: Transforming the Synagogue into a Learning Community*. New York: UAHC Press, 1995.

Augustine, St. *On Baptism against the Donatists*. Trans. J. R. King, rev. Chester D. Hartranft. In *Nicene and Post-Nicene Fathers of the Christian Church*, vol. 4, ed. Philip Schaff. Grand Rapids, Mich.: Wm. B. Eerdmans, 1956.

————. *City of God against the Pagans*. Ed. and trans. R. W. Dyson. Cambridge: Cambridge University, 1998.

————. *The Confessions of St. Augustine*. Trans. John K. Ryan. New York: Image Books, Doubleday, 1960.

Avila, Rafael. *Worship and Politics*. Maryknoll, N.Y.: Orbis, 1981, 1977.

Baillie, Donald McPherson. *God Was in Christ: An Essay on Incarnation and Atonement*. New York: Charles Scribner's Sons, 1948.

Balasuriya, Tissa. *The Eucharist and Human Liberation*. Maryknoll, N.Y.: Orbis, 1979, 1977.

Bass, Dorothy C., ed. *Practicing Our Faith: A Way of Life for a Searching People*. San Francisco: Jossey-Bass, 1997.

Bender, Sue. *Everyday Sacred: A Woman's Journey Home*. San Francisco: HarperSanFrancisco, 1995.

Berlin, Adele. "Ruth: Introduction." In *The HarperCollins Study Bible*, ed. Wayne A. Meeks. New York: HarperCollins, 1993.

Berry, Thomas. "The New Story: Comments on the Origin, Identification, and Transmission of Values." *CrossCurrents* (Summer/Fall 1987).

Black, Kathy. *A Healing Homiletic: Preaching and Disability*. Nashville: Abingdon, 1996.

Blaiklock, E. M., and A. C. Keys, trans. *The Little Flowers of St. Francis: The Acts of St. Francis and His Companions*. London: Hodder and Stoughton, 1985.

Boff, Leonardo. *Ecclesiogenesis: The Base Communities Reinvent the Church*. Trans. Robert R. Barr. Maryknoll, N.Y.: Orbis, 1986.

————. *Sacraments of Life: Life of the Sacraments*. Washington, D.C.: Pastoral Press, 1987.

The Book of Common Prayer. New York: Seabury Press, 1979.

The Book of Common Worship. Louisville: Westminster John Knox, 1993.

Bowers, C. A. *Educating for an Ecologically Sustainable Culture: Rethinking Moral Education, Creativity, Intelligence, and Other Modern Orthodoxies.* Albany: State University of New York Press, 1995.

Bowers, C. A., and David J. Flinders. *Responsive Teaching: An Ecological Approach to Classroom Patterns of Language, Culture, and Thought.* New York: Teachers College, 1990.

Boys, Mary C. *Has God Only One Blessing? Judaism as a Source of Christian Self-Understanding.* New York: Paulist, 2000.

Brock, Rita Nakashima. *Journeys by Heart: A Christology of Erotic Power.* New York: Crossroad, 1988.

Brock, Rita Nakashima, and Rebecca Ann Parker. *Proverbs of Ashes: Violence, Redemptive Suffering, and the Search for What Saves Us.* Boston: Beacon, 2001.

Browning, Robert L., and Roy A. Reed. *The Sacraments in Religious Education and Liturgy: An Ecumenical Model.* Birmingham: Religious Education Press, 1985.

Brueggemann, Walter. *Abiding Astonishment: Psalms, Modernity, and the Making of History.* Louisville: Westminster John Knox, 1991.

——. *Israel's Praise: Doxology against Idolatry and Ideology.* Philadelphia: Fortress, 1988.

Brueggemann, Walter, Sharon Parks, and Thomas H. Groome. *To Act Justly, Love Tenderly, Walk Humbly: An Agenda for Ministers.* Eugene, Ore.: Wipf & Stock, 1992, 1986.

Bullard, Robert D., ed. *Confronting Environmental Racism: Voices from the Grassroots.* Boston: South End, 1993.

Bushnell, Horace. *Christian Nurture.* New Haven: Yale University Press, 1960.

Cajete, Gregory. *Look to the Mountain: An Ecology of Indigenous Education.* Durango, Colo.: Kivaki, 1994.

Caldwell, Elizabeth Francis. *Come unto Me: Rethinking the Sacraments for Children.* Cleveland: United Church Press, 1996.

Calvin, John. *Calvin: Institutes of the Christian Religion.* Trans. Ford Lewis Battles. Library of Christian Classics 21. Philadelphia: Westminster Press, 1960.

Cannon, Katie G. *Katie's Canon: Womanism and the Soul of the Black Community.* New York: Continuum, 1995.

Carroll, Jackson W., and Wade Clark Roof. *Bridging Divided Worlds: Generational Cultures in Congregations.* San Francisco: Jossey-Bass, 2002.

Carroll, Jackson W., and Wade Clark Roof, eds. *Beyond Establishment: Protestant Identity in a Post-Protestant Age.* Louisville: Westminster John Knox, 1993.

Casel, Odo. *The Mystery of Christian Worship and Other Writings.* Ed. Burkhard Neunheuser, O.S.B. Westminster, Md.: Darton, Longman & Todd, Newman, 1962, 1932.

Castenell, Louis A., Jr., and William F. Pinar, eds. *Understanding Curriculum as Racial Text: Representations of Identity and Difference in Education.* Albany: State University of New York Press, 1993.

Chadwick, Nora. *The Celts.* London: Penguin, 1991, 1971.

Chung, Hyun Kyung. *Struggle to Be the Sun Again: Introducing Asian Women's Theology.* Maryknoll, N.Y.: Orbis, 1990.

Cooke, Bernard J. *Sacraments and Sacramentality.* Mystic, Conn.: Twenty-Third Publications, 1983.

Costen, Melva Wilson. *African American Christian Worship.* Nashville: Abingdon, 1993.

Council of Trent. "Canon XII." *The Canons and Decrees of the Council of Trent* (1547). Trans. Philip Schaff. *The Creeds of Christendom*. Grand Rapids, Mich.: Baker Book House, n.d.

Couture, Pamela D. *Seeing Children, Seeing God: A Practical Theology of Children and Poverty*. Nashville: Abingdon Press, 2000.

Crossan, John Dominic. *The Dark Interval: Towards a Theology of Story*. Sonoma, Calif.: Polebridge, 1988.

———. *In Parables: The Challenge of the Historical Jesus*. New York: Harper & Row, 1973.

De Waal, Esther, comp. and ed. *The Celtic Vision*. London: Darton, Longman & Todd, 1988.

Deloria Jr., Vine. *For This Land: Writings on Religion in America*. New York: Routledge, 1999.

Dewey, John. *The Child and the Curriculum*. Chicago: University of Chicago Press, 1971.

———. *Experience and Education*. New York: Collier Books, 1977, 1938.

Dewey, John, and Evelyn Dewey. *Schools of Tomorrow*. New York, E. P. Dutton, 1962, 1915.

Didache. Trans. Willie Rordorf et al. In *The Eucharist of the Early Christians*. Trans. Matthew J. O'Connell. New York: Pueblo, 1978.

Dykstra, Craig. *Growing in the Life of Faith: Education and Christian Practices*. Louisville: Geneva Press, 1999.

Edwards, Tilden. *Sabbath Time*. Nashville: Upper Room, 1992.

Eiesland, Nancy. *The Disabled God*. Nashville: Abingdon, 1994.

Elaw, Zilpha. "Memoirs of the Life, Religious Experience, Ministerial Travels, and Labours of Mrs. Zilpha Elaw, an American Female of Colour; Together with Some Account of the Great Religious Revivals in America [Written by Herself] (1846)." In *Sisters of the Spirit: Three Black Women's Autobiographies of the Nineteenth Century*, ed. William L. Andrews. Bloomington: Indiana University Press, 1986.

Eusden, John Dykstra, and John H. Westerhoff, III. *Sensing Beauty: Aesthetics, the Human Spirit, and the Church*. Cleveland: United Church Press, 1998.

Evans, Alice Frazer, Robert A. Evans, and William Bean Kennedy. *Pedagogy for the Non-Poor*. Maryknoll, N.Y.: Orbis, 1987.

Everist, Norma Cook. *The Church as Learning Community: A Comprehensive Guide to Christian Education*. Nashville: Abingdon, 2002.

Fishburn, Janet F. *People of a Compassionate God*. Nashville: Abingdon, 2003.

Forsyth, Peter Taylor. *The Church and the Sacraments*. London: Independent Press, 1953, 1917.

Freire, Paulo. *Pedagogy in Process*. New York: Seabury, 1978.

———. *Pedagogy of the Oppressed*. Trans. Myra B. Ramos. New York: Herder & Herder, 1970.

Freire, Paulo, ed. *The Politics of Education: Culture, Power, and Liberation*. Trans. Donaldo Macedo. Westport, Conn.: Bergin & Garvey, 1985.

Freire, Paulo, and Antonio Faundez. *Learning to Question: A Pedagogy of Liberation*. Trans. Tony Coates. New York: Continuum, 1989.

Furlong, J., and T. Maynard. *Mentoring Student Teachers*. London: Routledge, 1995.

Gopin, Marc. *Between Eden and Armageddon: The Future of World Religions, Violence, and Peacemaking*. New York: Oxford University Press, 2000.

———. *Holy War, Holy Peace: How Religion Can Bring Peace to the Middle East.* New York: Oxford University Press, 2002.

Grant, Jacquelyn. *White Women's Christ and Black Women's Jesus: Feminist Christology and Womanist Response.* Atlanta: Scholars Press, 1989.

Greenberg, Irvin. "Cloud of Smoke, Pillar of Fire: Judaism, Christianity and Modernity after the Holocaust." In *Auschwitz: Beginning of a New Era?*, ed. Eva Fleischner. New York: KTAV, 1977.

Greene, Dana. *Evelyn Underhill: Artist of the Infinite Life.* New York: Crossroad, 1990.

Grimes, Howard. *The Church Redemptive.* New York: Abingdon Press, 1958.

Groome, Thomas H. *Christian Religious Education.* San Francisco: Jossey-Bass, 1999, 1980.

———. *Sharing Faith: A Comprehensive Approach to Religious Education.* San Francisco: HarperSanFrancisco, 1991.

Gudorf, Christine E. "The Power to Create: Sacraments and Men's Need to Birth." *Horizons* 14 (1987).

———. *Victimization: Examining Christian Complicity.* Philadelphia: Trinity Press International, 1992.

Gutiérrez, Gustavo. *The God of Life.* Trans. Matthew J. O'Connell. Maryknoll, N.Y.: Orbis, 1991.

———. *On Job: God-Talk and the Suffering of the Innocent.* Trans. Matthew J. O'Connell. Maryknoll, N.Y.: Orbis, 1987.

———. *We Drink from Our Own Wells: The Spiritual Journey of a People.* Trans. Matthew J. O'Connell. Maryknoll, N.Y.: Orbis, 1984.

Haig-Brown, Celia, Kathy L. Hodgson-Smith, Robert Regnier, and Jo-ann Archibald. *Making the Spirit Dance Within: Joe Duquette High School and an Aboriginal Community.* Toronto: James Lorimer & Company, 1997.

Hallie, Philip P. *Lest Innocent Blood Be Shed: The Story of the Village of Le Chambon, and How Goodness Happened There.* 1st Harper Colophon ed. New York: Harper Colophon, 1980, 1979.

———. "Major Julius Schmahling. In *The Courage to Care: Rescuers of Jews during the Holocaust.* Ed. Carol Rittner and Sondra Myers. New York: New York University Press, 1986.

Harris, Maria. *Dance of the Spirit: The Seven Steps of Women's Spirituality.* New York: Bantam Doubleday Dell, 1989.

———. *Proclaim Jubilee! A Spirituality for the Twenty-first Century.* Louisville: Westminster John Knox, 1996.

———. *Teaching and Religious Imagination: An Essay in the Theology of Teaching.* San Francisco: Harper & Row, 1987.

———. *Women and Teaching: Themes for a Spirituality of Pedagogy.* New York: Paulist Press, 1988.

Hellwig, Monika K. *The Eucharist and the Hunger of the World.* New York: Paulist, 1976.

Heschel, Abraham Joshua. *The Earth Is the Lord's and the Sabbath.* New York: Harper & Row, 1962.

———. *God in Search of Man: A Philosophy of Judaism.* New York: Farrar, Straus & Cudahy, 1955.

———. *Man Is Not Alone: A Philosophy of Religion.* New York: Farrar, Straus and Giroux, 1951.

Hess, Carol Lakey. *Caretakers of Our Common House: Women's Development in Communities of Faith.* Nashville: Abingdon, 1997.

Heyward, Carter. *God in the Balance: Christian Spirituality in Times of Terror.* Cleveland: Pilgrim, 2002.

———. *The Redemption of God: A Theology of Mutual Relation.* Washington, D.C.: University Press of America, 1982.

Hilkert, Mary Catherine. *Naming Grace: Preaching and the Sacramental Imagination.* New York: Continuum, 1997.

hooks, bell. *Communion: The Female Search for Love.* New York: William Morrow, 2002.

———. *Salvation: Black People and Love.* New York: William Morrow, 2001.

Hull, John M. "Blindness and the Face of God: Toward a Theology of Disability." In *The Human Image of God,* ed. Hans-Georg Ziebertz et al. Leiden: Brill, 2001.

———. *On Sight and Insight: A Journey into the World of Blindness.* Oxford: Oneworld Publications, 1997, 1990.

Isasi-Díaz, Ada María. *En la Lucha: In the Struggle: A Hispanic Women's Liberation Theology.* Minneapolis: Fortress, 1993.

———. *Mujerista Theology: A Theology for the Twenty-first Century.* Maryknoll, N.Y.: Orbis, 1996.

James, William. *The Varieties of Religious Experience: A Study in Human Nature.* New York: University Books, 1963, 1902.

Jantzen, Grace M. *Julian of Norwich: Mystic and Theologian.* New ed. New York: Paulist Press, 2000.

———. *Power, Gender and Christian Mysticism.* New York: Cambridge University, 1995,

John Chrysostom. *The Homilies of St. John Chrysostom on the Gospel of St. Matthew.* Oxford: John Henry Parker, 1852.

Johnson, Elizabeth A. *She Who Is: The Mystery of God in Feminist Theological Discourse.* New York: Crossroad, 1992.

Jones, Cheslyn, Geoffrey Wainwright, and Edward Yarnold, S.J., eds. *The Study of Liturgy.* New York: Oxford University Press, 1978.

Julian of Norwich. *Showings.* Classics of Western Spirituality. Trans. Edmund Colledge, O.S.A., and James Walsh, S.J. Mahwah, N.J.: Paulist, 1978.

Kaufman, Gordon D. *The Theological Imagination: Constructing the Concept of God.* Philadelphia: Westminster Press, 1981.

Keely, Barbara Anne, ed. *Faith of Our Foremothers: Women Changing Religious Education.* Louisville: Westminster John Knox, 1997.

Keller, Catherine. *Face of the Deep: A Theology of Becoming.* New York: Routledge, 2003.

Kincheloe, Joe L., and William F. Pinar, eds. *Curriculum as Social Psychoanalysis: The Significance of Place.* Albany: State University of New York Press, 1991.

King Jr., Martin Luther. *I Have a Dream: Writings and Speeches That Changed the World.* Ed. James Melvin Washington. San Francisco: HarperSanFrancisco, 1992.

———. *Strength to Love.* Minneapolis: Fortress, 1981, 1963.

Knowles, Malcolm S. *The Modern Practice of Adult Education: Andragogy versus Pedagogy.* New York: Association Press, 1970.

Krondorfer, Björn. *Remembrance and Reconciliation: Encounters between Young Jews and Germans.* New Haven: Yale University Press, 1995.

Kwok, Pui-lan. *Introducing Asian Feminist Theology.* Cleveland: Pilgrim Press, 2000.

Law, Eric H. F. *The Bush Was Blazing but Not Consumed: Developing a Multicultural Community through Dialogue Liturgy.* St. Louis: Chalice, 1996.

———. *Inclusion: Making Room for Grace.* St. Louis: Chalice, 2000.

———. *Sacred Acts, Holy Change: Faithful Diversity and Practical Transformation.* St. Louis: Chalice, 2002.

Lee, James Michael. *The Sacrament of Teaching: A Social Science Approach.* Birmingham: Religious Education Press, 2000.

L'Engle, Madeleine. *Madeleine L'Engle Herself: Reflections on a Writing Life.* Comp. Carole F. Chase. Colorado Springs, Colo.: WaterBrook, 2001.

Levy, Steven. *Starting from Scratch: One Classroom Builds Its Own Curriculum.* Portsmouth, N.H.: Heinemann, 1996.

Livingstone, E. A. *The Oxford Dictionary of the Christian Church.* Oxford: Oxford University Press, 1997.

Long, Thomas G. *Beyond the Worship Wars: Building Vital and Faithful Worship.* Bethesda, Md.: Alban Institute, 2001.

Luther, Martin. *A Catechism for the People, Pastor, and Preacher.* Manchester: A. Brothers, for the Holbein Society, 1892, 1553.

———. *Doctor Martin Luther's Small Catechism: Explained for Children and Adults.* Ed. C. Gausewitz. Milwaukee: Northwestern Pub. House, 1956, 1941.

———. *Getting into Luther's Large Catechism: A Guide for Popular Study.* Ed. F. Samuel Janzow. St. Louis: Concordia, 1978.

Lutheran Book of Worship. Minneapolis: Augsburg Publishing House, 1978.

Matthaei, Sondra Higgins. *Faith Matters: Faith-Mentoring in the Faith Community.* Valley Forge, Pa.: Trinity Press International, 1996.

Mayer, Gabriele. *Post-Holocaust Religious Education for German Women.* Münster: LIT Verlag, 2003.

Maynard, Jane Frances. "Finding Religious and Spiritual Meaning in AIDS-Related Multiple Loss: A Comparative and Constructive Theological Analysis of Communal Bereavement." Ph.D. diss., Claremont School of Theology, 2001.

McCarthy, C., and W. Crichlow. *Race and Identity in Education.* New York: Routledge, 1994.

McConnell, Taylor. "Family Ministry through Cross-Cultural Education." *Religious Education* 76, no. 3 (May–June 1981).

McFague, Sallie. *The Body of God: An Ecological Theology.* Minneapolis: Augsburg Fortress, 1993.

———. *Life Abundant: Rethinking Theology and Economy for a Planet in Peril.* Minneapolis: Fortress Press, 2001.

———. *Metaphorical Theology: Models of God in Religious Language.* Philadelphia: Fortress, 1985, 1982.

———. *Models of God: Theology for an Ecological, Nuclear Age.* Philadelphia: Fortress, 1987.

Mead, George H. *The Philosophy of the Present.* LaSalle, Ill.: Open Court, 1932.

———. *The Social Psychology of George Herbert Mead.* Chicago: University of Chicago Press, 1956.

Menzies, Lucy, ed. *Collected Papers of Evelyn Underhill.* London: Longmans, Green and Co., 1946.

Merton, Thomas. *Bread in the Wilderness.* Collegeville, Minn.: Liturgical Press, 1986, 1953.

———. *What Is Contemplation?* Springfield, Ill.: Templegate, 1978.

Miles, Margaret R. *Desire and Delight: A New Reading of Augustine's Confessions.* New York: Crossroad, 1992.

Miller-McLemore, Bonnie J. *Let the Children Come: Reimagining Childhood from a Christian Perspective.* New York: Wiley, 2003.

Miller-McLemore, Bonnie J., and Brita L. Gill-Austern, eds. *Feminist and Womanist Pastoral Theology.* Nashville: Abingdon, 1999.

Mitchell, David D. *Black Theology and Youths at Risk.* New York: Peter Lang, 2001.

Mitchell, Ella Pearson, ed. *Those Preachin' Women: More Sermons by Black Women Preachers.* Vol. 2. Valley Forge, Pa.: Judson, 1988.

Moltmann, Jürgen. *The Church in the Power of the Spirit: A Contribution to Messianic Ecclesiology.* New York: Harper & Row, 1977.

———. *The Crucified God: The Cross of Christ as the Foundation and Criticism of Christian Theology.* Trans. R. A. Wilson and John Bowden. San Francisco: HarperSanFrancisco, 1991, 1974, 1972.

———. *Hope for the Church.* Nashville: Abingdon, 1979.

———. *Theology of Hope: On the Ground and the Implications of a Christian Eschatology.* Trans. James W. Leitch and preface trans. Margaret Kohl. San Francisco: HarperSanFrancisco, 1991, 1975.

Moltmann-Wendel, Elisabeth. *Rediscovering Friendship.* London: SCM, 2000.

Moore, Allen J. "Religious Education as a Discipline." In *Changing Patterns of Religious Education,* ed. Marvin J. Taylor. Nashville: Abingdon, 1984.

Moore, Mary Elizabeth."Beyond Poverty and Violence: An Eschatological Vision." *International Journal of Practical Theology* 7, no. 1 (Summer 2003).

———. *Covenant and Call: Mission of the Future Church.* Nashville: Discipleship Resources, UMC, 2000.

———. *Education for Continuity and Change.* Nashville: Abingdon, 1983.

———. "Richness in Religious Education: Ethnic, Religious and Biodiversity." In *The Fourth R for the Third Millennium: Education in Religion and Values for the Global Future,* ed. Leslie J. Francis, Jeff Astley, and Mandy Robbins. Dublin: Lindisfarne Books, 2001.

———. "Sacramental Teaching: Mediating the Holy." In *Forging a Better Religious Education for the Third Millennium,* ed. James Michael Lee. Birmingham: Religious Education Press, 2000.

Moore, Mary Elizabeth Mullino. "Dynamics of Religious Culture: Theological Wisdom and Ethical Guidance from Diverse Urban Communities." *International Journal of Practical Theology* 2 (1998).

———. "New Creation: Repentance, Reparation, and Reconciliation." In *Wesleyan Perspectives on the New Creation,* ed. Douglas M. Meeks. Nashville: Abingdon, Kingswood, 2004.

———. "Poetry, Prophecy, and Power." *Religious Education* 93, no. 3 (Summer 1998).

———. *Teaching from the Heart: Theology and Educational Method.* Valley Forge, Pa.: Trinity Press International, 1998.

Nouwen, Henri J. M. *Can You Drink the Cup?* Notre Dame, Ind.: Ave Maria, 1996.

O'Connor, June. "Sensuality, Spirituality, Sacramentality." *Union Seminary Quarterly Review* 40, nos. 1–2 (1985).

O'Hare, Padraic. *The Enduring Covenant: The Education of Christians and the End of Antisemitism.* Valley Forge, Pa.: Trinity Press International, 1997.

Oliner, Samuel, and Pearl Oliner. *Embracing the Other.* New York: New York University Press, 1995.

Palmer, Parker J. *The Courage to Teach: Exploring the Inner Landscape of a Teacher's Life.* San Francisco: Jossey-Bass, 1998.

Park, Andrew Sung. *The Wounded Heart of God: The Asian Concept of Han and the Christian Doctrine of Sin.* Nashville: Abingdon, 1993.

Park, Andrew Sung, and Susan L. Nelson, eds. *The Other Side of Sin: Woundedness from the Perspective of the Sinned-Against.* Albany: State University of New York Press, 2001.

Parker, Evelyn L. "Hungry for Honor: Children in Violent Youth Gangs." *Interpretation: A Journal of Bible and Theology* 55, no. 2 (April 2001).

———. *Trouble Don't Last Always: Emancipatory Hope among African American Adolescents.* Cleveland: Pilgrim Press, 2003.

Parks, Rosa. *Rosa Parks: My Story.* New York: Puffin Books, 1992.

Parks, Rosa, with Gregory J. Reed. *Quiet Strength: The Faith, the Hope, and the Heart of a Woman Who Changed a Nation.* Grand Rapids, Mich.: Zondervan, 1994.

Parks, Sharon Daloz. *Big Questions, Worthy Dreams: Mentoring Young Adults in their Search for Meaning, Purpose, and Faith.* San Francisco: Jossey-Bass, 2000.

Pazmino, Robert W. *God Our Teacher: Theological Basics in Christian Education.* Grand Rapids, Mich.: Baker, 2001.

Peter Lombard. "Peter Lombard: The Four Books of Sentences, IV." Trans. Owen R. Orr. In *A Scholastic Miscellany: Anselm to Ockham.* Library of Christian Classics 10. Ed. Eugene R. Fairweather. Philadelphia: Westminster Press, 1956.

———. *Peter Lombard and the Sacramental System.* Trans. Elizabeth Frances Rogers. Merrick, N.Y.: Richwood Publishing Co., 1976.

Pollard, Alton B. *Mysticism and Social Change: The Social Witness of Howard Thurman.* New York: P. Lang, 1992.

Procter-Smith, Marjorie. *In Her Own Rite: Constructing Feminist Liturgical Tradition.* Akron, Ohio: OSL Publications, 2000; Nashville: Abingdon Press, 1990.

Proffitt, Anabel Colman. "The Importance of Wonder in Religious Education." *Religious Education* 93, no. 1 (1998).

Quick, Oliver Chase. *The Christian Sacraments.* London: Nisbet, 1929, 1927.

Rahner, Karl. *Theological Investigations* 4. Baltimore: Helicon, 1966.

———. *Theological Investigations* 14. London: Darton, Longman & Todd, 1976.

Ramsey, Arthur Michael. *God, Christ and the World: A Study of Contemporary Theology.* London: SCM, 1969.

Ramsey, A. M., and A. M. Allchin, eds. *Evelyn Underhill: Anglican Mystic.* Oxford: Sisters of the Love of God Press, 1996.

Riggs, Marcia, ed. *Can I Get a Witness? Prophetic Religious Voices of African American Women — An Anthology.* Maryknoll, N.Y.: Orbis, 1997.

Rittner, Carol, and Sondra Myers, eds. *The Courage to Care: Rescuers of Jews during the Holocaust.* New York: New York University Press, 1986.

Roof, Wade Clark. *Spiritual Marketplace: Baby Boomers and the Remaking of American Religion.* Princeton, N.J.: Princeton University Press, 1999.

Roof, Wade Clark, Jackson W. Carroll, and David A. Roozen, eds. *The Post-War Generation and Establishment Religion: Cross-Cultural Perspectives.* Boulder, Colo.: Westview, 1995.

Ross, Susan A. "God's Embodiment and Women: Sacraments." In *Freeing Theology: The Essentials of Theology in Feminist Perspective,* ed. Catherine Mowry LaCugna. San Francisco: Harper, 1993.

Ruether, Rosemary Radford. *Women and Redemption: A Theological History.* Minneapolis: Fortress, 1998.

———. *Women-Church: Theology and Practice of Feminist Liturgical Communities.* New York: Crossroad, 1985.

Saliers, Don E. *Worship and Spirituality.* 2nd ed. Akron, Ohio: OSL Publications, 1996, 1984.

———. *Worship as Theology: Foretaste of Glory Divine.* Nashville: Abingdon, 1994.

———. *Worship Come to Its Senses.* Nashville: Abingdon, 1996.

Santmire, Paul. *Nature Reborn.* Minneapolis: Fortress, 2000.

Scharper, Philip and Sally. *The Gospel in Art by the Peasants of Solentiname.* Maryknoll, N.Y.: Orbis, 1982.

Schillebeeckx, Edward. *Christ the Sacrament of the Encounter with God.* New York: Sheed and Ward, 1965.

Schmemann, Alexander. *The Eucharist: Sacrament of the Kingdom.* Trans. Paul Kachur. Crestwood, N.Y.: St. Vladimir's Seminary Press, 1988, 1987.

———. *For the Life of the World: Sacraments and Orthodoxy.* Crestwood, N.Y.: St. Vladimir's Seminary Press, 1973.

———. "Theology and Eucharist." In *Liturgy and Tradition,* ed. Thomas Fisch. Crestwood, N.Y.: St. Vladimir's Seminary, 1990, 1961.

Schüssler-Fiorenza, Elisabeth. *The Book of Revelation: Justice and Judgment.* Minneapolis: Augsburg/Fortress, 1998.

———. *In Memory of Her: A Feminist Theological Reconstruction of Christian Origins.* New York: Crossroad, 1994, 1983.

———. *Jesus: Miriam's Child, Sophia's Prophet — Critical Issues in Feminist Christology.* New York: Continuum, 1994.

Sebba, Anne. *Mother Teresa: Beyond the Image.* New York: Doubleday, 1997.

Shaw, Susan M. *Storytelling in Religious Education.* Birmingham: Religious Education Press, 1999.

Simpkinson, Anne, Charles Simpkinson, and Rose Solari, eds. *Nourishing the Soul: Discovering the Sacred in Everyday Life.* San Francisco: HarperCollins, 1995.

Smith, Joanmarie. *Teaching as Eucharist.* Williston Park, N.Y.: Resurrection Press, 1999.

Smith, Lillian Eugenia. *Killers of the Dream.* New York: Norton, 1994, 1949.

Smith, Luther. *Howard Thurman: The Mystic as Prophet.* Washington, D.C.: University Press of America, 1981.

Smith, Yolanda Y. *Reclaiming the Spirituals: New Possibilities for African American Christian Education.* Cleveland: Pilgrim, 2004.

Snyder, Martha, Ross Snyder, and Ross Snyder Jr. *The Young Child as Person: Toward the Development of Healthy Conscience.* New York: Human Sciences, 1980.

Song, Choan-Seng. *The Believing Heart: An Invitation to Story Theology.* Minneapolis: Fortress, 1999.

————. *Tell Us Our Names: Story Theology from an Asian Perspective.* Maryknoll, N.Y.: Orbis, 1984.

Steindl-Rast, David. *Gratefulness, the Heart of Prayer: An Approach to Life in Fullness.* New York: Paulist, 1984.

————. *A Listening Heart: The Spirituality of Sacred Sensuousness.* New York: Crossroad, 1999, 1983.

Suchocki, Marjorie Hewitt. *The End of Evil: Process Eschatology in Historical Context.* Albany: State University of New York Press, 1988.

————. *The Fall to Violence: Original Sin in Relational Theology.* New York: Continuum, 1994.

Tamez, Elsa. *The Amnesty of Grace: Justification by Faith from a Latin American Perspective.* Trans. Sharon H. Ringe. Nashville: Abingdon, 1993.

————. *Bible of the Oppressed.* Trans. Matthew J. O'Connell. Maryknoll, N.Y.: Orbis, 1982.

Tamez, Elsa, ed. *Through Her Eyes: Women's Theology from Latin America.* Maryknoll, N.Y.: Orbis, 1989.

Thandeka. *Learning to Be White: Money, Race, and God in America.* New York: Continuum, 1999.

Thomas Aquinas. *Summa Theologica,* Part III. Trans. Fathers of the English Dominican Province. New York: Benziger Brothers, 1947.

Thurman, Howard. *With Head and Heart: The Autobiography of Howard Thurman.* New York: Harcourt Brace Jovanovich, 1979.

————. *The Inward Journey.* Richmond, Ind.: Friends United Press, 1961.

Tinker, George. *Missionary Conquest: The Gospel and Native American Cultural Genocide.* Minneapolis: Fortress, 1993.

Townes, Emilie M. *In a Blaze of Glory: Womanist Spirituality as Social Witness.* Nashville: Abingdon, 1995.

Tracy, David. *The Analogical Imagination: Christian Theology and the Culture of Pluralism.* New York: Crossroad, 1981.

Tutu, Desmond Mpilo. *No Future without Forgiveness.* New York: Doubleday, 1999.

Underhill, Evelyn. *Man and the Supernatural.* London: Methuen, 1927.

————. *Mysticism: A Study in the Nature and Development of Man's Spiritual Consciousness.* 12th ed., rev. London: Methuen, 1930, 1911.

————. *Theophanies: A Book of Verses.* London: J. M. Dent & Sons, 1916.

————. *Worship.* New York: Crossroad, 1982, 1936.

The United Methodist Book of Worship. Nashville: United Methodist Publishing House, 1992.

Vassiliadis, Petros. *Eucharist and Witness: Orthodox Perspectives on the Unity and Mission of the Church.* Geneva: WCC Publications, 1998.

Victorin-Vangerud, Nancy M. *The Raging Hearth: Spirit in the Household of God.* St. Louis: Chalice, 2000.

Vogel, Dwight W., and Linda J. Vogel. *Sacramental Living: Falling Stars and Coloring Outside the Lines.* Nashville: Upper Room Books, 1999.

von Hügel, Baron Friedrich. *Essays and Addresses on the Philosophy of Religion, Second Series.* London: J. M. Dent & Sons, 1930, 1926.

Wand, John William Charles. *The Development of Sacramentalism.* London: Methuen, 1928.

Weil, Simone. *Waiting for God.* New York: Harper Colophon, 1973, 1951.

Wesley, Charles. *Hymns for the Nativity of our Lord.* Intro. and notes, Frank Baker. Madison, N.J.: Charles Wesley Society, 1991.

———. *Hymns on the Trinity.* Preface, S. T. Kimbrough Jr., intro., Wilma J. Quantrille. Madison, N.J.: Charles Wesley Society, 1998.

Wesley, John. *The Bicentennial Edition of the Works of John Wesley.* Nashville: Abingdon, 1984–.

———. *A Collection of Hymns, for the Use of the People Called Methodists.* London: John Mason, 1864.

Wesley, John, and Charles Wesley. *A Selection of Hymns on the Lord's Supper.* Preface, Donald G. Rogers. Exeter: Methodist Sacramental Fellowship, 1995.

Westerhoff, John H. *Building God's People in a Materialistic Society.* New York: Seabury, 1983.

———. *Will Our Children Have Faith?* Rev. ed. Harrisburg, Pa.: Morehouse, 2000, 1976.

Westerhoff, John, and Gwen Kennedy Neville. *Learning through Liturgy.* New York: Seabury, 1978.

White, James F. *Introduction to Christian Worship.* Rev. ed. Nashville: Abingdon, 1990, 1980.

———. *Sacraments as God's Self-Giving.* Nashville: Abingdon, 1983.

———. *The Sacraments in Protestant Practice and Faith.* Nashville: Abingdon, 1999.

Whitehead, Alfred North. *Process and Reality: An Essay in Cosmology.* Ed. David Ray Griffin and Donald W. Sherburne. New York: Free Press, Macmillan, 1978.

Williams, Charles, ed. *The Letters of Evelyn Underhill.* London: Longmans, Green, 1943.

Williams, Delores S. *Sisters in the Wilderness: The Challenge of Womanist God-Talk.* Maryknoll, N.Y.: Orbis, 1993.

Wimberly, Anne Streaty. *Soul Stories.* Nashville: Abingdon, 1994.

Wimberly, Anne E. Streaty, and Evelyn L. Parker, eds. *In Search of Wisdom: Faith Formation in the Black Church.* Nashville: Abingdon, 2002.

Wire, Antoinette Clark. *The Corinthian Women Prophets: A Reconstruction through Paul's Rhetoric.* Minneapolis: Fortress, 1990.

Yates, Miranda, and James Youniss, eds. *Roots of Civic Identity: International Perspectives on Community Service and Activism in Youth.* Cambridge: Cambridge University Press, 1999.

Youniss, James, and Miranda Yates. *Community Service and Social Responsibility in Youth.* Chicago: University of Chicago Press, 1997.

Zarnecki, George. *Art of the Medieval World: Architecture, Sculpture, Painting, the Sacred Arts.* Englewood Cliffs, N.J.: Prentice-Hall, 1975.

Zeldin, Michael, and Sara L. Lee, eds. *Touching the Future: Mentoring and the Jewish Professional.* Los Angeles: Rhea Hirsch School of Education, Hebrew Union College–Jewish Institute of Religion, 1995.